# Naked Before God

Medieval European Studies III

# Naked Before God

## Uncovering the Body in Anglo-Saxon England

Edited by

Benjamin C. Withers

and

Jonathan Wilcox

West Virginia University Press

Morgantown 2003

West Virginia University Press, Morgantown 26506


First edition published 2003 by West Virginia University Press
Printed in the United States of America

10 09 9 8 7 6 5 4 3

ISBN 0-937058-68-8 (alk. paper)

**Library of Congress Cataloguing-in-Publication Data**

Naked before God. Uncovering the body in Anglo-Saxon England / edited by Benjamin C. Withers, Jonathan Wilcox.
p. cm. – (Medieval European Studies ; 3)
1. Social history Medieval, 500-1500. 2. Anglo-Saxons–Intellectual life. 3. Civilization, Anglo-Saxon, in literature. 4. Civilization, Anglo-Saxon, in art. 5. Civilization, Medieval, in literature. 6. Christian literature, English (Old)–History and criticism. 7. English literature–Old English, ca. 450-1100–History and criticism. 8. Art, Anglo-Saxon 9. Art, Medieval–Great Britain. I. Title. II. Withers, Benjamin C. III. Wilcox, Jonathan, 1960. IV. Series.
IN PROCESS

Library of Congress Control Number: 2003104078

Cover design by Alcorn Publication Design
Cover motif based on image of Adam and Angel in Oxford,
Bodleian Library, MS Junius 11, page 31
Typeset by P. W. Conner
Printed in USA by DeHART's Printing Services Corp.

# Table of Contents

List of Illustrations ........ vii
List of Abbreviations ........ xi
Acknowledgments ........ xii

Forward: Uncovering the Body in Anglo-Saxon England
*Benjamin C. Withers, Indiana University South Bend* ........ 1

Introduction: Medieval Bodies Then and Now: Negotiating Problems of Ambivalence and Paradox
*Suzanne Lewis, Stanford University* ........ 15

1. The Wanton Hand: Reading and Reaching Into Grammars and Bodies in Old English Riddle 12
*Sarah L. Higley, University of Rochester* ........ 29

2. The Key to the Body: Unlocking Riddles 42-46
*Mercedes Salvador, Universidad de Sevilla* ........ 60

3. The Body as Text in Early Anglo-Saxon Law
*Mary P. Richards, University of Delaware* ........ 97

4. The Sacrificial Synecdoche of Hands, Heads, and Arms in Anglo-Saxon Heroic Story
*John M. Hill, United States Naval Academy* ........ 116

5. Nudity on the Margins: The Bayeux Tapestry and Its Relationship to Marginal Architectural Sculpture
*Karen Rose Mathews, University of Washington* ........ 138

6. The Donestre and the Person of Both Sexes
*Susan M. Kim, Illinois State University* ........ 162

7. Exiles from the Kingdom: The Naked and the Damned in Anglo-Saxon Art
*Catherine E. Karkov, Miami University, Ohio* .............................. 181

8. Breasts and Babies: The Maternal Body of Eve in the Junius 11 *Genesis*
*Mary Dockray-Miller, Lesley University*........................................ 221

9. Penitential Nakedness and the Junius 11 *Genesis*
*Janet S. Ericksen, University of Minnesota—Morris*...................... 257

10. Naked in Old English: The Embarrassed and the Shamed
*Jonathan Wilcox, University of Iowa* ............................................ 275

Index................................................................................................ 310

# Illustrations

*Following page 180*


Figure 1. Vatican, Biblioteca Apostolica, Barberini lat. 570, fol. 1 (Barberini Gospels): figure in canon tables. [*Copyright Biblioteca Apostolica Vaticana*]

Figure 2. Bayeux Tapestry: nude male and female. [*By special permission of the City of Bayeux*]

Figure 3. Bayeux Tapestry: nude male with board and axe. Bayeux, Musée de la Tapisserie (photo: Erich Lessing/Art Resource, NY)

Figure 4. Bayeux Tapestry: nude male. Bayeux, Musée de la Tapisserie (photo: Erich Lessing/Art Resource, NY)

Figure 5. Bayeux Tapestry: nude male and female. Bayeux, Musée de la Tapisserie (photo: Erich Lessing/Art Resource, NY)

Figure 6. Bayeux Tapestry: nude male and female. Bayeux, Musée de la Tapisserie (photo: Erich Lessing/Art Resource, NY)

Figure 7. Dublin, Trinity College MS. 58 (Book of Kells), fol. 200r: male figure. [*The Board of Trinity College Dublin*]

Figure 8. Kiltinane Church: sheela-na-gig relief (photo: Anthony Weir)

Figure 9. Loctudy, Brittany: exhibiting couple

Figure 10. Saint-Front-sur-Nizonne: exhibiting couple (photo: Anthony Weir)

Figure 11. Marignac, St. Supice: embracing couple (photo: Benjamin and Nurith Kedar Archives)

Figure 12. Champagnolles: embracing couple

Figure 13. Poitiers, Sainte-Radegonde: male exhibitionist (photo: James Austin)

Figure 14. Ballycloghduff: male exhibitionist

Figure 15. Semur-en-Brionnais: exhibitionist atlas figure (photo: Anthony Weir)

Figure 16. Conques, Sainte-Foi, west portal tympanum: Last Judgment

Figure 17. British Library, MS Cotton Tiberius B. v, fol. 83v: Donestre. [*By permission of the British Library*]

Figure 18. British Library, MS Cotton Vitellius A. xv, fol. 103v: (lower) Donestre. [*By permission of the British Library*]

Figure 19. British Library, MS Cotton Tiberius B. v, fol. 82r: Blemmyae. [*By permission of the British Library*]

Figure 20. The Rothbury Cross Shaft, base: hell scene. [*Copyright Department of Archaeology, University of Durham. Photographer T. Middlemass*]

Figure 21. The Rothbury Cross Shaft, top: group of figures. [*Copyright Department of Archaeology, University of Durham. Photographer T. Middlemass*]

Figure 22. Vatican, Biblioteca Apostolica, Reg. lat. 12 (Bury Psalter), fol. 62v: Psalm 51. [*Copyright Biblioteca Apostolica Vaticana*]

Figure 23. British Library, MS Cotton Claudius B. iv (Illustrated Hexateuch), fol. 6v: Creation of Eve. [*By permission of the British Library*]

Figure 24. British Library, MS Cotton Claudius B. iv (Illustrated Hexateuch), fol. 7r: Adam and Eve eat fruit. [*By permission of the British Library*]

Figure 25. British Library, MS Cotton Claudius B. iv (Illustrated Hexateuch), fol. 7v: (upper) Adam and Eve hide; (lower) Expulsion of Adam and Eve. [*By permission of the British Library*]

Figure 26. Oxford, Bodleian Library, MS Junius 11, page 9: Creation of Eve. [*By permission of the Bodleian Library, University of Oxford*]

Figure 27. Oxford, Bodleian Library, MS Junius 11, page 10: Adam and Eve. [*By permission of the Bodleian Library, University of Oxford*]

Figure 28. Oxford, Bodleian Library, MS Junius 11, page 11: Creation: God resting. [*By permission of the Bodleian Library, University of Oxford*]

Figure 29. Oxford, Bodleian Library, MS Junius 11, page 13: Adam and Eve. [*By permission of the Bodleian Library, University of Oxford*]

Figure 30. Oxford, Bodleian Library, MS Junius 11, page 16: Fall of the Angels. [*By permission of the Bodleian Library, University of Oxford*]

Figure 31. Oxford, Bodleian Library, MS Junius 11, page 17: Fall of the Angels. [*By permission of the Bodleian Library, University of Oxford*]

Figure 32. Oxford, Bodleian Library, MS Junius 11, page 24: Eve tempted. [*By permission of the Bodleian Library, University of Oxford*]

Figure 33. Oxford, Bodleian Library, MS Junius 11, page 28: Adam and Eve tempted. [*By permission of the Bodleian Library, University of Oxford*]

Figure 34. Oxford, Bodleian Library, MS Junius 11, page 31: (upper) Eve tempts Adam; (lower) Adam and Eve's remorse. [*By permission of the Bodleian Library, University of Oxford*]

Figure 35. Oxford, Bodleian Library, MS Junius 11, page 34: (upper) Adam and Eve know nakedness; (lower) Adam and Eve hide. [*By permission of the Bodleian Library, University of Oxford*]

Figure 36. Oxford, Bodleian Library, MS Junius 11, page 36: Tempter returns to Hell. [*By permission of the Bodleian Library, University of Oxford*]

Figure 37. Oxford, Bodleian Library, MS Junius 11, page 45: Expulsion of Adam and Eve. [*By permission of the Bodleian Library, University of Oxford*]

Figure 38. Oxford, Bodleian Library, MS Junius 11, page 46: Expulsion of Adam and Eve. [*By permission of the Bodleian Library, University of Oxford*]

Figure 39. Oxford, Bodleian Library, MS Junius 11, page 47: Eve at childbed. [*By permission of the Bodleian Library, University of Oxford*]

Figure 40. Oxford, Bodleian Library, MS Junius 11, page 53: (upper) Jared's unnamed wife in labor; (center) Maviael's unnamed wife with baby Mathusal. [*By permission of the Bodleian Library, University of Oxford*]

Figure 41. Oxford, Bodleian Library, MS Junius 11, page 54: (lower) Adam and Eve with infant Seth. [*By permission of the Bodleian Library, University of Oxford*]

Figure 42. Oxford, Bodleian Library, MS Junius 11, page 56: Seth's unnamed wife with Enos. [*By permission of the Bodleian Library, University of Oxford*]

Figure 43. Oxford, Bodleian Library, MS Junius 11, page 57: Cainan's unnamed wife with baby Malalehel. [*By permission of the Bodleian Library, University of Oxford*]

Figure 44. Oxford, Bodleian Library, MS Junius 11, page 78: drunkenness of Noah. [*By permission of the Bodleian Library, University of Oxford*]

Figure 45. London, British Library, MS Add. 49598 (Benedictional of Æthelwold), fol. 22v: Naming of Christ. [*By permission of the British Library*]

# Abbreviations

| | |
|---|---|
| ASE | *Anglo-Saxon England* (cited as a periodical by volume and year) |
| ASPR | Anglo-Saxon Poetic Records |
| Bodl. Lib. | Bodleian Library |
| BL | British Library |
| BT(S), Bosworth and Toller: | Joseph Bosworth *An Anglo-Saxon Dictionary Based on the Manuscript Collections of the late Joseph Bosworth* (Oxford, 1898) and *Supplement*, edited and enlarged by T. Northcote Toller (Oxford, 1921); repr. with enlarged addenda and corrigenda by Alistair Campbell (Oxford, 1972). |
| CCSL | Corpus Christianorum, series Latina |
| CH I | Ælfric's First Series of *Catholic Homilies* |
| CH II | Ælfric's Second Series of *Catholic Homilies* |
| DOE | *Dictionary of Old English*, ed. Angus Cameron, Ashley Crandell Amos, Antonette diPaolo Healey, et al. (Toronto, 1986–) |
| EEMF | Early English Manuscripts in Facsimile |
| EETS | Early English Text Society |
| | o.s. original series |
| | s.s. supplementary series |
| Junius 11 | Oxford, Bodleian Library, MS Junius 11 |
| l., ll. | line(s) |
| MLN | *Modern Language Notes* |
| OED | *Oxford English Dictionary*, ed. J. A. Simpson, et al, 2nd edn., 20 vols. (Oxford, 1989). |
| PG | Patrologia Graeca, ed. J.-P. Migne |
| PL | Patrologia Latina, ed. J.-P. Migne |
| PMLA | *Publications of the Modern Language Association of America* |

# Acknowledgments

We wish to thank the libraries and individuals who hold the copyrights for allowing us to publish the illustrations that uncover the body within this book. Three institutions helped defray the costs of purchasing images and permissions: Mary Dockray-Miller thanks Janet Schulte, Dean of the School of Undergraduate Studies at Lesley University; Jonathan Wilcox thanks the Glick Fund of the Department of English at the University of Iowa; and Benjamin Withers thanks Dean Thomas C. Miller and the Research and Development Committee of Indiana University South Bend. Jonathan Wilcox is also grateful to the Department of English at the University of Iowa and Young Hee Kwon, John Pendell, Amy Spellacy, and Keith Wilhite for research assistance at varying stages of editing the collection. Both editors and contributors owe a great debt of gratitude to the two anonymous reviewers for West Virginia University Press who made helpful and perceptive comments about the individual essays and the book as a whole.

Benjamin C. Withers
Jonathan Wilcox

# FORWARD
# Uncovering the Body in Anglo-Saxon England

BENJAMIN C. WITHERS

THOUGH ANGLO-SAXON ENGLAND is better known for its penitents than peep-shows, glimpses of unclothed bodies peek through in surprising places in the surviving sources. As the essays that follow demonstrate, the spectacle of the unclothed body, at once scandalous and seductive, exposes more than just bare flesh. Like all representations, those of the naked body partake in larger cultural conversations. If some glimpses of naked forms provoke feelings of shame and embarrassment, others signal defiance and triumph, and still others figure as the ambiguous and passing cipher at the crux of a riddling joke. While the body in general occupies an important site at the intersections of many discourses, the naked body, because it so readily captures both attention and censure, can provoke the reevaluation of those discourses in ways that the clothed body cannot.

Seen not so very long ago as unlikely to support discussions of the body and its attendant discourses of sexuality, gender, and subjectivity, the rich vernacular culture of Anglo-Saxon England suddenly appears as fertile ground for studies that uncover once-hidden Anglo-Saxon bodies. Much of the best work in this regard stems from Allen J. Frantzen's book, *Desire for Origins*, which demands that we reevaluate the boundaries that scholarship has traditionally drawn between past and present, between what is seen to be appropriately "Anglo-Saxon" and what is not.[1] His own examination of little-known texts such as the penitentials demonstrates the value of searching through marginalized sources for categories that otherwise "we know nothing about," in this case for ways of

[1] Allen J. Frantzen, *Desire for Origins: New Language, Old English, and Teaching the Tradition* (New Brunswick, N.J., 1990).

thinking of gender as mutable and non-binary, or for expressions of sexuality that differ from our own.[2] Complementing and extending Frantzen's challenge, Clare A. Lees exposes representations of the body in Old English literature that operate as crucially important matrices of the discourses (desire, chastity and marriage) that produce sexuality.[3] Her attention to the body derives from a central proposition, namely that sensual knowledge is a tool used in the service of worship, as she observes "knowledge of the senses is linked to Christian knowledge of, and desire for God." For Lees, Anglo-Saxon art and literature represent the body in a paradoxical way. In her view, this paradox arises from the culture's emphasis on restraint; restraint, she argues, simultaneously acknowledges the importance of the material body even as it works to make the material body absent as it is translated into writing.[4]

The desire to question the accepted relationship of early medieval bodies to modern regimes of power and control also underlies Katherine O'Brien O'Keeffe's examination of the changes in the operation of law in Late Anglo-Saxon England. Focusing primarily on the *Anglo-Saxon Chronicle*, law codes, and the Life of St Swithun, she determines that from roughly 970 to 1036 Anglo-Saxon secular and religious leaders effected a major change in the punishment of criminals. As in Lees's study, but here in relation to judicial discourse, the body emerges as "a sign of something other than itself." Anglo-Saxon penalties for crimes, O'Keeffe demonstrates, changed from those involving "external, in some ways communal responsibility," such as the payment of wergilds and/or sentences of death, to punishments that mandated mutilation of the body, such as branding, amputation of the nose or ears. "The mutilated

[2] Allen J. Frantzen, "Between the Lines: Queer Theory, The History of Homosexuality, and Anglo-Saxon Penitentials," *Journal of Medieval and Early Modern Studies* 26 (1996): 255-96.

[3] Clare A. Lees, "Engendering Religious Desire: Sex, Knowledge, and Christian Identity in Anglo-Saxon England," *Journal of Medieval and Early Modern Studies* 27 (1997): 17-45.

[4] Lees, "Engendering Desire," pp. 18 and 39.

bodies of criminals," O'Keeffe shows, "became texts of their behavior and its lawful consequences."[5]

Though not explicitly addressed, the naked body revealed and re-concealed haunts the operations that these studies uncover. As O'Keeffe notes, the law-codes implicitly rely on the sight of the bared body since "injuries which are visible are more heavily compensated than those which are not seen."[6] Discussions of the ramifications of King Alfred's use of nakedness as a metaphor for knowledge plays a key role in Lees's "Engendering Desire," and in Frantzen's recent study, *Before the Closet,* while the possibilities and problems presented by the display of the bare body of female saints run like a thread through Lees's work.[7] For example, in what was until the present collection the most extended discussion of surviving representations of the unclothed body from Anglo-Saxon England, Lees collaborates with Gillian Overing to address the provocative yet elusive nature of the nakedness of the tortured female martyrs described by the writers Aldhelm and Ælfric.[8] They demonstrate that the appearance of the naked saint arouses a voyeuristic desire that is simultaneously met and denied by the vocabulary and structure of the texts under consideration. Though these texts tell us that the saints are despoiled of clothes, tortured, even penetrated by swords, and that their torturers often put those bodies on public display, Lees and Overing contend that:

> We never see the tortured body of Lucy, and all the female Lives appear defended against the unregulated gaze; Agnes' nudity is miraculously concealed; Agatha's breast, cut off from her torturers, is miraculously healed

[5] Katherine O'Brien O'Keeffe, "Body and Law in late Anglo-Saxon England," *ASE* 27 (1998): 209-32.

[6] O'Keeffe, "Body and Law," p. 215.

[7] Lees, "Engendering Desire," pp. 26-27; Allen J. Frantzen, *Before the Closet Same-Sex Love from Beowulf to Angels in America* (Chicago, 1998), p. 103.

[8] Clare A. Lees and Gillian Overing, "Before History, Before Difference: Bodies, Metaphor, and the Church in Anglo-Saxon England," *Yale Journal of Criticism* 11 (1998): 315-34.

> in a blaze of light that prevents any gaze on her new, spiritual wholeness....[9]

In short, the descriptions of naked saints are "accompanied by the kinds of cultural ambivalences and evasions" that not only complicate theories of gender and subjectivity but also significantly challenge the relevance of other modern notions, such as vision, voyeurism, and the gaze that we may seek to project back onto these texts.[10]

Situated in this manner by Lees and Overing "before history, before difference," the spectacle of the naked female saintly body denies the possibility of framing the early Middle Ages as "other," or separating it out as a "pre-history" for modern categories of thought and behavior which we impose on the past in a search for origins. Once uncovered in this way, Anglo-Saxon bodies in general challenge modern classification and indeed do present those "categories we know nothing about" called for by Frantzen and, in another context, by Caroline Walker Bynum.[11] In modern theory, especially in art history, "naked" and "nude" are carefully distinguished and defined, nowhere more eloquently and influentially than in Kenneth Clark's masterful book tellingly entitled *The Nude.* For Clark, the naked body (wrinkled, ugly, and particular) is "no more than a point of departure" for the nude. In a defintion well-known to art historians, he declares "[t]o be naked is to be deprived of our clothes and the word implies some embarrassment which most of us feel in that condition" while a nude is clothed in art, a "balanced, prosperous, and confident body: the body re-formed."[12] A seemingly innocuous, commonsensical, and acceptable differentiation, except as Lynda Nead has

[9] Lees and Overing, "Before History, Before Difference," p. 328.

[10] Lees and Overing, "Before History, Before Difference," p. 323; see also Lees, *Tradition and Belief: Religious Writing in Late Anglo-Saxon England* (Minneapolis, 1999), pp. 146-50.

[11] Caroline Walker Bynum, "Why all the Fuss about the Body: A Medievalists' Perspective," *Critical Inquiry* 22 (1995): 1-33.

[12] Kenneth Clark, *The Nude: A Study in Ideal Form, The A.W. Mellon Lectures in the Fine Arts 1953* (1956; repr. Princeton, 1990), p. 3.

recently argued, while Clark's study is purportedly "concerned with a specific classical and idealizing tradition of representation... within the book this particularity gains the force of a general cultural norm against which all other modes of representation of the nude (Gothic, Baroque, non-European) are categorized as transgressive, as a cultural other."[13] Clark's history of the body draws upon a purposeful and familiar trajectory, one that connects the art of Antiquity to the Renaissance and both of these revered cultures in turn to the Masters of Modern Art. Underneath this rhetorical clothing, however, the perception and identification of the Nude relies on its display of a negative difference: the Nude is not natural, it is not overly concerned with the base, material aspects of the body, it is not the "merely" naked. More importantly for this discussion of Anglo-Saxon bodies, it cannot be medieval, as Clark himself acknowledges: "[g]iven my initial distinction between the nude and the naked, it may be asked by what excuse the Gothic body is included in this book at all."[14] When medieval bodies do appear in Clark's work, they exist primarily to define "The Alternative Convention" (the name of his penultimate essay) that appears before, and thus helps define, the ultimate appearance of "The Nude as an End in Itself" in the book's final chapter. In essence, as Clark formulates his category of the Nude, he projects it back on the medieval past and finds that past wanting. So, when Clark asks (rhetorically), "Why, then, does it [the nude] never appear [in the Middle Ages]?" the answer can only be because the category of the Nude depends on a relationship to an ideal, classical form which, when applied retroactively to medieval art, renders the bare, exposed bodies we find there, even those of the classically inspired Gothic artist Villard de Honnecourt, "ugly" and too close to nature, hence merely naked.[15] There can be few better examples of Carolyn Dinshaw's provocative argument that the

[13] Lynda Nead, *The Female Nude: Art, Obscenity, and Sexuality* (New York, 1992), p. 12.

[14] Clark, *The Nude*, p. 308.

[15] Clark, *The Nude*, p. 12.

modern world fashions the medieval as an abject realm, a place where culturally prescribed practices are assigned so that modernity might be seen to emerge through a dialectic of difference and origin.[16] Thus modern studies which follow Clark's categorization of unclothed forms, such as Edward Lucie-Smith's recent discussion of the male nude, can dispense with the Middle Ages in a few dismissive words: "[b]efore the Renaissance, art of the Christian era found it almost impossible to represent male genitalia."[17] Such views surely contribute to the lack of studies of the naked body in Anglo-Saxon England: why spend time looking for and studying what we are told does not exist?

In Clark's definition, "naked" (the Modern English reflex and a reliable cognate to the Old English *nacod*) occupies a lesser term in a cultural hierarchy, and is used to indicate a lower-class or more "earthy" circumstance, while the Latinate "nude" connotes something more aristocratic or cultured and hence properly belonging to the higher realm of art. The presence of the word "Naked" in our title "Naked before God," counters the standard distinction in art historical scholarship between naked and nude.[18] By highlighting a descendant of an Old English word in our title, we do not seek to reverse Clark's binary hierarchy as much as to stress a key component of Anglo-Saxon society, its dependence on its own vernacular, and to acknowledge a continuity between that past and our present. The other words of our main title, "before God," suggest the ever-important Christian register in which human's clothed or unclothed state is a theological issue which implicates the body as concrete metaphor of both innocence and sexual desire. It is the need to question how the body is sited variously at the

[16] Carolyn Dinshaw, "Getting Medieval: Pulp Fiction, Gawain, Foucault," in The Book and the Body, ed. Dolores Warwick Frese and Katherine O'Brien O'Keeffe (Notre Dame, 1997), pp. 116-63. Portions of this essay can also be found in Dinshaw, *Getting Medieval: Sexualities and Communities, Pre- and Post-Modernism* (Durham, NC, 1999).

[17] Edward Lucie-Smith, *Adam: The Male Figure in Art* (New York, 1998), p. 115.

[18] Compare Margaret R. Miles, *Carnal Knowing: Female Nakedness and Religious Meaning in the Christian West* (New York, 1991), pp. 12-17.

intersection of religious, social, and cultural formations that unifies this collection of individual essays.

By calling attention to some of the representations of unclothed bodies that survive in Anglo-Saxon art and literature, the essays gathered here provide new perspectives on familiar sources and help bring other, less well-known, works into the spotlight. This collection provides the first extensive catalogue to date of surviving representations of unclothed bodies and bare body parts from Anglo-Saxon England: these unexpectedly diverse sources range from biblical translations (both prose and poetic) and their illustration to secular epics, from homilies to worldly marvels, from embroidered histories to punning riddles, from saints' lives to legal codes. In these works we can survey the kinds of characters that Anglo-Saxon artists and scribes were willing to portray as naked: from the damned in hell and/or demons to biblical characters; from sexual aggressors to penitent sinners; and from beautiful, dark haired Welsh girls to ugly, mutilated victims and criminals. Informing as it does the risky familiarity of the strange monsters imagined at the edge of the world to the risqué strangeness of familiar objects such as common household keys, nakedness marks both the center and edge of the potential for knowledge and interpretation. The appearance of descriptions or representations of the naked body in so many different kinds of discourses signals a cultural role that we should be embarrassed to look away from or ignore.

Focus on the naked body permits this collection to reach across what still today are too often seen as mutually exclusive or at least contrasting scholarly domains. In order to facilitate the exploration of interdisciplinary connections, there has been no attempt to impose a single overarching viewpoint or common methodology on the authors. Instead, we have structured this collection as a sequence of paired essays, seeking to create a series of open-ended dialogues between and across individual studies. Likewise, aside from a focus on the Anglo-Saxon period, our organization breaks away from any chronological implication altogether, instead aiming for a rich set of thematic and theoretical resonances. Thus, after the general introduction by Suzanne Lewis, the reader will find two essays with distinctly different views on the well-known and ambiguously sexual riddles of the tenth-century Exeter Book. Sarah L. Higley's "The Wanton Hand: Reading and Reaching Into Grammars and Bodies in Old English Riddle 12" sweeps around, over and through the body at the center of a riddle whose solution infamously depends on how we interpret the nighttime activities of a drunken Welsh woman. She demonstrates that the potential for an innocent or obscene reading of the riddle hinges on lexical and grammatical ambiguities presented by the rare Old English verb *swifeð* (with the possible meanings of "moves" as well as "fucks"). More than a rumination of a word's meaning or even the propriety or impropriety of one particular interpretation, Higley's stimulating essay introduces what is in effect a new solution to the riddle, one that requires us to paradoxically question the difference between scholarly need and desire while calling for a renewal of our commitment to philology. The second study of the Exeter Book's riddles also demands that we consider the reader's orientation to larger issues of reading and interpretation even as it takes a different scholarly approach to the task. In her "The Key to the Body: Unlocking Exeter Book Riddles 42-46," Mercedes Salvador examines a group of consecutive riddles whose seemingly blatant references to sexual intercourse and male genitalia are notoriously some of the most sexually explicit texts from Anglo-Saxon England. For Salvador, the secret to the solution of these riddles lies not so much in their double meanings (as with Riddle 12, each of the texts Salvador examines can be seen to have at least one innocent and one obscene solution) as in their structure and sequence. Casting these riddles as part of the larger cultural impetus of the Benedictine reform, Salvador argues that the body and its potentially pornographic activities materialize as kinds of instructional citations that warn of the dangers posed by the absence of a proper, spiritual reading of the literal text.

Salvador's concern with spiritual interpretation begins a trajectory toward the traditional center of Anglo-Saxon culture that is continued by the next pair of essays, devoted to law and epic poetry, respectively. Mary P. Richards in her "The Body as Text in Early Anglo-Saxon Law" concentrates on the "body tariffs" found in the law codes of Kings Æthelberht and Alfred. These tariffs, from the early seventh and late ninth centuries, likely reflect oral sources and derive from early continental practices which were meant to deflect blood-feud by requiring compensation for a victim's wounds. Richards mines these seemingly dry and heavily formulaic texts to reveal, in a wonderfully unexpected way, how the wounded, naked body was subject to a series of legal examinations in the process of the administration of justice. The body emerges as text on whose surface the slashes and bruises of a violent society are read and re-read as evidence of a crime, its severity, and thus its compensation. Though it required repeated display of the victim's body before witnesses, this "textuality" was meant for the protection of the victim because it called attention publically to the wounds and differentiated them from those resulting from the officially-sanctioned punishment of criminals. This simultaneous linking and differentiating of victim from criminal drops away as the tariffs themselves disappear from later law codes written by churchmen; this change, Richards argues, illuminates just how "the church moves from peripheral influence to major force" in the construction of laws and the Anglo-Saxon subjects they govern. Another unexpected link between the body and Anglo-Saxon culture — in this case the violently fragmented parts of the heroic body — emerges in John M. Hill's contribution, "The Sacrificial Synecdoche of Hands, Heads, and Arms in Anglo-Saxon Heroic Story." Heroic literature, Hill argues, is obsessed with certain body parts not just because appendages such as the hand or arm support sword and shield but because "the heroic feat itself is concentrated in the warrior appendage, much as the 'professional' thief's or slanderer's crimes are written on to him." In effect, Hill's emphasis on the metaphoric aspects of the heroic body casts raking light on the issues of mutilation advanced by Richards; by focusing on where the naked body is represented minimally and anxiously, as a few bared parts in *Beowulf*, the *Battle of Maldon*, and in the few surviving echoes of Germanic legend,

Hill helps us understand how the body, or in this case its severed appendages, can be seen to define the psycho-sexual boundaries of one type of particularly male performance.

From this focus on the heroic/legal center, the next four essays examine the naked body's role in the definition of the culture's margins and boundaries. This section is introduced by an essay by Karen Mathews, "Nudity on the Margins: the Bayeux Tapestry and Its Relationship to Marginal Architectural Sculpture," where Mathews examines fives scenes of actively-engaged naked women and men (the latter with prominently-depicted genitalia) who are present in the borders of the famous, late-eleventh-century embroidery depicting the events leading to the battle of Hastings. As Mathews shows, these particular scenes lack parallels in Anglo-Saxon manuscripts, the sources usually associated with the creation of the Tapestry; instead, she argues that in terms of composition and meaning, the scenes resemble the marginal sculpture found on later, Romanesque architecture. Her study thus broadens the chronological and temporal borders of our understanding of these enigmatic figures and our perception of the intersection of Anglo-Saxon and continental cultures that produced them. The genital exhibitionism found on the Tapestry not only compares to the acrobatic exhibitionists found on churches, but such a comparison provides a visual context for the Tapestry as a whole, helping make the case for its perception by multiple audiences. Mathews' concerns with margins and boundaries are in turn taken up and extended by Susan M. Kim in her sharply focused essay, "The Donestre and the Person of Both Sexes." The Donestre is a hybrid creature, part monster and part human, that would have been encountered by the readers of either one of the two late Anglo-Saxon illustrated texts of the *Marvels of the East.* The "person of both sexes" meanwhile, is described at the beginning of the related text known as the *Liber Monstrorum,* where it is counted as a verifiable marvel, though one that in Kim's analysis becomes a hybrid that strangely occludes any clear point of definition and demarcation. Although the text does not call for it, the illustration of the Donestre is depicted with prominently articulated male genitalia (in one case marked in red ink), a feature complemented by a similarly unexplained presence of a naked female who simultaneously conceals and exposes her own sexual organs. For Kim, this display of genitalia supplements the difference between monstrous and human that lies at the heart of both the *Liber* and the *Marvels* with that of male and female; it is a textual encounter which "make[s] literal, or naked — anxieties which underlie not only these monstrous texts, but also the cultures which generate and read them."

Catherine E. Karkov's essay, "Exiles from the Kingdom: The Naked and the Damned in Anglo-Saxon Art," moves us from a consideration of monsters to well-endowed, marginal creatures of another sort: demons, fallen angels, and condemned criminals exiled from the courts of God and man. She focuses on the depiction of male genitalia on the fallen angels in Junius 11 (in its illustrations of the Old English poems *Genesis A* and *B*) and demons in the Harley Psalter. Linking these graphic sexual markers to other literary, diplomatic, and legal practices, including the burial of criminals, her essay complements the connections of the body with legal discourse first established by O'Keeffe and extended in this volume by Richards. Karkov combines attention to the body with a particular focus on gender to elucidate how the ambivalence, fear, and erasure of the female form that characterizes much of medieval culture manifests itself in Anglo-Saxon England through the addition of "the male genitals and human bodies of demons in the drawings of the fall of the angels ... as part of the largely male discourse of crime and punishment." Noting that the genital exhibitionism seen in the illustration of the exiled angels reminds of the stripped bodies of legally-punished criminals, traditionally displayed on the boundaries between political jurisdictions, Karkov establishes the functional role of the unclothed body as marker of the margins of power and community. The appearance of the feminine body as a site of identity and difference also occupies Mary Dockray-Miller's essay, "Breasts and Babies: The Maternal Body of Eve in the Junius 11 *Genesis*." At play here is the boundary not between the known and unknown but between text and illustrations;

Dockray-Miller builds her argument on the observation that the visual and verbal aspects of this extensively illustrated text are often split apart and isolated in modern scholarly studies. This disjuncture results in a failure to appreciate the richness and multivalency of the "full-text" created when text and illustrations are seen simultaneously. Without the illustrations the poems exhibit a different meaning. Dockray-Miller points to the use of the breast, particularly the nipple, to differentiate the otherwise undifferentiated and sexless bodies of the prelapsarian Adam and Eve in the illustrations. Seen as a marker of the maternal function of breast-feeding, the nipple calls attention to Eve's role as a mother, and prompts closer attention to the unusually prominent mothers depicted in the genealogies that follow the Fall; these illustrations, Dockray-Miller contends, counter the centrality of the masculine body in the poetic text and problematize the dominant masculinist interpretations of poems in modern scholarship.

The final two essays bring the collection round toward the full circle. Janet S. Ericksen's "Penitential Nakedness and the Junius 11 *Genesis*" continues the discussion of that manuscript begun by Karkov and Dockray-Miller, though the focus now becomes how the unclothed bodies of Adam and Eve suggest the need for "clothing" in confession and penance. The links forged here are between the illustrations and dogmatic homilies and pentitentials; in a patristically-inflected reading, the naked, vulnerable bodies of Adam and Eve express not just the literal nakedness of the sinners after their Fall but also, more metaphorically, the state of their spiritual vulnerability as well. In the last essay in the collection, "Naked in Old English: the Embarrassed and the Shamed," Jonathan Wilcox offers one final, summarizing look at the question of nakedness. Wilcox utilizes a broad range of sources to explore a homiletic motif of a sinner at the Last Judgement who stands before Christ as if naked before the people, a motif that depends on the act of looking at the naked body to link and yet differentiate the emotions of embarrassment and shame. The relationship of shame ("an internalized breach of a moral code") and embarrassment ("more situational, more spontaneous, more dependant on an observer") is very close in Old English, Wilcox admits. But he argues that the two emotions can be distinguished by carefully reading and looking at surviving representations of the naked body encompassed by the vocabulary for shame and genitalia (linked by OE words such as *sceamu*) and the poetic and exegetical treatments of the stories of Adam and Eve, and Noah. If in these examples the sight of the naked body causes embarrassment, this tie is defeated by pious bodies, such as the saints, in whose lives we can perceive a miraculous transcendence of the body and its bond to embarrassment and shame.

As the reader picks and chooses his or her path through the collection, it is hoped that our organization encourages the emergence of other dialogues as well. Lewis's general introduction, magisterially wide-ranging and theoretical in scope, must be read alongside Higley's careful, detailed rumination of the meaning of a single word. Wilcox, Karkov, and Mathews provide much needed surveys of the representations of nudity in literature and art that call into question many of our current views of the traditional role of nudity/nakedness in Anglo-Saxon culture. Ericksen's argument for the penitential dimension of the Adam and Eve story corresponds to and complements Salvador's argument for a spiritual interpretation of the most explicitly sexual Exeter Book riddles. The force of Kim's reading of the display of the Donestre's genitalia and the role of this display in the construction of identity gains when read alongside Dockray-Miller's investigation of the breast as sign of difference and Richards' study of the wounded, naked body, subject to legal examination. Mathew's link of the sexually aggressive nudes from the Bayeux Tapestry to the enigmatic, deformed discourse of continental marginal sculpture resonates with Hill's examination of the violently-severed arms, hands, and heads scattered about in epic poems.

Although the essays that follow will discuss a considerable proportion of the representations of the naked body or its constituent parts that survive from Anglo-Saxon England, they by no means uncover them all. Thus, this collection should be seen as the first step toward creating a broader interpretive context for these representations, and thereby stimulating further research on both the unknown and well-known. An important part of this goal is the ensuing introduction written by Suzanne Lewis. Her broadly-pitched survey contextualizes the collection by placing it within the broader field of medieval studies, demonstrating, for example, just how much there is to learn about the multivalence of the body, its representations, and its effects. The investigation of the medieval body has arisen only recently and those studies that do exist have been directed toward either the conditions of its formation in Late Antiquity or toward its most "flamboyant" expression in the High and Late Gothic eras, leaving the period between the decline of Roman society and the late-eleventh century relatively unexplored and obscure. The variety of approaches and scholarly techniques utilized by the authors of the essays presented here demonstrate not only how a concern for the body adds to our understanding of Anglo-Saxon England but also how Anglo-Saxon England can help us rethink the importance of the body for the study of the Middle Ages as a whole and for our own culture as well.

# INTRODUCTION
# Medieval Bodies Then and Now: Negotiating Problems of Ambivalence and Paradox

SUZANNE LEWIS

SITUATED at the intersection of contemporary discourses about identity, sexuality, gender, and subjectivity, the body (or em-bodiment) dominates the center of many conversations we are now having about the Middle Ages. We never encounter the body unmediated by the meanings that cultures, including our own as well as medieval, give to it.[1] Yet, as some writers have complained, so much has been written about the body within a variety of historical and theoretical contexts, that the body has dissolved into pure language — "the postmodern body is no body at all."[2] Further complicating our subject, contradictions produced by earlier discourses, as well as by hundreds of years of controversy, confront us with a multiplicity of bodies in the Middle Ages.[3] In the face of what appears to be the disappearance of the body behind obscuring layers of text and crowds of other bodies, the rescue of the medieval body as lived experience lies at the core of current historical perspectives.

*Body/Embodiment*

In the Christian West, nakedness is not a "natural" but an assumed state. In a dressed society, the unclothed body is always problematical but at the same time meaningful.[4] Although

1 See Gayle S. Rubin, "Thinking Sex: Notes for a Radical Theory of the Politics of Sexuality," in *The Lesbian and Gay Studies Reader*, ed. Henry Abelove, et al. (New York, 1993), pp. 3-44, at 10.

2 See Caroline Bynum, "Why All the Fuss about the Body? A Medievalist's Perspective," *Critical Inquiry* 22 (1995): 1-33, at 1; Susan Bordo, "Feminism, Postmodernism and Gender-Scepticism," in *Feminism/Postmodernism*, ed. Linda Nicholson (New York, 1990), p. 145.

3 See Bynum, "Why All the Fuss?" p. 33.

4 Anne Hollander, *Seeing Through Clothes* (New York, 1978, repr. Berkeley, 1993), pp. 83-84.

thoroughly committed to associating nakedness with sin and shame, the Middle Ages also had its origins in Mediterranean cultures devoted to the celebration of physical beauty. If nudity were idealized to represent anything good, its transformation had to accommodate a requisite sense of shameful sexuality, that is, to invent costumes of nudity itself. In the belief that humankind's naked state had been perfect and innocent before the Fall, clothes were seen as unnatural or profane — the visible result of Adam and Eve's shame.[5]

As modified versions of Mediterranean classical dress combined with Northern garb, early medieval draped clothes were shapeless and loose. Intended to cover the body more fully and effectively, draped rectangles were sewn into "baglike garments" with sleeves and openings for the hands.[6] When conditioned to observing the body filtered through clothing, the eye tends to reconceptualize nudity automatically, editing the visual evidence to conform to a current sense of the undressed body — widening or sloping the shoulders, elongating or shortening the waist, thinning or fattening here and there.[7] Hence the distinctive but rare Anglo-Saxon representations of the nude bodies of Adam and Eve in Junius 11 — elongated, tubular and inarticulate, replete with sagging breasts and abdomen marked by the residue of their usual appearance beneath falling drapery. Uncovered bodily movements are grossly exaggerated as if still performing largely hidden under concealing clothes. Enlarged but expressive hands and feet then seem to emerge as salient appendages to situate the body within a spatio-temporal, narrative context. As Ann Hollander reminds us, nakedness undergoes fashion changes not only in artistic tradition but in living experience.

[5] Hollander, *Seeing Through Clothes,* p. 85.

[6] Hollander, *Seeing Through Clothes,* p. 17.

[7] On the concept of "corporeal style," see Judith Butler, *Gender Trouble: Feminism and the Subversion of Identity* (New York, 1990), pp. 139-141; also Hollander, *Seeing Through Clothes,* pp. 86-87.

There is, however, no direct correlation between representation and the real without the mediation of ideology.[8] Distanced from nature by a multiplicity of social, political, sexual, and psychic codes, bodies exist within intellectual conceptualizations or "frames."[9] Systematic coding renders bodies as much the product as the site of experience. In the last two decades, history has turned away from the history of ideas toward the exploration of "material culture," and thus toward the history of the body and embodied ideas.[10] Whereas studies inspired by cultural anthropology center on rituals and symbolic gestures of acting bodies as visible agents of potential meaning, our present focus tends toward a historical understanding of embodiment.[11] Overlapping Lacanian psychoanalysis and poststructualism, the embodied nature of consciousness stages the body as a unity and the identity of self as bodily coherence. However, if the body is conceived as a totality, a product of psychic investment, the totalizing ideology of the singular body has been increasingly challenged and subverted by a poststructualist and feminist insistence on multiplicity, fragmentation, "otherness," and abjection.[12] Merleau-Ponty has given us the

[8] Clare Lees and Gillian Overing, "Before History, Before Difference: Bodies, Metaphor, and the Church in Anglo-Saxon England," *Yale Journal of Criticism* 11 (1998): 315-339, at 318.

[9] Sarah Kay and Miri Rubin, *Framing Medieval Bodies* (Manchester, 1994), p. 1.

[10] Roy Porter, "History of the Body," in *New Perspectives in Historical Writing*, ed. Peter Burke (University Park, PA, 1991), pp. 206-232, at 207, who points to various stimuli ranging from the *Annalistes* to cultural anthropology in shaping a discourse of symbolic meanings of the body as contextualized within systems of social exchange; see B. S. Turner, *The Body and Society in Social Theory* (Oxford, 1984). Related to the history of medicine, social histories of the body explore the underlying conditions for a variety of practices in material and everyday life.

[11] See Jean-Claude Schmitt, *La Raison des gestes dans l'Occident médiéval* (Paris, 1990); François Garnier, *Le Langage de l'image au moyen âge: Signification et symbolique*, 2 vols. (Paris, 1982-89); also Jean-Claude Schmitt, "The Ethics of Gesture," in *Fragments for a History of the Human Body*, ed. Michel Feher, et al., 3 vols. (New York, 1989), I, 128-47.

[12] As pointed out by Kay and Rubin, *Framing Medieval Bodies*, p. 3, who cite Luce Irigary, *Speculum: Of the Other Woman*, trans. Gillian C. Gill (Ithaca,

most explicit and influential exploration of the embodied nature of consciousness, as well as the subjectivity of intention, enacted through a body knowable only through language and social systems.[13]

As the history of the body has emerged essentially as the shifting "representation" of the embodied self in discourse analysis and textual deconstruction,[14] the subtle elucidation of any small corpus of texts and images may be seen to fail in producing important insights into the problems and paradoxes of experience at large.[15] This brings us to a growing and pervasive theoretical concern with the inherent tensions between cultural constructions of the body and phenomenological embodiments of experience – the body as text (metaphor) vs. the body as lived experience. Although not necessarily mutually exclusive, constructivist and phenomenological discourses on the body clearly diverge in conceptualizing the *corpus* as a changing symbol or cultural construction as opposed to a stable, tangible, and material form — multiplicities of bodies vs. a single unitary body. As it focuses on the constitutive processes of mediating the structure of language, constructivist theory emphasizes the inaccessibility of direct experience. Textual analysis thus attempts to bring the ontology of essences into the dynamic sphere of concrete subjects fragmented by culture.[16] In contrast, the appeal of phenomenology lies in its potential for opening up and destabilizing language in the very process of its description of experience. Embodiment allows us a place from which to speak, the unique and social ground of the lived-body. At the same time, phenomenological reflection

1985); Butler, *Gender Trouble*; and Julia Kristeva, *Powers of Horror: An Essay on Abjection*, trans. Leon S. Roudiez (New York, 1982).

[13] Maurice Merleau-Ponty, *Phenomenology of Perception*, trans. Colin Smith (London, 1962), pp. 174-99.

[14] Roland Barthes, *Le Plaisir du texte* (Paris, 1973); Jacques Derrida, *Writing and Difference*, trans. Alan Bass (London, 1978).

[15] See Porter, "History of the Body," pp. 208-09.

[16] See Vivian Sobchack, *The Address of the Eye: A Phenomenology of Film Experience* (Princeton, 1992), p. xiv.

reaffirms language as "rooted in the existential and embodied significance of being."[17] In my view, the most pressing issue now facing us is how we come to terms with interfacing constructivist, phenomenological, and material approaches to the medieval body. Clearly inflected by cultural and ideological constructs, both present and past subjectivities, and above all by its material and visual presence, the human body should be explored as a dynamic site of being in all its multiplicities.

As Caroline Bynum remarks, medieval ideas and images of the body are largely considered in light of our present preoccupation with identity and the self, with carnality and desire.[18] As we have become increasingly involved with Lacanian notions of the self as integration within the symbolic order, the distinction between the self as subject (seeing and consciousness of being seen) and "other" (perceived or objectified according to the way in which what is seen is constructed by the viewer's gaze or imagination) becomes blurred.[19] The body is at the same time a metaphor for our locatedness in space and time, as well as the locus of human perception, consciousness, and knowledge. As bodies face the external world, they are visual forms for the gaze. At the same time, however, they are subjective and integral to the internal self.[20] If the body can be conceived as an intermediary between the self and society, how did individuals and social groups experience, control, and project their embodied selves? How did people understand the link between the "self" and its culturally constructed bodily extensions?[21] To return to our initial theoretical concern with tensions between constructivist and phenomenological approaches to the body, we might recast the question in terms of the lingering dichotomous regimes of mind/body or soul/body, for the two are not unrelated. In the words of Jacques Le Goff,

[17] Sobchack, *Address of the Eye*, p. xviii.

[18] Bynum, "Why All the Fuss?" p. 31.

[19] See Margaret R. Miles, *Carnal Knowing: Female Nakedness and Religious Meaning in the Christian West* (Boston, 1989).

[20] Porter, "History of the Body," pp. 223-24.

[21] See Porter, "History of the Body," p. 211.

> For the men of the Middle Ages the sacred often revealed itself in ... disconcerting interactions between the spiritual and the corporeal. ... not the least paradoxical thing about medieval Christian ideas is that the soul itself was envisioned in corporeal form.[22]

The territories of mind and body are not fixed but are assigned boundaries subject to negotiation within different systems of values, judgments, and expectations. The apportionment of function and responsibility between body and mind, body and soul, differs according to century, class, circumstances, and culture. As Roy Porter points out, societies often possess a plurality of competing meanings.[23] Although the body/soul opposition was regularly deployed in medieval rhetoric to denote "a troubling proximity of incommensurate yet coexisting entities,"[24] the relationship between body and soul was subject to constant redefinition.[25] One of the major projects of recent theoretical shifts to the historical elucidation of "material culture" has been to subvert and demolish old cultural hierarchies that privileged mind over body, thus discarding dualistic Cartesian notions largely inherited from the Enlightenment.[26] The hierarchical subordination of body to mind/soul systematically degrades the body into a blind, anarchic, sinful prison of the soul.[27] As Bynum has shown, medieval thinkers either blurred the soul/body distinctions or used ternary rather than binary models. Discourses on knowing

[22] Jacques Le Goff, *The Medieval Imagination*, trans. Arthur Goldhammer (Chicago, 1988), pp. 84-85.

[23] Porter, "History of the Body," pp. 215 and 224.

[24] Kay and Rubin, *Framing Medieval Bodies*, p. 5; see also Robert W. Ackerman, "The Debate of the Body and the Soul and Parochial Christianity," *Speculum* 37 (1962): 541-65.

[25] See G. S. Rousseau and Roy Porter, "Introduction: Toward a Natural History of Mind and Body," in *The Languages of Psyche: Mind and Body in Enlightenment Thought* (Berkeley, 1990), pp. 3-44.

[26] See Bynum, "Why All the Fuss?" p. 13.

[27] Porter, "History of the Body," p. 213.

and seeing used three categories of the body, spirit, and soul that located perception, dreams, and visions in the *corpus* or *spiritus*, not in *anima.*[28] Medieval writings about the body were as multiple and multivalent as the various discourses encountered in modern writing.[29] In the Middle Ages there were many bodies, experienced and conceived within a complex and unstable nexus of dissenting multiplicities.

### *Anglo-Saxon Bodies*

Anglo-Saxon England seems an unpromising, if not unlikely, venue for the exploration of the naked human body in texts and images. Reticence, even prudery, formed the ideologically dominant attitude towards the body that in turn provided a context of repudiation and denial.[30] As Hugh Magennis observes, Anglo-Saxon writers appear more comfortable with the asexual Germanic heroic world than with the world of the Old Testament. Clare Lees further asserts that "Anglo-Saxon art does not take as its subject the human body . . . [W]hat Anglo-Saxon writing captures is the paradox whereby the passage of the body into writing, into culture, is a passage into signification that renders the material body absent."[31] Notwithstanding the apparent paradoxical status of our subject, the collection of essays clearly engages in an ongoing conversation that intersects with other discourses on the body present, centered on gender, sexuality, and law.

[28] Bynum, "Why All the Fuss?" p. 13; also see Bynum, *Fragmentation and Redemption: Essays on Gender and the Human Body in Medieval Religion* (New York, 1991), pp. 226-27, for a further discussion of the blurring of the soul/body dichotomy.

[29] Bynum, "Why All the Fuss?" p. 33.

[30] See Hugh Magennis, "'No Sex Please, We're Anglo-Saxons'? Attitudes to Sexuality in Old English Prose and Poetry," *Leeds Studies in English* n.s. 26 (1995): 1-27, at 15.

[31] Clare A. Lees, "Engendering Religious Desire: Sex, Knowledge, and Christian Identity in Anglo-Saxon England," *Journal of Medieval and Early Modern Studies* 27 (1997): 17-45, at 23 and 39.

When we think of Anglo-Saxon culture, we tend to think in terms of a familiar but unwieldy binary opposition between Germanic tribal life and Christian Latin culture.[32] If Anglo-Saxon attitudes toward the body form a specific aspect of a distinctive cultural dynamic, what emerges as remarkably consistent in both Christian and non-Christian contexts is profound ambivalence: what Lees terms "a firm insistence on the material presence of the body" coupled with an equal insistence on its devaluation.[33] Silence and restraint produce not only regulation and repression but "a precise cultural logic" that facilitates the displacement of the material body into the spiritual realm. As Lees has shown, the process is a simple maneuver of "metaphoric substitution or *translatio,* which can be seen ... as the linguistic counterpart to sublimation."[34] In Lacanian terms, the body most often negotiates its transformation into the symbolic through metaphor.[35] However, the general medieval process of *translatio* becomes "distinctively Anglo-Saxon in its ambivalent stance toward both the materiality of the sign and its referent."[36] As the site of temporality, sin, and death, the living body was sometimes conceived as a container for the spirit or soul *(sawulhus, feorhus),* as in the Old English poem, *The Soul's Address to the Body,* in which the body is depicted as the prison of the soul, the inferior exterior shell which surrounds an immortal spiritual being.[37] Within the context of the saintly or heroic life, death provided the critical catalyst for a dense metaphoric transformation (*translatio*) of the body into a signifier of the embodied life of the spirit.[38]

[32] Lees, "Engendering Religious Desire," p. 22.

[33] Lees, "Engendering Religious Desire," pp. 22-23.

[34] Lees, "Engendering Religious Desire," p. 19.

[35] Lees, "Engendering Religious Desire," p. 24.

[36] Lees, "Engendering Religious Desire," p. 25.

[37] See Michelle Hoek, "Violence and Ideological Inversion in the Old English *Soul's Address to the Body,*" *Exemplaria* 10 (1998): 271-85; Lees, "Engendering Religious Desire," p. 24.

[38] Lees, "Engendering Religious Desire," p. 25.

In the great social rituals of Old English heroic literature as well as in the rituals of liturgical worship, there are abundant traces of the material body. But it is the fragmented body, as signifier of material death and spiritual life that tends to dominate the discourse. Parts of the body are scattered throughout Anglo-Saxon literary and cultural texts. In the extremely complex relation between bodies and body parts, connections between bodily and controlling systems of organization are most powerfully encoded by the semiotics of any given part — "where the tensions between the metaphoric and the metonymic, between the floating and the firmly contextualized, or more generally between conditions of autonomy and dependence are powerfully articulated."[39] The part becomes a subject imagined to take on the attribution of agency and subjectivity, as with Grendel's arm or St. Agatha's breast.[40] As Katherine O'Brien O'Keeffe has admirably demonstrated in her investigation of the body as subject in Anglo-Saxon law, body parts figure as commodities of exchange within an economy of pain, loss, payment and value.[41] Within legal codes that compensated visible injuries more heavily than those not seen, the efficacy of punishment was thought to reside in the spectacle of the criminal's mutilated body.[42] Absent arms, legs, hands, feet, noses, or ears mapped ineradicable signs of guilt upon the criminal body. As O'Keeffe points out, the Anglo-Saxon notion that forensic action on the guilty body should be "readable" crosses ecclesiastical and secular boundaries in some interesting ways. For example, in contrast to the common early medieval death penalty for theft, Æthelred's law code V (1008) specified that punishments should be devised that spare the

[39] David Hillman and Carla Mazzio, eds., *The Body in Parts: Fantasies of Corporeality in Early Modern Europe* (New York, 1997), p. xii.

[40] See Gilles Deleuze and Félix Guattari, *Anti-Oedipus: Capitalism and Schizophrenia* (1977, repr. Minneapolis, 1983), who seek to replace the uniquely privileged phallus with the diverse dynamics and flux of the *corps morcelé.*

[41] Katherine O'Brien O'Keeffe, "Body and Law in Late Anglo-Saxon England," *Anglo-Saxon England* 27 (1998): 209-32, at 212.

[42] O'Keeffe, "Body and Law," pp. 215 and 227.

lives of criminals in the interest of their salvation.[43] Such punishments taking the form of mutilation enacted on the bodies of criminals formed a significant development in the construction of the Anglo-Saxon legal subject where the notion of punishments that assisted salvation were sought to extend the reach of the law into the soul, thus rendering the body as a site in which secular law and divine power meet.[44]

Although Anglo-Saxon England can now be perceived as a richly promising terrain for the exploration of the human body, naked or otherwise, we must nevertheless still confront the widely held perception that characterizes its temporal place as different from other periods of English history, as located in a period "before history." Lees and Overing argue, however, that the prevailing tendency to alienate Anglo-Saxon culture from the current debates in medieval studies on the nature of subjectivity and identity, the body, gender, and sexuality, representation and power, is based on a false premise of differentiation from the later Middle Ages.[45] Seen in this conventional context, Anglo-Saxon England is defined by periodization (pre-Conquest), social formation (tribal), language (Old English, not Latin), and religion (pagan and Christian). Although, as Lees and Overing remind us, it is imperative to engage modern concerns when we confront the past, we need not project our explorations forward until "the medieval world starts to resemble, however precariously, the modern."[46] If we reason by analogy rather than merely re-writing or rejecting history, Bynum argues, "the present will help us see past complexity and the past will help us to under

[43] O'Keeffe, "Body and Law," p. 216. Such punishments allowing the transgressor an opportunity to save his soul were described by the phrase *per penas salvandi [sunt]*.

[44] O'Keeffe, "Body and Law," pp. 230 and 218-19.

[45] Lees and Overing, "Before History," pp. 315-19.

[46] Lees and Overing, "Before History," p. 315.

stand ourselves."[47] We do not seek identity by attempting to locate ourselves within a spatio-temporal continuity. Our concern is rather to account for the simultaneous strangeness and familiarity of medieval bodies, "to find some way of touching those afflicted, desiring, mysterious medieval bodies across time's distance," however great, as in the case of Anglo-Saxon England.[48]

When we reject the totalization of the Middle Ages as unitary and seamless, we find ourselves left with a Foucauldian retotalizing on the grounds of its dissenting multiplicities. As Valerie Allen has observed, "Why the body?" has become inextricably bound up with "Why the Middle Ages?" In the historical discourse constructed by Foucault, consideration of the physical human body and the chronological body of the Middle Ages is driven by perceptions and conceptualizations of difference. Foucault understands that history is difference, that alterity is an epistemological category. Meaning is produced in the process of differentiation between history and now. "The medieval is medieval," Allen notes, "because out of it we write fables of difference." In our desire to restore meaning to present bodies,

> we inquire into the past not in order to see it in itself, but to see as if in a mirror what is impossible for us to see without a mirror. The past emerges as meaningful insofar as it is what we, in the present, are not.[49]

Foucault's radical reading of history as *différance* raises the problem of boundaries – of the body, textuality, and language.[50] Boundaries are not simply there, waiting to be transgressed; they have to be constructed, and new ones erase the old. But if

[47] Bynum, "Why All the Fuss?" p. 31.

[48] Valerie Allen, "Middle-Aged Bodies," *Envoi* 7 (1998): 1-17, at 1.

[49] Quoted by Allen, "Middle-Aged Bodies," p. 12, who notes that Gilles Deleuze read these lines aloud at Foucault's funeral; see James Miller, *The Passion of Michel Foucault* (New York, 1993), pp. 35-36.

[50] See Peter Stallybrass, "Boundary and Transgression: Body, Text, Language," *Stanford French Review* 14 (1990): 9-23, at 9.

we begin to comprehend the contingency of limits, to what extent do boundaries remain invisible? To know the boundaries of our own being, we would have to stand outside ourselves, comparing the known and the unknown, our perspective and the perspective that transgresses ours.[51] As Wittgenstein argued, however, those boundaries are the very horizons of the obvious, of what is taken for granted:

> The aspects of things that are most important for us are hidden because of their simplicity and familiarity .... We fail to be struck by what, once seen, is the most striking and the most powerful.[52]

To understand trangression, we need to understand that the formation of boundaries is contingent and unstable.[53] As Peter Stallybrass argues, if boundaries are vulnerable, they also suggest potential metamorphosis: "transgressions of bodily boundaries map transformations of the psychic economy, of spatial division, and of the hierarchies of social formation."[54]

Boundary problems are implicit in medieval definitions of gender. According to Genesis 1:27, the whole world had to be considered as gendered ("male and female he created them"). In medieval discourse, however, gender is never grounded in the sense that a stable division was fixed between male and female. As boundaries were produced and trans-

[51] Stallybrass, "Boundary and Transgression," pp. 10-11, who cites Ludwig Wittgenstein, *Tractatus Logico-Philosophicus* (London, 1961), p. 117. Transgression and transformation constitute the conditions necessary to making boundaries visible. For example, see Joyce Lionarons, "Bodies, Buildings, and Boundaries: Metaphors of Liminality in Old English and Old Norse Literature," *Essays in Medieval Studies* 11 (1994): 43-50.

[52] Ludwig Wittgenstein, *Philosophical Investigations*, trans. G. E. M. Anscombe (Oxford, 1968), p. 50.

[53] Stallybrass, "Boundary and Transgression," p. 11.

[54] Stallybrass, "Boundary and Transgression," p. 16. Mary Douglas, *Purity and Danger: An Analysis of the Concepts of Pollution and Taboo* (London, 1969), p. 21, postulates that any structure of ideas is vulnerable at its margins. We should expect the orifices of the body to symbolize its specially vulnerable points.

formed rather than biologically given, the body was shaped and imagined through discursive categories that problematize inside and outside, body and identity.[55]

The cultural problematics of boundary and transgression bring us back to one of Foucault's most important contributions to the history of the medieval body. In the first volume of his *History of Sexuality*,[56] Foucault asserted that for the Middle Ages, the *actus* formed the center of identity, but that acts are multiple and discursive. He reimagines sexual difference as identity in the making, under construction, as formative, fluid, and reversible. As this notion was formulated by Aristotle in the *Nicomachean Ethics* (II.4.1), the reiteration of deeds into habits defines our moral being. The medieval *actus* presupposes the agency of the body, for there are no actions without bodies and no moral natures without habitual actions. In rethinking the subject, the body is necessarily reconsidered. The medieval *actus*, whether moral, sexual or both, performs and affirms identity and defines the body.[57] The body can thus be construed as a site of resistance and challenge, involving the transcendence or deconstruction of seemingly fixed dichotomies, such as male/female, human/beast, body/soul, at the same time as the body itself seems to delineate the contours of such culturally constructed oppositions.

### *The Present Collection*

In the following collection, the essays are uniformly focused on a dead language (Old English) in a remote area of the medieval spectrum (Anglo-Saxon England). But the collaboration is consciously framed around the still-living, ever present human body that we all share. Each author engages in critical self-consciousness to extend the boundaries of a medieval culture, so circumscribed in time and space, by invoking contemporary

[55] Stallybrass, "Boundary and Transgression," pp. 17-19.

[56] Michel Foucault, *History of Sexuality, vol. 1: An Introduction*, trans. Robert Hurley (London, 1978).

[57] See Allen, "Middle-Aged Bodies," pp. 13, 15-16.

theoretical approaches to reading, writing, and imaging — whether Foucauldian, Lacanian or Derridean. While all the essays in this collection "read" texts and images, they do so in order to see them as embodiments of cultural forces that critical analysis can dislodge, scrutinize, and identify. Their goal has not been to "apply" theory to the same small Anglo-Saxon corpus of visual and textual representations of the body but to test the flexibility of theoretical paradigms.[58]

What emerges when this collection is viewed as a whole is not only multiplicity and ambiguity in representing Anglo-Saxon bodies. It is the stunning realization of the culture's self-consciousness and awareness of the body's paradoxical nature. Revealed in a procession of vivid and diverse rhetorical strategies drawn from an impressive accumulation of evidence, Anglo-Saxon constructions confront the body's indeterminacy and transgressions in a disparate range of contexts, both real and imagined. Although *Naked Before God* might appear to suggest a unifying syntax, Anglo-Saxon bodies will be seen to resist any kind of totalizing coherence, offering instead multiple sites of morphing, transformation, instability, fragmentation, exposure, and negotiation.

[58] See Allen J. Frantzen, ed., *Speaking Two Languages: Traditional Disciplines and Contemporary Theory in Medieval Studies* (Albany, NY, 1991), pp. ix-xv.

# The Wanton Hand: Reading and Reaching into Grammars and Bodies in Old English Riddle 12

SARAH L. HIGLEY

THIS ESSAY is a study of the Old English word *swifeð* as it is used in the much talked of Riddle 12.[1] Although it is not a *hapax legomenon,* as it occurs five other times in the entire Anglo-Saxon corpus, its use here is a curious one, made all the more so by its rarity. In place of the ordinary usage of *swifeð* (intransitive) "moves," I propose that it mean something else in Riddle 12, something more akin to the meaning (transitive) that it developed in Chaucer's day. This puts it in the realm of what C.S. Lewis might have called a "dangerous sense" (d.s.),[2] since it can so easily bend to one's desire to make it have this meaning, make it solve the problem of its difficult grammar, make it prove the salaciousness of its context, and the contemned activity of the woman who is the centerpiece of the riddle. In short, I want to make *swifeð me* yield its probable, vulgar, and most "dangerous sense" of unveiled coitus, and to show that it may exhibit not only a double meaning in an obscene riddle but double valency — that is, in linguistic

[1] I want to thank all the scholars who responded to the questions I raised about Riddle 12 in the summer of 1997 on electronic listservs ANSAX and MEDFEM — Paul Acker, Norman Hinton, Susan Granquist, Lorraine Stock, and the late Ted Irving, and especially Nina Rulon-Miller, my partner in riddling, who has also recently written on this text, and who has been so generous in sharing ideas to which I hope I will give good credit.

[2] "The dominant sense of any word lies uppermost in our minds. Wherever we meet the word, our natural impulse will be to give it that sense. When this operation results in nonsense, of course, we see our mistake and try over again. But if it makes tolerable sense our tendency is to go merrily on. We are often deceived. In an old author the word may mean something different. I call such senses dangerous senses because they lure us into misreadings. In examining a word I shall often have to distinguish one of its meanings as its *dangerous sense*, and I shall symbolize this by writing the word (in italics) with the letters *d.s.* after it." *Studies in Words* (Cambridge, 1960), p. 13.

terminology, an extra argument and transitive force. If the Riddles represent naked and clothed meaning (to invoke Ælfric's familiar *nacedan gerecednisse*), I want to see, as I think the Exeter Book riddlers did, both word and woman revealed. The swiving woman may not be "naked before God," but she is naked, one presumes, before the servants of God in a poem recorded and read by learned men. This essay, then, has two thrusts: it tackles the problems of both grammar and solution in Riddle 12, and also the fraught issues of hermeneutics and sexuality that inform our readings of it. It strives to locate the tension between critical desire and careful philology, a difficult task when the latter may not easily serve the former, especially given the rare words and *double entendres.* Before I begin an analysis of this poem from the Exeter Book, let me start by invoking a much later text, one that raises the question of contemplation, distraction, and desire.

Walter Hilton's fourteenth-century *Scale of Perfection,* dedicated to an unknown anchoress, is a study of right meditation of Christ's divine body, and in Chapter 52 of Part I he begins to talk of a counter-image that will preoccupy the meditator and draw her away from her vision.[3] It takes the form of a thing the author calls "nought," or nothing, but it becomes clear that it has some kind of vile body that spouts limbs and rivers. Sarah Stanbury identifies the evil of the "murk ymage" with medieval biases against swarthy complexions, often given to the demons who appear in medieval illuminations as tormentors of the white-faced Christ.[4] Although *The Scale of Perfection* post-dates The Exeter Book by several hundred years, I find its preoccupation with a mysterious dark idol, emblem of self and sinfulness, to be peculiarly resonant with the distracting, mysterious, and dark body of the *wale,* perhaps reflecting a corresponding Anglo-Saxon fear of

[3] See the edition by Evelyn Underhill (London, 1923), and the translation by John P.H. Clark and Rosemary Dorward (New York, 1991). A TEAMS edition by Thomas H. Bestul (Kalamazoo, 2000) is now available.

[4] "Seductions of the Dark Image in Walter Hilton's *Scale of Perfection,*" unpublished paper delivered at the University of Rochester on April 2, 1999.

foreign faces, foreign coloring, and the foreign terrain of female sexuality. Following is W. S. Mackie's edition of the poem (chosen for its manuscript fidelity and avoidance of punctuation),[5] and my overly literal interlinear translation. This translation is intended as an interim gloss and not a "final" modern English equivalent (hence the alternative meanings in enclosed parantheses), and for that reason I make the translations of other scholars available for comparison. In my essay, I will focus in particular on lines 7b to 13a, as these have been most troubling to interpretation.

*The Riddle*

1 ***Fotum ic fere foldan slite***
on foot I go earth [I] tear
2 ***grene wongas þenden ic gæst bere***
green fields when I a spirit bear
3 ***gif me feorh losað fæste binde***
if from me life gets loose (i.e., "I die"), firmly [I] bind
4 ***swearte wealas hwilum sellan men***
dark Welshmen sometimes better men.
5 ***hwilum ic deorum drincan selle***
Sometimes I to brave ones give drink,
6 ***beorn[e] of bosme hwilum mec bryd triedeð***
to men from [my?] bosom; sometimes me the woman treads
7 ***felawlonc fotum hwilum feorran broht***
proud [wanton] one with feet. Sometimes from afar brought
8 ***wonfeax wale wegeð ond þyð***
dark-haired Welshwoman supports and presses [me?]
9 ***dol druncmennen deorcum nihtum***
stupid drunken servant in the dark nights
10 ***wæteð in wætre wyrmeð hwilum***
wets [me?] in water, warms [me?] sometimes
11 ***fægre to fyre me on fæðme sticaþ***
nicely by the fire; in my depths sticks [*me* = dative of

[5] W.S. Mackie, *The Exeter Book: Part II*, EETS o.s. 194 (London, 1934; repr. 1958), pp. 100-02.

possession] *or*: sticks me in depths? *me* = obj. of *sticaþ*? *fæðm* = dat. "bosom, lap, depths"

12 ***hygegalan hond    hwyrfeð geneahhe***
wanton's hand [NOM],    turns often enough
*or*: wanton hand [ACC], obj. of *sticaþ*?

13 ***swifeð me geond sweartne    saga hwæt ic hatte***
sweeps [me?] through dark thing; say what I am called, Tanke: moves through me, the dark one (postposition *geond*; see below). Mackie: sweeps across my blackness (*me* = dative of possession; see below).

14 ***þe ic lifgende    lond reafige***
I who living    [the] land plunder

15 ***ond æfter deaþe    dryhtum þeowig : – :7***
and after death    serve lords.

Here is John Tanke's translation of lines 7b to the end:

> ...sometimes a dark-haired *wale*, brought from afar, silly drunken slave, moves and presses (me) on dark nights, wets (me) in water, warms (me) at times, fairly by the fire; the lustful one's hand sticks in my embrace, turns often, moves through me, the dark one. Say what I am called, I who, living, plunder the land and, dead, serve people.[6]

Here is W.S. Mackie's, with *hygegalan hond* as object of *sticaþ*:

> Sometimes a dark-haired Welsh-woman,
> brought from far, a foolish drunken servant-girl,
> on dark nights lifts and presses me,
> wets me in water, sometimes warms me
> well at the fire, sticks into my bosom
> her wanton hand, turns me round often,
> sweeps across my blackness. Say what I am called,
> who when living despoil the land
> and after death serve men.[7]

[6] "*Wonfeax wale*: Ideology and Figuration in the Sexual Riddles of the Exeter Book," in *Class and Gender in Early English Literature: Intersections,* ed. Britton J. Harwood and Gillian R. Overing (Bloomington, 1994), pp. 21-42, at 33.

[7] *The Exeter Book*, pp. 101-03.

Paull F. Baum's translation makes *hygegalan hond* plural and restores it as subject of *sticaþ*:

> Sometimes the Welsh girl,
> dark-haired slave  brought from afar,
> stupid and drunk,  on dark nights
> lifts me and presses me,  soaks me in water,
> warms me sometimes  kindly by the fire,
> her wanton hands  thrust in my bosom;
> turning often  sweeps through the dark.
> Say what my name is  who living ravage
> the land, and dead  am of service to men.[8]

Craig Williamson gives a more liberal translation (omitting the object pronoun):

> Sometimes the dark-haired, drunken slave
> Lifts me up near the night fire
> With hot hands — turns, teases,
> Presses, thrusts, warm and wet,
> Down dark ways.[9]

Kevin Crossley-Holland's translation makes *me* of line thirteen the object of a transitive *sticaþ*:

> Sometimes a slave-girl, raven-haired, brought far from Wales, cradles and presses me–some stupid, sozzled maidservant, she fills me with water on dark nights, warms me by the gleaming fire; on my breast she places a wanton hand and writhes about, then sweeps me against her dark declivity.[10]

Nina Rulon-Miller also interprets *sticaþ* as transitive in both her "innocent" and "obscene" translations. In the former she attempts to "minimize ... the sexual innuendo and its preoccupation with servitude," and in the latter emphasizes the fixation on "binding and fetters." In the meantime, she marks the

[8] *Anglo-Saxon Riddles of the Exeter Book* (Durham, 1963), p. 24.

[9] *A Feast of Creatures: Anglo-Saxon Riddle-Songs* (Philadelphia, 1982), p. 70.

[10] *The Exeter Book Riddles* (Harmondsworth, 1979), p. 34.

presence of the object pronoun *mec* in one and its absence in the other, adjusting the meaning of *hygegalan* accordingly):

*Innocent Version:*

> Sometimes brought from afar, a dark-haired Welsh woman, a foolish, drunken maid, on dark nights lifts and presses me, moistens me with water; at times she heats me, carefully, over a fire; she pierces my surface with her skillful hand; she turns me often, rotates me through a black substance. Say what I am called, I, who living break up the soil, and after death, serve men.

*Obscene Version:*

> Now, carried off from far away, a dark-haired Welsh slave-woman shakes and squeezes me, stupid, drunken slave, in the dark of night she becomes moist with wetness, now gets nicely hot by the fire; with her wanton hand she thrusts me into her womb; she writhes excessively, she swivels me all around her blackness. Say what I am called, I, who living violate the land, and after death, serve men.[11]

In short, the deceptively readable line — *swifeð me geond sweartne* "sweeps me through the dark" — presents a host of problems that arise when its grammar is scrutinized. It is curious that the "popular" translations, like those offered by Crossley-Holland and Rulon-Miller, yield to a common-sense insight that has a logic that the grammar does not support, and which is belabored by the more "correct" translations like that by Mackie and Tanke. This is the conundrum I intend to address.

*The Solution*

At the end, or at the center, of Old English Riddle 12 is a *sweartne*, a "dark thing." Like Walter Hilton's "murk ymage" it

[11] "Sexual Humor and Fettered Desire in Exeter Book Riddle 12," in *Humour in Old English Literature*, ed. Jonathan Wilcox (Cambridge, 2000), pp. 99-126; translations at 125.

draws us down a funnel of confusion, down and away from the literal interpretation of this riddle about an ordinary ox and into the contemplation of a woman's dark glamor. *Sweart* in Old English carries powerfully negative connotations; for instance, in *Christ III* it is the demons that are black, the angels that are white:

þær gemengde beoð
onhælo gelac engla ond deofla,
beorhtra ond blacra. Weorþeð bega cyme,
hwitra ond sweartra, swa him is ham sceapen
ungelice, englum ond deoflum. (lines 894b-98)[12]

Further on in *Christ* it is the "swarthy fire" of hell that burns the damned ("Seoþeð swearta leg synne on fordonum," l. 994). *Swearte*, as adverb, indicates evil intent: "darkly, dismally, evilly," according to Bosworth and Toller.[13] So when the word appears in a poem about a foreign slave-woman who is determined by her dark hair (and by implication her "swarthy" complexion; her fellow Welshmen in line 4 are explicitly *swearte*), and shown engaging in a covert activity late at night, it draws us darkly, like a magnet. After decades of perusal, finding the solution to Riddle 12 (what is the speaking subject?) has given way to identifying and discussing the activity of this drunken, black-haired, Welsh servant woman and her wanton hand, pressing the subject, wetting it, warming it at the fire and sweeping (it?) through something black. Our attention has wandered, it seems, from the central question to the peripheral one, enticing us to bend the rules of Old English grammar in some of the more difficult and suggestive passages — to stretch the mean-

[12] George Philip Krapp and Elliot Van Kirk Dobbie, eds., *The Exeter Book*, ASPR 3 (New York, 1936), p. 28.

There shall be mingled
the entire host of angels and devils,
of bright ones and dark. Both are come
of white ones and black, as a home is shaped for them,
for angels and devils diversely.

[13] Joseph Bosworth and T. Northcote Toller, *An Anglo-Saxon Dictionary* (1898; repr. Oxford, 1991), s. v. *swearte*.

ing of *stician*, to turn the rare verb *swifeð* into a transitive, to fill in the missing *mecs*, to revise the meaning of *hygegalan* and *hond*. Center and periphery are precisely the issues that fool us in this and other texts. The Old English Riddles offer some of the best quarry for insight into our own contemporary preoccupations and reading practices, especially the Old English salacious riddles. Already intentionally opaque as riddles, they add another layer of opacity in their double meanings. They focus our own desires and obsessions as well as our hermeneutics. What is it that we are seeing in Riddle 12 that others have missed or have refused to see, and why? Which is the "naked text" in an obscene Old English riddle — the prurient or the innocent solution? What absence in this poem entices us to fill it with a presence of our own making? Years of critical theory have stressed that it is not enough sometimes to ask what is *in* an ancient text, but rather what the tools and assumptions are that we bring to deducing what we *think* is in it.

When it was assumed that the riddlers had only one solution in mind, especially when we compared them to Aldhelm's Latin counterparts (which give the solutions in the title), scholars argued over the answers and the clues given. F. Dietrich, Moritz Trautman, Frederick Tupper, Jr. and W. S. Mackie all agreed on "leather" or "oxhide";[14] Craig Williamson felt this answer was too general and suggested "ox,"[15] in its services both living and dead — in other words, all the parts of an ox in all its uses. When it was felt that the solutions were more or less discovered, or that finessing them could go on indefinitely, then scholars discussed open-endedness and the role of the reader in making meaning, along with the subtle traps laid by translation, the social and political implications of the Exeter Riddles, their participation in an Anglo-Saxon

[14] F. Dietrich, "Die Rätsel des Exeterbuch," *Zeitschrift für deutsches Altertum und deutsche Literatur* 11 (1859): 463; Trautman and Tupper cited in Craig Williamson, ed., *The Old English Riddles of the Exeter Book* (Chapel Hill, 1977), p. 166; W.S. Mackie, in Appendix A to *The Exeter Book*, p. 240.

[15] *Old English Riddles of the Exeter Book*, pp. 166-68.

aesthetic, and issues of center and margin.[16] When race, class, and gender became a focus, attention has turned in Riddle 12 to the activity of the woman, a riddle within a riddle, and its revealed attitudes towards slavery, ethnicity, and sexuality in the figure of this servant, derided not only for her activity, whatever it is, but her darkness and her lack of breeding. Now that it has become licit to discuss sex openly in articles, and even *de rigeur*, what the servant girl is doing takes center stage. The body has again become, as it was in the Middle Ages, a revered and reviled object of critical scrutiny, mysterious and compelling, beautiful and repellant, closed and permeable, and inextricably associated with glossing. Interpretation was and is an unclothing of a passive and silent corpus.

John Tanke's splendid article, "*Wonfeax wale*: Ideology and Figuration in the Sexual Riddles of the Exeter Book," attempts to undress not merely Riddle 12 and its dark body, but the Old English obscene riddles in general.[17] His focus on the

[16] Seth Lerer examines the Exeter Book Riddles in terms of their contexts, i.e., "the multiple environments contributing to an English riddling poetic." One of his major claims is that the Riddles constitute catalogue poetry, or a "book of lists." See his *Literacy and Power in Anglo-Saxon Literature* (Lincoln, 1991), p. 98, 99. In *Between Languages: The Uncooperative Text in Early Welsh and Old English Nature Poetry* (University Park, PA, 1993), I have examined the Old English Riddles from the standpoint of their context within an aesthetic of "deliberate obscurity," to which I compare certain Middle Welsh poems; Pauline E. Head looks to the Riddles primarily to demonstrate her arguments about the disjunct uses of chronology and space in Old English poetry, the conflation of center and margin, past and present (*Representation and Design: Tracing a Hermeneutics of Old English Poetry* [Albany, 1997], pp. 40-45). Prior to these studies, decades of work have been devoted to reader-response theory — shifting the analysis away from the text and on to the reading of the text — perhaps best summed up by Wolfgang Iser, *The Act of Reading: A Theory of Aesthetic Response* (Baltimore, 1978), and Umberto Eco, *The Role of the Reader: Explorations in the Semiotics of Texts* (Bloomington, 1979); and not only has the process of translation been minutely pored over and defined, but extensive examinations have been made of the thorny problem of the modern reader of medieval texts — far too many for a short note to name. My point: prevalent theories about texts will often dictate what it is we find important in texts.

[17] "*Wonfeax wale*," see note 6 above.

*wale* leads him to differ with Edith Whitehurst Williams[18] and Craig Williamson,[19] both of whom offer interpretations of the poem that are based on assumptions they have drawn about the treatment of women, servility, and female sexuality (discussed below). My own essay, then, is a response to these interpretations, but also a comment on the temptations of sex and translation — in which case it deals just about equally with grammars and bodies as the title indicates. It is more a process of investigation than a piece of exposition, wherein I thread my own way through this labyrinth and its temptations. As such, I do not mean to offer a solution or a definitive translation of the riddle, nor am I sure what it is we reveal of it when we have unraveled these layers and gotten tangled in them.

*The Problems*

Edith Whitehurst Williams strives to show that the Old English sexual riddles present "wholesome and spontaneous" attitudes towards female sexuality: this belief colors her interpretation of the *wonfeax wale* whom she declares is ridiculed not because she is a woman, but because she is a slave.[20] But then, in the seventies and early eighties, Old English feminist criticism was invested in finding positive images of women.[21] Craig Williamson's interpretation in *A Feast of Creatures* assumes that the

[18] "What's So New About the Sexual Revolution? Some Comments on Anglo-Saxon Attitudes Toward Sexuality in Women Based on Four Exeter Book Riddles," *The Texas Quarterly*, 18.2 (1975): 46-55. Reprinted in *New Readings on Women in Old English Literature*, ed. Helen Damico and Alexandra Hennessey Olsen (Bloomington, 1990), pp. 137-45.

[19] *A Feast of Creatures: Anglo-Saxon Riddle-Songs*; see note 9 above.

[20] "What's So New About the Sexual Revolution?"; see note 18 above.

[21] I am thinking in particular of the influential "double" book by Christine Fell, and Cecily Clark and Elizabeth Williams, *Women in Anglo-Saxon England and the Impact of 1066* (Bloomington, 1984). See especially Fell's discussion of the obscene riddle, p. 71. Readers may wish to contrast this treatment of the obscene riddles to the current study in this volume by Mercedes Salvador who looks upon them as negative images issued by a primarily ecclesiastical body of writers intended to remind readers of the strife between body and soul and warn them of the dangers of sin.

woman's cryptic sexual actions include pleasuring her lord, and not herself. But then, *A Feast of Creatures* is a poetic reinterpretation of Old English poems with which Williamson takes liberties in his inventive language, including producing a philandering lord that is not there. Both readings capitulate to the inventions and assumptions of the reader/translator and the context in which they read. All readings do. While taking issue with these prior interpretations, Tanke sees the woman's auto-eroticism in the empowering light of her autonomy. She is the agent of her own pleasure. I have my own more outlandish readings, but I also ponder in general the implications of reading cryptic sexual texts for contemporary readers and translators. The riddle at this point, both in its grammar and its imagery, becomes coyly unclear, and all of us have to reach into the words that are there, the words that might be there, and the words that are not in order to get what we want out of it.

Let us take a closer look: the speaking creature, a beast who renders its services while alive and dead, "slits the earth, and the green fields when it goes on foot, when it bears a spirit," presumably as a living ox drawing a plow. When life is "loosed" from it, it binds dark Welshmen [*wealas*] or foreign slaves, sometimes better men [freemen?], presumably when it is the leather rope made from its hide. It gives drink to brave men from its bosom, presumably when it is a leather bottle. It is under the foot of a proud or wanton (*felawlonc*) woman when it is presumably a hide rug, or shoes; and then, line 7b: "At times, brought from afar, the *wonfeax wale*, or dark-haired Welsh or foreign woman, supports and presses" [one must supply the object pronoun, *me/mec*, as in so many of the other riddles], *dol druncmennen*, "stupid drunken servant," in dark nights, wets ["me" understood] in water, warms ["me" understood] at times nicely by the fire. It is disconcerting how this *mec* simply drops out of sight as if it, or its writer, cannot bear to be the recipient of so much female carnality and manipulation. This *hygegalan hond*, or hand of the wanton one, sticks in the speaker's bosom [the first use of the pronoun is a dative of possession — "bosom with respect to me, bosom of mine"].

Here we must stop and examine this *hapax*. The compound *hyge* and *galan* occurs only in this poem. *Hyge* means "mind" or "thought"; *gal*, according to Bosworth and Toller, means "lust, wantonness, lightness, folly" as a noun, and "light, pleasant, wanton, licentious, and wicked" as an adjective, which I take to be either a substantive adjective in the genitive case, or an adjective agreeing with accusative *hond*. Most translators have chosen to see it as a transgressive hand, an unpleasant or undisciplined hand, or the hand of someone transgressive and foolish. It seems to mirror the use in Riddle 45, another obscene riddle, of *hygewlonc hondum*, "the proud/wanton one with her hands" — a different grammatical construction, which employs the same metrical space. (Metrically and grammatically, *hygewlonc hondum* is the same as *felawlonc fotum* in our poem; the Old English poetic formula allows for a lot of swapping around of construction and connotation). This hand belongs to a *wale*, a word that means both "foreigner" and "Briton" in Old English. Drawing on prior study of the subject, Rulon-Miller gives us the most succinct discussion of the negative image of the Welsh slave in Old English in her article. I need not rehearse it here except to repeat her fascinating observation that "in the riddles Welsh people appear almost without fail in some relation to binding, or bovines, or both."[22] In lines 12 and 13, the hand of this wanton turns often ["me"? understood] and — here's the clincher —

> Swifeð me geond sweartne

— sweeps ["me"? direct object of an otherwise intransitive verb?] through the dark or black thing [*sweartne*, acc. masculine]. Or: it sweeps through the dark thing *of mine* [dative of possession]. I will get to the important perusal of *swifeð* shortly. Meanwhile, we have already entered a deep grammatical and interpretive bog.

[22] Rulon-Miller, "Sexual Humor and Fettered Desire," p. 117.

*Dildoes, Condoms, and the Problem of Stician*

The obscene riddles, as it has been observed, operate on our being aware of an overt and covert solution to what they describe: an innocent activity which it is the joke of the riddler to make us think is prurient. That this section of Riddle 12 participates in the conventions of other more obviously "obscene" riddles is evident from its use of the stock OE vocabulary for innuendo–*hygegalan,* "wanton" and other compounds with *hyge* and *wlonc* that are suggestive of prurient-mindedness; *hond* or *hondum,* "hand," "with hands"; *þyð,* "presses," *fæðm,* "bosom," "breast," "lap," "depths," "embrace"; *sticaþ,* "stick" — and we assume that like the other riddles devoted to *double entendres,* this description also has an innocent interpretation. So what is it, on the level, that this woman is doing with a piece of leather? August Prehn wrote that it was a *Wamms,* "jerkin," doubling as the maiden's lover;[23] Tupper offered "glove";[24] Christine Fell said "bed covering";[25] Paull F. Baum "shoes" (the very ones worn by the *felawlonc*),[26] and Williamson "shoes" or "shirt."[27] The fact that her hand sticks in its depths and sweeps [verb intransitive] through a dark thing has made most critics favor something hollow, and Rulon-Miller suggests that what the woman is doing in the innocent version is making a bottle using a technique known later on as *cuir bouilli,* or "boiled leather."[28] This is an ingenious solution, and a fitting one, so to

[23] "Komposition und Quellen der Rätsel des Exeterbuches," *Neuphilologische Studien* 3 (1883): 176: "Vielleicht bezeichnet ersteres ein Wamms und deutet auf den Geliebten der schwarzlockigen Welschen hin, u.s.w.," quoted by Frederick Tupper, Jr., ed., *The Riddles of the Exeter Book* (Boston, 1910), pp. 95-96.

[24] *Riddles of the Exeter Book,* p. 96.

[25] *Women in Anglo-Saxon England,* p. 67.

[26] *Anglo Saxon Riddles of the Exeter Book,* p. 24.

[27] *A Feast of Creatures,* p. 170.

[28] "Sexual Humor and Fettered Desire," pp. 119-21: "If we follow the *wonfeax wale* at work, step-by-step, we find, first of all, that she is using bovine hide, the preferred material for *cuir bouilli.* She also may be stretching and fitting the leather onto a mold (*wegeð ond þyð,* "moves and presses," line 8b); then moistening the leather to keep it damp *(wæteð in wætre,* 10a); then

speak, but I prefer the more available and commonplace image of a servant using a piece of leather as a washrag to clean a cooking vessel — rather like Shakespeare's "greasy Joan."[29] It seems more reasonable to me to think that the *wonfeax* is wetting it, she is warming it at the fire, and she is wrapping it around her hand where her fingers *sticaþ* in its *fæðme* because she is washing up. The dark thing, *sweartne*, through which she sweeps, could easily be a cauldron charred by the fire. The fact that it is night suggests that it is a postprandial chore, as does the woman's tipsy state. I like the idea of the dark cauldron because it presents such an available metaphor for the womb, and retains the same grammar and the same sense of *fæðm* on either side of the innocent/obscene polarity.

Rulon-Miller goes on, however, to make the bolder suggestion that what the woman is doing on a prurient level is using her leather bottle like a dildo. As far as I know, this interpretation has not yet been offered. I second this insight about the dildo (if not the bottle) and have a few suggestions of my own. Tanke was the first to suggest "female masturbation" as the obscene answer to the woman's late night activity. His understanding, however, is that the speaking leather subject is doubling as the woman's vagina. In sticking her wanton hand into its depths (*fæðme*), a word that Ann Harleman Stewart declares is used as well in Riddle 63 with the prurient meaning,[30] she is putting her fingers into herself, and he remarks

heating it from time to time (*wyrmeð hwilum*, 10b), carefully (*fægre*, 11a) so as not to singe it, over a fire (*to fyre*, 11a); then tooling, embossing, and/or sewing it before it becomes too hard to work with (*me on fæðme sticaþ*, 11b)."

[29] Who "doth keel the pot." *Love's Labours Lost*, V.ii. 909. Of course what Joan is doing in "keeling" the pot is stirring it so that it will not boil over.

[30] "Double Entendre in the Old English Riddles," *Lore and Language* 3 (1983): 39-52, at 49. The text, however, is so badly damaged at this point that one has to reconstruct it. I give Mackie's emendations (pp. 202-05):

þær wit tu beoð
fæðme [on folme fin]grum þyð
wyrceð his willa[n] ... ??

... where we are together ...
presses me with his fingers in his hand's embrace,
carries out his desire ...

that "the sexual identity of this object (female genitalia) and the sexual activity engaged in by the *wonfeax wale* (masturbation) have never, to [his] knowledge, been named."[31] Clearly, something onanistic is going on in this riddle that perhaps good taste (until now) has prevented disclosing, though long recognized. In *The Old English Riddles of the Exeter Book,* Williamson writes somewhat obscurely that "though the riddle itself is not usually classified as 'obscene,' the double entendre of these lines should be clear."[32] It is not. While Tanke admits in a note that the leather thing itself could function as something to masturbate *with,* he never fully explores this possibility in his article. In fact, what light do the Middle Ages shed on female masturbation? There are a number of references to dildoes in early medieval literature, one of the most famous being the *Vingull* in *Volsa Þáttr* of *The Flateyjarbók.*[33] In this story, the son lewdly suggests to the serving women that they use the cut-off penis of a dead horse as a sexual aid. The mother preserves it in linen and herbs, and venerates it as a fertility object. According to Pierre J. Payer, there is mention in *The Penitential of Bede* of a *machina* or device used by lesbian nuns for mutual pleasur-

[31] Tanke, "*Wonfeax Wale,*" p. 33.

[32] *Old English Riddles of the Exeter Book,* p. 167.

[33] E.O.G. Turville-Petre, *Myth and Religion of the North: The Religion of Ancient Scandinavia* (New York, 1964), pp. 256-57: "One autumn a fat draught-horse died and, pagan as they were, the family cut him up and stewed him. When the horse was skinned, the farmer's son, full of boisterous humour, picked up the generative organ (*vingull*), ran into the house and shook it in front of the women, saying:

| *Hér meguþ sjá* | Here you can see |
|---|---|
| *heldr roskligan* | a good stout *vingull* |
| *vingul skorinn* | chopped off from |
| *af viggs föður* | the horse's father. |
| *þer er, ambátt,* | For you, serving-maid, |
| *þessi Völsi* | this Volsi (phallus) will be |
| *allódaufligr* | lively enough |
| *innan læra* | between the thighs." |

I am indebted to Susan Granquist on ANSAX for providing this reference.

ing.[34] And we learn from Reay Tannahill that third-century B.C. women of Greece used dildoes made either of wood or of padded leather."[35] In fact, I do not think we hear much about women's masturbation in medieval writings unless they are using some kind of penile aid. Payer says as much, at least about the penitentials. In *The Canons of Theodore*, a woman gets three years penance for *ipsa coitum habet*, "having sex with herself," a phrase which suggests, he says, the use of an instrument; hence the long penance.[36] There was no word in the Penitentials, writes Payer, for "masturbation." This activity was described using expressions like *propriis membris se ipsum violaverit* ("has violated himself with his own members"). The use of the term *coitum* or *fornicatum*, especially when speaking of female masturbation, implies an imitation of the sexual act between a man and a woman with a surrogate penis; this was apparently a more serious sin than the "wanton hand."

I have to admit that a dildo was not what I immediately thought of when I first read this riddle. Given the hollow nature of the speaking object ("the wanton one's hand sticks in my depths"), I had two suggestions for the use of the object: soft leather washrag that she wraps around her fingers (innocent level) and, either leather washrag that she uses to clean herself with (prurient level), or a contraceptive made of the animal's bladder into which she might also put her fingers. What are the depths of a dildo, unless it, too, is hollow? Crossley-Holland's translation seems to suggest either "wash-

[34] *The Penitential of Bede*, in *Die Bussordnungen der abendländischen Kirche,* ed. F. W. H. Wasserschleben (Halle, 1851), p. 223, cited in Pierre J. Payer, *Sex and the Penitentials: The Development of a Sexual Code, 550-1150* (Toronto, 1984), p. 43.

[35] *Sex in History* (New York, 1980), pp. 98-99. I am indebted to Rulon-Miller for this reference.

[36] *Sex and the Penitentials*, p. 46, note 158: "*Si sola cum se ipsa coitum habet sic peniteat*," *Canons of Theodore U* 1.2.13 (Finst 291). 'If she has coitus alone with herself she shall do penance thus.' The 'sic' refers to the penance of three years in the preceding canon. I suggest the use of an instrument both because of the length of the penance and because of the expression 'coitum habet'" (p. 173).

rag" or "bottle," making itself into its own *double-entendre.* He implies that the woman is taking a scrub-bath, something I am merely deducing from his translation: she is filling the leather object with water, as though it is a bottle she can upend over herself, warming it at the fire, grasping its bosom with her wanton hand and "writhing" it (or herself?) about (as she pours the hot water over herself, perhaps?) then sweeping it against "her dark declivity." He translates *me on fæðme* as "on my breast" rather than "in my bosom or depths," and *sweartne* as the accusative substantive adjective that it is. But there are some grammatical puzzlements here. Is *me,* in line 11, as it is so sensible to assume, really the dative of possession? *Mec* is used in line 6 as an unquestionable accusative, which does have the variant *me* with some frequency within the riddles. And how are the *mes* of line 11 and 13 really functioning? In a series of lines where the accusative *mec* is conspicuously left out, both *mes* could possibly receive the action of the verbs *stician* and *swifan,* if there were grammatical precedent in Old English. Rulon-Miller solves the problem by just leaving them out in her "obscene" version to suggest that it is the *wale* herself who is growing warm and wet as she becomes aroused. Craig Williamson leaves them out, too. But *mec* and other pronouns, usually the possessive, are routinely left out in other obscene riddles, notably 61 and 62, where the sense would call for it, probably for metrical reasons, although one is moved to wonder if scribal prudery is a factor.

Of *stician*: when did this word start acquiring the meaning of "insert (something)"? Perusing the dictionaries and the concordance I note that one can say in Old English "my hand sticks in this," or "I stick a pig," but not, according to extant records, "she sticks me into that." The word *stingan,* "to thrust (into)," supplies that meaning instead, as in this sentence from *Leechdoms* that wonderfully illustrates the difference between these two verbs: "sting þin seax on þa wyrte, læt stician ðæron" ("Stick your knife in the plant and let it stick there.")[37] On the

[37] *Leechdoms, Wortcunning, and Starcraft in Early England,* 3 vols., ed. Thomas Oswald Cockayne (London, 1864-66), II, 346, 12.

contrary, *stician*, used transitively, means "to stab, pierce, prick, kill, or poke out" (as in eyes: *sticode him mon þa eagan ut*). Used intransitively it means "to remain fixed." With *on* it means "to lie adjacent to." But somewhere along the line it replaced the meaning of *stingan*, as in Chaucer's "Love hath his firy dart so brennyngly / Ystiked thurgh my trewe, careful herte." It underwent a change in valency, acquiring a third argument. Verbs commonly do this; witness Mod.E *fail*: "I failed the course; Miss Otis failed me in the course." Furthermore, nominative and accusative forms in certain noun classes look alike in Old English, and W.S. Mackie translates "siðþan me on hreþre heafod sticade" in Riddle 61 as "afterwards he stuck his head into my interior" ("head" as object instead of subject of *sticade*).[38] He follows suit in his translation of the similar line in Riddle 12: "sticks into my bosom her wanton hand," again probably because *hygegalan hond*, if seen as adjective and noun, can be accusative. To read *hygegalan hond* as nominative, one must interpret the adjective *hygegalan* as substantive: "the hand of the wanton (one)," or "the hand with respect to the wanton (one)." If Mackie's use is correct, and if valency change with *stician* has occurred or is occurring in Old English, then these lines from the Riddles seem to offer the only evidence that *stician* is being used as *stingan*, with accusative of inserted thing and dative of place inserted.

It is tempting to try to go even further and translate "The wanton's hand sticks *me* into [her] depths," which is what several translators have, and which would facilitate both the dildo and the contraceptive interpretations. But there are other problems, not the least of which is the entrenched formula with the dative of possession ("sticks in my depths"; "sticks in my bosom") which inveighs against *me* as the object of the sticking, and we could argue this indefinitely, spiraling ever downward into a sea of grammatical minutiae. "My depths," "her depths," what does it matter, one might say, what we do with *me*, when the word *fæðm* is used in Riddle 63 to suggest vagina, is used, even in *Christ II* of The Exeter Book, to mean

[38] Mackie, *Exeter Book*, p. 203. Riddle 61 is discussed in detail below, pp. 48-50.

the virgin's womb?[39] The naked meaning *seems* clear, even if the grammar wrestles with it. Was this intentional on the part of the poet or the scribe? Are sentences being fudged or unfinished out of coyness, carelessness, or sensibility? Or is part of the joke that there is an alternative grammar (one that makes use of dialect or vernacular) along with an alternative meaning that can distract?

This issue of contraception at least deserves a closer look. John Riddle remarks that mention of condoms, either male or female, are very rare in medieval lore.[40] He is of course quoting Norman E. Himes' well-known 1936 study of the medical history of contraception who states that the "linen sheath" of Fallopius in 1564 was the precursor of the condom as we know it.[41] Himes does remark, however, that the goat bladder may have been used by the Romans as a male or female sheath for the collection of semen, and that we have a curious reference in the *Metamorphoses* of Antoninus Liberallis to the goat bladder used as protection against the poisonous semen of King Minos.[42] Commenting on this story, Carl Friedrich Helbig remarks that "if religious legends reflect in any degree the practices and customs of an epoch" then "in imperial Rome the bladders of animals were used" as a prophylactic.[43] Himes does not dismiss the possibility that a skin sheath of this sort was used in Rome, only that "we know nothing of the extent of such use" and must assume "that it was not in common use."[44]

[39] "Us secgað bec / hu æt ærestan eadmod astag / in middangeard mægna goldhord, / in fæmnan fæðm" (lines 785b-88, "Books tell us how in the beginning the treasury of might [Christ] humbly descended to earth into the virgin's womb").

[40] John M. Riddle, *Contraception and Abortion from the Ancient World to the Renaissance* (Cambridge, 1992), p. 5.

[41] Norman E. Himes, *Medical History of Contraception* (Baltimore, 1936), pp. 187-90.

[42] Himes, p. 187.

[43] C. F. Helbig, "Ein Condom im Altertume," *Reichs-Medizinal-Anzeiger* 25 (1900): 3, cited in Himes, *Medical History of Contraception,* pp. 187-88.

[44] Himes, *Medical History of Contraception*, p. 188.

Overwhelmingly, the contraceptives described in premodern medical manuals refer to pessaries made from herbs wrapped in linen, so I offer my suggestion with extreme reservation. Could contraceptive measures be as crude as a soft leather obstruction, however?

We must also take into consideration what a predominantly male, monastic, and misogynistic context for the composition of riddles would have focussed on in a satire about a slave woman's intimate activities, and "using a dildo" seems more obviously available to the male homosocial imagination than "using a contraceptive." Craig Williamson's interpretation, bent as it is on supplying that absent lover, hints at the use of something like a condom: In his notes he states that

> ... it offers its supple skin as a pleasure to man. It brings wine to the warrior ... [and] thrusts against the lecherous slave-girl who comes to warm, wet, and work over her lord's new skin. Whether this last bit of leather is shoe or shirt seems lost in the burgeoning sexual play of the riddle.[45]

And whether Williamson means also to hint that on the covert level she is sheathing her lord's penis ("new skin") in preparation for intercourse is still unclear.

However, before I lay the fragile notion of contraception to rest, I want to look at the aforementioned Riddle 61, where a man puts on either a helmet, a shirt, or a coat of mail drawn out of a box and given to him by a woman:

> Oft mec fæste bileac   freolicu meowle
> ides on earce   hwilum up ateah
> folmum sinum   ond frean sealde
> holdum þeodne   swa hio haten wæs
> siðþan me on hreþre   heofod sticade
> nioþan upweardne   on nearo fegde
> gif þæs ondfengan   ellen dohte
> mec frætwedne   fyllan sceolde
> ruwes nathwæt   ræd hwæt ic mæne[46]

[45] Williamson, *A Feast of Creatures*, p. 170.

[46] Often a noble/beautiful maiden, a woman,
firmly locked me up in a box; at times drew [me] up

On a literal level, the man is obviously pushing his head through some kind of ornamented garment, and the joke here is probably just another old chestnut about intercourse: the lovely lady is there, she is doing his bidding, his hairy *nathwæt* (lit. "I know not what") is sticking in a narrow place that it will fill if the owner's courage avails. But if we look with a little more complexity into this riddle and assume that the riddler intended us to do so (with at least as much complexity as Tanke asks of the prurient meaning of Riddle 12) then what is being described here is a man's penis encased in something the woman draws out of a box with her hands. I wonder if the prurient solution is not after all an item that the sexually experienced were well-acquainted with in Anglo-Saxon England. As I said, there is very little written about prophylactics in

with her hands and gave [me] to a lord,
a loyal prince, as she was commanded.
Then, in my depths the head stuck
from beneath; [I] joined the upward-facing [thing]
[i.e., the man's upturned face] in confinement.
If the receiver's courage availed,
the hairy "whatnot" would have to fill
adorned me. Interpret what I mean.

Mackie, *Exeter Book*, p. 202, again chosen for his lack of punctuation. Mackie's translation (203) is a bit loose, however. He ignores *nioþan* ("from beneath"), taking *heofod* as object instead of subject of *sticade*, probably because he sees the accusative substantive in the next line as adverbial: "Afterwards he stuck his head into my interior, / fixed me on tightly while I pointed upwards (*upweardne*)." What is the subject of *fegde* (= "unite," "join")? If it is "head" or "man," then we have the problem that these subjects are already the "upward-turned thing" with which they are uniting. Mackie seems to be influenced by his interpretation of the speaking subject which he envisions as turned upward, like a helmet. I am influenced, of course, by my sense that the speaking subject is flaccid, like a shirt or a sheath, which has joined (*fegde*) with the upward turned thing or head (*upweardne*). Ignoring *fegde*, Paull F. Baum *Anglo-Saxon Riddles of the Exeter Book* , p. 59, has: "then he thrust his head well inside me, / Up from below, into the narrow part," and interprets "ornamental shirt."

either this or ancient times. The argument that religious men would be unfamiliar with sexual practices is countered by the fact of the Penitentials. For the record, though, Riddle 61 uses very similar vocabulary to Riddle 12 (*hreþer* instead of *fæðm*) with a similar, if simpler, conundrum. The most obvious difference is that in Riddle 12 there is no man on the scene. The woman is alone; whether she is pleasuring herself, washing herself, or preparing for intercourse in front of a late night fire, we cannot know, although Williamson's imagination seems to have run along lines similar to mine.

In order to maintain his version of her activity, though, I note that he loses the *fæþm* altogether in his translation. It is not the woman's pleasure that he foregrounds, but the man's, and for this reason Tanke derails his reading, which he calls a "wholesale rewriting of the text."[47] "The text," reminds Tanke, "makes no mention of a lord who owns this 'new skin', and that is precisely the point; the *wale* here is the riddle subject's master. She is, in fact, her own master; far from serving her lord, she serves herself."[48] Tanke's wording, though ("she is her own master"), suggests that he is invested in restoring autonomy and power to the *wale* in her self-pleasuring. This is a natural contemporary impulse, given how maligned the woman is in this poem, but it comes as a surprise to me that he should ignore the appearance of *swifeð* in line 13a — a word that eventually came to mean "have sexual intercourse with."

### *The Word Swifeð*

This verb jumped off the page at me and inspired this essay, which is also about the dangers of tracing the evolution of words in pursuit of one's own meaning. *Swifan* in Old English is the etymological root of Chaucer's bawdy *swiven,* "fuck," attested with this meaning only in his day. It found its way into agriculture: *to swiven a tree to childe* meant in the fifteenth-century *Palladium* "to make a barren tree fruitful." In Old

[47] Tanke, "*Wonfeax Wale,*" pp. 34-35.

[48] "*Wonfeax Wale,*" p. 35.

English it appears a frustrating five other times in the corpus (four if you discount the example taken from *The Panther*), always with intransitive force, never with sexual connotation. One other Exeter Book Riddle uses it to describe the gliding motion of a ship on the waves:

Næfde sellicu wiht    syne ne folme,
exle ne earmas;    sceal on anum fet
searoceap *swifan*,    swiþe feran,
faran ofer feldas.
Riddle 32, ll. 5-8a[49]

It seems to mean "move," "pass," "sweep" — or a motion the panther makes when he falls asleep:

Symle fylle fægen,    þonne foddor þigeð,
æfter þam gereordum    ræste seceð
dygle stowe    under dunscrafum;
ðær se þeodwiga    þreonihta fæc
*swifeð* on swefote,    slæpe gebiesgad.
"The Panther," ll. 35-39.[50]

[49] Krapp and Dobbie, *The Exeter Book,* pp. 196-97.

The strange creature had neither sight nor hands,
shoulders nor arms; on one foot it must,
curious thing, *sweep,* travel quickly,
go over the plains.

[50] Krapp and Dobbie, *The Exeter Book,* p. 170.

When pleased with his fill of the meal he tastes his food,
after the dinner he seeks a bed,
a secret place under hill caves
where the warrior for three nights' time
*slips* into sleep, overcome by slumber.

This use of *swifeð*, here, is questionable, as it may be a variant spelling of *swefeð* from *swebban,* "to sleep, lull." Mackie has certainly seen it that way in his translation: "the warrior drowses in slumber" (*The Exeter Book,* p. 65). I am not ready to consider that the use of *swifeð* in Riddle 12 is a variant spelling of some other verb, but the watchful scholar should be mindful of the possibility. *Swæfan,* another *hapax,* is a verb that is used with *swearte* in *The Meters of Boethius* (8. 46-50), but no one knows what it means:

Efne sio gitsung    þe nænne grund hafaþ
swearte swæfeð    sumes onlice
efne þam munte    þe nu monna bearn

In *Boethius*, the river pursues a course like the ship: "Hwæt, eac se broc, þeah he swife of his rihtryne ..." (VI, l. 15: "Lo, also the torrent, though it may sweep along its straight course ..."),[51] and in *The Meters of Boethius* the sky "turns" or "sweeps" on one axis:

> On ðære ilcan eaxe    hwerfeð eall
> ruma rodor    recene scriðeð
> suðheald *swifeð*,    swift, untiorig
> (28.15-17)[52]

With the prefix *on-* it can mean "swing, turn aside," or "strike in," "intervene," as it appears in *Charters* 1445: "þa swaf Eanulf Penearding on — wæs gerefa — þa genom eal þæt yrfe him on þæt he ahte to Tyssebyrig" ("When [after the commission of a crime], Eanulf Penearding who was reeve, intervened, he took all the property from him [the criminal] which he owned at Tisbury").[53] Mostly, however, it seems to describe a gentle motion, a movement not made by lumbering feet. In Old Icelandic, its cognate is *svífa*, "rove," "turn," "sweep." In Old

> Etne hatað.    Se on iglonde
> Sicilia    swefle byrneð

"The greed that has no bottom blackly *swæfeþ* even like the mountain that the sons of men call Aetna, that burns with sulphur (*swefle*)" (according to the translation of Bosworth and Toller, s.v. *swæfan*, who posit the alternative reading *swæleð?*) Burns? Swallows? As one can see, there are several nefarious homonyms that can complicate our dark word *swifeð*, suggesting various obscene or hellish associations with a slave-woman's *fæðm*.

[51] *King Alfred's Old English Version of Boethius'* De Consolatione Philosophiae, ed. W.J. Sedgefield (Oxford, 1899), p. 14. Again, the use of this word is problematic, as the original MS has *swiðe*, emended by Sedgefield and others to *swife*, which makes better sense in context.

[52] *The Paris Psalter and the Meters of Boethius,* ed. George Philip Krapp, ASPR 5 (New York, 1932), p. 197.

> On the same axis turns all the
> wide heaven,    quickly glides,
> southward sweeps,    swift, unceasing ...

[53] *Select English Historical Documents of the Ninth and Tenth Centuries,* ed. F. E. Harmer (Cambridge, 1914), pp. 30-33, at 32, for text and translation.

High German it is *sweibon,* used to gloss *volvere,* "turn," and *incitari,* "incite, rouse, spur on." In Gothic, *sweiban* has the meaning "to cease," "leave off"; and in Old Frisian, *swífa* means "to be uncertain." Tracing its evolution up to Chaucer's day is even more difficult, given the absence of a Middle English Concordance, but one can see how it might have taken the path it did. *Swivier,* glossing *flabellum* in 1450, meant "fan" or "whisk" for driving away flies.[54] Our word *swivel* comes from *swifan.* Both show that at some point this term acquired a repetitive turning or back and forth movement that could have easily lent itself to obscene imaginings — in perhaps a development similar to that pursued by our word *screw* — from Latin *scrofa,* "sow," to West Germanic *scruva* to Old French *escroue,* maintaining both innocent and obscene meanings (i.e., the cylinder that receives the male screw in carpentry, and the act of screwing, influenced pejoratively by Latin *scrobis*: "ditch," "pudenda"). Yet there appear to be no instances of the use of *swifan* in twelfth- and thirteenth-century writings. Without clear prior development, it springs up in the fourteenth-century in all its vulgar glory.[55] Larry Benson has written, however, in "The 'Queynte' Punnings of Chaucer's Critics," that obscene words were often omitted or obscured in the early manuscripts.[56] Its prominent absence, then, including its rarety in Old English, might suggest that *swifan* had already acquired a prurient meaning earlier than the fourteenth century, perhaps even as early as the tenth century, along with transitive force.

Tanke is mindful that *swifeð* is intransitive, but consequently has a bit of a struggle with *me* and *sweartne* in line 13a. He follows the practice of "the majority of editors" who, he

[54] *The Middle English Dictionary,* ed. Robert E. Lewis, et al. (Ann Arbor, 1990), Part S. 14, p. 1253.

[55] Paul Acker wrote the entry for *swiven* in the Middle English Dictionary, and he has assured me privately that were there appearances of this word before the fourteenth century he would have cited them.

[56] *Studies in the Age of Chaucer, Proceedings* 1 (1984): 23-47. I am indebted to Paul Acker for this reference.

declares, read *sweartne* as "governed by the preceding *me*,"[57] but this statement is a little vague. Does "governed by the preceding *me*" mean that *me* is another dative of possession? Mackie translates "sweeps across my blackness." Tanke makes *me* and *sweartne* as apposite accusatives: "moves through me [*swifeð me geond*], the dark one [*sweartne*]."[58] This is very muddled. What is the dark or black one? The *fæðme*, which *sweartne* agrees with in gender and logic but not in case? Or *me*, the speaking object, which *sweartne* agrees with perhaps in case and possibly gender, but not in logic? I don't buy Mackie's "blackness"; the word *sweartnes* supplies that meaning, whereas *sweartne*, a substantive adjective, means "black one or thing." Logically and poetically speaking (given that her kinsmen are *sweart* in line 4), the *wonfeax wale* is the black one. Tanke's translation only makes sense if we accept his interpretation of the speaking object and its *fæðm* as the woman's genitalia. Perhaps he takes a precedent from Riddle 54, whose answer, "churn," is a feminine noun.[59] *Sweartne* is masculine, a fact, Tanke admits, that troubles his interpretation, but this is not the problem; Germanic languages have routinely ignored the link between natural and grammatical gender and Old English was no different. The problem is that the subject in Riddle 12 is speaking, whereas it is expressed in the third person in Riddle 54. The problem, for me at least, lies in merging the *speaking* subject with the woman who wields it, making it become a part of her body when she is

[57] Tanke, "*Wonfeax Wale*," p. 42, n. 35: "There is also the curious word *sweartne* in line 13, which the majority of editors read as governed by the preceding *me*. If this reading is correct, the riddle subject is represented as masculine!"

[58] Tanke, "*Wonfeax Wale*," p. 33.

[59] In none of the riddles, with the possible exception of Riddle 61, "shirt," does the speaking subject mimic female anatomy in the first person. Where the prurient answer could be a woman's womb or vagina, the object is usually spoken of in the third person (Riddle 54, "churn"; Riddle 37, "bellows," Riddle 87, "bellows"), whereas the riddles whose prurient answers could be a man's penis are twice written in the first person: Riddle 25, "onion"; Riddle 62, "poker." There are exceptions of course, like Riddles 44 ("key") and 45 ("dough"), where male sexual images are spoken of in the third person.

more obviously *using* it on her body. Why should the speaking leather subject identify itself, even momentarily, with part of the woman, and not with the boisterous male image of the dildo and the plowing ox? For similar reasons I have the same reservations about seeing the speaking subject of Riddle 61 as a double for the woman's anatomy ("she drew me out of a box" — now where does that image fit in with the obscene interpretation?). It makes better sense to keep the leather subject leather, even on the prurient level. And despite "the majority of editors," it may be simpler and more logical for the adposition *geond*, which can take an accusative of motion, to precede its object rather than follow it — even with the freer syntax of poetry, even with the Old English penchant for *tmesis* or "broken grammar," even with the early evidence of the Anglo-Saxon postposition (a holdover from the old OV typology of Indo-European). What if, defying good Old English grammatical precedent, and understanding that *me* is a common variant for accusative *mec*, I were to assume that the verb *swifeð* had acquired a new argument (as an obscenity) and translate it transitively as Crossley-Holland and Rulon-Miller do: "moves or sweeps me through or up to the dark thing" — with the additional *entendre* "swives me"? *Swifeð me geond sweartne.* Heard or even seen on the page, these forbidden words might have given a delicious jolt to any monk with a bit of the country tongue in him; that is, if my speculation is correct. But what does it mean to good scholarship and interpretation to take such a liberty?

Both Paull Baum and Reinhard Gleissner note the provocative appearance of *swifeð* in an obscene Old English Riddle so many decades earlier than its appearance in the fourteenth century. Baum is much more confident than Gleissner that *swifeð* is an obscenity: "Sweeps," he writes in a note on his translation, "is Chaucer's word *swive* and probably carries a salacious innuendo."[60] Gleissner notes the connection, but declares that because it is intransitive in its other uses it cannot

[60] *Anglo-Saxon Riddles of the Exeter Book*, p. 24.

take *me* as object.[61] What slim evidence do we have that *swifan* could have been used transitively, much less that it carried sexual connotations? What if this Riddle offers the only textual proof of either a transitive version of *swifan* or a sexual one? Transitivity and valency change in early English verbs were in a state of development, as we can see from the evolution of *stiked his firy dart.* The problem is that whenever one tries to suggest a potential *hapax legomenon* based on a *double entendre*, one chases chimeras, the bane of the lexicographer. We are still in a bog. But I note that the transitive interpretation of *swifeð* clears up the innocent meaning quite nicely: "the wanton hand swivels me through the dark thing: pot, bottle, or whatnot."

Of course I make this suggestion to promote my interpretation of the poem, which is that the speaking object is something the woman puts into herself or washes her rear end with, perhaps by wrapping the rag around her fingers. Nina Rulon-Miller does the same, even altering the meaning of *hygegalan* to mean "skillful" in her "technological" interpretation. Tanke's suggestion is a good one, and he admirably makes the received grammar the basis of his translation instead of the other way around, but it calls for a jolting distortion of identification. It also downplays the emphasis given in the poem to warming and wetting the speaking thing, i.e., making it pliable for entrance into either the cauldron or the body. I am willing to consider that the riddler is playing grammatical games in this poem, perhaps taking words and phrases that are in the process of expanding their meanings and valencies, and teasing the hearer to stretch them. He, or she, has certainly teased us: it doesn't escape me that reading this poem is equivalent to reaching into both grammars and bodies — and thus capitulating to the manipulations of the riddler and his disingenuous

[61] *Die "zweideutigen" altenglischen Rätsel des* Exeter Book *in ihrem zeitgenössischen Kontext* (Frankfurt am Main, 1984), p. 342: "Bedeutung von *swifan* wesentlich allgemeinerer Natur ist: 'drehen, fegen, wenden', bzw. 'to move in a course, wend, sweep', bzw.: 'Of a course of action "to come" to take part in a matter'. Auch zeigen sämtliche Belege für *swifan* im altenglischen intransitiven Gebrauch ohne Objekt. So ist es ratsam, Rä 12, 13a, wie hier geschehen, mit einem intransitiven Verb wiederzugeben."

use of language. Like Petrarch's readers, who in discovering the meaning of the text "lift its veil," or Lacan's readers who derive *jouissance* from interpretation, what are we if not sticking our wanton hand into the dark fathom of this riddle — as it invites us to do? Innuendo raises questions about the central and the peripheral, the subject and the margin. The joke of the riddle is that it makes us compromise our sense of the order of things: what should be peripheral (what the woman is doing instead of what the solution to the riddle is) becomes central, causing us to contemplate something that we, pious monks that we are, would do better to ignore. After all this scrambling around after the grammatical valencies of objects that stick or are stuck into other objects, the final joke may be that the clues to the prurient meanings of these riddles were not nearly so well-organized as the clues to the innocent meanings, and we are getting into a sweat over "nought." Again, I am reminded of that "murk ymage" of Hilton's, that *sweartne*, that abject thing that is nothing and that will draw us away from divine contemplation, that reveals the wrong text, much less the naked one, and yet which demands our examination and handling because of what it reveals to us about ourselves, as much as what it suggests about medieval xenophobia and misogyny. On the other hand, the ridiculous and the sublime are so often conflated in medieval aesthetic, and one could read the woman and her activity as central to the poem, and an outright rather than a covert indictment of female masturbation or contraception: neither activity leads to fruitful generation, as do the services of an ox ... as does the *swiving of a tree to childe.* Tanke observes this truth in his dismissal of Edith Williams' reading, but his own reading is subtly optimistic. I believe that trying to find in this poem an exercise in female autonomy and transgression is almost as fruitless as trying to find "fucks" (d.s.) in OE *swifeð.* This woman may have control of the speaker, she may be pushing the boundaries of what is allowed, she may be worshipping a *vingull*, but in this poem (as Tanke and others point out) she is controlled by the riddler, held up for scrutiny and derision by a male audience in her most intimate of activities — her race, her morals, even her color laughed at. As Mercedes Salvador points out in her study of other obscene riddles in this volume, she may stand as a warning to readers of The Exeter Book (and its decidedly didactic bent), of the dangers and the dead-endedness of the body. She is as unfree as the beast of burden who serves lords and washes pots. There might even be something of bestiality in her portrayal here: coitus is an activity that joins humans, but in swiving the speaking subject, the elusive *mec*, it is hinted that like the monstrous wife of Minos she mates with an ox, if that is what the creature is who supplies his leather, the final irony being that an ox, a gelded animal, is barren.

### *Grammar and Glamor*

We are all driven by our readings of the Riddle and what we want to see in it. We are all a little undone by the grammar of line thirteen. The need to be good linguists and translators fights at times with the need to promote our reading of the text, and what I want to suggest, finally, is that Old English grammar — so often the invisible marker of scholarly competence and a source of anxiety that threatens to unclothe our expertise, noted and hated when we make mistakes in it, a necessary evil in the process of interpretation, often left to the "pedants" who obsess over it, and deferred to the "majority of editors"[62] — is in itself a kind of dark body that can amaze and elude us, that can be subject to our manipulations, inspire our fantasies and our glosses, and provide us a source of transgressive pleasure. The truth of the matter is that we still do not know how some of these words and phrases were used in Old English, especially those words for which there is simply not

[62] Reliance on the authority of other scholars to help us solve a difficult grammatical conundrum in a dead language is a natural and respected critical move, especially when we need to get on with things; but it is a deferral: Tanke's deferral to "other editors" does not deal with the intricate problem of *me* and *sweartne.* Rulon-Miller's indebtedness for her idea about the *cuir bouilli* to F.N. Whitman's translation of line 13a ("making me black all over") does not acknowledge the severe problems of the looseness of this rendition (*Old English Riddles* [Ottawa, 1982], p. 171). But we also defer when we trust the dictionary definitions.

enough textual evidence. It is hazardous to make grammatical experiments, and if we interpret the words of a dead language we should do so carefully, consciously, and mindful of all its known rules. We are products of a generation of scholars obsessed with sex, and newly pious about it in our preoccupation with women's power or lack thereof. While obsessed as any other human being with sex, I am almost more preoccupied with understanding the liberties and limitations of language. I wonder, given how unfairly Old English language study has been rejected in favor of psychoanalytic and cultural studies, and increasingly dropped from the curriculum in our universities, if we may see ourselves as we enter a new millennium as a generation of scholars mindful of the laws of a dead language and the implications of tinkering with its corpse. That is why I invoke this old metaphor of body and grammar hoping to revive something of the sexiness, the *glamor*, so to speak, that was philology. I take risks in sticking my swiving hands into these sentences, turning them to my liking, imagining myself arousing in them double and triple meaning. I would not be surprised, however, to learn that the Old English riddler was just as tantalized by the ambiguous edges of his words and even more transgressive. Or maybe his scribe was just plain wrong. But that is a veil we will never lift, and a naked text we will never expose despite our best efforts.

# The Key to the Body: Unlocking Riddles 42-46

Mercedes Salvador

Riddle 44 (key) in the Exeter Book, with its blunt description of the male genitalia plus the reference to the "familiar hole," possibly stands out as the most explicit allusion to sex and sexual body parts in the extant corpus of Old English literature.[1] It is one of several riddles in the Exeter Book which have traditionally been labelled as "obscene" due to metaphorical allusions to body parts and/or the relatively veiled description of sexual intercourse by means of *double entendre*.[2] The majority of these pieces appear occasionally and rather haphazardly in the collection. We might infer that the compiler took care to camouflage their presence in a poetic anthology beginning with a conspicuous religious focus.[3] The obscene riddles could thus easily go unnoticed in an extensive *enigmata* with a great variety of themes. Furthermore, the *double entendre* is at times skilfully dissimulated among the other clues, as for instance occurs with the description of the sword in Riddle 20.

[1] The numbering of the riddles is that of George Philip Krapp and Elliott van Kirk Dobbie, eds., *The Exeter Book*, ASPR 3 (New York, 1936) and all citations are from this edition. Quotations of other poems in the Exeter Book will also be from this edition.

[2] In *Die "zweideutigen" altenglischen Rätsel des* Exeter Book *in ihrem zeitgenössischen Kontext* (Frankfurt, 1984), Reinhard Gleissner has offered a thoroughgoing monographic sudy of the obscene riddles. He provides a detailed analysis of Riddles 25, 42, and 46 but he has also included the study of riddles which are wholly or partially based on sexual or *double entendre* clues: nos. 11, 12, 20, 30a, 37, 44, 45, 54, 61, 62, 63, 75-76, 91, and 95.

[3] This is evident as the *Christ* poems open the manuscript, and are followed by *Guthlac, Azarias, The Phoenix,* and *Juliana.* Bernard J. Muir suggests that "the *Guthlac* poems and *Juliana* respectively offer exemplary models for contemporary male and female Christian witnesses to emulate," *The Exeter Anthology of Old English Poetry: An Edition of Exeter Dean and Chapter MS 3501*, 2 vols. (1994; repr. Exeter, 2000), I: 23.

On the basis of this, it is not surprising that occasional obscene riddles may have been preserved in the Exeter manuscript with no traces of censorship, unlike, for example, four of the Cambridge lyrics in which words and expressions which are sexually explicit have been erased.[4] However, Riddle 44 is one of a notorious group of riddles — Riddles 42, 44, 45, and 46 — which have a clear sexual component. Riddle 42 opens with the image of two copulating fowls; in the presentation of the rising dough, the *double entendre* of Riddle 45 hardly hides the answer "penis"; in turn, Riddle 46 alludes to incest, a strongly condemned sexual practice throughout the Middle Ages.

The close proximity of these riddles to Riddle 40, a solemn poem on divine Creation, is at best puzzling, and so is the presence of this obscene group among the contents of what seems to be "an instructional manual or a schoolroom anthology."[5] We should also bear in mind that the compilation of the Exeter Book was affected by the Benedictine Reform, which imposed an increasingly strict ecclesiastical control of social habits resulting in what Anthony Davies appropriately calls "the Church's loathing of the body and its abhorrence of sensuality."[6] Enclosed in the manuscript's third booklet in

4 Lyrics 27, 28, 39, and 49 have clearly undergone censorship in Cambridge, University Library, Gg.5.35. See the commentary in Jan M. Ziolkowski, ed. and trans., *The Cambridge Songs (Carmina Cantabrigiensia)*, Medieval and Renaissance Texts and Studies 192 (1994; repr. Tempe, AZ, 1998).

5 Seth Lerer, *Literacy and Power in Anglo-Saxon Literature* (Lincoln,1991), p. 103. He asserts this on the basis of the analogy of the Exeter Book's contents with those of the Cambridge Songs codex. See his arguments on pp. 103-06.

6 Anthony Davies, "Sexual Behaviour in Later Anglo-Saxon England," in *This Noble Craft: Proceedings of the Xth Research Symposium of the Dutch and Belgian University Teachers of Old and Middle English and Historical Linguistics*, ed. Erik Kooper, Costerus n.s. 80 (Amsterdam, 1991), pp. 83-105, at 85. He also notes that "with the impetus of the monastic revival, the growth of ecclesiastical influence in administrative government, and the insistence that priests should use penitentials for confession and guidance, sexual behaviour became even more closely scrutinized. Ecclesiastical and civil legislation, penitential injunctions, pastoral letters, and homiletic precepts attempted to regulate the Anglo-Saxons' sexual conduct." For the influence

which the reformist influence can already be perceived, a whole riddle sequence indulging in descriptions of body parts and bodily actions cannot simply have been overlooked.[7]

This prompts a number of questions: what was the function of these obscene themes in the collection, and how is it that they were preserved given that, as a group, their presence in the manuscript was more visible than single occurrences? Also, if the Exeter Book was a didactic compilation, what were the sexual riddles supposed to teach? This essay aims at providing answers to these questions, starting from the hypothesis that the consecutive appearance of those motifs is due to the fact that they were originally conceived as a section. Although some thematic links have occasionally been noted by several scholars,[8] there has been no serious attempt by

of the Church on medieval sexuality, see Reay Tannahill, *Sex in History* (1980; repr. London, 1995), pp. 128-54.

7 Although Conner describes the third booklet as transitional between the earlier poetic modes (represented by poems such as *Deor* and *Wulf and Eadwacer*, and *The Wife's Lament*), the majority of the texts contained in this booklet (*Homiletic Fragment II, Soul and Body II, Judgment Day I, Resignation A, Resignation B, The Descent into Hell*, among others) clearly denote the dramatic impact provoked by the Benedictine Reform. For a detailed account of the layers of influence from the Benedictine Reform in the contents of the manuscript, see Patrick W. Conner, *Anglo-Saxon Exeter: A Tenth-Century Cultural History* (Woodbridge, 1993), especially pp. 148-64. See also Mechthild Gretsch, *The Intellectual Foundations of the English Benedictine Reform* (Cambridge, 1999).

8 Baum, for instance, acknowledges a slight degree of arrangement noting that the sexual topic is more frequent in the first block of riddles (Riddles 1-59) and also points out the presence of two "obscene" pairs: "Of the seven 'obscene' riddles five (25, 37, 44, 45, 54) are among the first fifty-nine; the other two, 61, 62, form a pair, like 44 and 45," Paull F. Baum, *Anglo-Saxon Riddles of the* Exeter Book (Durham, 1963), p. xx. James E. Anderson argues, in "Two Spliced Riddles of the Exeter Book," *In Geardagum* 5 (1983): 57-75, and in *Two Literary Riddles in the* Exeter Book*: Riddle 1 and The Easter Riddle* (Norman, 1986), p. 23, that the lack of strong punctuation between Riddle 42 and 43 is due to the fact that they are thematically akin. John Wayne Conlee, "Artistry in the Riddles of the *Exeter Book*" (unpub. Ph.D. diss., University of Illinois, 1968) also suspects that Riddles 44, 45, and 46 might be related on the basis of their obscene contents. I have elsewhere aimed at demonstrating that the Exeter Riddles, as well as

others to demonstrate that Riddles 42-46 were concatenated in the manuscript to provide a cohesive series. The main concern of these compositions might have been to present the notion of the body in an instructional context, illustrating the conflictive twofold nature of human beings — carnal and spiritual, rational and irrational, female and male, and so forth. Riddle 43 (soul and body), though devoid of sexual content, could perfectly fit this thematic section, which might have focused on the concept of the body, rather than on sheer interest in sexual matters. In the light of this, instead of being regarded as a sample of pornographic material deliberately concealed in the obscure context of a riddle collection, this series could have been designed to be read allegorically, presenting a warning against the dangers of the body, as expressed in Riddle 43. An individual analysis of these texts will show that they make use of well-known symbols and metaphors which are present in both the scriptures and medieval exegetical commentaries. The reading of these poems according to the allegorical method of interpretation may justify the presence of explicit descriptions of body parts and sexual intercourse in the Exeter anthology.[9]

### *Riddle 42 (cock and hen)*

Riddle 42 starts with an explicit sexual image, with no parallel in Anglo-Saxon poetry nor in Latin *enigmata*,[10] which has motivated its inclusion in the "obscene" category:

medieval Latin *enigmata*, were compiled according to thematic criteria, although there are no visible signs in the manuscript indicating the different sections. Without taking into account occasional exceptions, the Exeter collection opens with the storm riddles, which are followed by a fairly consistent group made of animal motifs; the thematic arrangement continues with an extensive section on diverse tools. Riddle 40 (Creation) apparently closes this first block. See further my "The Compilation of the Old English Riddles of the *Exeter Book*" (unpub. Ph.D. diss., University of Seville, 1997).

9 For a parallel discussion of the allegorical function of nakedness in the Anglo-Saxon *Genesis* poem, see Ericksen's "Penitential Nakedness and the Junius 11 *Genesis*" in this volume.

10 No Latin analogues have been found for this riddle. Aldhelm's Riddle 26 ("gallus") has nothing to do with the clues offered by Exeter Riddle 42.

Ic seah wyhte wrætlice twa
undearnunga ute plegan
hæmedlaces; hwitloc anfeng
wlanc under wædum, gif þæs weorces speow,
fæmne fyllo. Ic on flette mæg
þurh runstafas rincum secgan,
þam þe bec witan, bega ætsomne
naman þara wihta. Þær sceal Nyd wesan
twega oþer ond se torhta Æsc
an an linan, Acas twegen,
Hægelas swa some. Hwylc þæs hordgates
cægan cræfte þa clamme onleac
þe þa rædellan wið rynemenn
hygefæste heold heortan bewrigene
orþoncbendum? Nu is undyrne
werum æt wine hu þa wihte mid us,
heanmode twa, hatne sindon.[11]

The "obscene" quality is manifest in the vocabulary deployed at the beginning of the text. The terms "plegan" (2b) and "hæmedlaces" (3a) are listed by Coleman among other Old English words for which the euphemistic expressions "to

There is however a riddle (no.10) in the collection known as Pseudo-Bede's *Flores* which bears a certain resemblance to Riddle 42, although the obscene context is missing: "vidi filium non natum sed ex tribus personis suscitatum et eum nutritum donec vivus vocaretur." As Frederick Tupper, Jr., states, "the 'three persons' of the riddle are, therefore, the cock, the hen who lays, and the hen who hatches the egg," in "Riddles of the Bede Tradition: The 'Flores' of Pseudo-Bede," *Modern Philology* 2 (1904): 561-72 at 564.

[11] "I saw two strange creatures openly enjoy sexual intercourse outside; if the deed was successful the proud fair-haired woman gained fullness under her clothes. Here on the floor I can tell, by means of letters, to men that know books, the names of both of those creatures together. Need (N) shall be there twice over, and the bright Ash (Æ), one only in the line, two Oaks (A), and two Hail-storms (H) also. Which letter unlocked, with the power of a key, the fastenings of the treasury-door, which in determined fashion guarded the riddle, its heart concealed by means of cunning bonds, against solvers? Now it is revealed to men at their wine, how those two mean-spirited creatures are named among us." The translation of the Exeter Riddles and other poems of the Exeter Book cited in this essay is by W. S. Mackie, ed., *The Exeter Book: Part II*, EETS o.s. 194 (London, 1934) unless otherwise indicated.

cohabit" and "cohabitation" have been traditionally provided by dictionaries.[12] However, they bluntly refer to sexual intercourse, and might have been close to the contemporary colloquial register.[13]

Interestingly, the two words also appear in Ælfric's homily on Midlent Sunday ("Dominica in media Quadragesime," CH II.12), in which the sin of lechery is expounded:

> Se oðer heafod-leahter is gecweden forliger oððe galnyss, þæt is þæt se man ungehealdsum sy on *hæmede*, and hnesce on mode to flæsclicum lustum. Of ðam leahtre cumað modes mægenleast, and ungemetegod lufu, hatung Godes beboda and higeleas *plega*, fracodlic spræc, and eagena unstæððignys.[14]

The use of such words is not incompatible with the enlightening purpose and the religious scope which are natural in the homiletic genre to which the passage belongs. Similarly, the presence of colloquial "plegan" (2b) and "hæmedlaces" (3a) does not hinder the didactic intention underlying the presentation of the sexual scene in Riddle 42. As occurs in the homily, the colloquial and the learned seem to blend in Riddle 42, just as the obscene elements conflate with the instructional ideas that will be discussed further in this essay.

[12] Julie Coleman, "Sexual Euphemism in Old English," *Neuphilologische Mitteilungen* 93 (1992): 93-98.

[13] This idea is contended by Bogislav von Lindheim, "Traces of Colloquial Speech in OE," *Anglia* 70 (1951): 22-42. He also points out that "the remarkable compound *hǣmedlāc* 'coitus' is nowhere else instanced in poetry" (p. 34).

[14] "The second deadly sin is called fornication or sexual desire, that is that a person is immoderate in sexual intercourse, and inclined to give in to physical lusts. From this sin comes feebleness of mind, passion, hating God's commandments, thoughtless amusement, obscene speech, and weak eyes." This passage is quoted by Davies, "Sexual Behaviour," p. 88 and n. 46, from whom the translation is cited. Gleissner, *Die "zweideutigen" altenglischen Rätsel*, p. 137, also cites this excerpt. It is from *Ælfric's Catholic Homilies: The Second Series; Text*, ed. Malcolm Godden, EETS s.s. 5 (London, 1979), homily 12, lines 500-05 (p. 124), emphases mine.

Significantly, the learned quality of the text is immediately perceived as the names of the two creatures are spelt out by means of runic clues, giving the twofold solution "hana" (cock) and "hæn" (hen).[15] The riddler probably did not employ *double entendre*, as in other obscene compositions, since the cryptographic clues point to the fact that the two creatures committing the sin of fornication are animals, not human beings.[16] The didactic aim can also be perceived as the clues of Riddle 42 insist on the irrational quality of these creatures. In this sense, the paronomastic pair "wihta/witan" is here used to underline the difference between beasts — "wihta" (8a) — indulging openly in sexual pleasure, and human beings who "bec witan" (7a), in other words, the ones characterized by reason.[17]

Further on, the clues dwell on the idea that only learned people can provide a solution for the riddle, that is, the distinction between irrational behaviour and intellectual thought is continued (11b-15a). In that passage, the phrase "cægan cræfte" (12a) refers to the commonplace notion that letters are the key to knowledge — and, by extension, of spiritual life.[18] The metaphorical implication suggested in the riddle is therefore that literacy leads to salvation.[19]

[15] The solution "cock and hen" was first pointed out by F. Dietrich in "Die Räthsel des Exeterbuchs: Würdigung, Lösung und Herstellung," *Zeitschrift für deutsches Alterthum* 11 (1859): 448-90.

[16] However, despite the absence of *double entendre*, the riddle deliberately plays on ambiguity as clues like "hwitloc" (3b) are provided: we need to decode the runic clues to find out that the creatures are two birds instead of a human couple. I owe this idea to Jonathan Wilcox.

[17] The differentiation between learned and illiterate beings is pervasive in the riddle, as Gleissner, *Die "zweideutigen" altenglischen Rätsel*, pp. 250-52, has pointed out. See also Lerer, *Literacy and Power*, pp. 112-13, and "The Riddle and the Book: Exeter Book Riddle 42 and Its Contexts," *Papers in Language and Literature* 25 (1989): 3-18.

[18] In Lerer's words, the expression *cægan cræfte* "securely situates the Riddle's interpretive concerns in a learned, and possibly monastic conception of understanding," *Literacy and Power*, p. 118.

[19] This symbolic function of the key is also a well-known theme in Christian iconography as it is St. Peter's attribute, which opens or locks Heaven's

The notion of the key as the instrument of literacy and the vehicle of salvation is attested to elsewhere in Old English literature. As Lerer notes, Ælfric uses this metaphor at the beginning of his *Grammar* in a way that resembles the passage in Riddle 42: "Đe stæfcræft is seo cæg, ðe ðæra boca andgit unlicð" ("The knowledge of letters [grammar] is the key which unlocks the meaning of books").[20] There is also a parallel use of this motif in a passage from the Old English *Exodus* which is particularly revealing for the interpretation of Riddle 42:

Gif onlucan wile  lifes wealhstod,
beorht in breostum,  banhuses weard,
ginfæsten god  Gastes cægon,
run bið gerecenod,  ræd forð gæð;
hafað wislicu  word on fæðme,
wile meagollice  modum tæcan,
þæt we gesne ne syn  Godes þeodscipes,
Metodes miltsa.  He us ma onlyhð,
nu us boceras  beteran secgað
lengran lyftwynna. (523-32) [21]

This passage provides a reflection on the the ways to decode the message of the poem. With regard to the phrase "gastes

doors, and is thus related to man's salvation. The idea is based on Matthew 16:19: "I will give you the keys of the kingdom of heaven, and whatever you bind on earth shall be bound in heaven, and whatever you loose on earth shall be loosed in heaven." All citations from the Bible in this essay are from Herbert G. May and Bruce M. Metzger, *The New Oxford Annotated Bible with the Apocrypha* (New York, 1977).

[20] Ed. Julius Zupitza, *Ælfric's Grammatik und Glossar* (Berlin, 1880); my translation. For further examples of the metaphor of the key in Old English literature, see Lerer, *Literacy and Power*, pp. 118-19.

[21] "If the faculty which interprets life's meaning, the body's tenant, radiant within the breast, has the will to unlock the ample benefits with the keys of the spirit, the mystery will be explained and wisdom will issue forth. It has wise words in its keeping and it earnestly desires to instruct our minds so that we may not be lacking in God's law and the Lord's mercy. He will enlighten us further: for the present, scholars tell us of the better, more lasting joys of heaven." The edition is by Peter J. Lucas, *Exodus* (1977; repr. Exeter, 1994); this translation is from S. A. J. Bradley, *Anglo-Saxon Poetry* (London, 1982), p. 64. Dorothy Haines provides a detailed analysis of this passage in "Unlocking *Exodus* ll. 516-532," *JEGP* 98 (1999): 481-98.

cægon," Lucas notes that "one of the standard interpretations [of this image] was as the 'key of the scriptures,' i.e. typology itself."[22] As for the expression "boceras," he states that it possibly refers to "the Church Fathers (rather than just the evangelists) who, after Christ has ensured the salvation of mankind (*nu*), can teach the rewards of heaven (*beteran*) through the interpretation of the scriptures."[23]

The "gastes cægon" in the *Exodus* passage thus recalls the expression "cægan cræfte" in Riddle 42, and the men who "bec witan" are equivalent to the *Exodus* "boceras." We can therefore infer that Riddle 42 is actually alluding to these two ideas, so that the full meaning of the riddlic imagery will only be released by means of a key (typology) and by scholars trained to unveil the allegorical component of texts. At the time this composition was included in the Exeter Book, the learned people *par excellence* — who were most likely the producers and recipients of this type of literature — were the members of the ecclesiastical profession, to which the author of Riddle 42 surely belonged.

Although the fowls are not dealt with separately but as a pair of creatures throughout the riddle — "wyhte wrætlice twa" (1) and "heanmode twa" (17a) —, each bird might have also conjured up further allegorical allusions in the minds of a monastic audience, since the rooster and the hen constitute well-known symbols deriving from ancient learned and popular tradition. In this sense, it is worth noting that the hen was regarded the allegorical representation of spiritual life, or the soul, as in patristic literature it frequently symbolized the "intelligence or wisdom of God which led the elect to salvation,"[24] a notion which evinces clear affinities with the

[22] Lucas, *Exodus*, p. 143 (note to line 525). In *Literacy and Power* Lerer agrees with Lucas' interpretation of this phrase: "exemplified in the *gæstes cægon* of *Exodus* are the exegetical methods of their interpretation" (p. 119).

[23] Lucas, *Exodus*, p. 143 (note to line 531).

[24] Beryl Rowland, *Birds with Human Souls: A Guide to Bird Symbolism* (Knoxville, 1978), p. 77. In *Allegoriae in sacram scripturam* (*PL* 112), Rabanus Maurus asserts: "Gallina est sapientia Dei" (939). In *De universo*, the same author extends this idea to the Church: "Gallina significat sapientiam, sive sanctam

context of this poem. In turn, the cock was a traditional emblem of lechery, thus, possibly assumed as a symbol of the body in Riddle 42.[25] According to this, the joint image of the cock and hen might then point to the traditional conflict between carnal desire and spiritual aspirations. The two creatures involved in the "war of love," as "hæmedlaces" (3a) suggests,[26] could have been meant to conform the allegorical representation of the body and soul, thus anticipating the theme of Riddle 43.[27]

However, if the hen represents the spiritual quality of human beings, this idea seems contradictory as the hen of Riddle 42 is clearly described as a lecherous bird, since "wlanc" (4a) is an adjective that characterizes sensual women in the obscene context of other riddles — notably, nos. 12 (ox) and

Ecclesiam ..." (VIII.vi). See *De universo libri viginti duo* (*PL* 111, 248). Similarly, as Rowland observes (p. 77), for St. John Chrysostom (*PG* 58, 682-83) the hen was a symbol of the church, while "the wandering chickens were the people of God following evil pleasures and wordly desires." Rowland explains that the analogy is based on Christ's words on his way to Jerusalem for the last time: "O Jerusalem, Jerusalem, killing the prophets and stoning those who are sent to you! How often would I have gathered your children together as a hen gathers her brood under her wings, and you would not!" (Matt. 23:37; also Lk. 13:34).

25 This idea possibly derives from Pliny's *Historia Naturalis* (X.xxiv), which describes how a cock fights to protect his "wives." Chaucer's Chaunticleer in *The Nun's Priest's Tale* is thus a good illustration of the uxoriousness of the cock.

26 It is significant that *lac* in the *hapax legomenon* "hæmedlaces" (3a), as Gleissner, *Die "zweideutigen" altenglischen Rätsel,* pp. 236-38, points out, is frequently found in kennings related to war — *beadulac,* and *heaðolac* — and to the clashing of weapons and shields — *ecga gelac, sweorda gelac, bordgelac, lindgelac,* and so on.

27 Anderson also noted the thematic relationship between these two riddles: "[Riddle 42] plays on widely distributed folklore motifs of the cock and hen as both fleshly and spiritual marriage partners. The riddlic word *orþoncbendum* 'bonds of skillful thought' then links the copulating cock and hen in the implicit farmyard of *Riddle 42* to the nobler marriage of 'body and soul,' figuratively confined *in geardum* — that is, within the nature of Man — in *Riddle 43*," *Two Literary Riddles*, p. 23.

25 (onion).[28] In this sense, the lustful character of the cock likewise contrasts, for instance, with its exegetical function as the allegorical representation of the doctors of the church.[29] According to this, both birds might have been regarded simultaneously as symbols of lechery, an idea which could simply stem from folklore and direct experience, and as representatives of wisdom and spiritual life leading to salvation as attested to in patristic literature.[30] This assumption is consistent with the general mode of the riddle in which the colloquial and the lewd are blended with the learned and the instructional. As Lerer appropriately points out, Riddle 42 "rephrases the potentially obscene in terms of the patently religious."[31]

In the light of this discussion, Riddle 42 evinces a clear didactic function that goes beyond the mere indulgence in sexual imagery. In an instructional context, the copulating birds of Riddle 42 would therefore have been intended to illustrate the lustful irrational behaviour of animals — and, by extension, of human sinners. This idea is quite evident at the end of the riddle, when the two birds are referred to as

[28] See Sarah L. Higley's comments on this word in "The Wanton Hand: Reading and Reaching into Grammars and Bodies in Old English Riddle 12" in this volume, pp. 39-40.

[29] This idea is present, for example, in Rabanus Maurus's *De universo libri viginti duo* VIII.vi: "Gallus virum sanctum aut doctorem evangelicum significat ..." (*PL* 111). See also the notes to Chaucer's *The Nun's Priest's Tale* in Larry D. Benson's *The Riverside Chaucer* (Boston, 1987), p. 936, in which the allegorical function of Chauntecleer as a representation of the preacher and the holy man is pointed out.

[30] In Chaucer's *The Nun's Priest's Tale*, the ending lines urge the reader to go beyond the literal meaning of the fable in order to consider the allegorical role of the cock and the hen:

> But ye that holden this tale a folye,
> As of a fox, or of a cok and hen,
> Taketh the moralite, goode men.
> For Seint Paul seith that al that writen is,
> To oure doctrine it is ywrite, ywis;
> Taketh the fruyt, and lat the chaf be stille. (3438-43)

[31] *Literacy and Power*, p. 119.

"heanmode twa" (17a), i.e. wretched or miserable due to their sinful condition.[32] Characterizing the two birds as "heanmode," the poet was at the same time anticipating the twofold solution "hana" and "hæn" by means of wordplay. In a typically Isidorian fashion,[33] the riddler was associating those words with the sinful quality of the animals which would thus contrast with the pious behaviour of learned men (most probably clerics), those capable of decoding the runic clues by means of the "cægan cræfte." The cock and hen could therefore illustrate the allegorical fight between the body and the soul, which will in turn be supplemented with the soul-and-body motif of Riddle 43.

In this context, literacy and spiritual life are thus clearly exalted in Riddle 42 as a possible exemplary reference to the conduct expected in the consumers of this type of literature. We might also assume that this poem implicitly warns potential riddlees of the dangers of the sins of the flesh which can be triggered by the contemplation of animals or human sinners surrounding them. In this line of thought, the notion of the "power of literacy," using Lerer's expression, as the best pro-

[32] Note that Adam's postlapsarian state — i.e., naked, needy of clothing, and prone to bodily lust — in the Old English poetic *Genesis* is described thus: "*hean* hleoþrade hrægles þearfa" (859) and "*hean* hygegeomor, þæt þe sie hrægles þearf" (878). See the discussion of this passage in this volume in Ericksen's "Penitential Nakedness and the Junius 11 *Genesis*," pp. 268-69, and Wilcox's "Naked in Old English: The Embarrassed and the Shamed," pp. 292-93.

[33] This kind of clue based on far-fetched etymological association derives from Isidore's *Etymologiae* and is pervasive in Aldhelm's Riddles. In "Aldhelm's *Enigmata* and Isidorian Etymology," *ASE* 14 (1985): 37-59, Nicholas Howe cites numerous examples of this:

> Aldhelm also offers etymologies which seem to be of his own devising. A case in point is 'Scnifes' (*Enigma* no.xxxvi), which he describes as ascending above high places: '*Scando catervatim volitans super ardua pennis*' (line 2). That he sought to teach the derivation of *scnifes* from *scando* is rendered all the more likely by his spelling of the title word with *sc* rather than *c*, which is more common. In 'Cribellus' (*Enigma* no. lxvii), Aldhelm explains that the sieve contains *crebris . . . fenestris* (line 1) and thereby points to its etymology: it is named for its most ovious feature, its numerous holes. (p. 47)

tection of the spirit against the sins of the body seems to be patent in the text.

*Riddle 43 (soul and body)*

The soul-and-body motif, allegorically present in Riddle 42, is the topic of Riddle 43. A reccurrent theme in medieval literature, two poetic dialogues between soul and body are found in Old English literature — one in the Exeter Book and another in the Vercelli Book. Riddle 43 presents several commonplaces which frequently occur in literary works dealing with this well-known motif. Thus, the religious overtones of Riddle 43 are undeniable, as its opening lines stress the different nature of the soul, which is not affected by hunger, thirst, old age, nor by other torments that the body, on the contrary, must endure.

Ic wat indryhtne æþelum deorne
giest in geardum, þam se grimma ne mæg
hungor sceððan ne se hata þurst,
yldo ne adle. Gif him arlice
esne þenað, se þe agan sceal
on þam siðfate, hy gesunde æt ham
findað witode him wiste ond blisse,
cnosles unrim, care, gif se esne
his hlaforde hyreð yfle,
frean on fore. Ne wile forht wesan
broþor oþrum; him þæt bam sceðeð,
þonne hy from bearme begen hweorfað
anre magan ellorfuse,
moddor ond sweostor. Mon, se þe wille,
cyþe cynewordum hu se cuma hatte,
eðþa se esne, þe ic her ymb sprice.[34]

[34] "I know of a lordly, nobly brave guest in the courts, whom grim hunger cannot harm, nor hot thirst, nor old age nor disease. If the servant who must always go with him on his journey serves him honestly, they, safe at home, will find food and gladness appointed for them, abundant plenty, but sorrow, if the servant obeys his lord and master badly upon the way. The one brother must not be a cause of fear to the other; that will do them both harm when they, bound elsewhere, both leave the bosom of their one kinswoman, who is their mother and their sister. Let the man who will declare in noble words what the guest or the servant, whom I speak about

The instructional mood of Riddle 43 can be observed for instance in the allusion to the body and soul as travelling companions, as it is stated that the body must follow his lord (the soul) "on þam siðfate" (6a). In the Exeter Book, the beginning of *Soul and Body II* likewise presents the relationship between soul and body in similar terms: "hu þæt bið deoplic þonne se deað cymeð, / asundrað þa sibbe, þa þe ær somud wæron, / lic ond sawle!" (3-5a, "how serious it is when death comes and parts then the kinsmen who before were united, the body and the soul").[35] Just as the body and soul are considered kinsmen ("sibbe") in this passage, Riddle 43 establishes the close connection between body and soul by means of family clues, stating that they are brothers (11a). The presentation of earth as mother and sister of the two brothers constitutes a typical paradox which is explained by Williamson as follows: "Since body, soul, and earth were all created by God, they are siblings; thus, earth is a sister to her brothers, body and soul. Since the whole man, both body and soul, was created from the earth, earth is mother to both body and soul."[36]

here, is called." The comparison of body and soul to house and guest is a cliché in Anglo-Saxon literature. The terms *lichama* or *banhus* — literally, "body-house" and "bone-house," respectively — are typical kennings referring to the physical body that illustrate this well-known metaphorical association.

[35] Mackie's translation. As Craig Williamson, ed., *The Old English Riddles of the* Exeter Book (Chapel Hill, 1977), p. 278, notes, the motif of the soul and body travelling together is also found in *Juliana* (695-703).

[36] *The Old English Riddles*, p. 280. Williamson also supports this reading with a citation from Isidore's *Etymologiae*, which relates the word *homo* (man) to *humus* (earth):

> Homo dictus, quia ex humo est factus, sicut [et] in *Genesi* dicitur (2,7): 'Et creavit Deus hominem de humo terrae.' Abusive autem pronuntiatur ex utraque substantia totus homo, id est ex societate animae et corporis. (XI.i.4)

All citations from this work are from the edition by J. Oroz Reta and M.A. Marcos Casquero, *Etimologías* (Madrid, 1983). The notion of earth as Adam's mother is present in Old English prose dialogues as for example, in *Adrian and Ritheus*, no. 28:

A further significant aspect of Riddle 43 is the use of the term "frea" as a reference to the soul, which is characterized as lordly and noble — "indryhtne" (1a) and "æþelum" (1b) — at the beginning of the poem.[37] Conversely, the term "esne," whose first meaning is "a man of the servile class" in Bosworth-Toller's dictionary, occurs three times in the poem (5a, 8b, and 16a) as an allusion to the body.[38] This insistence on the subservience of the body to the soul, the intellectual and spiritual part of human beings, is significant as it reveals the didactic aim which is clearly consonant with the ideas presented in Riddle 42.[39] The instructional overtones are

> Saga me, hwilc man wære dead and nære acenned and æfter þam deaðe wære eft bebyried in his moder innoðe.
>
> Ic þe secge, þæt wæs Adam se æresta man, for þam eorðe wæs his moder and he wæs bibiriged eft in þære eorðan.

("Tell me which man died and was not born, and after death was later buried in his mother's womb. I tell you, that was Adam the first man, because the earth was his mother and he was buried afterwards in the earth"), James E. Cross and Thomas D. Hill, ed. and trans., *The Prose Solomon and Saturn and Adrian and Ritheus* (Toronto, 1982), p. 38. For further information and parallel passages in other works, see Cross and Hill, pp. 76-77.

[37] In *The Old English Riddles*, Williamson notes: "the soul has an excellent lineage since (as we know from the *Soul and Body* poems) it comes from God ..." (pp. 278-79).

[38] Although the term "esne" can also mean "man," there are numerous examples provided by Bosworth-Toller which make clear that the term was frequently employed with the meaning "servant." As Bosworth-Toller indicates, "the esne was probably a poor freeman from whom a certain portion of labour could be demanded in consideration of his holdings, or a certain rent [gafol, q.v.] reserved out of the produce of the hives, flocks or herds committed to his care. He was a poor mercenary, serving for hire, or for his land, but was not of so low a rank as the þeów or wealh," in Bosworth and Toller, p. 258. Also, see this entry in *Dictionary of Old English*, ed. Angus Cameron, et al. (Toronto, 1986–).

[39] The notion of the body dominating the soul is present in many medieval works. For instance, the character Mankind introduces this idea in his first appearance in the homonymous morality play:

> My name ys Mankynde. I haue my composycyon
> Of a body and of a soull, of condycyon contrarye.

particularly evident in lines 4b-10a which emphasize the positive effect of a life grounded on spiritual aims, not on carnal interests, a plea which also finds an echo in the preceding composition. In this sense, Riddle 43 also warns potential readers of the disastrous consequences that will be endured by those who allow the body to rule their lives, just as in Riddle 42 lechery and irrational behaviour in general were contrasted with spiritual life based on learning.

This riddle continues the carnal/spiritual reflection initiated in Riddle 42. We may infer that Riddle 43 has been juxtaposed to the preceding composition due to their ostensible thematic connection and the didactic overtones shared by them. In the same way the cock and hen of Riddle 42 allegorically represent the battle between fleshly desires and spiritual aspirations, Riddle 43 presents this conflictive dichotomy in a literal dimension.[40] A further outstanding characteristic which supports the thematic connection between these two compositions is the fact that, in the manuscript, there is no space nor strong punctuation separating Riddle 42 from Riddle 43 although the latter begins with a small capital.[41] Williamson interprets the lack of punctuation as a mistake on

Betwyx þem tweyn ys a grett dyvisyon;
He þat xulde be subjecte, now he hath þe victory. (194-97)

Mark Eccles, ed., *The Macro Plays*, EETS o.s. 262 (London, 1969).

[40] This idea is frequently present in medieval literature. In *Mankind*, for example, Mercy advises Mankind to fight against the sins of the flesh alluding to the battle between the soul and the body citing from Job 8:1: "The temptacyon of þe flesch ye must resyst lyke a man, / For þer ys euer a batell betwyx þe soull and þe body: / 'Vita hominis est milicia super terram'" (226-28).

[41] See fol. 112r in R. W. Chambers, Max Förster, and Robin Flower, eds., *The* Exeter Book *of Old English Poetry: A Complete Photographic Facsimile of the Manuscript* (London, 1933). In "Two Spliced Riddles of the Exeter Book," Anderson proposes reading Riddle 42 and Riddle 43 as a single poem on the basis of the thematic relationship between the two texts and the absence of strong punctuation. However, this hypothesis has been discarded by the majority of editors, who print the two riddles separately. As Williamson fittingly states, "each riddle disguises a pair of creatures, but the pairs are certainly unlike (p. 276)."

the part of the scribe who was probably misled by the fact that the two riddles deal with a pair of creatures.[42] However, it is plausible that the omission of end-punctuation may be due to the compiler's acknowledgment of the thematic association between Riddle 43 and Riddle 42.[43] The capital letter beginning Riddle 43 might have been meant to indicate that the two riddles were independent texts but thematically interrelated, as the allegorical symbology of the cock and hen in patristic literature must have been known by the monastic audience to which the riddle was most likely addressed.

*Riddle 44 (key)*

With its explicit description of the male sexual organ in its first three lines, Riddle 44 has traditionally been included in the "obscene" category. The remainder of the text refers to the metaphor of the key and the lock alluding to male and female pudenda, a motif which was well-known in medieval literature.[44]

Wrætlic hongað bi weres þeo,
frean under sceate. Foran is þyrel.
Bið stiþ ond heard, stede hafað godne;
þonne se esne his agen hrægl
ofer cneo hefeð, wile þæt cuþe hol
mid his hangellan heafde gretan
þæt he efenlang ær oft gefylde.[45]

[42] *The Old English Riddles*, p. 276.

[43] Anderson arrived at a similar conclusion: "The scribe seems to have acknowledged the joint themes with a sly graphic trick of his own: he copied both riddles as one text but also 'separated' them with a bold raised point and a somewhat elongated small capital in the middle of the manuscript line," *Two Literary Riddles*, p. 23.

[44] See Gleissner, *Die "zweideutigen" altenglischen Rätsel,* pp. 356-59, for German analogues.

[45] "A strange thing hangs by a man's thigh under its master's clothes. It is pierced in front, is stiff and hard, has a good fixed place. When the man lifts his own garment up above his knee, he wishes to visit with the head of this hanging instrument the familiar hole which it, when of equal length, has often filled before."

In one of the Cambridge Songs (no. 49), the key motif is used with similar sexual connotations:

> Ven[i], d[ilectissim]e,
> et a et o,
> gratam me [in] uisere,
> et a et o et a et o!
> . . . . . . . . . . . . . . .
> Si cum claue ueneris,
> [et a et o],
> [mo]x intrare poteris,
> et a et o et a et o! (1-4, 13-16) [46]

Spanke has noted that the lock and key in the last part of the Cambridge lyric suggest female and male sexual organs respectively, just as occurs with Riddle 44.[47] The explicitness of this song is thus very much in the line of the imagery found in the Exeter riddle. However, despite the evident sexual connotations of the images, there are also religious overtones underlying the Cambridge text. As Ziolkowski observes, the *a et o* refrain is probably intended "to convey the sighs of the woman," but it may also "allude playfully to alpha and omega: 'Come, beloved, my alpha and omega.'"[48] Scholars have likewise noted that the erotic metaphors found in the Cambridge lyric present clear affinities with those present in the Song of Songs. Ziolkowski, for example, states that "the metaphor of sexual love being like the unlocking of a door is

[46] "Come, dearest love, with ah! and oh! to visit me — I will please you, with ah! and oh! ... If you come with the key, with ah! and oh! You will soon be able to enter, with ah! and oh! and ah! and oh!" The text and translation of lyric 49 is from Jan M. Ziolkowski, *The Cambridge Songs (Carmina Cantabrigiensia)* (New York, 1994), pp. 126-27. The reconstruction of the obliterated text, as indicated by square brackets, is in turn based on Peter Dronke's reading in *Medieval Latin and the Rise of European Love-Lyric,* 2 vols., 2nd ed. (Oxford, 1968), I, 274. See also Clifford Davidson, "Erotic 'Women's Songs' in Anglo-Saxon England," *Neophilologus* 59 (1975): 451-62.

[47] See Hans Spanke, "Ein lateinisches Liederbuch des 11. Jahrhunderts," *Studi Medievali* n.s. 15 (1942): 111-42, and *Deutsche und französische Dichtung des Mittelalters* (Stuttgart, 1943), p. 51.

[48] *The Cambridge Songs,* p. 310.

prominent in the Song of Songs itself (5.2, 5.4-6)."[49] If we pay attention to the second biblical passage pointed out by Ziolkowski, the parallelism with the imagery and the sensual mood found in both the Cambridge lyric and Exeter Riddle 44 is significant: "My beloved put his hand to the latch, and my heart was thrilled within me. I arose to open to my beloved, and my hands dripped with myrrh, my fingers with liquid myrrh, upon the handles of the bolt."[50]

In the traditional exegesis of the Song of Songs, erotic imagery and sexual love have been interpreted as an allegorical reference to "the love of Christ for his bride, the church (Rev. 21.2, 9), or as symbolizing the intimate experience of divine love in the individual soul."[51] Also, as Ferguson points out, "the most influential interpretation [of the Song of Songs] in patristic times took the bride as the individual human soul."[52] If we assume that the erotic description of Riddle 44, like that of Cambridge lyric 49, recalls the allegorical reading of the Song of Songs, it would not be too far-fetched to suppose that the key (as the lover) and the lock (representing the bride) might be a metaphor alluding to Christ and the human soul, an idea closely related to the preceding dichotomy of the body and soul in Riddle 43.

The consecutive order of Riddle 43 and Riddle 44 in the manuscript could have been intended to present a further thematic association, since their pairing seems to echo contemporary texts in which the image of the key appears as a

[49] *The Cambridge Songs*, pp. 310-11.

[50] As Ziolkowski mentions, Pollmann has also contended that the allusion to the key in the Cambridge song is in the line of Ambrose's comments on this passage from the Song of Songs: "Cubiculum Ecclesiae corpus est Christi. Introduxit eam Rex in omnia interiora mysteria, dedit ei claves; ut aperiret sibi thesauros scientiae sacramentorum." See Leo Pollmann, "*Iam, dulcis amica, venito* und die Hoheliedtradition," *Romanische Forschungen* 74 (1962): 265-80, at 280. For Ambrose's commentary, see *Opera Omnia, In Psalmum 118, Sermo* 1.16 (*PL* 15, 1271).

[51] This citation is from the introduction to the *Song of Songs* in *The New Oxford Annotated Bible*, p. 815.

[52] Everett Ferguson, et al., eds., *Encyclopedia of Early Christianity* (London, 1990; repr. New York, 1997), s.v. "Song of Solomon," p. 860.

tool related to the salvation of the human soul. This symbolic association is, for example, present in *Christ I,* in which Jesus is characterized as the guardian of the key which opens the lock leading to eternal life.[53]

> Eala þu reccend ond þu riht cyning,
> se þe locan healdeð, lif ontyneð,
> eadga[n] upwegas, oþrum forwyrneð
> wlitigan wilsiþes, gif his weorc ne deag. (18-21) [54]

The key is also a motif which frequently accompanies the soul in coeval eschatological literature. Brandished by St. Peter, it appears as a decisive symbolic instrument for the fate of human souls, for instance, in a passage from Vercelli Homily 15:

> ⁊ þonne gesamniað ða dioflu hie tosomne, ⁊ hie ðonne drifað þa synfullan ⁊ þa cearfullan sawla to helle. ⁊ se halga Petrus gæð mid ⁊ bereð helle cægan on handa. ... ⁊ þonne wendeð sanctus Petrus þanon fram þære helle / dura, ⁊ he beluceð þa helle duru syðþan þa earman sawla bioð in ða ecan helle ⁊ in ða ecan cwylmnesse, ⁊ ða deofla mid him. ⁊ þonne wendeð him

[53] This idea is based on Stanley B. Greenfield's reading of this passage in "Of Locks and Keys — Line 19a of the O. E. *Christ,*" *MLN* 67 (1952): 238-40. Jackson J. Campbell cites a passage by Amalarius commenting on the significance of the "Clavis David" antiphon from which this notion derives; see Campbell's discussion of this passage in his edition, *The Advent Lyrics of the* Exeter Book (Princeton, 1959), pp. 82-83. As Burlin notes, "like Amalarius, (CV 1268), who associated the Clavis David antiphon with the 'spiritus intellectus,' the Old English poet thought of the 'Key' as unlocking the meaning of Holy Writ," *The Old English Advent: A Typological Commentary* (New Haven, 1968), p. 76.

[54] "You, O Ruler and rightful King, Who guard the lock, Who open life, the blessed ways to heaven, [yet] withhold from another that bright, longed-for journey, if his work does not merit." The edition and translation is by Burlin. This passage seems to be based on Psalm 118:20: "This is the gate of the Lord; the righteous shall enter through it." With regard to the excerpt from *Christ I,* Burlin states: "Through the power of Christ, the secrets of the divine law are open to the faithful and closed to unbelievers. . ." (p. 75). This idea is paralleled in Riddle 42 in which a similar distinction is made alluding to the ones who know books — "þe bec witan" (7a) — and will be able to reveal the mystery by means of the key — "cægan cræfte"(12a).

> sanctus Petrus þanon fram þære helle dura, ⁊ he þonne weorpeð ða cearfullan cæge ofer bæc in on ða helle. Đis he deð for þam þe he ne mæg locian on þæt mycle sar ⁊ on þam myclan wanunge ⁊ on ðam myclan wope þe þa earman sawla dreogað mid ðam deoflum in helle tintrego. Eala, broðor mine, hu mycel ⁊ hu hlud bið se cnyll þonne seo cæge fealleð in þa helle. (184-99)[55]

The link between the key and the soul is also present elsewhere in medieval literature, notably in the story of the monk of the monastery of St. Peter at Cologne, preserved in an eleventh-century Latin collection of Marian miracles.[56] This version describes a monk who had led a sinful life, and had even engendered a son. When death occurs all of a sudden, without allowing the monk to repent of his sins ("sine confessione uel Christi corporis sacra communione"), the devils capture his soul. The monk then begs the angels and saints to help him save his soul and, finally, it is St. Peter who intercedes for him putting to flight the devil with the power of his great key: "sanctus petrus magna clave quam tenebat diabolum terrens eum in fugam vertit, et animam fratris quam tenebat eripuit." St. Peter then frees the soul which comes back

[55] "And then the devils gather them together, and drive the sinful and the sorrowful souls to hell. And the holy Peter goes with them, and bears in his hands the key of hell. . . . and then from there Saint Peter turns from the doors of hell, and he then locks the door of hell once those poor souls are inside that perpetual hell, and in that eternal affliction, and the devils with them. And then Saint Peter turns away from the doors of hell and throws that sorrowful key backwards into hell. He does this because he cannot look at the great sorrow, and on that great lamentation, and on that great weeping that those poor souls must suffer with the devils in the punishment of hell. Alas, my brothers, how great and how loud is the knell when the key falls into hell." For the edition of this passage and that of the parallel text in BL, Cotton Faustina A.ix, see D.G. Scragg, ed., *The Vercelli Homilies and Related Texts*, EETS o.s. 300 (Oxford, 1992), pp. 260-61. The translation is my own.

[56] For the edition of the whole miracle, see Elise F. Dexter, ed., *Miracula Sanctae Virginis Mariae*, University of Wisconsin Studies in the Social Sciences and History 12 (Madison, 1927), pp. 21-22. Also, this version is cited and commented on by M. José Mora, "The Power of the Keys: A Parallel to the Line Drawings in BL MS Stowe 944," *SELIM* 3 (1993): 57-71. I want to thank Professor Mora for pointing out this passage to me.

to the body of the monk whose life is thus spared to tell the miracle.[57] This account, which must have been well-known and exemplary in the monastic context, thus supplies a further example of the connection between the symbol of the key and the human soul.

According to this reading, Riddle 44 was most probably meant to continue the didactic allegorical aim established with Riddle 42, in which a sensual image is used to offer ideas related to learning, spiritual life, and salvation. It is also quite possible that, as a continuation of this metaphorical mode, the obscene description found in Riddle 44 owes much to the allegorical interpretation of erotic imagery in the Song of Songs. We should therefore infer that the typological reading suggested for Riddle 42 might extend to the immediately following riddles. Interestingly enough, the male lover (the key) and the bride (the lock) of Riddle 44 correspond to the copulating cock and hen of Riddle 42, and the soul and body union in Riddle 43. Also, note the master/servant dichotomy as used in Riddle 44 — "frean" (2a) for the owner of the key, and "esne" (4a), the key — which is parallel to the presentation of the soul and body in the preceding poem. The concatenation of Riddles 42, 43, and 44 thus supports the idea that the riddler was deliberately providing the key of Riddle 44 with the learned connotations found in contemporary texts which were surely well-known to a monastic audience. In this sense, Riddle 44 should not be considered a mere obscene piece deriving from popular tradition as it could well have been included here as an erotic lyric dealing with a well-known allegory. Possibly this

[57] The connection between the key and the soul as described in this miracle is also observable in a drawing found on fol. 6v of BL MS Stowe 944 in which St. Peter appears brandishing the key as a weapon to release a soul whose arm is seized by a demon. This motif has been analyzed by David F. Johnson, "A Scene of Post-Mortem Judgment in the New Minster *Liber Vitae*," *Old English Newsletter* 34.1 (Fall 2000): 26-30. Johnson supplies textual evidence — alluding to the passage from Vercelli Homily 15 as well as two excerpts from *Christ III* — to demonstrate the relationship of this pictorial representation with the notion of individual judgment, rather than the Final Judgment with which it has traditionally been associated. I want to thank Prof. Johnson for having allowed me to have access to an earlier version of this essay. Mora (cited above, n. 56) provides further literary support for this hypothesis with medieval versions of the story of the monk of St. Peter's at Cologne.

allegorical motif served as an excuse to give free rein to the sexual *double entendre*, probably rooted in popular lore, but also likely subject to learned allegorical commentary, similar to Latin erotic lyrics.

*Riddle 45 (dough)*

The clues of Riddle 45 can be read at two levels, as usual in *double entendre* riddles, so that the activity of the woman kneading, and the process of the dough being baked in the oven are paralleled with the sexual act:[58]

> Ic on wincle gefrægn weaxan nathwæt,
> þindan ond þunian, þecene hebban;
> on þæt banlease bryd grapode,
> hygewlonc hondum, hrægle þeahte
> þrindende þing þeodnes dohtor.[59]

The *double entendre* of Riddle 45 is similar to that in Riddle 44. Thus, expressions such as "banlease" (3a) and "þrindende þing" (5a) favor the ambiguous description, as they can apply to both the dough and the male sexual organ. The term "þrindende"

[58] Aldhelm's Riddle 70 ("tortella") also presents the image of the rising dough in slightly obscene *double entendre*, although it mainly concentrates on the comparison between the round form of the pancake and that of a shield: "De terris orior candenti corpore pelta / Et niue fecunda, Vulcani torre rigescens . . ." (1-3, "I arise from the earth, shield-shaped with a gleaming body of rich snow, growing hard in the heat of Vulcan [i.e. the oven]," trans. Michael Lapidge and James L. Rosier, *Aldhelm: The Poetic Works* [Cambridge, 1985], p. 85.) The edition of all Latin riddles presented in this essay is that of *CCSL* 133-133A. For information about bread making in the Anglo-Saxon period, see Ann Hagen, *A Handbook of Anglo-Saxon Food: Processing and Consumption* (Pinner, Norfolk, 1992; repr. 1998), pp. 17-20. For a recent essay on Riddle 45, see Thomas D. Hill, "The Old English Dough Riddle and the Power of Women's Magic: The Traditional Context of Exeter Book Riddle 45," in *Via Crucis: Essays on Early Medieval Sources and Ideas in Memory of J.E. Cross*, ed. Thomas N. Hall (Morgantown, 2002), pp. 50-60. I want to thank Prof. Hill for allowing me to have access to an earlier version of this essay. See also Edith Whitehurst Williams, "What's So New About the Sexual Revolution? Some Comments on Anglo-Saxon Attitudes Toward Sexuality in Women Based on Four Exeter Book Riddles," *Texas Quarterly* 18.2 (1975): 46-55, who examines the active role of the riddlic woman of this poem.

[59] "I have heard of something growing in a corner, swelling and standing up, raising its covering. At that boneless thing a proud-hearted bride grasped with her hands; a prince's daughter covered that swelling thing with her robe."

(5a) in Riddle 45 is evidently used in the text to refer to the literal swelling of the dough, due to the fermentation provoked by yeast, and to the figurative erection.[60]

As occurs in the preceding riddles, there are further metaphorical connotations in the image of the rising dough which echo passages in poems with a clear religious aim. In *Vainglory*, the verb "þrinteð" occurs in an excerpt presenting the image of the vainglorious person swelling with pride and drunkenness: "Sum on oferhygdo / þrymme þringeð, þrinteð him in innan / ungemedemad mod" (23-25, "In arrogance one pushes haughtily forward; there swells within him immoderate pride"). In his comments on this passage, Huppé notes the uniqueness of both "þrinteð" (23b) and "ungemedemad" (25a), the first occurring elsewhere only in Riddle 37 and Riddle 45: "The poet's use of these special forms seems to mark his intention of establishing in the concept of 'swelling' and 'lack of moderation' a base for a metaphoric picture of the vainglorious man as drunkenly gluttonous...."[61] Further in *Vainglory*, the man affected by excess of pride is described as "þrymme gebyrmed" (42b) — "leavened with pride" is Mackie's translation for the phrase. As Huppé notes, this expression parallels the preceding swelling image in *Vainglory* (23-25), stating that "*gebyrmed*, 'fermented,' (42) is the metaphoric equivalent of *þrinteð*, putting in a homely image what is implied

[60] In Riddle 37, in which the mechanical movement of the bellows in likewise presented as a *double entendre* suggesting sexual intercourse, the form "aþrunten" (2b) is used to refer to the swelling of the artifact, also hinting at penis erection:

Ic þa wihte geseah; womb wæs on hindan
þriþum aþrunten. Þegn folgade,
mægenrofa man, ond micel hæfde
gefered þæt hit felde, fleah þurh his eage. (1-4)

"I saw the creature. Behind it was its belly, hugely distended. It was served by an attendant, a man of great strength, who had accomplished much when what filled it flew out through its eye."

[61] Bernard F. Huppé, *The Web of Words; Structural Analyses of the Old English Poems: Vainglory, the Wonder of Creation, the Dream of the Rood, and Judith* (Albany, 1970), p. 16.

by the swelling of the immoderate soul: the vainglorious man is a vat of fermenting, swelling malice."[62]

For contemporary learned readers of Riddle 45, the image of the rising dough would surely conjure up metaphorical connotations similar to those found in Exeter *Vainglory*, thus linking fermentation and swelling with the bodily sin of lechery. This association is attested to in the Bible, and is also frequently expounded in patristic commentaries. In the first letter to the Corinthians, surely a well-known text for a monastic audience, St. Paul condemns the permissiveness with which certain sexual perversions are overlooked by the Christian Church at Corinth. Having received news about a case of incest being passively tolerated by the Corinthian brethren, St. Paul reprimands them for not having taken serious measures against the sinful conduct of a member of their community, warning them of the easy spreading of corruption and evil by means of the leaven metaphor:

> Do you not know that a little leaven leavens the whole lump? Cleanse out the old leaven that you may be a new lump, as you really are unleavened.... Let us, therefore, celebrate the festival, not with the old leaven, the leaven of malice and evil, but with the unleavened bread of sincerity and truth. (1 Cor. 5:6-7)

Evil is thus compared to leaven affecting a whole piece of dough, i.e. a whole community, whereas spiritual brethren are compared to unleavened bread, that is, free from corruption.[63]

The adjective "hygewlonc" (4a) is also worth discussing in the instructional context underlying the riddle. Although the term *wlonc* has traditionally been translated into MnE as "proud" or "proud-hearted," von Lindheim contends that it

[62] Huppé, *The Web of Words*, p. 18.

[63] Sedulius Scotus, in his commentaries to St. Paul's epistle to Galatians — namely, to the verse "A little leaven leavens the whole lump" (5.9) — extends the metaphor to explain that the corruption of the whole church may originate with an insignificant crime: "Ostendit quod modicum erroris fermentum totam possit Ecclesiae massam corrumpere,"*Sedulii Scoti Collectanea in omnes B. Pauli epistolas, In epistolam ad Galatas* (V), *PL* 103, 191.

should actually be rendered as "wanton" or "lustful" instead of "proud."[64] The word might however suggest both ideas, for the association of pride with lust is pervasive in religious literature. In this sense, it is worth noting that "wlanc" (4a) describes the lecherous hen of Riddle 42. Also, the lascivous slave of Riddle 12 is described as "felawlonc"(7a),[65] while the woman handling the onion, in the *double entendre* context of Riddle 25, is said to be "modwlonc" (7a). Significantly, in *Soul and Body II* the soul accuses the body of wantonness, excessive pride, and drunkenness by means of the term "wlonc": "Wære þu þe wiste wlonc ond wines sæd, / þrymful þunedest"(36-37a, "Thou wast flushed with food and sated with wine, thou didst vaunt in thy glory").

In Riddle 45 there are further images which might fit in an instructional context. For example, the allusion to the woman kneading bread would possibly remind an ecclesiastical audience of the parable of the leaven in which the eventual growing and spreading of God's kingdom is described in similar terms: "The kingdom of heaven is like leaven which a woman took and hid in three measures of flour, till it was all leavened" (Matt. 13:33)."[66] The image of the lewd woman of Riddle 45 covering the swelling dough with her clothes — "hrægle þeahte / þrindende þing þeodnes dohtor" (4b-5) —

[64] "The contextual analysis ... of *wlonc* in the *Riddles* confirms that the meaning 'lust, greed' was undoubtedly part of the original semantic nucleus of the word ...," von Lindheim, "Traces of Colloquial Speech," p. 35.

[65] See Higley's discussion of Riddle 12 in this volume. For another recent analysis of this riddle, see Nina Rulon-Miller, "Sexual Humor and Fettered Desire in Exeter Book Riddle 12," in *Humour in Anglo-Saxon Literature*, ed. Jonathan Wilcox (Cambridge, 2000), pp. 99-126.

[66] Also in Lk.13:20-21.

might conjure up that of the biblical woman hiding the leaven in the flour. [67] According to this, Riddle 45 might have possibly been intended to reflect on the different allegorical meanings of the leavened bread, which is a recurrent image in the scriptures. Riddle 45 therefore constitutes a further illustration of the combination of the prurient and the instructional as observed in Riddle 42 and Riddle 44.

In the light of this discussion, Riddle 45 is clearly a thematic companion to Riddle 44. In both compositions, the literal reading describes a pair of domestic items such as the key and the lock, and the dough and the oven.[68] The two texts also make use of *double entendre* to suggest sexual intercourse and the implicit sexual solution "penis." Finally, they both seem to lend themselves to allegorical interpretation, since they could be alluding to well-known metaphors found in the Bible and exegetical literature.

*Riddle 46 (Lot and his daughters)*

A popular theme in both literary and folklore tradition,[69] Riddle 46 would immediately remind a monastic audience of the biblical episode found in Genesis 19:30-38. Having been

[67] Williamson, *The Old English Riddles*, p. 282, has also noted that Riddle 45 is "an elaborate conceit based upon the role of the Anglo-Saxon wife as *hlæfdige*, 'lady, mistress of the house' (B-T, p. 539), literally 'kneader of the dough'."

[68] The comparison of houseware tools with human genitalia, and the metaphorical equivalence of domestic activities to the sexual act are ancient themes in folklore and literature. The preparation of bread has frequently been associated with sexuality in literature. Note, for example, the miller's wife and daughter in Chaucer's *The Reeve's Tale*. Likewise the miller's daughter is a commonplace figure in French fabliaux.

[69] As J. B. Friedreich, *Geschichte des Räthsels* (Dresden, 1860), pp. 98-103, notes, a version of this ancient motif can be found in the second query of the Queen of Sheba to King Solomon, which is contained in the Talmud (Midras Mishlae). See also Gleissner, *Die "zweideutigen" altenglischen Rätsel*, pp. 303-06, and Dina Stein, "A King, a Queen, and the Riddle Between: Riddles and Interpretation in a Late Midrashic Text," in *Untying the Knot: On Riddles and other Enigmatic Modes*, ed. Galit Hasan-Rokem and David Shulman (New York, 1996): 125-47.

warned by two angels of the imminent destruction of the vicious city of Sodom, Lot is urged to escape with his family without ever looking back. Disregarding this command, Lot's wife turns to look back at the city and becomes a pillar of salt. Lot and his daughters take refuge in a cave, in which the latter contrive a plan to seduce their father in order to bear him offspring; they make him become drunk and sleep with him. As a result, two sons — Moab and Ammon — are born.[70]

This riddle presents the outcome of this incestuous relationship which ends up in a confusing family structure:

> Wer sæt æt wine   mid his wifum twam
> ond his twegen suno   ond his twa dohtor,
> swase gesweostor,   ond hyra suno twegen,
> freolico frumbearn;   fæder wæs þær inne
> þara æþelinga   æghwæðres mid,
> eam ond nefa.   Ealra wæron fife
> eorla ond idesa   insittendra.[71]

The man (Lot) is thus said to have two wives (i.e. his two daughters), and two sons from his two daughters. The

[70] For a similar Anglo-Saxon relationship query, see Max Förster, "Die Lösung des ae. Prosarätsels," *Archiv für das Studium der neueren Sprachen und Literaturen* 60 (1906): 367-71. The Lot theme is a frequent motif in riddling dialogues, as these indulge in queries based on the knowledge of the Bible. For example, in one of the versions of the Latin *Adrian and Epictetus*, we find one of these riddles: "Quis nepos patris matri factus est frater? — Filii Loth." This is no. 29 (p. 32) of Walther Suchier's edition, *Das mittellateinische Gespräch Adrian und Epictitus* (Tübingen, 1955). See also Gleissner, *Die "zweideutigen" altenglischen Rätsel*, pp. 306-07, for other versions of this motif in riddlic dialogues. Frederick Tupper, Jr., detects an analogue to Riddle 46 in "The Holme Riddles (MS. Harl. 1960)," *PMLA* 18 (1903): 211-72:

> Q[uestion]. 2 sisters standing on a tombe thus bewaled the dead ther is alas here lys our mothers husbant our husband our childrens father & our father how can this bee
>
> A[nswer]. it is ment lots daughters on the tombe of ther father. (No. 10, p. 221)

[71] "A man sat at wine with his two wives, and his two sons and his two daughters, as also sisters and their two sons, noble first-born children. The father of each of these princes was there with them, and an uncle and a nephew. In all there were five men and women sitting within."

daughters are therefore sisters to their own sons, and the two boys are in turn uncle and nephew to each other. Despite the allusion to different family members, the riddle at the end clarifies that there are only five people involved. Just as in Riddle 43 the body and soul are said to be brothers whose mother (earth) is also their sister, Riddle 46 presents a similar paradoxical situation, since the category of daughter is incompatible with that of wife, a grandson cannot be a son at the same time, and so forth. As Barley explains, "the paradox [in Riddle 46] results from the assumption of the kinship system that incest will not occur. If it does, then different mutually exclusive slots will be filled by the same people."[72]

Riddle 46 does not seem an "obscene" composition at first sight, since there is no apparent description of sexual intercourse nor of body genitalia, as occurs in the preceding poems. However, Riddle 46 clearly alludes to incest, which is one of the sexual practices prohibited in Leviticus 18: "None of you shall approach any one near of kin to him to uncover nakedness . . . . You shall not uncover the nakedness of your father, which is the nakedness of your mother" (18:6-7).[73]

After commenting on numerous passages from patristic literature condemning incest, Gleissner concludes that Riddle 46 must be regarded an obscene composition to which allegorical interpretation might have been applied.[74] Among the passages cited by Gleissner, it is worth considering Bede's commentaries to Genesis in which the allegorical reading of the episode of Lot may serve to understand the context in which Riddle 46 might have been interpreted by a contemporary learned audience. Since Lot's condition as patriarch made this biblical

[72] Nigel F. Barley, "Structural Aspects of the Anglo-Saxon Riddle," *Semiotica* 10 (1974): 143-75 at 164.

[73] The notion of incest as a sin of the body is reflected in Ælfric's *Glossary*, in which Latin "incestus" is glossed as Old English "unclæne," literally meaning "unclean" or "impure." By contrast, Latin "castus" corresponds to Old English "clæne." This idea echoes the definition of incest found in Isidore's *Etymologiae*, as Latin *incestus* is associated with *incastus*: "Incestus, propter inlicitam conmixtionem vocatus, quasi incastus" (X.i.148).

[74] Gleissner, *Die "zweideutigen" altenglischen Rätsel*, p. 326.

episode a thorny issue for exegesis, patristic authors frequently sought to justify his misconduct. Thus, Lot's behaviour is exonerated by Bede's *In Principium Genesis*, pre-senting his daughters as the typical female temptresses. Accord-ing to Bede, these represent "carnales etiam sublimium uirorum cogitationes," i.e. the carnal thoughts which affect great men.[75] Following Bede's line of argument, the biblical episode of Lot should be viewed as a representation of the difficulties endured by spiritual men who are tempted by fleshly sins. Also, as Gleissner notes, Lot's sons would then constitute the resulting sins and vices engendered by his carnal thoughts (his daughters).[76] Under this light, Lot prefigures the anchorite who, withdrawn in the wilderness like St. Anthony, is tempted by the sins of the flesh. Such reflection would certainly be consonant with the soul-and-body conflict which serves as a leitmotif for the riddlic section.[77]

Lot's sinful behaviour was often justified by his inebriated state. In the Old English version of the *Heptateuch*, Lot's drunkenness and unawareness are clearly underlined: "Eft hi fordrencton ðone unwaran Loð, ⁊ seo gingre dohtor eode to hys bedde, ⁊ se fæder nyste hu he befeng on hi, ne hwænne heo aras, for hys druncennysse" ("They made unaware Lot get drunk again, and the younger daughter went to his bed, and the father did not know how he grasped onto them, nor when

[75] Bede, *In Principium Genesis* (IV.xix), *CCSL* 118A; this passage is also cited and discussed by Gleissner, *Die "zweideutigen" altenglischen Rätsel*, p. 321.

[76] "Ja, Moab und Ammon stehen für die Sünde und alle Laster überhaupt," *Die "zweideutigen" altenglischen Rätsel*, pp. 321-22.

[77] In a much more straightforward way than Riddle 46, Boniface's enigma no. 3 ("De cupiditate") alerts a potential monastic audience of the dangers of carnal desire, describing how *Cupiditas* seeks members of the different ecclesiastical orders to tempt them, misleading them from the spiritual way to heaven:

> Pontifices multos temptans per deuia duxi,
> Candida ut meritis non scandant atria caeli;
> Presbiterosque sumul uastans per lucra peremi.
> Ordinibus sacris degentes sterno phalanges;
> Cum semel agrediens comitabor fraude monachos (25-29).

she arose, because of his drunkenness").[78] In this sense, this biblical episode might have served as an exemplary account of the negative consequences of drunkenness, an idea that is superficially hinted at in line 1a of Riddle 46 ("Wer sæt æt wine"). Besides, drunkenness has traditionally been considered a bodily sin, associated with lechery.[79] Boniface's Riddles, for example, clearly relate these two vices, as enigma no. 6 ("De ebrietate") is juxtaposed to no. 7 ("De luxoria").

As commented with regard to Riddle 45, in *Vainglory* excessive pride is presented by means of images of swelling and drunkenness. In this sense, it is worth quoting another passage from this work describing the vainglorious man, fermenting with wine and pride, which somewhat parallels the presentation of Lot as "Wer sæt æt wine" (1a): "siteþ symbelwlonc, searwum læteð / wine gewæged word ut faran, / þræfte þringan þrymme gebyrmed ..." (40-42, "He sits flushed with the feast, deluded by wine, designedly lets his words go forth, crowd out provocatively, leavened with pride ..."). In this sense, "wlonc" (from "symbelwlonc") is once more used in the context of the excesses of the body, as occurs with other obscene riddles. This passage similarly presents the association of carnal sins and drunkenness with the image of fermentation ("gebyrmed"). The conflation of these ideas is also discernible in the juxtaposition of Riddle 45 and Riddle 46, since the former

[78] This passage is also cited by Williamson, *The Old English Riddles*, p. 284. The text is edited by S. J. Crawford, *The Old English Version of the Heptateuch: Ælfric's Treatise on the Old and New Testament and his Preface to Genesis*, EETS o.s. 160 (London, 1922), p. 134. The translation is mine.

[79] Lot's drunkenness is paralleled by the Genesis episode in which another Old Testament patriarch, Noah, lay naked in the presence of his sons due to intoxication from wine (Gen. 9:20-23). The exposure of Noah's naked body as a result of inebriation is found in one of the drawings of the Junius manuscript, Israel Gollancz, *The Cædmon Manuscript of Anglo-Saxon Biblical Poetry* (Oxford, 1927), p. 239. For a fuller discussion of Noah's nakedness, see comments on this episode and its pictorial representations in the essays by Karkov and Wilcox in this volume, pp. 191-92 and 295-98. For a discussion on drunkenness in Anglo-Saxon texts, see Hugh Magennis, *Anglo-Saxon Appetites: Food and Drink and Their Consumption in Old English and Related Literature* (Dublin, 1999), especially pp. 103-10.

describes the swelling image of leavened bread, and the latter presents the consequences of Lot's committing incest with his daughters. In this context, the subsequent concatenation of Riddle 45 and Riddle 46 shows the same association of incest and fermentation as appears, for example, in St. Paul's first letter to Corinthians.[80]

As a final reflection on Riddle 46 and the whole section, it is worth taking into account the use of *double entendre* in Latin *enigmata* providing ideas similar to those suggested by the Anglo-Saxon riddles. Aldhelm, the same author who composed the treatises on virginity, supplied some of his riddles with evident sexual connotations. In Riddle 78 ("cupa uinaria"), the wine-cask, like Lot's daughters, is presented as a temptress intoxicating men with wine and leading them astray: "En, plures debrians impendo pocula Bacchi ..." (1, "Look, I dole out cups of wine, making many men drunk ..." trans. Lapidge). The riddle then offers the image of the wine-cask containing fermenting must compared to a woman swelling with lechery: "Sic mea turgescunt ad plenum uiscera musto, / Et tamen inflatum non uexat crapula corpus, / Quamuis hoc nectar centenis hauserit urnis" (5-7, "Thus my inwards swell to the full with must, yet inebriation does not trouble my swollen body, even though someone might draw off this nectar in a hundred jars").

Aldhelm's Riddle 80 ("calix uitreus") is also a good illustration of *double entendre* in the context of drunkenness. After presenting some clues describing the manufacturing of a glass cup, the action of seizing a cup of wine and drinking from it is paralleled to that of a man caressing and kissing a woman's body:

> Nempe uolunt plures collum constringere dextra
> Et pulchre digitis lubricum comprendere corpus;

[80] As cited above, p. 84, St. Paul urges the members of the Christian community at Corinth to punish a case of incest and so cleanse the old leaven.

Sed mentes muto, dum labris oscula trado
Dulcia compressis impendens basia buccis,
Atque pedum gressus titubantes sterno ruina. (5-9)[81]

The description of the wine cup relates the negative consequences of alcohol intoxication to an illicit sexual encounter with a woman, thus linking drunkenness and lechery as in Exeter Riddle 46.[82] The slightly moralizing tone of the Latin *enigma* seems to be enough to justify the use of the sexual *double entendre.*

These examples demonstrate that the didactic aim of Latin riddles was by no means hindered by the presentation of erotic imagery. Furthermore, the presence of sexual innuendo seems to have been perfectly tolerated in the instructional context of *enigmata*, as none of these riddles have been censored in the manuscripts in which they appear. Although the moralizing and instructional aim of Exeter Riddles 45 and 46 is not as obvious as in Aldhelm's Riddle 80, the consecutive occurrence of the description of the fermenting dough, and

[81] Lapidge's trans.: "To be sure, many people wish to grasp my neck with their right hands and to seize my delightfully smooth body with their fingers. But I change their minds as I give kisses to their lips, applying these sweet kisses to their tightly-pressed mouths: and (thus) I strike down the tottering advances of their feet with disaster."

[82] It is also significant that Exeter Riddle 63 (beaker of wine), though partially obliterated, shows clear parallels with Aldhelm's Riddle 80:

Hwilum mec on cofan cysseð muþe
Tillic esne, þær wit tu beoþ,
fæðme on folm[......]grum þyð,
wyrceð his willa[......]ð l[.......]

(4-7, "Sometimes in a chamber, where we are together, a good man kisses me with his mouth, presses me with his fingers in his hand's embrace, carries out his desire").

Riddle 63 might be emulating the *double entendre* present in Aldhelm's composition. As Tupper points out, "in both poems [Riddle 63 and Aldhelm's Riddle 80] the drinking-vessel is a woman who yields readily to caresses," Frederick Tupper, Jr., ed., *The Riddles of the* Exeter Book (Boston, 1910), p. 203.

the anomalous family relationship as a result of incest due to wine inebriation is unlikely to be haphazard.[83]

*Conclusions*

This discussion began with several questions which directed our attention to the reasons underlying the preservation of explicit erotic descriptions contained in some riddles occurring in a sequence. This essay has tried to demonstrate that these riddles survived thanks to the instructional aims that were usually associated with the enigmatic genre. Beyond the metaphorical reading of the *double entendre* clues as pointing to sexual intercourse, an allegorical reading of these texts might have been required. In this sense, the two traditional methods employed in the interpretation of the scriptures, as pointed out by Mitchell and Robinson, could have been at work with these riddles as well:

> When a medieval scholar like Ælfric read the Bible, he saw behind the literal sense of the words a host of allegorical and typological meanings which had been discerned by biblical commentators from early Christian times to his own day. These meanings make up the "spiritual sense" (*þæt gastlice andgit*) as opposed to the literal meaning (*seo nacede gerecednis*) of the Bible and are one of the means by which medieval Christians reconciled the sometimes bizarre and violent events of the Old Testament with the doctrine of the New.[84]

It is well-known that the two methods were employed with works other than the scriptures, as most editors agree that a great deal of the metaphors, and images found in poems such

[83] As mentioned above, in *Artistry in the Riddles of the* Exeter Book (p. 194), Conlee had already established a possible connection between Riddle 46 and the preceding Riddles 44 and 45.

[84] Bruce Mitchell and Fred C. Robinson, *A Guide to Old English*, fifth edn. (Oxford, 1992), p. 190.

as *Christ*, or *The Phoenix* contain allusions to well-known exegetical allegories.[85] The allegorical and instructional elements are also undoubtedly present in the riddle collections composed by ecclesiastical authors such as Aldhelm, Eusebius, Tatwine, and Boniface.[86] Even in Symphosius' *enigmata*, with no clear Christian background, many of the themes seem to lend themselves to exegetical interpretation as, for example, incense (no. 47), myrrh (no. 48), bell (no. 81), or apple (no. 85).[87]

With the precedent established by Latin riddles, and the images and metaphors (the cock and hen, the key, the fermenting dough, and so on) that have been detected in the

[85] For patristic and learned allusions in Old English literature, see for example J. E. Cross, "The Literate Anglo-Saxon — On Sources and Disseminations," *Proceedings of the British Academy* 58 (1972): 67-100.

[86] As an illustration, note, for instance, this passage from Aldhelm's Riddle 76 ("melarius"):

> Ex me tunc priscae processit causa ruinae,
> Dulcia quae rudibus tradeban mala colonis.
> En iterum mundo testor remeasse salutem,
> Stipite de patulo dum penderet arbiter orbis
> Et poenas lueret sobloes ueneranda Tonantis. (3-7)

"The cause of the original sin came then from me, who was dispensing sweet apples to the new inhabitants (of Paradise). I am a witness that salvation returned once more to the world (5), when the Judge of the World was hanged from a spreading tree and this glorious Son of the Thundering God washed away our sins" (trans. Lapidge). These lines obviously allude to the connection of the apple-tree with the Genesis episode narrating the fall (3-4), but also present this tree as a symbol prefiguring the cross of redemption (5-7). With the term "mala" (4), the text even provides the well-known wordplay with Latin *malum*, meaning both "evil" and "apple," thus associating this fruit to the origin of evil in the world. Significantly, this riddle is followed by Riddle 77 ("ficulnea"), linking "Apple-tree (lxxvi), the source of man's downfall, alongside Fig-tree (lxxvii), which supplied the covering for his shame," Lapidge and Rosier, *Aldhelm: The Poetic Works*, p. 64.

[87] As Frank Herbert Whitman notes, "The riddles of Symphosius, though they appear to have been composed without Christian influence, were probably read from a Christian point of view. The practice of turning secular works to Christian ends was not uncommon throughout the whole medieval period," *The Influence of the Latin and the Popular Riddle Traditions on the Old English Riddles of the* Exeter Book (Madison, 1968), p. 190.

components of the series, it could be easily inferred that a contemporary audience of the Exeter Riddles, most probably belonging to the monastic "learned elite," would be trained to recognize the literal and allegorical dimensions of these texts. From a literal point of view, the compiler seems to have assembled these riddles according to a simple criterion: each of these compositions alludes to a pair of creatures, which are clearly assigned male and female roles:

Riddle 42: cock and hen
Riddle 43: soul and body
Riddle 44: key and lock
Riddle 45: dough and oven
Riddle 46: Lot and his daughters[88]

This double pattern cannot be sheer coincidence, as it conforms to what I think is one of the major thematic links connecting these riddles: the concern with the body. This idea is discernible in those riddles describing the body or body parts. Thus, Riddle 43 presents the body proper as a companion of the soul, while Riddles 44 and 45 provide allusions to female and male sexual organs. Some of the compositions of this series — notably Riddles 42, 44, and 45 — contain impudent descriptions of sexual intercourse which again focus on the corporeal. Riddle 46 also forms part of this group as incest was obviously considered a sin of the body.

The section as a whole might have been intended as a reflection on the spiritual and bodily nature of human beings. Under this light, the series evinces further thematic consistency as it fittingly starts with the cock and hen which constitute an allegorical prelude to the soul-and-body theme of Riddle 43. In turn, Riddle 42 also underlines the rational or spiritual as the human quality that should prevail over the irrational (animal)

[88] It is also noteworthy that three of these riddles allude to pregnancy or offspring as a result of the sexual intercourse suggested: in Riddle 42, the hen is said to gain fullness under her garments; in Riddle 45, the bread inside the oven clearly stands for the pregnant woman; and Lot's sons are referred to as the outcome of an incestuous relation.

or carnal instincts. In this sense, Riddle 42 clearly extols the intellectual gifts of learned men (monks) who are capable of decoding the mysteries of literacy and typology, therefore anticipating that the allegorical method will be necessary for the following riddles. The allusion to the key in Riddle 42 thus prepares the audience for the allegorical symbology present in the following riddles, insisting that a spiritual reader should not rely on the literal meaning or the *nacede gerecednis* of the scenes described, but should know how to interpret them by means of the *gastlice andgit.* Riddle 45 and Riddle 46 might then possibly be read allegorically, just as was usual with the Song of Songs, and the biblical episode of Lot. In sum, the sequence formed by Riddles 42-46 seems to have been conceived as a section focused on the body, ultimately warning a potential audience against the dangers of relying on the carnal/literal dimension of the texts and, by extension, of life.

# The Body as Text in Early Anglo-Saxon Law

Mary P. Richards

In her recent article "Body and Law in Late Anglo-Saxon England," Katherine O'Brien O'Keeffe explores new ground about the meaning of mutilation during the late tenth and early eleventh centuries in England.[1] Using evidence drawn from the *Anglo-Saxon Chronicle*, the *Translatio et miracula S. Swithuni* by Lantfred, and contemporary legislation, O'Keeffe elucidates the use of physical punishment as a means to reveal both the crime and its recompense on the material body, which therefore becomes the text of both. In addition, she shows how such punishment becomes interpreted as a means for saving the soul. As she notes, the phenomena portrayed in events and writings associated with the Benedictine Revival and beyond have their roots in a much earlier tradition of Anglo-Saxon lawgiving that itself is influenced by continental formulations. But these earlier perceptions of the body have a focus and meaning different, I would stress, from the evolved interpretations post-*Renovatio*. The Kentish and West-Saxon injury tariffs and related statements surviving in law codes from the seventh through ninth centuries portray the material body as victim. Their purpose is more to establish appropriate compensation than to assign punishment. Although condign penalties for certain offences such as rape and theft likely were enacted during this period, the injury tariffs preserve the motive to avoid vendetta by settling disputes through arbitration and payment of fines.

Nevertheless, in their assumption of a message in the wounded body, these tariffs foreshadow the later interpretation of the material body as the medium for inscription of culpabil-

[1] Katherine O'Brien O'Keeffe, "Body and Law in Late Anglo-Saxon England," *ASE* 27 (1998): 209–32.

ity and redemption. For as we will see, the unclothed, wounded body in early Anglo-Saxon law conveyed both the evidence of a crime and the means to determine restitution. Whereas a victim might be twice victimized, first in the wounding and then in the unclothing and potential embarrassment, the process of reading the material body, implied by the injury tariffs, was essential to differentiate a victim from a punished criminal. The problem involved separating the nakedness and shame of the sinner, as elucidated in the essays of Catherine Karkov and Jonathan Wilcox, from the victim's pursuit of justice.[2] Wilcox, for example, surveys a wide variety of literary and visual evidence to demonstrate that the publicly exposed naked body was, for the Anglo-Saxons, the subject of embarrassment within a broader context of shame, yet unclothing before witnesses was necessary to describe many injuries. We cannot know exactly how these early laws were observed and implemented, but we can look for themes and patterns in the injury tariffs and other laws regarding wounding to tell us how the injured body was interpreted in this earlier period. In so doing, we can begin to answer questions, such as those posed by Roy Porter, about how individuals and cultures have "ascribed meaning to their limbs and organs, their constitutions, their flesh."[3]

To begin, an injury tariff is a list specifying types of wounds and their assigned monetary compensation to the victim. As Patrick Wormald has shown, such lists are traditional features of Merovingian law codes and they served as alternatives to the blood feud.[4] Several features prevail among the varying versions: the tariffs ordinarily do not specify social status as a factor in determining compensation, though in some instances there

[2] See Catherine E. Karkov, "Exiles from the Kingdom: The Naked and the Damned in Anglo-Saxon Art," and Jonathan Wilcox, "Naked in Old English: the Embarrassed and the Shamed," in the present volume.

[3] See Porter's "History of the Body" in *New Perspectives on Historical Writing*, ed. Peter Burke (Cambridge, 1991), pp. 206-32, at 224.

[4] Patrick Wormald, "*Exempla Romanorum*: the Earliest English Legislation in Context," in *Rome and the North*, ed. Alvar Ellegård and Gunilla Åkerström-Hougen (Jonsered, Sweden, 1996), pp. 14-27.

is a direct statement about them applying to freemen;[5] they are often arranged in rough head-to-toe order, though wounds to the generative organs may come last; they normally occur in one or two parts within a longer set of legal statements; and wounds affecting the victim's generative organs or physical appearance tend to be compensated more highly than other types. Furthermore, the syntax of the individual items within the tariff is simple and repetitive, at times resembling a primitive shorthand. This could indicate a mnemonics reflecting the oral origins of such lists, but it could also simply be the traditional written format for this information. Injury tariffs appear in the two English royal codes bearing the strongest resemblances to continental legislation, those of Æthelberht and Alfred.[6]

Whether these tariffs cover crimes by and against women is an issue addressed recently by Carole Hough.[7] She notes the generic use of the term *man* through the time of Alfred, and draws evidence from both legal codes to demonstrate that *man* could refer to both sexes separately or together. Equally important, Hough shows how Æthelberht's items 73 and 74, immediately following the statements of injuries and fines, serve as a coda to the tariff applying it to women. Hough argues convincingly that 73 and 74 "define the penalty for physical assault by females of free birth, dealing first with adult women and then

[5] Stanley Rubin, "The *Bot*, or Composition in Anglo Saxon Law: A Reassessment," *Journal of Legal History* 17 (1996): 144-54, esp. 148. In a private communication Lisi Oliver comments that the Old Irish laws do distinguish the injury tariff by the rank of the victim.

[6] The edition quoted is that of Felix Liebermann, *Die Gesetze der Angelsachsen,* 3 vols. (Halle, 1903-1916; rpt. Aalen, 1960), I: Text und Übersetzung. Æthelberht's laws are on pp. 3-9; Hlothhere and Eadric's laws are on pp. 9-11; and Alfred's laws are on pp. 16-89. The translations are my own, but I have consulted those offered by Dorothy Whitelock in *English Historical Documents, c.550-1042,* 2nd ed. (London, 1979), pp. 391-94, 394-95, and 407-16, and F. L. Attenborough in *The Laws of the Earliest English Kings* (Cambridge, 1922), pp. 5-17, 18-23, and 63-93.

[7] "Two Kentish Laws Concerning Women: A New Reading of Æthelberht 73 and 74," *Anglia* 119 (2001): 554-78.

with unmarried girls."[8] This type of statement appears in certain Germanic codes, but is not reproduced by Alfred, perhaps because it was assumed. Even so, Karkov's caveat about the largely male discourse of crime and punishment in Anglo-Saxon England remains valid.[9] Although injuries to male genitalia are specified in detail and assigned a high valuation, there is no mention of female genitalia in the tariffs, nor are any statements directed specifically toward female bodies. Sexual transgressions are dealt with elsewhere in the codes.

The early seventh-century legal code attributed to the Kentish king Æthelberht follows the pattern of continental Germanic examples, especially the Alaman and Bavarian codes.[10] Typical of these "barbaric" codes, the list of compensations for injuries amounts to more than one-third of the statements in the Kentish compendium. The list occurs in the middle of Æthelberht's code (#34-72) with no special introduction or termination. In the legal statements preceding the list we find scattered penalties for various types of murder, such as killing someone on the king's premises (#5), a total of nine in all. In contrast to the injury tariffs, these penalties often are characterized by the social status of the person killed and the place or circumstances, for example during a robbery. The penalty is most often related to the *wergild* (monetary value) of

[8] Hough, "Two Kentish Laws," p. 577.

[9] See her essay in this volume.

[10] Patrick Wormald, *The Making of English Law: King Alfred to the Twelfth Century; vol. 1: Legislation and its Limits* (Oxford, 1999), pp. 95-101 and table 2.3. See also Patrizia Lendinara, "The Kentish Laws," in *The Anglo-Saxons from the Migration Period to the Eighth Century: An Ethnographic Perspective*, ed. John Hines, Studies in Historical Archaeoethnology 2 (San Marino and Woodbridge, 1997), pp. 211-42. Lendinara calls attention to similarities in the injury tariffs between Æthelberht's laws and those issued by Rothari in 643 for the Lombards. For an analysis of the importance of Frankish connections to Kent, see Barbara Yorke, *Kings and Kingdoms of Early Anglo-Saxon England* (London, 1990), pp. 39-41. The unique copy of the Kentish laws is preserved in the *Textus Roffensis*, a twelfth-century manuscript from Rochester Cathedral Priory. A facsimile has been edited by Peter Sawyer, *Textus Roffensis: Rochester Cathedral Library Manuscript A. 3. 5*, EEMF 7 (Copenhagen, 1957).

the deceased, as seen in #26, where compensation is specified by degree within a rank.

> 26. Gif læt ofslæhð, þone selestan LXXX scll' forgelde; gif þane oþerne ofslæhð, LX scillingum forgelde; ðane þriddan XL scilling[um] forgelden.
>
> (26. If [a man] slays a *læt* of the best class, let him pay 80 shillings; if he slays one of the second class, let him pay 60 shillings; for the third class, let him pay 40 shillings.)

Although both types of offenses specify monetary compensation, violent crimes are treated separately in Æthelberht's code from the injury tariff, which covers mutilation rather than death.

When we look at the injury tariff itself, therefore, we see something quite different from the statements regarding capital crimes. First, few circumstances about an injury are mentioned–never, for example, the site where the wounding took place. Based upon the attention to social status in the penalties for murder, we might expect to find that the arm of an *eorl*, say, was worth more than that of a *ceorl*. But following Germanic tradition, no such distinction is made. Furthermore, the Kentish injury tariff is relatively complete in its coverage of the body. Although a number of the wounds cited are itemized as well in the *Lex Salica*, the legal code associated with Clovis that inspired the later Frankish codes, one finds substantially fuller coverage in the Kentish material.[11] Æthelberht's list is not, then, simply a traditional holdover but a feature seemingly developed for its utility. There is as well some independent logic to the arrangement of this list. Bone injuries precede those of the skull and shoulder, and thereafter come all manner of wounds to the head, arm, hand, belly, generative organs, legs, and feet in a kind of top-to-bottom hierarchy paralleling the social one that informs the larger code. The injuries listed require consideration in more detail. We ask, why are these

[11] See, for example, *Lex Salica*, ed. Karl August Eckhardt, Monumenta Germaniae Historica, Legum Sectio I, IV, pt. Ii (Hannover, 1969), Text D, XLVIII, §§1-14, pp. 84-88; Text S, XV, §§1-11 and XVI, §§1-19, pp. 205-06.

wounds mentioned in particular, why the specificity of description in some cases, and what did they mean to the Anglo-Saxons?

Using Æthelberht's tariff as our entrée, let's begin by imagining a wounded person in seventh-century England seeking retribution. How was he/she wounded? Æthelberht's laws indicate fighting, house-breaking, and robbery as three criminal contexts in which injuries might happen, not to mention more general malicious behavior. What types of weapons were used? The kinds of injuries described indicate weapons that could pierce or slash, blunt objects such as clubs, and bare hands as the agents. These inflict bone damage, skull breaking, piercing of various organs, severing of organs and limbs, and loss of teeth. The actual agent of injury is mentioned, however, in only two statements on the list:

> 57. Gif man oþerne mid fyste in naso slæhð, III scill'.
> 58.1. Gif he heahre handa dyntes onfehð, scill' forgelde.
>
> (57. If one person strikes another with a fist in the nose, three shillings [in compensation]. 58.1. If he receives a blow from a raised hand, let a shilling be paid.)

Oliver has speculated that some of the injuries may result from private torture, especially where the thumbnail is struck off.[12]

Next in our imagined scenario, the injured person and/or friends brings the charge against the attacker for arbitration and, it is hoped, recompense. A three-step process, similar to what may have been followed in Æthelberht's time, is described in the Kentish laws of Hlothhere and Eadric (statements 8-10) dating from the late seventh century. First, in response to a charge, the accused must give surety, a pledge to abide by the law, and be prepared to submit to the judgment of the tribunal (*Cantwara deman*). If the accused refuses to give surety, he must pay twelve shillings to the king and still face arbitration. Secondly, an arbitrator must be agreed upon within three days

[12] Lisi Oliver, *The Beginnings of English Law* (Toronto, 2002), p. 101. My thanks to Professor Oliver for use of this material before publication and for helpful comments on the present essay.

unless the accuser prefers a delay. Finally, within seven days after arbitration, the accused must either pay the accuser the amount assessed or swear an oath of innocence. If the accused will do neither, he/she must pay 100 shillings the day following the arbitration. This process must have been available to any freeman, since social status does not enter into the description.

Æthelberht's injury tariff implies that the complainant must bring the charge promptly in order to display the evidence to the arbitrator. Statements 59 and 60, for instance, refer to the placement of bruises, which likely are the first of the injuries mentioned to disappear.

> 59. Gif dynt sweart sie buton wædum, XXX scætta gebete.
> 60. Gif hit sie binnan wædum, gehwylc XX scætta gebete.
>
> (59. If the bruise be dark outside the clothes, let 30 sceattas be paid.
> 60. If it be inside the clothes, let 20 sceattas be paid for each.)

Judging from these statements, unclothing and public examination would seem to have been the preliminary steps in the process of accusation. Just who would have been called upon to view the wounds and determine their extent is uncertain, but presumably there would have been at least one person on hand with experience and/or medical knowledge sufficient to render a description. A doctor is mentioned explicitly in certain Germanic codes and may be implied in Æthelberht's tariff.[13]

> 62. Gif man gegemed weorðeþ, XXX scill' gebete.
>
> (62. If the person becomes cured, let him be paid 30 shillings.)

The need for such a role and examination is obvious from the injury list. Statements 34 and 35 determine the amount of compensation based upon whether the bone is merely exposed or actually damaged in a wound.

> 34. Gif banes blice weorðeþ, III scillingum gebete.

[13] See Katherine Fischer Drew's translation of the *Edictum Rothari* in *The Lombard Laws* (Philadelphia, 1973), pp. 66-67, where statements 82, 83, 84, 87, and 89 stipulate that additional compensation is to be paid for the doctor's fee.

35. Gif banes bite weorð, IIII scillingum gebete.

(34. If a bone is laid bare, let three shillings be paid.
35. If a bone is damaged, let four shillings be paid.)

There is a similar, but obscure, distinction made in types of skull wounds (#36 and 37). Assessing the extent of these types of injuries, where extensive bleeding would be a factor, is not a task for the inexperienced observer. And, in fact, many of the assessments require the ability to make precise descriptions. A cut or gashed ear is compensated at twice the rate for a pierced ear (#40 and 41). A wound in the abdomen is compensated less than a piercing (#61). And stab wounds in the thigh are compensated based upon their depth (#67).

67. Gif man þeoh ðurhstingþ, stice gehwilce VI scillingas.
67.1. Gyfe ofer ynce scilling, æt twam yncum twegen, ofer þry III scll'.

(67. If a someone pierces a thigh right through, let him pay six shillings for each stab.
67.1. For a stab over an inch deep, one shilling; for two inches, two shillings, over three inches, three shillings.)

There would be an immediate need, then, for an experienced examiner to unclothe the body and become its interpreter.

At this point we are envisaging at least four people at the scene of the unclothing: the wounded person, the accused, an arbitrator, and a medical examiner, but friends and kinsmen of the victim could also be involved. Statement 65.1 indicates as much:

65.1 Gif he healt weorð, þær motan freond seman.

(65.1 If he becomes lame [from a broken thigh], friends/kinsmen may settle the matter.)

Although such a viewing might be uncomfortable for many reasons, the arbitration process, not to mention the health of the victim, would seem to require it. In fact, many of the wounds mentioned in the tariff seem to be there precisely because they imply medical judgment to determine their severity and, hence, the appropriate compensation.

Whereas the extent of some wounds could be ascertained by visual examination, in other cases additional measures and even the passage of time might be required to learn the full damage. An injured shoulder or leg could be permanently lamed (#38, 65). A person could be rendered deaf in one or both ears (#39), or lose the power of speech (#52). Although the body would still carry information about its condition, the full story might wait to be revealed. This could certainly be true of wounds to the male genitalia. A partially or completely pierced scrotum could be observed, but determining whether it (or its powers) had been destroyed might take longer (#64). The size of the penalty for destruction, three times the *wergild*, is a sign of the significance attached to this type of injury.

> 64. Gif man gekyndelice lim awyrdeþ, þrym leudgeldum hine man forgelde.
>
> (64. If anyone destroys the generative organ, let him pay three wergilds for it.)

Oliver suggests that the compensation reflects the worth of the future offspring the man would not be able to generate.[14] We should not overlook, however, the factors of shame and embarrassment such a wound might involve and the possibility, therefore, of compensatory damages beyond those for other catastrophic injuries.

It is one thing for a person with medical knowledge to evaluate a wound to determine the appropriate compensation, and others with direct involvement in the case to be on hand for the examination. But moving from the material to the metaphoric body, what of the stigma conveyed by the maiming in a society where mutilation may have punished crimes such as thievery, especially when the perpetrator was unable to pay restitution?[15] Perhaps as an answer to this problem, wounds

[14] Oliver, *Beginnings of English Law*, p. 99. Rubin, "The *Bot*," p. 151, draws a connection between this unusual dependence of compensation upon social status and the risk of severing family lineage.

[15] A relevant discussion of the stigmatized body focusing on the location of hospitals in the Middle Ages appears in Roberta Gilchrist, "Medieval Bodies in the Material World: Gender, Stigma and the Body," in *Framing Medieval*

that mar a person's appearance tend to receive high compensation, and loss of a limb is in a class by itself. An eye taken out is worth twice the loss of hearing in one ear (#39, 43). A broken jawbone likewise is highly compensated (#50). The front teeth have the highest value (#51) among dental losses, and damage to the mouth, eye, or nose rates more than an injured (but not dismembered) ear (#40-42, 44, 45, 48). In fact, a separate statement addresses the matter of disfigurement:

> 56. Æt þam lærestan wlitewamme III scillingas ond æt þam maran VI scill'.
>
> (56. For the least disfigurement in appearance, three shillings, and for the greater, six shillings.)

As mentioned earlier, a dark bruise showing outside the clothes is compensated fifty per cent higher than one inside the clothes (#59 and 60). It mattered, then, whether a person had to bear the text of the encounter for all to see and interpret. This could be especially problematic for those who suffered the striking off of a limb, since such a loss could be read as punishment for a crime rather than the result of victimization. As may be the case with the large compensatory amounts for grievous harm to the genitalia, damage to one's appearance seems to carry a premium that acknowledges and compensates the public embarrassment beyond the physical trauma.

Apart from their potential metaphoric signification, however, physical wounds also have utilitarian value. Just as the injury list is arranged roughly from head to toe, statements concerning lost or disfigured limbs are separated into those involving the hand (#54-55) and those for the foot (#69-72). Again, the detail devoted to specifying possible wounds and determining relative compensation would imply the need for such guidelines. The hand itself is not addressed, but the fingers seem to be priced according to utility, with the thumb valued the highest and the middle finger the least. Why the loss of the little finger receives the second highest compensation is

*Bodies*, ed. Sarah Kay and Miri Rubin (Manchester, 1994), pp. 42-61, at 46-49 and 58-59.

not immediately clear. The explanation could be, as Oliver suggests, that after the thumb, it would be the most noticeable loss in a society which measures in handspans.[16] Turning to the foot, if struck off it has the same high value as an eye, but the toes are valued at half the compensation of the corresponding fingers. Oliver remarks that a foot without one or more toes is more usable than a hand without the corresponding number of fingers.[17] Toenails can be worth more than fingernails, further suggesting that utility as well as appearance is a guiding factor in determining compensation. The loss of a toenail might impair one's ability to wear shoes, or it might be considered more painful than the loss of a fingernail, but it is not likely to be more visible than a missing fingernail.

To return to the procedure implied by Æthelberht's injury tariff, after examination and description the wound would provide the basis for an accusation that the defendant would have to answer. Each side might have witnesses and oath-takers to bring to the arbitration. So few records of lawsuits survive, and those that do tend to involve property, that it is hard to be more specific about the actual process, especially since the status of the persons involved undoubtedly would have played a role in it.[18] Powerful supporters could also be a factor. In the statement quoted above dealing with the matter of permanent lameness from a thigh wound, friends or kinsmen of the accuser are called upon to negotiate a settlement (#65.1). Having known the victim in a healthy state, and perhaps now obligated to maintain this person and his/her dependents, these supporters could play a crucial role in negotiating the appropriate recompense. Dozens of people, then, might examine the marked body in the course of the suit and draw

[16] Oliver, *Beginnings of English Law*, p. 101.

[17] Oliver, *Beginnings of English Law*, p. 99.

[18] See the descriptions of the lawsuits through 900 A.D. in Patrick Wormald, "A Handlist of Anglo-Saxon Lawsuits," *ASE* 17 (1988): 247-81; rpt. with additional notes in Wormald's *Legal Culture in the Early Medieval West: Law as Text, Image, and Experience* (London and Rio Grande, Ohio, 1999), pp. 253-87.

inferences from it before the victim had to deal with the longer-term damage to appearance, mobility, ability to work, and even reputation. Wounding thus could lead to a person's exposure on many levels, making the assignment of payment a fraught but vital process intended in part to avoid vendetta but also to demonstrate victimization. It is no wonder that the earliest written codes gave such attention to the tariffs.

The second and final injury tariff in Anglo-Saxon legislation occurs in the West-Saxon laws of King Alfred, composed c. 895. As he states in the preface, Alfred drew upon earlier legislation, including Æthelberht's laws, in producing his *domboc*, but he may also have been influenced directly by Frankish codes.[19] The result is a list (#44-77) of thirty-three statements covering many of the same injuries but updated in terms of compensation figures and expanded by some new items. Clearly the need for such a tariff continued at least through the ninth century. This one actually concludes the main body of Alfred's laws, thereby calling attention to its status as a separate element within the longer code and perhaps allowing the possibility of additions. As in Æthelberht's code, however, the list is not introduced, nor are the circumstances of the wounding or the social status of the victims described.

Other features remain constant, or are even strengthened, in the West Saxon list. The bulk of Alfred's tariff follows the head-to-toe order of its Kentish predecessor. Visible wounds continue to receive higher compensation than those hidden from sight, as indicated in this new statement:

[19] Wormald, *The Making of English Law*, pp. 280-85.

45. Gif in feaxe bið wund inces lang, geselle anne scill. to bote.
45.1 Gif beforan feaxe bið wund inces lang, twegen scill. to bote.

(45. If a wound an inch long be within the hair, let one shilling be paid as compensation.
45.1 If a wound an inch long be in front of the hair, two shillings as compensation.)

Moreover,

66.1 Æghwelcere wunde beforan feaxe ⁊ beforan sliefan ⁊ beneoðan cneowe sio bot bið twysceatte mare.

(66.1 For every wound in front of the hair and below the sleeve and beneath the knee, the compensation will be doubled.)

Despite this continuing concern with the long-lasting physical and emotional effects of a visible wound in terms of scars and possible damage to psyche and reputation, the valuation of teeth and appendages in Alfred's tariff has been revised to accord better with their utility. The front teeth continue to be worth more than the molars, but the incisors are given the highest value (#49). Among the fingers, the thumb of course continues to be most valuable, but now the little finger has fallen to last place (#56-60). No mention is made of toenails.

The role of medical treatment is made even more explicit than in the Kentish list:

69. Gif mon oðrum þa hond utan forslea, geselle him XX scill. to bote, gif hine mon gelacnian mæge.

(69. If someone damages another's hand outwardly, let 20 shillings be given as compensation, if he can be healed.)

75. Gif mon ða greatan sinwe forslea, gif hie mon gelacnian mæge, þæt hio hal sie, geselle XII scill. to bote.

75.1 Gif se mon healt sie for þære sinwe wunde, ⁊ hine mon gelacnian ne mæge, geselle XXX scille. to bote.

> (75. If the large sinew be damaged, and if it can be healed so that it be sound, let 12 shillings be paid as compensation.
> 75.1 If the person be lamed from a wound of the sinew, and it cannot be healed, let 30 shillings be paid as compensation.)

These items remind us that after attempts at healing had taken place, an assessment of the residual damage, and therefore another unclothing, remained to be done.

Furthermore, the final statement in Alfred's list provides an additional hint about the workings of the arbitration process:

> 77. Gif mon oðrum ða geweald forslea uppe on þam sweoran ⁊ forwundie to þam swiðe, þæt he nage þære geweald, ⁊ hwæðre lifie swa gescended, geselle him mon C scill. to bote, buton him witan ryhtre ⁊ mare gereccan.
>
> (77. If someone damages the strength of another's neck and wounds him so severely that he no longer has control of it, and nevertheless he continues to live thus damaged, let him be given 100 shillings as compensation, unless the councillors award him a more just and larger amount.)[20]

Despite the straightforward nature of the tariff lists, apparently there could be some wiggle room in the assigned compensation if the tribunal saw fit. Alfred, as we know, was concerned about the issue of just judges, and this statement reflects that position.

Reading the injury tariff as the culmination of Alfred's code highlights the potential influence of embarrassment and shame upon compensatory payments. Elsewhere in his laws we find references to condign punishment and the exchange of money for a limb. For instance, a thief who is to lose a hand for the crime may redeem it, with permission, by paying a fine commensurate with his *wergild* (#6.1). Likewise, a convicted perjurer may ransom his tongue with a similarly-determined payment (#32). Injuries that coincide with such penalties carry a very high price. Two new head injuries illustrate this point:

[20] The high compensation for this condition underlines the embarrassment caused to the victim who cannot control his neck or, by implication, his head.

> 51. Gif monnes ðrotbolla bið þyrel, gebete mid XII scill.
> 52. Gif monnes tunge biþ of heafde oþres monnes dædum dón, þæt bið gelic ⁊ eagan bot.
>
> (51. If someone's throat be pierced, let him be paid 12 shillings.
> 52. If someone's tongue be removed from his head because of another's doing, compensation will be equal to that for an eye.)

The latter is the only instance in either tariff where an equivalency (66 shillings, 6 pence, and 1/3 of a penny) is stated in terms of body parts, and it is a high price indeed. In this example, the criteria implied for such compensation would seem to be loss of an essential function (sight or speech) and discernible damage to an organ. But given that the tongue, and possibly one or both eyes, could be removed as punishment for a crime, the embarrassment factor must figure as well into the fine. By contrast, the pierced throat in statement 51 receives the same, considerably lesser, price as a broken chin bone. Statement 71 reinforces the implication that maiming of certain types, namely those associated with physical penalties, receives special compensation:

> 71. Gif monnes eage him mon ófaslea oððe his hand oððe his fot, ðær gæð gelic bot to eallum: VI pæningas ⁊ VI scill. ⁊ LX scill. ⁊ ðriddan dæl pæninges.
>
> (71. If a person's eye be struck out or his hand or his foot struck off, the same compensation applies to all: 6 pennies, 66 shillings, and the third part of a penny.)

It seems clear that part of a victim's restitution could be intended to address any potential confusion with criminal punishment.

The last portion of Alfred's tariff, statements 65-77, forms a miscellaneous addendum to the head-to-toe listing. This supplement deals primarily with injuries to the genitalia displaced from the first group along with additional types of limb loss and other injuries caused by strong force. In general, the statements convey the need for greater definition among injuries and increased attention to the condition of the wounded person. There are two statements concerning genitalia here, allowing for more specificity regarding the location and severity of the injury:

> 65. Gif mon sie on þa herðan to ðam swiþe wund, þæt he ne mæge bearn [gestrienan], gebete him ðæt mid LXXX scill.
> 67. Gif sio lendenbræde bið forslegen, þær sceal LX scill. to bote.
> 67.1 Gif hio bið onbestungen, geselle XV scill. to bote.
> 67.2 Gif hio bið ðurhðyrel, þonne sceal ðær XXX scill. to bote.
>
> (65. If a man be so badly wounded in the testicles that he cannot beget children, let him be compensated 80 shillings for that.
>
> 67. If the scrotum be damaged, 60 shillings shall be paid as compensation.
>
> 67.1 If it be pierced, 15 shillings be given as compensation.
>
> 67.2 If it be pierced through, then 30 shillings shall be paid as compensation.)

Not only are the payments considerably higher than those specified in Æthelberht's legislation, but a new category, that of being unable to conceive children, has been added explicitly. Beyond the embarrassment associated with unclothing, the humiliation of infertility and the economic and social disadvantages of having no children figure into the compensation for wounded testicles.

These statements concerning wounds to the genitalia appear among others addressing catastrophic wounds: loss of the forearm (#66), loss of the leg at the knee (#72), smashing or hacking of the shoulder (#68, 73, 74). Somewhat less severe are broken ribs (#70), maimed hands (#69), and damaged sinews, presumably of the leg (#75-76). Here, as mentioned previously, we are given additional insight into the process of healing and judgment. Phrases such as "gif hine mon gelacnian mæge" ("if he can be healed") and "gif se mon cwic sie" ("if the person be alive") indicate that medical care in addition to examination is part of the process involved in seeking compensation for a wound during Alfred's time. So the initial inspection of the material body is not its only appearance as metaphoric text. Survival after the wounding and determination of the cause of death are also factors to be observed. After attempts at healing occur, the extent to which they are successful must be assessed. It's one thing to see if a person has lost half the hand, but quite another to decide whether a game leg or a wobbly neck deserves extra compensation. These types of outcomes could be faked, of course, but in reality they occur with varying degrees of severity. Someone must render an opinion based upon examination of the victim and then, with an understanding of what long-term effects such an injury carries in their society, the arbitrator hearing the case can award the damages. Alfred's code makes clear that there is some latitude in determining fair compensation based upon the "text" of the case presented.

To sum up, with the injury tariffs in the laws of Æthelberht and Alfred, we are obviously dealing with the remnants of oral tradition. The statements are set out in the formulaic phraseology we associate with mnemonic aids. Because they originated in attempts to ward off feuds and vendettas, injury lists express the primitive eye-for-an-eye concept that fades away with time and centuries of Christianization. Alfred is the last king who would need to itemize compensation for injuries, though the references in later royal codes to *seo domboc* make us suspect that his list, or one very much like it, continued as a reference point until the Conquest. As we have seen, the focus in these early laws is very much on the victim. However, by Alfred's time we can begin to detect the influence of condign punishment, in reference to the penalties for thievery and slander, on the compensatory amounts for wounds of similar nature. More detailed than Æthelberht's, Alfred's list emphasizes the factors of embarrassment and shame in determining compensation. Given the types of potential injuries covered by the tariff, the possibility of misreading the material body was ever-present.

This analysis is, by the nature of its sources, far less subtle than that offered by O'Keeffe for the late tenth/early eleventh centuries. The meaning of punishment written on the body no doubt was understood in the earlier periods, but the larger concern seems to have been with the body as evidence of a crime. We can see this perspective operating in *Beowulf*, for example, where Grendel's arm, hand, and nails become evidence of a feud to be avenged by his mother — a life for a life.[21] Æschere's head, found at the mere, is avenged by the retrieval of Grendel's head. The poet comments, perhaps ironically, that Grendel (and presumably his family) has no idea about paying restitution for crimes against Hrothgar's men the way that civilized people would do.[22]

Indeed, another way to view the process of unclothing and inspection implied by the injury tariffs would be as a means of protection for victims. The presence of witnesses, along with the procedure itself, insures that the nature of the wounding or maiming is known publicly and is understood not to result from officially-sanctioned punishment. And, finally, the public assignment of compensation provides yet another guide to the proper interpretation of the body as the text of victimization. There seems to be no spiritual dimension to the process other than instances involving the ordeal for the accused.

But a change in emphasis is underway. Royal legislation after Alfred's time begins to make more direct responses to social and religious concerns and to convey royal initiatives.[23] Compensation for injury certainly does not disappear, but it is no longer expressed in tariffs attached to legal codes, if the

[21] As Clare A. Lees observes, "these instances suggest first that the language of the body is simultaneously material and metaphoric, and second that the body part can be used to symbolize violence and death," "Engendering Religious Desire: Sex, Knowledge, and Christian Identity in Anglo-Saxon England," *Journal of Medieval and Early Modern Studies* 27 (1997): 17-45, at 24.

[22] *Beowulf and the Fight at Finnsburh*, ed. Friedrich Klaeber , 3rd ed. (Boston, 1950), lines 156-58. See A. R. Bridbury, "Seventh-Century England in Bede and the Early Laws," in *The English Economy from Bede to the Reformation* (Woodbridge, 1992), pp. 56-85, at 66-67.

[23] See Wormald, *The Making of English Law*, esp. pp. 133-34, and the discussion of Æthelstan's legislation, pp. 305-8. See also Simon Keynes, "Crime and Punishment in the Reign of King Æthelred the Unready," in *People and Places in Northern Europe, 500-1600: Essays in Honour of Peter Hayes Sawyer*, ed. Ian Wood and Niels Lund (Woodbridge, 1991), pp. 67-81.

surviving materials can be trusted. As O'Keeffe demonstrates, punishment assumes prominence in the later codes owing to its spiritual implications of restitution before death. Restitution can be read on the punished body as cannot be done on a victim. The lesson, therefore, becomes the focus of physical examination, both for the criminal and the observers. This evolution in viewing the body from the perspective of the law reflects changes in the nature of the codes themselves, culminating in the hortatory materials drafted by Archbishop Wulfstan for Æthelred and Cnut. As the church moves from a peripheral influence to a major force in the governance and national identity of England, so the barbaric elements of the earlier phase become subsumed within a new Christian, activist vision of the law. The punished body then takes on a major role in the plan for the salvation of the English people.

# The Sacrificial Synecdoche of Hands, Heads, and Arms in Anglo-Saxon Heroic Story

JOHN M. HILL

BECAUSE I DO NOT analyze an Anglo-Saxon approach to the naked body, my essay differs somewhat from the rest of this collection. Indeed, "nacod" does not occur often in heroic story, not at all in *The Battle of Maldon* and only three times in *Beowulf* (twice describing unsheathed swords, once the dragon, ll. 539, 2273, 2585). Still, my concern is with an Anglo-Saxon focus on heroic limbs and their functions, centrally with Anglo-Saxon depictions of bodily force and strength in combat. That combat is usually in defense of hearth and home, in the martial and always contestable establishing of physical as well as ethical boundaries, and in the ending, the unbinding, of reigns of terror.

Insofar as some sort of righteous thinking, of right personhood is involved in a martial act, an embodied self, that is, a psychology of values and asserted identity is involved. For a character such as Wiglaf in *Beowulf*, that psychology and the transactional development of self is complex — something I analyze at length elsewhere.[1] Space does not permit an account of that psychology here, except to say that part of Wiglaf's identity is borrowed from his lord, Beowulf. That is, part of Wiglaf is an internalization of Beowulf's possible needs as sealed by the exchange of vows and gifts in the hall — an internalization willingly actualized in a moment of magnanimous assistance (Beowulf having dismissed his retainers from any bound obligation to fight the dragon). Such an inner identity, when successfully formed (as measured by action),

[1] John M. Hill, *The Anglo-Saxon Warrior Ethic: Reconstructing Lordship in Early English Literature* (Gainesville, 2000), chap. 1.

strengthens a value-laden conscience, a righteousness, that definitively distinguishes man from beast, hero from coward, and dear kin from the banished, former members, in Wiglaf's case, of his Geat cohort. To borrow some of Suzanne Lewis's phrasings from her introduction to this volume, the heroic warrior body, especially in its hands, arms, and head, is a "site of resistance." But instead of becoming a site that either transcends or complicates "seemingly fixed dichotomies, such as male/female, human/beast, body/soul," the heroic warrior body, in its actions as dramatized in Anglo-Saxon heroic story, asserts with righteous prejudice the "contours of ... culturally constructed oppositions." Those oppositions define social demands as shaped within embodied, psychological developments. Through action, the heroic warrior body asserts definitive differences between good man and beast, between hero and coward, between commitment and fear, renown and infamy, lawful warfare or what is right and terror. These dichotomies of course have a meeting ground — the tremendous, one might say monstrous, energy that both hero and baleful creature call up in their rage (hence the dual "aglæcean," l. 2592, used for Beowulf and the dragon)[2] — but crucially, that energy is drawn up, so to speak, for very different ends, dedicated in opposite ways (Beowulf is a principled people's guardian, the dragon an enraged treasure guardian).

Rather than further unfold these psychological aspects of heroic action, however, I will focus in this essay on what seems an unconscious topos for Anglo-Saxon heroic poets, a coherent set of concerns and signs, as centered in the potent parts of the warrior body — a body dedicated to righteous action. As such the discussion here anticipates a wider investigation of what we might call the mythical resonances of the heroic body — something that Celtic and Norse sources detail for us in ways the Anglo-Saxon do not. Consider only the bodily marks of a

[2] Quotations from *Beowulf* are to the magisterial edition of Friedrich Klaeber, *Beowulf and the Fight at Finnsburh,* 3rd ed. (Boston, 1950). Translations are my own.

Cuchulainn, for example, his juggling of eyeballs, that protrusion on his forehead; or else consider the ways in which Viking warriors projected threat through bizarre grimaces (as in the case of Egill facing King Æthelsteinn).[3] Perhaps in terms of entire body image, we would have to consider the shape-changing for which Odin is famous, whether berserkers went naked or not or just eschewed armor, and the bear shapes of heroes in folktale and saga (Bjarki in *Hrolfs saga kraka* comes to mind, as does an etymology for Beowulf as "bee-wolf" or bear). But the Anglo-Saxon stories do not go in this direction. Instead, they emphasize the hand, the arm, the head — the hand as having great potency, the head in both literal and figurative terms, both armed and not.

These emphases should not surprise us in accounts of battle, where hands indeed hold weapons and are vulnerable, along with helmeted heads, to counter blows. But more is at work here, I will argue. The warrior hand is a super-potent image having its clearest, northern avatar in the myth of Tyr's hand-pledge and the eventual loss or sacrifice of that hand in the cosmic wolf's (Fenrir's) mouth. As Snorri Sturluson tells it in *Gylfaginning,* that pledge involves the gods in tying up the quickly growing wolf with a third set of restraints (Fenrir having easily broken two other, incredibly massive sets). Tyr, the sky god of war and law, is the only god brave enough to place his hand in the wolf's mouth as a pledge that the bonds are not magical. He and the other gods promise that the new fetters will break. Of course, because of their magical ingredients, they do bind the wolf who, in his rage, devours Tyr's hand.[4] The

[3] A fascinating gathering of these and other attributes of the warrior can be found in Georges Dumézil, *The Destiny of the Warrior,* trans. Alf Hiltebeitel (Chicago, 1970), pp. 161-64.

[4] The main accounts of Tyr and Fenris Wolf are in Snorri Sturluson's *Edda,* in two places in the opening section, "Gylfaginning." A convenient translation is Jean I. Young, *Snorri Sturluson, The Prose Edda* (Berkeley, 1966), pp. 52 and 57-58. My interpretative commitment concerning Tyr or Tiu follows the line of commentary set forth by Georges Dumézil, *Gods of the Ancient Northmen,* trans. Einar Haugen (Berkeley, 1973) and *Mitra-Varuna: An Essay on Two Indo-European Representatives of Sovereignty,* trans. Derek Coltman (New York, 1988). Dumézil's *Mythes et dieux des Germains* came out in 1939.

resonance both of Tyr's sacrifice and of his nature and status is reflected, I will argue, in Old English. This is especially the case in the use of such words in heroic story as *tir* ("glory, fame, light"), in victory scene invocations of god's candle and of morning light, in such formulas for battle as "hand-play," and in the diction of various heroic encounters where terror is bound and reigns of terror unbound.[5]

Elsewhere in Anglo-Saxon culture body parts matter greatly. Codified law in the various kingdoms reflects three kinds of reciprocities: that of the blood feud, of wergeld payment (and compensation for theft), and of mutilation or else execution. From *Beowulf* to *The Battle of Maldon*, heroic injunctions urge strength of body and weaponry, courage and heart against the enemy and when in dire straits. How do these two domains — law and heroic encounter — intersect each other? While warfare involves the killing of others, that killing is not the same as either judicial mutilation or execution. Still, the Anglo-Saxons did think of warfare as a kind of law — as did Germanic peoples generally. This would be the law of armed might, expressed by the conclave of warriors Tacitus notes in the *Germania* and applied prominently in the poetic record to acts that either establish or defend hall, treasure, folk and land

His comparative and structuralist approach, by which he analyzes Indo-European divinity in tripartite terms (the high god or principle of sovereignty, the god of war and law, the god of productivity or fertility) notably found an adherent in Jan de Vries of *Altgermanische Religionsgeschichte* (Berlin, 1935-1937) fame, who reassessed some of his earlier work when publishing *Keltische Religion*, Die Religionen der Menschheit 18 (Stuttgart, 1961). Dumézil's influence in this country appears notably in Gerald J. Larson, ed., *Myth in Indo-European Antiquity* (Berkeley, 1974).

5 Richard North, *Heathen Gods in Old English Literature* (Cambridge, 1997), summarizes the best evidence for Tiu's presence in Anglo-Saxon England. Tiu, who probably has some association with light, may have died out of Anglo-Saxon mind and observance in the seventh century. A rebirth of sorts may have been the god's fortune, however, when the Danes bring him to England in the ninth or tenth century (pp. 231-32).

and that fix boundaries by the sword.[6] The former appears early in *The Battle of Brunanburh* — "þæt hi æt campe oft / wiþ laþra gehwæne land ealgodon, / hord and hamas" ("that they at battle often against the hateful foe, each one, defended land, hoard and homes," lines 8b-10a) — and in *The Battle of Maldon*: Byrhtnoth tells the Viking messenger that his warriors are here to defend "eþel þysne, / Æþelredes eard, ealdres mines, / folc and foldan" ("this native country, Æthelred's region, my lord's people and land," lines 52b-54a).[7] To establish boundaries by the sword is praise-worthy in *Widsith,* in the passage on the Anglian Offa. With his sword, Offa "made known" ("gemærde") the frontier against the Myrgingas at Fifeldore ("Ane sweorde / merce gemærde wið Myrgingum / bi Fifeldore" ["with his single sword he made known the boundary against the Myrgingas at Fifeldor," lines 41b-43a]). Offa's act is figuratively a forming of boundaries against the monstrous ("fifel"), at terror's door. The place called Dore in West Saxon times is a significant area for just this kind of establishing also. Alfred's grandfather, Egbert, said to be the eighth Bretwalda, marched in 829 to Dore, where he received the submission of the Northumbrians. This significant role for Dore continues among the West Saxons well into the time of Athelstan and Edmund.[8]

Still, while martial acts can have juridical overtones, something even more interesting lurks in scenes of heroic combat — as well as in conceptions of legal mutilation: somehow the heroic feat itself is concentrated in the warrior appendage, much as the "professional" thief's or slanderer's crimes are written onto him, through acts of judicial taking. While early law codes emphasize bodily wounds and mutilations on behalf of the victim, emphasizing the *victim's* losses and a consequent

[6] *Germania,* trans. M. Hutton, revised E. H. Warmington (1914, repr. Cambridge, Mass., 1970), chapter 11, p. 149.

[7] These lines from *Brunanburh* and *Maldon* are quoted from Elliott Van Kirk Dobbie, ed., *The Anglo-Saxon Minor Poems,* ASPR 6 (New York, 1942). Except for *Beowulf,* all quotation of Old English poetry will be to the editions in this series. Translations are my own.

[8] See Hill, *Warrior Ethic,* p. 108.

scrutiny of the victim's body in relation to levels of compensation (see Mary Richard's elegant treatment of this in the current volume), no doubt corporal punishment, such as flogging and mutilation for crime is practiced. In later codes, culminating in Cnut's, mutilations can be multiple, involving losses of hand, foot, or eye, the splitting of a nose, the taking of a tongue, scalping, or worse (mutilations that in Wulfstan's time form what we can call a "soul-saving" strategy).[9]

The body as a site for punishment must be more than ancient; psychologically the fear of mutilation is early indeed, exploding in pre-Oedipal times for the child, at the level of early and harsh super-ego formation. At least this is what Melanie Klein posits in her accounts of body destruction anxieties both projected onto the mother and also internalized in payment for wishing harm to the denying mother.[10] In corporal punishment we accordingly always return again both to our earliest fears and erupting righteousness. It is this fiercely righteous body, that of the super-ego hero, that underlies both judicial dismemberment and heroic exertion. The latter, however, has a sense of momentary omnipotence to it — the feeling that not only can one not be castrated (beheaded, cut asunder, killed) but in fact one is invulnerable during the particular action in question.[11] Judicial takings would be mainly

[9] See Patrick Wormald, *The Making of English Law: King Alfred to the Twelfth Century, I, Legislation and its Limits* (Oxford, 1999), pp. 125, 545. Katherine O'Brien O'Keeffe has notably amplified the idea of a living mutilation that produces the criminal body as text: "Mutilation designed for the living body serves multiple purposes. Whatever its function as deterrence, juridical mutilation produces a body about which things may be known.... [C]onstruing juridical mutilation as a mercy, by making it a happy alternative to eternal death, makes the criminal a partner in his punishment.... [extending] the power of the law (previously satisfied by external compensation) inward into the criminal's soul," "Body and Law in Late Anglo-Saxon England," *ASE* 27 (1998): 209-232, at 230.

[10] Melanie Klein, *Love, Guilt, and Reparation and Other Works, 1921-1945* (New York, 1984), pp. 190-91.

[11] Sigmund Freud, *Collected Papers*, IV, trans. Joan Riviere (New York, 1959), "The Poet and Daydreaming," pp. 179-80.

righteous, an overlay floating uneasily upon the ghost of early body destruction anxieties. Heroic exertion seems to allay those ghosts by partially succumbing to fear and then turning that succumbing into the invulnerability of successful sacrifice: as though to say, "alright, I do lose something but I thereby gain much more."

In this way, then, we can think of the summoning of monstrous heroic strength and courage as a sacrifice of sorts — a huge expenditure that demands and receives honor-enhancing compensation (otherwise that exertion would be the expenditure of a slave). The legendary formation of this hero-demand in Germanic myth would be what Georges Dumézil has called the two mutilations involving Odin and Tyr — Odin's loss of an eye and Tyr's loss of a hand, with Tyr then becoming the sky-god of war as law. The two sacrifices establish Odin as the paralyzing visionary and Tyr as the chief of legal procedure.[12] In my terms, Tyr becomes the sky god of luminously settled boundaries, of the binding of terror and the unbinding of reigns of terror. Any Anglo-Saxon history of the literary topos springing from Tyr's sacrifice of his hand in Fenris Wolf's mouth is a subject too far-ranging for discussion here. The key point right now is that Tyr loses his *right hand* in the angry, cosmic wolf's mouth and so becomes known ever after as the one-handed god. To some degree, the Germanic hero is a physical and psychological son of Tyr — a status in some sense marked in his body, in his strength of hand and arm, much as the Tiu rune as victory rune might appear on weapons and urns (especially in fifth- and sixth-century Kent).[13] This status is one the *Beowulf* poet inherits with his material — material infused with older meanings and perhaps responded to subconsciously rather than being something the poet draws out through a kind of typological thinking (although to know one righteous Northern warrior is to know another, perhaps all others). Nowhere, of course, is the mark of Tiu, so to speak, more

[12] Dumézil, *Mitra-Varuna*, p. 142.

[13] North, *Heathen Gods*, p. 231.

powerfully embodied than in the life and deeds of the Geat champion we know as Beowulf, who first appears among the Danes as larger than any warrior the coast watch has seen.

The poet has already introduced him to us as Hygelac's thane, a good man among the Geats, who was among mankind the strongest in might in those days of this life, noble and huge (ll. 194-98). This heroic body is, then, vaguely outlined as simply massive, mighty and noble — embodying a strength (of hand, as we shall see) equal to that of an entire warband. This hand strength, while gripping a sword, is something both Beowulf and Breca — young, boisterous heroes — rely upon when undertaking their ocean swimming contest, according to Beowulf in his reply to a verbal challenge from Hunferth, Hrothgar's officer. Protected by his breast armor, Beowulf stabs an angry sea beast who has him firmly in its grasp. Then the rush of battle, through Beowulf's own hand, took the mighty sea beast (l. 558). Other beasts attacked but Beowulf dispensed with them. In the morning those beasts lay in death's sleep on the beach, never again to trouble the movements of sailors. Light came from the east, Beowulf says, God's bright beacon. The seas calmed down and Beowulf saw the shore. This combination of armed hand strength, killing thrusts, and God's light reflects the Tyr-founded topos of victory over terror indicated above. Contrary to the claim in Hunferth's eloquent challenge — that Beowulf lost his foolhardy match with Breca and so can expect much worse against Grendel — Beowulf asserts both victory and a more complicated ending to the Breca event. A storm ended the competition, Beowulf says, turning his part into a time of heroic exertion and victory — an event that involves the restraining of sea beasts, the clearing of sea lanes and the emergence of a powerful warrior-hero, an unfated warrior saved by events and his own courage. This story leads to a boast in Heorot against Grendel, who expects no defense from the Danes, Beowulf says. When Grendel comes, Beowulf continues, he will show him the courage and strength of Geats in battle. Those who care to may come in high spirits to the meadhall in the morning, once the sun shines from the south over the sons of men (ll. 603-06). This boast, in its prominent reference to sun, to light as a metonymy for victory, nicely vocalizes the victory-focused purport of the heroic boast, and so of Beowulf's personal showing of "strength and valor" ("eafoð ond ellen," l. 602a) on behalf of the Geats. Beowulf's is a true boast from the mouth and heart of the mightiest of heroes in those days of this life.

Interestingly, Grendel forces his way brutally into Heorot through the hall's "mouth." He tears his way into the hall, thinking happily only about feasting upon sleeping warriors. Perhaps Grendel is understood as somehow projecting a powerful somnolence upon the gathered warriors in the hall. Whatever might be the case in that realm, he clearly enters the hall as though it were a constructed, bound-together body he intends to rip asunder and devour from the inside out.[14] For his repeated violations of Hrothgar's legal *mund*, for his violations of the hall as bodily construction, therein breaking both figuratively and psychologically into Hrothgar himself, with Hrothgar later saying that Grendel is his invader ("ingenga min," l. 1776b), and for his criminal refusal to settle the feud, to pay compensation to the Danes — for all of this Grendel will be dismembered righteously and juridically in the course of twisting away from Beowulf's stunning hold. But that will not happen before Grendel gluttonously seizes a sleeping Geat, biting body and drinking blood, consuming the warrior feet and hands (l. 745). Emboldened, he then steps further into the hall and reaches for a resting warrior, who reaches back. Instantly the guardian of crimes (Grendel) knows that never before has he met in this middle earth, in any other man, a greater "mundgripe" (l. 753a, with "mund" perhaps indicating protection, rightful possession, even as Beowulf has been given a special guardianship of Heorot for the night). This extended action articulates in its plot nearly exactly the binding of Fenris

[14] See Raymond P. Tripp, Jr., "Language, Archaic Symbolism, and the Poetic Structure of *Beowulf*," *Hiroshima Studies in English Language and Literature* 19:1 (1972): 1-21, for a fascinating notion of the "knot body" in the diction and imagery of the poem — such as in language for the fastened hall, Beowulf's body as a bone house, and the breaking of joints and sinew.

Wolf, with the hapless warrior standing in as the hand pledge Fenrir takes and then devours when gripped tightly in magical bonds. Of course the moment plays out as nighttime combat. We have no good reason to think that Beowulf deliberately sacrifices his retainer — later named Hondscio ("hand-shoe" or glove, as though the unarmed Beowulf has offered his retainer or glove, perhaps a wager of sorts!). For Hondscio's loss Grendel becomes sorely constrained, then mutilated as he departs eventually, life-sick. In his retelling of this combat to Hygelac later in the poem, Beowulf names Hondscio and then says that Grendel, the mouth slayer, the bloody-toothed killer, thought to put Beowulf into a craftily made, dragon-skin pouch, a pouch bound around with cunning spells. The motif of magical bonds is here transferred from the sinews that bound Fenris Wolf to the sack Grendel brings and into which he means to stuff Geat warriors. Beowulf says that he foiled that move by standing upright in anger. Then, skipping over some details, he says he dealt that evil person a hand-requital ("hondlean," l. 2094b — the MS reading — although many editions emend the compound to "ondlean"). Beowulf's hand-requital parallels Tyr's hand-pledge, coming as it does in two phases. The monster is bound tightly; in its rage it takes the hand; but the bonds hold and the gods triumph, just as Beowulf does when, after the inadvertent pledge named Hondscio goes down, he blocks Grendel's emboldened advance and instead seizes the creature with definitive force. Of course Beowulf does not then become the one-handed god of martial jurisprudence — the topos hardly requires such figurative morphing. Beowulf does become the most renowned of young heroes, his might and courage gloriously confirmed. In this he is certainly a son of Tyr.

In token of victory, and as a juridical sign, Grendel's shoulder, arm, and claw-like hand are hung up in Heorot. This display is like the punishment meted out in late Anglo-Saxon times to thieves — in Cnut's time a false monier might have his hand cut off without redemption (II Cnut, 8.1, a punishment drawn from II Athelstan, 14.1, which Dorothy Whitelock renders in this way: "And if a moneyer is convicted, the hand with which he committed the crime is to be struck off, and put up on the mint").[15] In *Beowulf* Grendel's body part is a token of his punishing defeat and a public spectacle for all to gaze upon in the morning light. After that sight, the order is given to refurbish the hall, to repair the badly damaged, shining building (ll. 991-97). Grendel's member displayed on high allows the making whole of Heorot — that fastened body for the indwelling splendor of Danish social life and for Hrothgar's personal as well as dynastic glory. Stained by his crimes, the creature has fled; it then is feast time in Heorot — in the housing for the Danish body politic. He who came from afar has purged Heorot ("Hæfde þa gefælsod se þe ær feorran com," l. 825); Beowulf, strong in mind and spirit, has ended a reign of terror.

So what is there in a hero's hand? In the hand as appendage — nothing. The appendage by whatever name can be a monster's paw, a man's sword-wielding gripper, or else a hand grip so powerful that instantly the creature or man grasped knows his doom (Beowulf will later in the poem, with his battle-grip, crush Dæghrefn [ll. 2507-08a] and otherwise destroy the Hugan champion's entire warband — single-handed, so to speak). Indeed, Edward B. Irving, Jr., has noticed that Beowulf's handgrip is "the mammoth central fact" in the narrative of Grendel's attack. The narrative keeps coming back to it and then moving on "to explore varied reactions that surround it," central among them being Grendel's stunned, unprecedented, finally life-sick surprise.[16] The Geats are surprised also, as are overhearing Danes. Only Beowulf is not surprised: for Irving, Beowulf "thinks with his hand, *in* his hand. It is the hot and centered focus of terrific intent."[17] Mentally, somatically, and as focused on Beowulf's sheer energy, that observation is quite right. The hero's hand, then, cannot be described. To attempt to do so would be to describe merely flesh or else a token, a

[15] Dorothy Whitelock, ed., *English Historical Documents, c. 500-1042* (London, 1955), pp. 384, 420.

[16] Edward B. Irving, Jr., *Rereading* Beowulf (Philadelphia, 1989), pp. 92-95.

[17] Irving, *Rereading*, p. 94.

sign only of the hero's might, of his crushing potency (or of his healing potency if a saint). As with the counselor's head and the lord's helmet, the hero's hand or handgrip is a synecdoche for his embodied strength, heart, and courage in this world, as well as being a guarantor of rightful governance. It is also a warrant for mythical sanction in the other world. The hero's hand or arm, when lopped off, as with his head perhaps, is sacral in some sense — much as is a saint's.

It is here in the sainted treatment of heroic body parts that the resonance of Tyr's sacrifice lives on most potently in Anglo-Saxon kingdoms, albeit transformed, taken up into the spirituality of popular cults. Relying on work by Peter Brown and others, Karen Jolly tells us that the "cult of saints, as established and fostered by church leaders, consciously or unconsciously" accommodated "the animistic beliefs of Germanic peoples . . . . The concept of saints' relics as a doorway between this world and the next developed in the late antique Roman-Christian synthesis but easily made itself at home in the world views of Germanic peoples in the early Middle Ages."[18]

Relics, sacred body parts, made their way into the surviving literature, especially in war-making contexts. Bede tells the story of King Oswald: Penda kills Oswald, then takes his head and hand and places them on stakes, where they stay until Oswiu comes a year later. Oswiu kills the pagan, Mercian king, Penda, beheading him — perhaps enacting what we might call the reciprocal "trophification" of royal remains.[19] Oswiu takes Oswald's head and has it buried at Lindisfarne. The severed right hand goes to Bamborough, the Bernician royal seat (for Bede's version, see *Ecclesiastical History*, III.12). In Ælfric's Life of St. Oswald we learn that the hand's flesh shows no sign of corruption; in both Bede and Ælfric we are told that the site of Oswald's death becomes a place of miracles. Oswald's bones

[18] Karen Louise Jolly, *Popular Religion in Late Saxon England: Elf Charms in Context* (Chapel Hill, 1996), p. 27.

[19] See John Edward Damon, "*Desecto Capite Perfido*: Bodily Fragmentation and Reciprocal Violence in Anglo-Saxon England," *Exemplaria* 13 (2001): 399-432.

and even splinters from the stake that impaled his severed hand become potent relics — Bede has a story from Willibrord about a plague-stricken, Irish scholar cured by drinking water in which Willibrord had placed a splinter from the stake (*EH*, III.13). Appropriately enough, given its potency like that of the True Cross, the splinter is called a "holy tree" ("halgan treowe") in Ælfric's Life.[20] The right hand is both royal power and a doorway to eternal life, to God's kingdom. Thus individual dedication to sacral sacrifice is what lives, immanently, in the warrior hand, in Beowulf's "mundgripe."

This sacral potential in the warrior body, resident in the hand in the synecdoche of handgrip and hand strength, appears in a scattered pattern across Anglo-Saxon heroic story. We see it first in *Beowulf* itself, as amplified above, and as repeated in the course of the dragon fight when Wiglaf's right hand receives severe burns ("ac sio hand gebarn / modiges mannes," ll. 2697b-98a). With a few stops elsewhere, we can then move to a certifiably late poem, to *The Battle of Maldon.* There a Viking cuts off Byrhtnoth's arm, inadvertently beginning what will become a tableau of dead warriors, as one dies on each side of Byrhtnoth — a grandly mute trinity for the edification of those English who gaze upon it. That trinity urges a formal recommitment for those who would remain loyal to Byrhtnoth. Then we can end with the post-Maldon, Byrhtnoth legend itself, with if not his sanctification at least with the replacement of his severed head — a ball of wax is fashioned in its place — and with his ascension indirectly to the status of a new Moses. In that image the fighting lord becomes the martial lawgiver who opposes terror (in the form of hostile raiders)!

The matter of the head is clearly important, given heroic language about the warrior leader and king as helm and protector of his people. Hrothgar's counselor and war companion is taken by Grendel's mother in her reprisal for Grendel's mortal wounding by Beowulf. She leaves Æschere's head by the

[20] Ælfric, "St. Oswald, King and Martyr," in *Lives of Three English Saints*, ed. G. I. Needham (London, 1966), p. 41, l. 216.

edge of the pool where she lives. Beowulf, after slaying her in their underwater fight, beheads the dead Grendel and brings his head back to Heorot — an exchange of heads that reasserts rightful rule through warrior reprisal.

In other stories, hands and arms figure prominently in both literal and metaphorical ways. In the *Waldere* fragments, a Beowulf-like attitude is struck and we have good reason to suppose that the (missing) ending of the poem included a scene in which Walter loses his right hand. That same hand has held a sword up as Walter speaks about god-given victory — before he and his opponents come to terms, establishing peace.[21] Along with a language of hand-play in *Brunanburh*, the English prevail sardonically at the expense of a combined Scottish and Viking army. The English successfully defend their land, hoard, and homes. Thus it is possible to see this affair of the heroic hand (or arm in Byrhtnoth's case in *The Battle of Maldon*) as a prelude to efforts at definitive settlement and victory, even accompanied by a language of heaven's light in *Brunanburh*. As such, the mythologically sanctioned resonance of heroic hand play has a remarkable life across the Anglo-Saxon centuries. In all cases the hero is god-blest, with the Christian God having replaced the original god of war as law, Tyr.[22] Should the hero die, as he does in the *Maldon* case and in Oswald's, a kind of sacrificial power arises.

The establishing of sacrificial power, however, does not occur whenever a hand or arm is mentioned in a martial context or as a martial gesture. A cluster of functioning ideas has to be present as aspects of a victory topos. As noted already, among

[21] Assuming, of course, that the *Waldere* fragments correspond to moments in the Latin legend of Walter of Aquitaine. See Karl Langesch, ed., *Waltharius: Ruodlieb Marchenepen*, 2[nd] ed. (Darmstadt, 1960), pp. 6-83, especially ll. 1401-34.

[22] This is true also in the Old English *Genesis*, l. 2057. In the immediate passage Abraham pursues the fleeing army, following lethally in its tracks. He is victorious because of god who gave Abraham glory of spears ("æsca tir") in the battle (l. 2108b). God's hands defend Abraham.

those ideas are words for light, glory, and victory, for binding and unbinding (binding terror, unbinding reigns of terror), for establishing boundaries, for defending hearth, home, and treasure (or some variation on that). Aspects of this cluster appear conspicuously in *Beowulf* whenever Beowulf seeks settlement (which distinguishes his violence from the seemingly random, free-floating strife others seek). A light appears and God decides the issue; or else this connection goes the other way around, when Beowulf strikes Grendel's mother with the gigantic sword (ll. 1565-72). The light is likened to a gleam as though from heaven, a gleam like God's candle. From the neck down, apparently, Beowulf's sword stroke slices through the mother's body, the blade going through her fated flesh. She is not dismembered in the way Grendel was, perhaps because she is not criminal. But no man aside from Beowulf with his tremendous strength and summoned savagery could have lifted that sword, borne it into battle. God has helped here, deciding for the right and called *rodera Rædend,* "Ruler of the skies." This ties what is right with heaven, with stupendous hand strength and with the light that follows a victorious stroke — surely the legacy of Tyr, originally the sky-god.

The theme of binding has already come up, concerning Grendel. In his account of the battle to Hrothgar, Beowulf almost apologizes when he says that he sought to hold Grendel in a hard clamp on the slaughter-bed, in twisted bonds. But Grendel escaped, leaving his hand and arm behind — an escape from which he will receive no solace, Beowulf quips mordantly. Pain now has Grendel in a terrible grip. Grendel is narrowly encompassed in baleful bonds (ll. 970-77) where, Beowulf adds, he will remain until the great Day when the bright, resplendent Measurer will judge him. When Beowulf finds Grendel lying dead in the mother's cave, he strikes the body again, this time to make sure perhaps and perhaps to recover the head in a corporal exchange for Æschere. Beowulf beheads the corpse and brings the head to the surface of the mere. So while Grendel's criminal hand and arm are a clear and repeatedly gazed upon, stunning sign of victory in Heorot, Grendel's head is surety that at least this creaturely source of terror has been definitively bound. The head, which is so large that four warriors stagger as they carry it, also is a kind of exchange, I would say, for Æschere, whose body the mother must have eaten, while leaving his head by the shore of the mere. In a psychological formula, by a kind of synecdoche, we might say that the right rule of the head is here symbolically asserted over a momentary, dark possession of the body (the mother's inchoate revenge need). After all, Æschere was Hrothgar's long-time counselor and shoulder-companion. Similarly it is Beowulf's strong grasp that is a kind of metonymy for his hand — for mainly words for hand in this section of the poem apply to Grendel. He does with his hands and claws what should not be done, including breaking open the mouth of the hall and downing a warrior hands and feet. Perhaps Hondscio's death is an unanticipated bond for Grendel that all is well — until he reaches for the next warrior, a wakeful Beowulf whose grip instantly causes Grendel to think of fleeing. But his hand is bound fast as Beowulf bursts the monster's fingers. For his crimes, Grendel's terrible hand, claws, and arm are rightly displayed, triumphantly — a grizzly token of terrible crime, something his mother reclaims when she flees from the hall with Æschere in her grasp.

We can do more with this kind of exchange material in *Beowulf*. Recall that Wiglaf has his right hand severely burned in the dragon's third attack on Beowulf. Yet Wiglaf manages a crucial blow, one that diminishes the dragon's fire and thus allows Beowulf to deliver the killing thrust. For his heroic actions in this episode, and implicitly as an exchange for his loss of a functioning hand, Wiglaf gains much — he becomes explicitly known as Beowulf's noble kinsman and beloved Wiglaf; moreover, he is now said to be battle-worthy, wise, and a leader of thanes. Beowulf gives him great war gear and urges that he use the dragon's hoard for the good of the people. In this Beowulf has nominated Wiglaf as his successor in every way (the passing on of war gear can even suggest a kind of adoption). I have discussed this episode extensively elsewhere[23] and

[23] Hill, *Warrior Ethic.*

so here will observe simply this: like Walter in the *Waltharius*, Wiglaf loses a hand but gains war goods, treasure, people to lead and, implicitly if he wants it, a kingdom. There is compensation, do with it what he will. (What he does is another story for another occasion.)

Outside of *Beowulf*, the two poems that in some way best reflect the topos outlined earlier — aside from the *Waldere* fragments — are *The Battle of Brunanburh* and *The Battle of Maldon*. In *Brunanburh* the chief reflection appears in images of light and the diction of battle. The theme of warfare as law is expressed in several phrases we might otherwise construe as bizarre description in one place or as a mere indication of time in another. Consider the lines describing the field of battle as resounding with men's blood: foes died cringing, Scots and Vikings fell fated; the field resounded ("dænnede") with the blood of men when in the morning tide the glorious star, God's bright candle, the eternal lord's, glided over the ground, until that noble creation sank to rest (*Brunanburh*, lines 10b-17a). As the poet develops his lines, he produces an image indicating the full noise and cry, the blood on the day of battle — and then that glorious star, God's bright Candle. The subsequent parsing of defeat for Norse and Scottish kings contains most strikingly the variable, probably Norse-inspired diction of battle as a meeting of spears, an assembly of men and an exchange of weapons played on the field of slaughter with Eadward's sons. That diction is less ironic than inherently legislative—being originally applied I would say to the armed conclaves of Tyr, god of war as law, but now understood as reflecting the rightful decisions of the Christian God, whose bright candle, the sun, oversees the day of English victory. This is the same God who, in *Beowulf*, ruled battle victory. Elsewhere in that poem the world's candle shines on the hero's triumphant return up the beach to Hygelac's hall (l. 1965b), much as earlier Beowulf said that God's bright beacon shone on his success in the Breca incident (l. 570a). Thus the legislative diction of battle as a meeting and exchange of weapons is congruent with the association of victory with heaven's candle, all presided over by the sky god who originally was Tyr in the Germanic pantheon. Finally, one should note that Athelstan and Eadmund are opposing a terrifying alliance in the clear, even "sacred" defense (as implicit in "ealgian," "to protect, defend" — cf. "ealh," "temple") of hearth, homes, and treasure.

That defense forms a useful link to *The Battle of Maldon*, where Byrhtnoth initially raises the customary grounds for fighting early in the poem. He speaks of a sacred duty when he says he would defend his folk, land, and home, the country of King Æthelred, his lord. This duty is especially acute given that the Vikings are characterized more as predatory, despicable creatures, as wolfish or even devilish, than as men. As "slaughter-wolves" they may even be linked to Matthew's tormentors, the famished, depraved characters in *Andreas* — cannibals all. But before the fighting begins, a Viking messenger offers peace by using the formalistic, legal terms "grið" and "frið," (ll. 35, 39). These terms require a pledge: the Vikings will leave all to Byrhtnoth's choice if he will accord self-judgment to the seamen; they will leave if given gold. Byrhtnoth wittily rejects that insulting offer, substituting spears for gold as what the Vikings can count on receiving. As the fighting develops, after Byrhtnoth allows the Vikings to cross over to where he has arranged his levy — a decision both the poet and many readers decry as foolish at best and damagingly foolhardy at worst — the time comes for Byrhtnoth to do his utmost and die. He thanks God for the opportunity to kill two Vikings before yet another Viking wounds him with a spear. A compatriot, Wulfmær the younger, pulls out the spear and kills Byrhtnoth's assailant. But then a fourth Viking advances and sorely checks Byrhtnoth's sword arm, crippling it. Although he has fought well and been avenged by a youthful retainer once, this moment marks the beginning of Byrhtnoth's death. He can no longer hold his yellow or golden-hilted sword, which drops to the earth. Whether he has overreached or not, in his dying moments he first exhorts his young retainers, urging them forward. After doing so he falls to the ground, looks to heaven and thanks God for the joys he has experienced.

This action unfolds in clear stages to show us what defense against armed, bodily terror affords and what it might cost — in this case and at this point the mortal wounding of a great, splendidly armed lord. Yet both that lord and, I believe, the poet would urge continuing engagement by that lord's hearth-retainers and assembled levy in the continuing need to fight for folk, home and land. At this point, however, while no longer able to resist terror with well-aimed spear or with his sword arm, Byrhtnoth's horizon of battle, of concern for terror, tilts upward. Instead of heathen slaughter-wolves, or Vikings, Byrhtnoth now seeks a defense for his soul against the bonds, narrow sufferings and torments imposed by hell-demons, which is how the work of hell-demons is understood in *Genesis* (ll. 694-97) and in *Christ I* (ll. 358-65). In those cases bad desire leads to bad bondage and torments only God can undo; in Byrhtnoth's case his desire is for a good, something for which he beseeches the Measurer, the lord of Angels. His prayer is essentially a petition for safe passage for his spirit or soul on its way to God's keeping; that his soul might pass in peace ("frið"), unharmed by hellish attackers — a prayer we assume God heard, the only Lord who can fashion a genuine and lasting peace. For his valiant defense — even if tactically impaired by battlefield decisions — Byrhtnoth, as noted above, loses sword arm and life. Yet he gains pious standing and fame as a good man who, in effect, put his arm in terror's way and lost it, yet whose soul can be safeguarded on its way to heaven by a God who can undo the bonds of terror. This is legislative compensation for loss against terror, albeit compensation in the spiritual realm — a compensation that has its martyrdom analogue in the Byrhtnoth stories composed at Ramsey and at Ely.

In an early-eleventh-century account of the Life of Saint Oswald, a section of which Calder and Allen render in their *Sources and Analogues of Old English Poetry*, Byrhtnoth stands tall, a type of new Moses sustained by the Lord's love rather than by the prophets Aaron and Hur — who in Exodus 17:12 hold up

Moses' hands as they grow heavy.[24] As long as Moses can hold his hands up, Joshua will prevail militarily over Amalek (presumably a marauder who attacks the wandering Israelites at a place called Rephidim). Amalek and his people may, then, be a type of marauding Dane for the Ely historian, who perhaps is following a line of allegorizing going back to a second-century Church Father, Justin the Martyr.[25] Along with the Amelikites, the Danes will eventually have all memory of them divinely blotted out. For this eleventh-century monastic historian that kind of fate for Byrhtnoth's attackers would be Byrhtnoth's best after-death revenge in this life. The ascension of his soul to heaven is his best revenge in the next.

With his right hand Byrhtnoth strikes repeatedly, heedless of his grey hair. We learn that with his left hand Byrhtnoth defends himself, strengthened by his alms and holy masses. Here the historian probably both praises Byrhtnoth's benefactions to the monastery at Ramsey as well as invokes an earlier Life (perhaps Ælfric's) of St. Oswald, whose prayers and good deeds supported him. Are the references to right hand and left merely fortuitous here and just an echo of Moses two hands? Perhaps. They may also partake of the cult of relics in that saintly bones were miraculously powerful and King Oswald, also of whom Byrhtnoth may be seen here as a type, was cut down by Penda — see Ælfric's Life of St. Oswald — who took Oswald's head and right hand. Something related in both cases to the force of Tyr might inhere in the original dismembering as well as in the subsequent retrieval of the body parts. A beheaded king is certainly dead, his displayed parts a warning to one's neighbors (and perhaps some sort of ritual sacrifice, Penda being pagan). But then too his head and hand can have both

[24] Daniel G. Calder and M. J. Allen, trans., *Sources and Analogues of Old English Poetry: The Major Latin Texts in Translation* (Totowa, New Jersey, 1976), pp. 188-89.

[25] R. P. C. Hanson, "Biblical Exegesis in the Early Church," in *The Cambridge History of The Bible*, vol. 1, ed. P. R. Ackroyd and C. F. Evans (Cambridge, 1970), pp. 412-53.

pagan and Christian power in them, the latter being indeed how Oswiu, Bede, and Ælfric think of Oswald's head.

In the late-twelfth-century *Ely Book*, Byrhtnoth's battle has grown to two engagements at Maldon, four years apart.[26] After the first and victorious fight, Byrhtnoth heroically fails in a second during the climax of which the large body of attacking Danes forms into a wedge and barely manages to cut off the fighting ealdorman's head — a head they flee with to their own land. The abbot of Ely hears about this outcome, recovers Byrhtnoth's beheaded body and replaces the head with a ball of wax. That arresting detail, the ball of wax, has few parallels elsewhere. In Old English prose, in an expansive personification allegory, the Pater Noster is said all alone to entwine and twist in its right hand all of creaturely creation into the likeness of a wax apple ("And se Pater Noster he mæg ana ealla gesceafta on his ðære swiðran hand on anes weaxæpples onlicnisse geðyn and gewringan"[27]). This is a small part of a long response to the question, what is the Pater Noster's beautiful heart like? The author of Byrhtnoth's wax head might well attribute some such literary or else allusive significance to the replacement ball, just as the originator of the prose passage on the Pater Noster seems to combine biblical, apocalyptic allegory, and Germanic material in his extended personification. Earlier in the passage, we learn that in the Pater Noster's right hand there is the likeness of a golden sword, a sword that gleams brighter than the heavens, its right edge being mild, the other angry and sharp. Then a few lines later that same right hand can bind all the creatures of the world into the likeness of a wax apple. Clearly enough this is a legislatively heterodox, cosmic hand. I think the Tyr topos lurks here and that the missing head has been replaced by a cosmic, figuratively manna-filled dummy. At any rate, the wax ball is how for years

[26] The relevant passage is presented in Calder and Allen, *Sources and Analogues*, pp. 190-92.

[27] J. M. Kemble, *The Poetry of the Codex Vercellensis*, with an English Translation (London, 1843), p. 150.

afterward people can recognize Byrhtnoth's honored body. In the Byrhtnoth legends, spiritual compensations play out the thread, I would argue, of Tyr's original loss in exchange for restraining the cosmic wolf until the day of doom, when both the heroes and gods will die. A head and arm here and there, a later ball of wax elsewhere — these are now the spiritualized signs of terror overcome and heaven's embrace received. They mark a definitive boundary to terror in this life and victory in the next — a marvelous translation of the Tyr legend into Christian hagiography.

So, while reflexes or resonances of the Tyr topos do not concern "nakedness" in the sense of an unclothed, exposed, and perhaps desiring and sinful body — as is the case elsewhere in this collection of essays — the deep force or spirit or emanating power of the body is present in both secular and hagiographic contexts where something like juridical or else sacral warfare exists. The construction of the Anglo-Saxon heroic body goes from fiercely dedicated hand to sacred relic, from the huge potency of awesome bodily strength and righteous dedication to the healing power of saintly hand, head, and blood.

# Nudity on the Margins: The Bayeux Tapestry and its Relationship to Marginal Architectural Sculpture

KAREN ROSE MATHEWS

IN THE ANCIENT world, representations of the nude body possessed overwhelmingly positive associations.[1] The display of the male nude form in ancient Greece conveyed notions of freedom and power, qualities that differentiated the Greeks from their political rivals.[2] In the transition from the ancient to the medieval world, the nude body continued to possess incredible power; indeed the meanings associated with nudity and the display of genitalia expanded to encompass a complex variety of ideas and emotions.[3]

1 Larissa Bonfante, "Nudity as Costume in Classical Art," *American Journal of Archaeology* 93 (1989): 543-70; Andrew Stewart, *Art, Desire, and the Body in Ancient Greece* (Cambridge, 1997), devotes an entire chapter, pp. 24-42, to a discussion to nakedness in ancient Greek society.

2 Bonfante, "Nudity as Costume," p. 557, notes how the civic nudity of the Greeks differentiated them from barbarians, that is, everyone who was not Greek. Christine Havelock, *The Aphrodite of Knidos and Her Successors: A Historical Review of the Female Nude in Greek Art* (Ann Arbor, 1995), pp. 30-35, discusses the power of nudity in Greek society.

3 There exists an enormous body of literature on the body and sexuality in the Middle Ages. The following references represent a selected list of works on this topic: Danielle Jacquart and Claude Thomasset, *Sexuality and Medicine in the Middle Ages*, trans. Matthew Adamson (Princeton, 1988); Thomas Laqueur, *Making Sex: Body and Gender from the Greeks to Freud* (Cambridge, Mass., 1990); Jean-Louis Flandrin, *Sex in the Western World: The Development of Attitudes and Behavior*, trans. Sue Collins (Chur, Switzerland, 1991); Sarah Kay and Miri Rubin, eds., *Framing Medieval Bodies* (Manchester, 1994); Jacqueline Murray and Konrad Eisenbichler, eds., *Desire and Discipline: Sex and Sexuality in the Premodern West* (Toronto, 1996); Merry Wiesner-Hanks, *Christianity and Sexuality in the Early Modern World: Regulating Desire, Reforming Practice* (London, 2000).

For the variety of attitudes towards representations of the nude body, see Margaret Miles, *Carnal Knowing: Female Nakedness and Religious Meaning in the Christian West* (Boston, 1989), p. 81; Michael Camille, *The Gothic Idol: Ideology and Image-making in Medieval Art* (Cambridge, 1989), pp. 92, 96; Karma Lochrie, Peggy McCracken, et al., eds., *Constructing Medieval Sexuality* (Minneapolis, 1997), pp. xiii-xiv. Caroline Walker Bynum, *Fragmentation*

Scholars have attributed a shift in attitude about the body to the patristic period of the early Church, when passages from the Bible pertaining to nudity were provided a particularly negative gloss.[4] In early medieval texts and images, there were forms of positive or innocent nudity. Children and souls ascending to heaven were often represented as nude, as were Adam and Eve in their prelapsarian state.[5] The practice of naked baptism in the early Church reiterated these positive associations of purity and innocence.[6] The newly baptized body was clean and pure, unmarked by sin.

In the Middle Ages, nudity presented negative associations, and it is in these types of representations that we most often see the display of female breasts and male and female genitalia.[7] These are sexualized bodies, defined by sin and excess. The postlapsarian Adam and Eve belong in this category, as do other representations of biblical figures. In an overwhelming majority of non-religious images, as well, when nudity appears, it is this negative, sexualized type. Often the representation of nudity in the Middle Ages was avoided altogether, as this type of image might encourage illicit behav-

*and Redemption: Essays on Gender and the Human Body in Medieval Religion* (New York, 1992), p. 182, has argued against the categorical equation of the female body with sexuality, claiming that "medieval images of the body have less to do with sexuality than with fertility and decay."

[4] See particularly Jacques LeGoff, *The Medieval Imagination*, trans. Arthur Goldhammer (Chicago, 1988), pp. 93-103. In *City of God*, Book 14, chap. 17, Augustine comments upon the Fall of Adam and Eve, in a passage that perhaps best characterizes this change in attitude; see Camille, *Gothic Idol*, pp. 87-88, for a discussion of Augustine's commentary. Miles, *Carnal Knowing*, pp. 89-99, addresses both the thought of Augustine and Ambrose on the sexuality of Adam and Eve after the Fall. The passages most often discussed in the patristic literature are Genesis 2:25, 3:7, 9:21-25; Leviticus 18.

[5] Miles, *Carnal Knowing*, p. xi; Camille, *Gothic Idol*, pp. 88, 98. Barbara Zeitler, "*Ostentatio genitalium*: Displays of Nudity in Byzantium," in *Desire and Denial in Byzantium*, ed. Liz James (Aldershot, 1999), pp. 185-201, esp. 196-97, discusses the nudity and genitalia of Adam and Eve in Byzantine art.

[6] Miles, *Carnal Knowing*, pp. 30-35.

[7] Camille, *Gothic Idol*, pp. 86-90.

ior.[8] When nude bodies were represented, their style and context made clear that they symbolized evil, and provided negative exempla concerning activities to be avoided.[9]

Though nudity might appear to indicate a lack, that is, a lack of clothing, culture, or morals, in medieval representations it might also serve as a costume in its own right, a canvas or blank page upon which various perceptions and significations can be inscribed.[10] In this essay, I will investigate the meanings and perceptions associated with a group of nude figures with prominent genitalia on the Bayeux Tapestry. Ignored by most scholars, censored by others, these images have been the object of intense non-seeing in modern research on the Bayeux Tapestry.[11] These figures are anomalous on the Tapestry, but

[8] Camille, *Gothic Idol*, pp. 96-97; Michael Camille, "Manuscript Illumination and the Art of Copulation," in *Constructing Medieval Sexuality*, ed. Lochrie and McCracken, pp. 58-91, especially 77-78.

[9] Michael Camille, *Image on the Edge: The Margins of Medieval Art* (Cambridge, Mass., 1992), pp. 73, 79-80.

[10] This idea of the body as garment, or blank page is expressed by various authors including Miles, *Carnal Knowing*, pp. 135, 169; Bynum, *Fragmentation and Redemption*, p. 202; E. Jane Burns, "Refashioning Courtly Love: Lancelot as Ladies' Man or Lady/Man," in *Constructing Medieval Sexuality*, ed. Lochrie and McCracken, pp. 111-34, especially 120, states that a noble woman's social status is defined by her skin, that is, the absence of a garment.

[11] The margins of the Bayeux Tapestry have begun to attract scholarly interest in the past two decades. The following list of references addresses the borders of the Tapestry in general; specific references to the figures analyzed in this study will be provided below. N. P. Brooks and H. E. Walker, "The Authority and Interpretation of the Bayeux Tapestry," *Proceedings of the Battle Conference on Anglo-Norman Studies* 1 (1978): 9; David Wilson, *The Bayeux Tapestry: The Complete Tapestry in Color* (New York, 1985), p. 209; David Bernstein, *The Mystery of the Bayeux Tapestry* (Chicago, 1986), pp. 82-88, 124-35; H.E.J. Cowdrey, "Towards an Interpretation of the Bayeux Tapestry," *Anglo-Norman Studies* 10 (1988): 49-65; J. Bard McNulty, *The Narrative Art of the Bayeux Tapestry Master* (New York, 1989), pp. 84-147; Wolfgang Grape, *The Bayeux Tapestry: Monument to a Norman Triumph* (Munich, 1994), pp. 41-44; Carola Hicks, "The Borders of the Bayeux Tapestry," in *England in the Eleventh Century: Proceedings of the 1990 Harlaxton Symposium*, ed. Carola Hicks, (Stamford, 1995), pp. 251-65; Daniel Terkla, "Cut on the Norman Bias: Fabulous Borders and Visual Glosses on the Bayeux Tapestry," *Word & Image* 11.3 (1995): 264-90; Richard Gameson, "The Origin, Art, and Message of the Bayeux Tapestry," in *The Study of the Bayeux*

comparisons with contemporary representations in other artistic media abound.

The Bayeux Tapestry is most often compared to manuscript illumination as scholars attempt to classify this unusual work.[12] In addition, scholarly research has come to emphasize the Englishness of the Bayeux Tapestry, as it is generally agreed that the Tapestry was made in England by English artists.[13] Though a score of representations in English manuscript illumination can be found where nude figures are depicted with exposed genitalia, these figures do not present compelling visual parallels to the Tapestry nudes. I will argue here that the nude border figures on the Tapestry bear a striking resemblance to marginal sculpture on the Continent.

Though the sculptural examples to be discussed date to a generation or so after the Tapestry, I believe that these two artistic media display affinities in iconography, placement, and reception. Both marginal sculpture and the nude figures on

*Tapestry*, ed. Richard Gameson (Woodbridge, 1997), pp. 159-60. See Madeline Caviness, "Obscenity and Alterity: Images that Shock and Offend Us/Them, Now/Then?" in *Obscenity: Social Control and Artistic Creation in the European Middle Ages*, ed. Jan M. Ziolkowski (Leiden, 1998), pp. 155-75, especially 168-71, for censored reproductions of the Bayeux Tapestry. Catherine Karkov, "Gendering the Battle: Male and Female in the Bayeux Tapestry," in *Harold II and the Bayeux Tapestry*, ed. Gale R. Owen Crocker and David Hill (Woodbridge, forthcoming), analyzes the gender relations in the main narrative zone and the margins. I thank Prof. Karkov for sending me a copy of this essay in advance of its publication.

12 Scholars have generally sought visual parallels to the Bayeux Tapestry in contemporary manuscript illumination. This approach has some validity given the general assumption that the Tapestry was produced in Canterbury, which was also a flourishing center for the decoration of manuscripts. For studies that illustrate iconographic similarities between the Bayeux Tapestry and contemporary manuscripts, see Wilson, *The Bayeux Tapestry*, pp. 208-12, who expresses some skepticism concerning the close relationship between manuscripts and the Tapestry; Bernstein, *The Mystery of the Bayeux Tapestry*, bases most of his arguments about iconography on comparative examples from manuscripts.

13 Bernstein, *The Mystery of the Bayeux Tapestry*, devotes two chapters to this issue. Chapter IV assesses the stylistic similarities between the Tapestry images and Anglo-Saxon manuscript illumination. Chapter V discusses the Englishness of the borders and figures that inhabit them. Grape, *The Bayeux Tapestry*, pp. 44-54, takes the opposing position and argues that the Tapestry was a Norman work created in Bayeux.

the borders of the Tapestry share analogous subject matter and highly emotional and dynamic styles of representation. In addition, the relationship established between main and marginal zones in architectural sculpture can provide innovative approaches to the interpretation of the border images on the Bayeux Tapestry. Scholars of the Tapestry have noted the internally coherent, historical, complex narrative of the main visual zone on the Tapestry, but have been confounded in their attempts to find meaning in the margins. Even attempts to study thematic groupings of border scenes, like the images from fables, have proven unsatisfactory, for some marginal images appear to comment upon the central narrative, but not all accommodate themselves to this totalizing reading.[14] Finally, audiences for the Bayeux Tapestry and marginal church sculpture would have been similar, as both were public monuments viewed by a variety of people over time in an open setting. The interpretation of the nude figures on the Tapestry in relation to these complex and multivalent architectural reliefs can broaden our understanding of the Bayeux Tapestry as an international, Romanesque monument, the product of the synthesis of French and English artistic cultures in post-conquest England.

Five groups of nude figures inhabit the borders of the Bayeux Tapestry. These images are exceptional in the confrontational nature of their nudity and the emphasis on male genitalia.[15] In the first border image, a nude man with an erect penis reaches out to a nude woman (figure 2).[16] His gesture of lewd invitation evokes one of resignation or fear by the woman.

[14] Terkla, "Cut on the Norman Bias," limits his study to the fable scenes in the borders, but does not successfully establish consistent relationships between this small group of images and the narrative they frame.

[15] There are other nude figures depicted on the Bayeux Tapestry, such as the warriors who are stripped of their armor in battle scenes, but these nude figures are not represented with genitalia. See Karkov, "Gendering the Battle?," for a discussion of the nude fallen warriors.

[16] Wilson, *The Bayeux Tapestry*, pp. 178-79; McNulty, *The Narrative Art*, p. 96; Camille, *Image on the Edge*, p. 126; Cowdrey, "Towards an Interpretation," 55; Suzanne Lewis, *The Rhetoric of Power in the Bayeux Tapestry* (Cambridge, 1999), p. 81.

Two more border scenes with nude figures follow in quick succession. A nude man bends over holding an axe and a board (figure 3).[17] As in the first image, this figure also has exaggerated genitalia, stitched in a different color to contrast with the rest of his body. A third figure, in the border below the famous Ælfgyva scene, exposes his genitals and points to the scene above (figure 4).[18] Near the end of the Tapestry the last two sets of images appear. A nude woman reaches out to a man in a gesture of welcome or farewell (figure 5).[19] The man, whose immense testicles protrude behind him, holds a bucket or lamp and an ax. Finally, a man sporting a dashing English mustache moves towards a woman with his right hand in a gesture of speech (figure 6). The woman, whose pubic hair and breasts are prominently delineated, appears to recoil from the man while countering with a speech gesture of her own.

These figures in the borders of the Tapestry are exceptional in their nudity and overt display of genitalia. No nude figures appear in the main narrative zone, and other nude figures in the borders are not represented with genitalia. A small number of visual parallels exist, however, in contemporary manuscript illumination. Figures with exposed genitalia are represented in both religious texts and secular works spanning the eighth to the twelfth centuries. Nude figures with exposed genitalia can be found in medical or pseudo-scientific texts, as they undergo medical procedures or represent medicinal (or magical) plants like the mandrake.[20] A set of images

[17] Wilson, *The Bayeux Tapestry*, p. 209, refers to this image as a genre scene of chopping wood; see also McNulty, *The Narrative Art*, pp. 55-57, 98.

[18] Gerald Bond, *The Loving Subject: Desire, Eloquence, and Power in Romanesque France* (Philadelphia, 1995), p. 27; Lewis, *The Rhetoric of Power*, p. 87.

[19] Wilson, *The Bayeux Tapestry*, pp. 188-89; McNulty, *The Narrative Art*, pp. 37-38, 76; Caviness, "Obscenity or Alterity," pp. 171-72.

[20] In a medical tract illustrated c. 1100, London, British Library MS Sloane 2839, fol. 1v., a nude male figure serves as a subject for the medical practice of cautery, or the application of red-hot irons to particular points on the body. This manuscript is discussed in C.M. Kauffmann, *Romanesque Manuscripts, 1066-1190*, A Survey of Manuscripts Illuminated in the British Isles, 3 (London, 1975), no. 12, pp. 58-59, illustrations 19-20.

illustrating the Marvels of the East, discussed elsewhere in this volume, depicts exotic peoples with exposed genitalia. [21] In biblical texts, we see nudity and genitalia in a limited variety of images: children, biblical figures like Noah, and demons and enemies of God.[22] The first category mentioned, that of nude children, is represented in one text, the *Stuttgart Psalter*, made in France c. 820-30. [23] The biblical figure of Noah is often depicted nude, and is shown with exposed genitalia in the manuscript Junius 11.[24] The largest category of figures displaying genitalia is that of demons and devils. Such demons can be

In the *Herbarium of Apuleius Barbarus*, Oxford, Bodleian Library MS Ashmole 1431, fol. 31, the mandrake plant is represented in human form. Kauffmann, *Romanesque Manuscripts*, no. 10, pp. 57-58, illustrations 22-25, discusses this manuscript and provides bibliographic references. A connection was made in medieval folklore between the shape of the mandrake's bifurcated root and the human form. For the powers and legends associated with the mandrake, see Robert Auty, et al., eds., *Lexikon des Mittelalters* (Munich, 1980) s.v. "Alraun(e)," by P. Dilg; Joseph R. Strayer, ed., *Dictionary of the Middle Ages* (New York, 1982-1989) s.v. "Herbals: Byzantine and Arabic," by John Scarborough, and "Herbals, Western European," by Linda Ehrsam Voigts, with bibliography.

[21] See Susan M. Kim's contribution to this volume, "The Donestre and the Person of Both Sexes," and Susan M. Kim, "Man-Eating Monsters and Ants as Big as Dogs," in *Animals and the Symbolic in Mediaeval Art and Literature*, ed. L.A.J.R. Houwen (Groningen, 1997), pp. 39-51. Kim's essay provides excellent bibliographic references for medieval representations of the monstrous races.

[22] Nikolaus Himmelmann, *Ideale Nacktheit* (Opladen, 1985), pp. 44-45, 123-25, provides a comprehensive list of Christian representations with naked figures.

[23] This manuscript is reproduced with commentary in Ernest De Wald, *The Stuttgart Psalter* (Princeton, 1930).

[24] A description of Oxford, Bodleian Library, MS Junius 11, with bibliography and commentary can be found in Thomas Ohlgren, ed., *Anglo-Saxon Textual Illustration* (Kalamazoo, Mich., 1992), pp. 10, 97, and Elzbieta Temple, *Anglo-Saxon Manuscripts 900-1066*, A Survey of Manuscripts Illuminated in the British Isles, 2 (London, 1976), no. 58, pp. 76-78. Catherine E. Karkov, pp. 191-92, discusses the Noah image in detail in her contribution to this volume. Himmelmann, *Ideale Nacktheit*, pp. 44, 124, notes other medieval monuments where this scene is depicted. Zeitler, "*Ostentatio genitalium,*" pp. 197-98, notes that Byzantine artists tended not to represent the transgressive display of Noah's genitalia to his children; they depict instead the reaction of his sons to Noah's behavior.

found in Psalter illustrations and other biblical texts. [25] The *Harley Psalter* was created in the early eleventh century with later additions, and possesses elaborate images of demons, devils, and fallen angels,[26] while an opening of Junius 11 depicts the Fall of the Rebel Angels.[27]

In two more miniatures we find nude figures that resemble those of the Bayeux Tapestry. The central decorative band separating the Canon Tables on folio 1 of the *Barberini Gospels* features a human figure placed within a background of twisting and biting animal forms (figure 1).[28] The male figure tugs at his beard with his left hand as his right hand reaches down to touch his genitals.[29] This figure forms an interesting parallel to

[25] In a particularly original image from the *Stuttgart Psalter*, the illustrator literally depicts the text of Psalm 78: "... and the Lord smote his enemies in the hinder parts, he put them in perpetual reproach" (... et percussit inimicos suos in posteriora, obprobrium sempiternum dedit illos ...). See Camille, *Image on the Edge*, pp. 106-07, for illustrations of this psalm in thirteenth-century manuscripts.

[26] William Noel's *The Harley Psalter* (Cambridge, 1995), is the most recent and authoritative monograph on this manuscript. Ohlgren, *Textual Illustration*, pp. 1-2, 19, also amply illustrates and comments upon the Harley Psalter, British Library MS Harley 603. See also Temple, *Anglo-Saxon Manuscripts*, no. 64, pp. 81-83 for commentary and bibliography on this manuscript. Noel, "The Utrecht Psalter in England: Continuity and Experiment," in *The Utrecht Psalter in Medieval Art: Picturing the Psalms of David*, ed. Koert van der Horst, et al. (Westrenen, 1996), pp. 125-26, argues that these figures are not angels, but more generic "instruments of God's wrath." Karkov discusses the demons in the Harley Psalter in her essay, and cites Louis Jordan, "Demonic Elements in Anglo-Saxon Iconography," in *Sources of Anglo-Saxon Culture*, ed. Paul Szarmach (Kalamazoo, Mich., 1986), pp. 283-317, for a catalogue of demonic images in Anglo-Saxon manuscripts.

[27] Ohlgren, *Textual Illustration*, pp. 90-91.

[28] Rome, Vatican, Biblioteca Apostolica, Barberini Lat. 570, fol. 1, published in J.J.G. Alexander, *Insular Manuscripts, 6th to the 9th Century*, A Survey of Manuscripts Illuminated in the British Isles, 1 (London, 1978), no. 36, pp. 61-62, illustrations 169-78. The Barberini figure is also mentioned by Catherine Karkov in her contribution to this volume.

[29] Anthony Weir and James Jerman, *Images of Lust: Sexual Carvings on Medieval Churches* (London, 1986), p. 75, discuss the figures from both the *Barberini Gospels* and the *Book of Kells*. They relate the *Barberini* image to images of men and women being punished for lust, where serpents bite at the breasts

one nude figure in the Bayeux Tapestry's margins, who also points to his genitals with one hand (figure 4).

A figure from the *Book of Kells* exists in isolation like the nude male in the *Barberini Gospels* (figure 7). On folio 200r, which lists the genealogy of Christ, a male figure sits at the end of the line that reads "qui fuit Naggae."[30] He is fully clothed and holding a shield and spear; below the shaft of his spear, however, we see his genitals exposed, outlined with red dots.[31] Iconographically, this figure resembles one of the Tapestry's nude males, who is represented in profile with an erect penis as he gestures to a reluctant female (figure 2).

This brief review of exposed genitalia in Anglo-Saxon and French manuscript illumination has itself exposed the paucity of painted examples. From a time period spanning three centuries, approximately sixteen images were identified which represented nude figures with genitalia.[32] These figures were meant to depict anatomical accuracy, the sub-human or non-human nature of the figures illustrated, the stain of sin or the innocence and purity of children. Of this limited number of examples, then, only the image of Noah and the figures from the *Barberini Gospels* and the *Book of Kells* relate even remotely to the Bayeux Tapestry's nude figures.

The exposure of genitalia in these manuscript examples was associated generally with supernatural and non-human

and genitals of these figures. The problem with such a moralizing reading of the *Barberini* image is that the man is certainly menaced by the creatures surrounding him, but they have not attached him yet.

[30] The text is from Luke 3:22-26. Bernard Meehan, *The Book of Kells: An Illustrated Introduction to the Manuscript in Trinity College Dublin* (London, 1994), pp. 22, 64, reproduces fol. 200r and a detail of this image. See also Alexander, *Insular Manuscripts,* no. 52, pp. 71-76, for his commentary on the *Book of Kells*, Dublin, Trinity College MS A.1.6 (58).

[31] Meehan, *The Book of Kells*, p. 64, interprets this genital display as an allusion to procreation and death, associated with the genealogy of Christ listed on the page.

[32] This survey does not claim to be exhaustive as it is based on an analysis of images available in published sources.

beings, not the human figures we see in the Tapestry.[33] In addition, their integration within a biblical narrative differentiates them from the discrete, almost iconic, marginal representations in the secular narrative depicted on the Bayeux Tapestry. These illuminated examples are also located in the main zone of representation, once again contrasting them with the marginal placement of the Tapestry's nudes. Finally, the nudity of the Tapestry figures makes specific gendered statements, and is aggressively and overtly sexualized, while the nude body in some of the manuscript imagery could be understood as innocent and non-sexual. In general, then, these examples from manuscript illumination appear to present more differences than similarities with the Bayeux Tapestry marginalia.

Though scholars have generally turned to manuscript illumination for iconographic parallels to the Bayeux Tapestry imagery, the medium of relief sculpture presents more compelling visual comparisons to the animated and aggressive nude figures in the Tapestry's margins.[34] In their confrontational nudity, lewd gestures, secular setting and audiences, the Bayeux Tapestry nudes resemble sculpture found on the exteriors of Romanesque churches throughout Europe.

A figural type prevalent in medieval Europe was the sheela-na-gig, or female exhibitionist.[35] The earliest sheelas

[33] The biblical figure of Noah and the male nude in the *Barberini Gospels* are exceptions to this general statement.

[34] Both Wilson, *The Bayeux Tapestry*, pp. 206-08, and Grape, *The Bayeux Tapestry*, p. 44, mention iconographic similarities with a relief from Winchester. See also Jane Hawkes, "The Rothbury Cross: An Iconographic Bricolage," *Gesta* 35.1 (1996): 77-94, especially 88-90, for her discussion of nude figures of the damned in hell represented at the base of the cross-shaft. She dates the cross to the second half of the eighth century, making this sculpted cross an early iconographic precedent for the Bayeux Tapestry images. It would, however, be roughly contemporary with the *Book of Kells*.

[35] Two of the most extensive discussions of this topic are found in Jørgen Andersen, *The Witch on the Wall: Medieval Erotic Sculpture in the British Isles* (Copenhagen, 1977), and Weir and Jerman, *Images of Lust*. Nurith Kenaan-Kedar analyzes only French examples of female exhibitionists in her study, *Marginal Sculpture in Medieval France* (Aldershot, 1995). Other recent publi-

date to the early twelfth century, and are particularly concentrated in the British Isles and northern France.[36] In these sheela-type images, female figures, nude or partially clothed, expose their breasts or genitalia. Many of these figures also make animated gestures or facial expressions. The three female figures on the Bayeux Tapestry with exposed breasts and pudenda may relate to this type of sculpted imagery. We clearly see the breasts of two nude females on the Bayeux Tapestry, and sheela figures frequently expose their breasts while displaying their genitalia.[37]

The nude female figures on the Tapestry gesture animatedly to their male companions in the margins, imitating some of the gestures made by sculpted sheelas. One sheela from the Kiltinane Church (figure 8) raises one hand to her head as the other is placed on her genital area, in an almost exact parallel to the gesture of one Tapestry figure (figure 2). Both the sheela reliefs and their stitched counterparts interact with other figures in some sort of nested narrative within the larger official narrative surrounding them. Female exhibitionist images were generally part of an extended series of reliefs, including male

cations on sheela-na-gigs include Robert Jacks, *The Divine Hag of the Christian Celts: An Illustrated Guide to Sheela-na-gigs of Britain and Ireland* (Cork, 2000); Barbara Freitag, "A New Light on the Sheela-na-gig (Celtic Mythology, goddess, fertility)," *Eire-Ireland* 33.3-4 (1998): 50-69; Eamonn Kelly, *Sheela-na-gigs: Origins and Functions* (Dublin, 1996); Irish Museum of Modern Art, *From Beyond the Pale: Sheela na gigs* (Dublin, 1994), pp. 43-52.

[36] Weir and Jerman, *Images of Lust*, p. 125, provide a series of maps that indicate the distribution of sexual carvings in various parts of Europe. They also indicate, p. 21, the chronological range of these marginal images, which extended from approximately 1080 to 1250. Andersen, *Witch on the Wall*, p. 70, and Eamonn Kelly, "Sheela-na-gigs in the National Museum of Ireland, together with a brief description of their origin and function," in *Irish Antiquities: Essays in Memory of Joseph Raftery*, ed. Michael Ryan (Wicklow, 1998), pp. 173-84, have both argued that in Ireland, where an extraordinary number of these images exist, sheela figures appear most frequently in areas where the Norman influence was strongest.

[37] Many sheela figures are depicted without breasts, as the general emphasis in these images is on the overt display of the vulva.

exhibitionists, animals, drunkards, acrobats, and fools.[38] Each nude female on the Bayeux Tapestry is paired with a nude male figure; and sheela reliefs are often accompanied by images of male exhibitionists. As Weir and Jerman have stated, the "function of the sheela is highlighted by an aroused male."[39] The sheela or female exhibitionist image, then, can only be understood in the context of the images that surround it.

There are some significant differences, however, between the female nudes on the Bayeux Tapestry and sheela-na-gig sculptures. The first obstacle in establishing any relationship between these two types of images is one of chronology. No sheela relief predates the Bayeux Tapestry, making an argument of direct artistic influence untenable. I would suggest that both types of artwork, textiles and architectural sculpture, reflect a synthesis of continental and indigenous English influences, a blending of artistic styles that simply manifested itself later in architecture.

The Tapestry's female nudes and sheela reliefs also differ in style. This may have a purely functional explanation based on the demands of the media employed, but it could be argued that the distinct styles of these sculpted and stitched images conveyed different messages, though the difference is perhaps one of degree. The sheelas overwhelmingly confront the viewer with an overt display of genitalia and often a grimacing or leering facial expression. One could say that the essential reason for the carving of these images was this grotesque and transgressive display of body parts. In contrast, none of the Tapestry's female nudes address the viewer; instead, they direct their attention to the other male figure in the scene. The nude females on the Tapestry could not be characterized as grotesque or aggressively sexual either, as they are not reduced to a grimacing face and exposed genitalia. Not all sheelas are so overt in their facial expressions and genital display, and some of the less extreme examples present compelling visual parallels

[38] Both Weir and Jerman, *Images of Lust*, pp. 17, 29, 38, and Kenaan-Kedar, *Marginal Sculpture*, pp. 36-37, 41, warn against studying these marginal images in isolation.

[39] Weir and Jerman, *Images of Lust*, p. 23.

with the Tapestry nudes. These images of female nude figures in sculpture and embroidery perhaps both reflect an international Romanesque style and subject matter recently imported to the British Isles.

In the Bayeux Tapestry images and the sheela-na-gig, or female exhibitionist reliefs, viewers are presented with a highly sexualized representation of women, but most scholars agree that these images were not meant to be seen as erotic or sexually stimulating.[40] The ambiguous nature of these two types of images, at once sexual, aggressive, pathetic, and repulsive, connects them as well. In addition, the multiple interpretations of sheela images may be extended to the nude females on the Tapestry. From the time of their earliest publication by antiquarians in the 1840s, sheelas have elicited diametrically opposed responses.[41] They have been interpreted as protective, benevolent spirits who ward off the evil eye, encourage fertility, or help women in childbirth.[42] This folkloric understanding of these images most likely reflects a modern, and not medieval, set of beliefs.[43]

The second interpretation is equally categorical, where these are images warning against the sin of lust, terrifying representations of sexually aggressive and predatory women.[44] The female nudes on the Tapestry may reflect this moralizing

[40] Weir and Jerman, *Images of Lust*, p. 11, and Patrick Ford, "The *Which* on the Wall: Obscenity Exposed in Early Ireland," in *Obscenity*, ed. Ziolkowski, p. 176.

[41] Andersen, *The Witch on the Wall*, pp. 9-21, provides the most comprehensive treatment of the antiquarian discovery of sheela images in the British Isles.

[42] Andersen, *The Witch on the Wall*, pp. 22-31. Andersen devotes an entire chapter of his work to the roles sheelas play in popular belief. More recently, Madeline Caviness, "Obscenity and Alterity," p. 166, has referred to the sheela-na-gig as a "polysemous sign, no doubt instilling fear and revulsion in some (to whom it is therefore obscene) but of comfort to women in childbirth."

[43] Weir and Jerman, *Images of Lust*, p. 15, argue against the apotropaic function of these images in the Middle Ages.

[44] Weir and Jerman, *Images of Lust*, pp. 61, 70-73; Ford, "The *Which* on the Wall," p. 181.

overtone, demonstrating inappropriate feminine behavior in hopes of encouraging more acceptable activities on the part of women who viewed the Tapestry. As it is generally believed that women were responsible for the Tapestry's manufacture, they would have had ample opportunity to reflect on these images as they worked on this embroidery.[45]

The female figures on the Tapestry are always pendants to a nude male, and these groupings may provide further clues to their significance for the Tapestry's audiences. Three male/female pairs interact in the borders of the Bayeux Tapestry, just as pairings of male and female exhibitionists form part of numerous ensembles of marginal sculpture. Exhibiting couples adorn a pillar in the church of Loctudy, Brittany, capitals at the church of Frómista in Spain and Saint-Front-sur-Nizonne in France, and a censored relief at Saint-Hilaire in Poitiers (figures 9, 10).[46] In an explicit pair of corbels from San Pedro de Tejada in Spain, clothed male and female figures lift up their tunics to expose their genitals. In the majority of these reliefs, both figures make animated gestures similar to the ones used by the nude pairs in the Bayeux Tapestry.[47] In the sculptural examples, however, these gestures are often directed out at the viewer and not to the other figure.

[45] Andersen, *Witch on the Wall*, p. 56. Scholars generally agree that women actually embroidered the Tapestry, though they ascribe the design of the imagery to a male, most likely a cleric. See, for example, Wilson, *The Bayeux Tapestry*, p. 212; Bernstein, *The Mystery of the Bayeux Tapestry*, pp. 26, 38-39; Grape, *The Bayeux Tapestry*, pp. 62-63; Caviness, "Obscenity and Alterity," p. 174.

[46] Andersen, *Witch on the Wall*, p. 63, discusses and reproduces the relief from Loctudy, and Weir and Jerman, *Images of Lust*, pp. 86-90, discuss the other exhibitionist pairs mentioned.

[47] Kenaan-Kedar, *Marginal Sculpture*, p. 17, has noted the extreme gestures and facial expressions that characterize these marginal images, and cites Roman sculpture as an iconographic source. C. R. Dodwell, *Anglo-Saxon Gestures and the Roman Stage* (Cambridge, 2000), has undertaken a similar study of gestures in Anglo-Saxon manuscripts, which he relates to the gestures employed on the Roman stage as recorded in Terence manuscripts. Le Goff, *The Medieval Imagination*, p. 86, states that "gesticulation reminded Christians of two things they abhorred and combatted: the theater and possession by the devil."

Another type of marginal sculpture related to the Tapestry's nude couples depicts lovers embracing. In reliefs from Spain and France, couples engage in sexual acts or embrace and kiss on corbels.[48] Particularly explicit examples can be found at Marignac, St. Supice, and Champagnolles, where the genitals of the male figures can be seen as couples interlock in acrobatic sexual positions (figures 11, 12). The couples on the Tapestry borders do not necessarily engage in such intimate acts, but it can be argued that at least in one case (figure 5: nude male and female), the gestures between the man and woman are welcoming and inviting, contrasting with the tense stand-offs between the other two pairs (figures 2, 6) The sculpted reliefs of lovers, then, may present the culmination of activities only hinted at in the Tapestry's border zone.

Finally, all five of the Tapestry scenes contain representations of nude males, and two images depict isolated male figures (figures 3, 4). Sculptural counterparts can be seen in the numerous ithyphallic or megaphallic men who adorn churches throughout Europe.[49] Though the female exhibitionist, or sheela figure, may be particularly prominent in the British Isles, there are at least twice as many male as female exhibitionists on churches in France and Spain.[50] Either these male figures are shown in an aroused state with an erect penis, or they are endowed with oversized genitalia. Several sculpted examples emulate the confrontational nudity of the male figure below the Ælfgyva scene on the Tapestry. This figure is represented frontally and points to his large genitals while gesturing to the scene above. Images of megaphallic men indicating or touching their genitals abound in marginal sculpture, as seen

[48] Andersen, *Witch on the Wall*, pp. 35, 59; Weir and Jerman, *Images of Lust*, p. 89; Kenaan-Kedar, *Marginal Sculpture*, pp. 23-24, reproduce these images of embracing pairs.

[49] Weir and Jerman, *Images of Lust*, pp. 91-99, devote an entire chapter to male exhibitionist sculpture.

[50] Weir and Jerman, *Images of Lust*, p. 11. Weir and Jerman's maps, pp. 126-28, which display the distribution of sexual carvings in Europe, show that no male exhibitionist reliefs have been found in England or Wales; Ireland possesses two such images.

in reliefs from Sainte-Radegonde in Poitiers and the church of Notre Dame in Semur-en-Auxois, both in France, and a gate-post in Ballycloghduff in Ireland (figures 13, 14). The other male nude on the Tapestry bends over with an axe and a board, as he displays grossly oversized genitalia detailed in a contrasting color of thread. In marginal sculpture as well, we see nude males carrying objects such as wine barrels or loaves of bread.[51] One example at Semur-en-Brionnais depicts a megaphallic male serving as an atlas figure, supporting the capital on which he is represented (figure 15).

Thus, Romanesque marginal sculpture presents numerous iconographic comparisons with the Bayeux Tapestry border images. In both media, the nudity is confrontational and the representations sexually explicit. These images abound in exposed and aroused genitalia, graphic sexual positions, and related images of vices such as gluttony and avarice.[52] The sculpted nude figures found on architectural monuments, however, appear to present a more exaggerated and explicit version of the Tapestry nudes. In their lack of eye contact with the viewer and their less dramatic actions and gestures, the Bayeux Tapestry's nude figures were perhaps not intended to elicit the depth and variety of emotions that their sculpted counterparts did.

The striking visual similarities between the Tapestry's nudes and marginal sculpture complemented the analogous physical settings and audiences for these images. Marginal sculpture would have decorated both the exterior and interior of churches, surrounding the "official," religious, narrative, and didactic sculpture on a Romanesque church portal.[53] These

[51] I have not found an example in the published sources of a relief where a nude figure carries a weapon. Nude barrel toters can be found at Givrezac and Béceleuf in France among other sites, and wafer or bread eaters adorn churches at Givrezac and Champagnolles. For a discussion of these types of images, see Weir and Jerman, *Images of Lust*, p. 92.

[52] Kenaan-Kedar, *Marginal Sculpture*, p. 73; Weir and Jerman, *Images of Lust*, p. 15.

[53] Kenaan-Kedar, *Marginal Sculpture*, pp. 4-5, employs the term "official art" as the antithesis of marginal artworks.

reliefs, carved on capitals, metopes, or corbels, would have been experienced both temporally and spatially, as the viewer moved around or through the church to view each image. There does not appear to have been a set sequence for viewing or understanding these marginal images, and this unconstrained reception of the imagery differed markedly from the controlled and orchestrated viewing at the church's main entrance.

Though there is no consensus among scholars concerning the original placement of the Bayeux Tapestry, it is certain that this image would have been on public display in an architectural setting. The Tapestry hung in the Cathedral of Bayeux for centuries, and some scholars believe that this was the intended context for this monumental textile.[54] Critics of this theory, notably C.R. Dodwell, have countered that the secular content of the main narrative zone and the nude figures in the borders precluded a religious setting for this work.[55] The argument that the "obscenity and lewdness" of the border images rendered the Tapestry inappropriate for display in a church completely ignores the sexually explicit carvings decorating the exterior and sometimes interior of countless churches throughout Europe. The placement of the Tapestry within a church interior would thus approximate the setting of much marginal sculpture on Continental churches.

These nationalistic and somewhat puritanical interpretations of the Tapestry have led many scholars to postulate a secular setting for the textile, as a noble audience hall would be a more appropriate setting for the decidedly secular and worldly imagery on the Tapestry.[56] Whether the Tapestry was displayed in a church or a manor hall, both settings would have

[54] Grape, *The Bayeux Tapestry*, pp. 77-80.

[55] C.R. Dodwell, "The Bayeux Tapestry and the French Secular Epic," *Burlington Magazine* 108 (1966): 549, first expressed reservations about the Tapestry hanging in a church, based on the "obscenity and lewdness" of some of the border scenes.

[56] See Richard Brilliant, "The Bayeux Tapestry: A Stripped Narrative for Their Eyes and Ears," *Word & Image* 7.2 (1991): 98-126, especially 99-100, for a recent presentation of this hypothesis.

been public, and the Tapestry would have been viewed communally by people of various nationalities and social classes.[57] A viewer would have had to move through time and space to experience the Tapestry, and this type of dynamic viewing parallels the perception of marginal sculptural imagery on ecclesiastical structures.

The spatial and temporal aspects of viewing and understanding the Tapestry have generally been downplayed by scholars who wish to highlight the book-like quality of the narrative flow. The Tapestry tells a story, its images and text both read from left to right, and the narrative has a beginning, middle, and end. Some art historians, however, feel that the comparison of experiencing the Tapestry to reading a book oversimplifies the reception of this multi-layered work. Richard Brilliant has emphatically stated that the Bayeux Tapestry was not "read" like a book.[58] In fact, Brilliant postulates that the images were viewed and interpreted by various audiences, or served as visual cues for an oral presentation by a learned interlocutor.[59] In other words, the story conveyed in the Tapestry was performed and not read. The terse Latin inscriptions above the main narrative zone, intelligible only to a literate elite, would have been the least informative element in the Tapestry's composition.

Though the narrative in the Tapestry's main zone flowed with relatively few pauses or stops, the upper and lower border zones follow an entirely different organizational principle. These images do not form part of a coherent, overall narrative of their own, nor do they elaborate on the main narrative zone in a consistent way. Indeed, the composition of the border zones militates against an overarching story presented in the margins. The numerous figures, animal and human, that decorate the borders are separated from each other by a series

[57] Gameson, "The Origin, Art, and Message of the Bayeux Tapestry," pp. 174-75, notes the inherent portability of the Tapestry, and theorizes that this textile was displayed in various contexts.

[58] Brilliant, "The Bayeux Tapestry," pp. 109, 117.

[59] Brilliant, "The Bayeux Tapestry," p. 109.

of diagonal bars creating a visual barrier between scenes. The border divisions would encourage viewers to see this imagery as a set of discrete scenes, like the marginal reliefs on medieval architectural structures.

Another similarity between the Tapestry and marginal sculpture lies in the relationship between the marginal images and the main or official decorative zones. Nurith Kenaan-Kedar has argued that marginal imagery must be understood in the context of the overall sculptural program on a church.[60] Thematic relationships existed between the marginal reliefs, and figures on separate corbels engage in shared activities. These marginal images also complemented and augmented the ideas presented in the "main narrative zone," that is, the official sculpted portal or capitals.[61] Though marginal reliefs can be viewed separately from the images on a portal, they were most likely not intended to stand alone as a discrete cycle of imagery. Indeed, scholars have argued against seeing these marginal zones as the expression of a subversive counter-narrative.[62] It is likely that these images were understood in small thematic groupings, and any holistic interpretations of these images could only be derived in conjunction with the more monumental, "official" sculptural decoration.

Kenaan-Kedar establishes a set of dichotomies between official art and marginal art, which I think pertain to the Bayeux Tapestry's main and marginal zones. Official art was hierarchical, symmetrical, and oppositional with specific

[60] Kenaan-Kedar, *Marginal Sculpture*, pp. 53-54.

[61] Both Kenaan-Kedar, *Marginal Sculpture*, pp. 4-6, 53-54, and Weir and Jerman, *Images of Lust*, p. 38, argue that these images must be seen in relation to official, narrative sculpture on church portals. Camille, *Image on the Edge*, has made similar arguments for manuscript illumination, which he analyzed with marginal sculpture in this work. Kenaan-Kedar, *Marginal Sculpture*, p. 3, critiqued his conflation of these two distinct media, arguing that the audiences and locations of marginal sculpture differ markedly from those of manuscript illumination.

[62] Camille, *Image on the Edge*, p. 127, has warned against interpreting marginal imagery as a site of liberation, stating that in the margins "the inversion and release of liminality works only for those in power, those who maintain the status quo and have something at stake in resisting change."

meanings meant to elicit particular responses.[63] For example, the gist of the Bayeux Tapestry's narrative is at once apparent; this is the story of the Norman Conquest from the victor's perspective. The hero of this tale, William the Conqueror, is represented throughout the Tapestry as a noble man with a rightful claim to the throne, and is accompanied by all the trappings of military and political power. His adversary, Harold of Wessex, is portrayed in a more ambivalent light. Some scholars have argued that the portrayal of Harold on the Tapestry is sympathetic, while others claim that Harold is ridiculed and feminized in contrast to the hyper-masculine William.[64]

This description of the main narrative zone corresponds to portal imagery on Romanesque churches in terms of its style rather than subject matter. Hieratic images of celestial figures, angels and saints, watch impassively over animated demons and the supplicating damned in hell on tympana at Autun and Conques to name just two portal scenes (figure 16). The marginal sculpture on Romanesque churches and the border images on the Bayeux Tapestry represent the antithesis of official art, as they are disorganized, fluid, emotional, and dynamic.[65] They are more iconic than narrative, and any narrative thread established among them is only sustained over a few discrete scenes or reliefs.[66] Both marginal sculpture and the nude figures on the borders of the Tapestry share highly emotional and dynamic styles of representation. Marginal

[63] Kenaan-Kedar, *Marginal Sculpture*, p. 4.

[64] McNulty, *The Narrative Art*, pp. 37-38; Caviness, "Obscenity and Alterity," pp. 172-74. Karkov, "Gendering the Battle?," also comments on the feminization of the English in the Tapestry.

[65] Kenaan-Kedar, *Marginal Sculpture*, pp. 3-5. Lucy Freeman Sandler, "The Study of Marginal Imagery: Past, Present, and Future," *Studies in Iconography* 18 (1997): 1-49, especially 13, 26, offers a recent overview of marginal imagery in Gothic manuscript illumination, and makes similar observations about the nature of marginal images in manuscripts.

[66] See Camille, *Image on the Edge*, pp. 42-43, and Sandler, "The Study of Marginal Imagery," p. 13, for similar relationships established between marginal scenes in manuscript illumination.

reliefs display grimaces, acrobatic postures, as well as gestures of joy, anger, and despair. The border images on the Tapestry are also more dynamic than the figures in the main zone, as psychological drama and moral questions inform the relationships between nude figures on the border. Only the Ælfgyva scene approaches the same level of prurient interest, but this episode is anomalous on the Tapestry.

Finally, audiences for the Bayeux Tapestry and marginal church sculpture would have been similar, as both were public monuments viewed by a variety of people over time in an open setting. The Bayeux Tapestry may have been displayed in a large secular hall, where members of the nobility, men and women, secular and religious, could view it at their leisure and in their own way. If it were displayed in a church, the audiences would have been even more inclusive, encompassing the same social groups who would have viewed architectural sculpture. The clergy may have been the primary audience, but the nobility, merchants, peasants, and the poor of the town would all have visited and used these religious spaces on a regular basis. What is not clear is whether any or all of these groups would have paid close attention to this imagery.[67]

It is impossible to view and understand the Tapestry in one glance, given its length and complex narrative. The various audiences for the Tapestry, however, could create relationships between main and marginal zones, between marginal images, or view images individually. Indeed, Kenaan-Kedar has argued that marginal sculpture was meant to convey different meanings to different audiences, expressing one thing to its patrons and another to the artists and their public.[68] She further argues that artists, and possibly the public viewing these images, related to the individual representations, while the patron, most likely an ecclesiastical official, perceived marginal reliefs as a unified series.

[67] See my "Reading Romanesque Sculpture: The Iconography and Reception of the South Portal Sculpture at Santiago de Compostela," *Gesta* 39.1 (2000): 3-12, for an analysis of audience responses to the architectural sculpture on this Romanesque structure.

[68] Kenaan-Kedar, *Marginal Sculpture*, p. 53.

Can we postulate a similar dichotomy of viewing for the Bayeux Tapestry borders? The patron of the Tapestry, Odo of Bayeux, was a cleric, and he might have interpreted the border images as a moralizing gloss on human behavior, the horrors of war, the virtues of the victorious, and just punishments for the defeated. They may have served as admonitions against violence and lascivious behavior during and after the Conquest. As males identified as both Norman and English display their genitals and make lewd advances at women in the Tapestry, the warnings against concupiscence were directed equally at the conquerors and conquered.

If the interpretations presented above may have approximated the reception of these images by the patron, other audiences may have had markedly different perceptions of this imagery. Noble audiences viewing the Tapestry in a secular hall may have interpreted these images in a more literal manner. Though many English families had their lands confiscated, there was also a considerable amount of intermarriage among the English and the Normans after the Conquest. It is likely, then, that at any gathering held within Odo's landholdings in Kent, a number of English nobles would have been in attendance. Might they have seen these border images as small genre scenes, vignettes of activities that actually took place during the military campaign? As such, the marginal images would blend imperceptibly into the martial imagery of the main zone, all of which demonstrated the heroic, mundane, and morally reprehensible actualities of war.

If the Tapestry adorned a church interior, then a greater variety of people would have had access to this work. People who frequented the Cathedral of Bayeux might not have had any direct knowledge of the battles that took place across the Channel. They might have chosen to read the images individually, relating them to folk legends, popular sayings, and stories circulated in the town about mythical or real characters.[69]

[69] The content of the margins has been equated with oral traditions, such as proverbs, jokes, riddles and tales. See Camille, *Image on the Edge*, p. 36; Kenaan-Kedar, *Marginal Sculpture*, p. 62; Sandler, "The Study of Marginal Imagery," p. 27.

These border scenes might have also represented actual inhabitants of the town, the drunkards, fools, beggars, and prostitutes who populated any medieval urban center.

Finally, any analysis of the reception of the Bayeux Tapestry nude figures must incorporate what might be considered the most immediate audience, the female embroiderers, most likely English, who viewed and stitched the Tapestry over a number of months, if not years. I have argued elsewhere that these images may have been understood by these English embroideresses as a subversive commentary on the male-dominated master narrative in the main zone concerning the political motives and consequences of the Norman Conquest.[70] These nude figures in the border may have presented themes of aggression and violence towards women as well as lewd and unacceptable behavior by men. The females threatened with sexual violence could represent symbolically the fate the English suffered at the hands of the Normans. They could also depict on a literal and individualized level the suffering of English women at the hands Norman invaders.

A comparison of the Bayeux Tapestry border images to marginal sculpture suggests that there might have been multiple and simultaneous perceptions of these images. Different viewers in various contexts may have perceived these scenes in a variety of ways, depending upon their social status, the location of the image, and the time and interest they devoted to the viewing of the work. Through this type of analysis, the enigmatic figures in the margins of sculpture and textiles can be liberated from a totalizing narrative that insists that they must all have some consistent, overarching meaning. In addition, the type of viewing (dynamic and multi-faceted) can be seen to correspond to the type of image, that is, the animated, gesticulating nude figures that inhabit the margins of the Bayeux

[70] Karen Mathews, "Subverting the Norman Narrative in the Borders of the Bayeux Tapestry," paper presented at the College Art Association Annual Meeting, Toronto, 1998.

Tapestry.[71] And, through a comparison of the Bayeux Tapestry to Continental architectural sculpture, we can broaden our understanding of the Tapestry as a complex artistic monument which displayed iconographic motifs and international influences from beyond the British Isles.

[71] Sandler, "The Study of Marginal Imagery," pp. 28-43, concludes her article with an overview of the meanings (or non-meanings) ascribed to Gothic marginal imagery.

# The Donestre and the Person of Both Sexes

Susan M. Kim

> ... [*In*] *more innocent times it was possible to create a grotesque by mingling human with animal or mechanical elements; but as we learn more about the languages of animals, and teach more and more complex languages to computers, the membranes dividing these realms from that of the human begin to dissolve, and with them go the potentiality for many forms of the grotesque. In short, the grotesque — with the help of technology — is becoming the victim of its own success: having existed for many centuries on the disorderly margins of Western culture and the aesthetic conventions that constitute that culture, it is now faced with a situation where the center cannot, or does not choose to, hold; where nothing is incompatible with anything else; and where the marginal is indistinguishable from the typical. Thus the grotesque, in endlessly diluting forms, is always and everywhere around us — and increasingly invisible.*
>
> –Geoffrey Galt Harpham, *On the Grotesque*[1]

The "Wonders of the East" survives in two illustrated manuscripts with texts in Old English: BL, Cotton Tiberius B. v, and BL, Cotton Vitellius A. xv.[2] Not only these two versions of the "Wonders of the East" but also the related texts of the

1 Geoffrey Galt Harpham, *On the Grotesque: Strategies of Contradiction in Art and Literature* (Princeton, 1982), pp. xx-xxi.

2 The text in the Vitellius version is in Old English; the text of the Tiberius is in Latin and Old English. The somewhat later manuscript, Oxford, Bodleian Library 614, contains a text in Latin only. The following provide surveys of these and other related manuscripts, and insight into the backgrounds and traditions which inform these texts and illustrations: Stanley Rypins, ed., *Three Old English Prose Texts in MS Cotton Vitellius A. xv*, EETS o.s. 161 (London, 1924); Rudolf Wittkower, "Marvels of the East: A Study in the History of Monsters," *Journal of the Warburg and Cortauld Institutes* 5 (1942): 159-97; Paul Gibb, "'Wonders of the East': A Critical Edition and Commentary" (unpub. Ph. D. diss., Duke Univ., 1977); John Block Friedman, *The Monstrous Races in Medieval Art and Thought* (1981: repr. Syracuse, 2000); Mary P. Campbell, *The Witness and the Other World: Exotic European Travel*

*Liber Monstrorum* contain descriptions of hybrid monsters called "Donestre."[3] In the verbal descriptions, the Donestre are partly human, and use their facility with human speech to lure their human victims to approach. Once the victims approach the Donestre, the monsters eat them. Mary B. Campbell reads the description of the Donestre as the "most active of all the descriptions of dubious human races in the *Wonders*" but adds that the activity is "infinitely repeating...like that of a peep show. It is the only action the Donestre perform, and it is not only unmotivated, but self-contradictory."[4]

Although she focuses on the text, Campbell's reading of the episode is also supported by the illustrations of the "Wonders of the East." The most marked common features of the Vitellius and Tiberius illustrations of the Donestre are the exposed genitalia of the monster (unmentioned by the text) and the dismemberment of the human victim. In the Tiberius illustration (figure 17: Donestre), the genitalia are emphatically clear, not only clearly marked, but also red. In the Vitellius illustration (figure 18: Donestre), the genitalia are similarly exposed. The Vitellius illustration, moreover, pairs the monster with a female figure unmentioned by the text, thus providing a context of sexual difference to underscore the exposure of the clearly male monster. As John Block Friedman has argued, "the monstrous races in medieval art were often shown naked or wearing only animal skins" in part as a "necessary convention in that it enabled the artist to show their anatomical peculiarities," but more importantly as "a sign of wildness and bestiality — of the animal nature thought to characterize those who lived beyond the limits of the Christian world."[5] The juxtaposition in both the Tiberius and the Vitellius illustrations of the naked

*Writing, 400-1600* (Ithaca, 1988); Andy Orchard, *Pride and Prodigies: Studies in the Monsters of the Beowulf-Manuscript* (Cambridge, 1995).

[3] On the *Liber Monstrorum*, see the above invaluable sources, in particular, Orchard, *Pride and Prodigies*, pp. 86-115.

[4] Campbell, *Witness and the Other World*, p. 73.

[5] Friedman, *Monstrous Races*, pp. 31-32.

monster and the clothed human supports Friedman's argument that the nakedness of the monster marks its bestiality, and its difference from the human victim as well as the human viewer.

The female figure in the Vitellius illustration, however, provides what appears to be a supplemental point of difference: the monster is not human because he is not clothed, like the human figure beside him; but the monster is also male, because his genitals reveal him to be so, and because viewers can *see* his difference from the female. This supplemental point, however, while it appears to reinforce categories of difference, draws attention to the absence of exactly the grounds for that difference. David Williams argues that,

> After the head, the most important index of monstrosity is the genitals and related ideas such as sexual distinction, the sexual act, and reproduction.... Selfhood, social structure — indeed our very sense of a logical reality — depend on this fundamental distinction between male and female. When it disappears or is confused, the necessary distinctions between all things evaporate with it, and the rational structures of the real begin to collapse and to meld one into another in a cascade toward the absurd.[6]

The Vitellius illustration presents the female figure as if to provide additional evidence of difference: difference between monstrous and human is supplemented by difference between male and female. By providing this supplement, however, the illustration reveals the fragility of the categories maintained by both differences. What appears to be an obvious difference, the difference between male and female, is immediately destabilized, in part by the woman's peculiar gesture of simultaneously revealing and concealing her genitals, and thus the illustration's insistence on obscuring exactly the actual point of difference which the figure of the woman might provide. If, as in Campbell's reading, the textual description and the illustra-

[6] David Williams, *Deformed Discourse: The Function of the Monster in Mediaeval Thought and Literature* (Montreal, 1996), p. 160.

tion suggest pornography, they do so because they reveal — they make literal, or naked — anxieties which underlie not only these monstrous texts, but also the cultures which generate and read them.

The "Wonders of the East" is a catalog of monsters and other "wonders." It is difficult to discern any consistent method behind the organization of the catalog. The Donestre episode, for example, occurs in the "Wonders" after the description of the balsam trees and before the description of the men with ears like fans. In constrast, the related *Liber Monstrorum* opens with a prologue in which the narrator explains how he will progress through his material.[7] Describing the progress of his text as a movement down the body of a female monster, the *Liber's* narrator writes,

> And first I will discuss those things which are in some part to be trusted, and then let each judge for himself the following material, because throughout these monster-filled caverns I shall paint a little picture of a sea-girl or siren, which if it has a head of reason is followed by all kinds of shaggy and scaly tales.[8]

[7] Paul Gibb argues for an ultimately Christian symbolism and a coherent structure for the "Wonders," however: "The author seems to have structured his work so as to be an exploration of the bivalent nature of Christian symbolism, of the conflicting possibilities of interpreting the same concepts" (p. 76). The *Liber Monstrorum* exists in five manuscripts from the ninth and tenth centuries. Orchard argues that "the Latin texts which lie behind the vernacular renderings of *The Wonders of the East* and *Alexander's Letter to Aristotle* were clearly known to the author of the *Liber monstrorum*" and that the *Liber* is "the rather subtle and sophisticated work of a learned author who drew on and cunningly manipulated a number of disparate texts to offer a cogent (if uncomforting) view of the monstrous in nature"; see *Pride and Prodigies*, p. 87.

[8] "Prologue" to the *Liber Monstrorum, Pride and Prodigies*, pp. 256-57: "Et de his primum eloquar quae sunt aliquo modo credenda et sequentem historiam sibi quisque discernat, quod per haec antra monstrorum marinae puellae quandam formulam sirenae depingam, ut sit capite rationis quod tamen diuersorum generum hispidae squamosaeque sequuntur fabulae." All references to the *Liber* will be to Orchard's edition and translation.

In the verbal description of the sirens which appears as the sixth entry in the *Liber*, the sirens are "sea-girls, who deceive sailors with the outstanding beauty of their appearance and the sweetness of their song, and are most like human beings from the head to the navel, with the body of a maiden, but have scaly fishes' tails, with which they always lurk in the sea."[9] In both the metaphor and the following description, that which is reasonable, "to be trusted," and *attractive*, is that which is most recognizably human. What manifests itself below the navel, however, reveals the instability of both "appearance" and "song": it also exposes the corollary that viewers, listeners, and readers who allow themselves to feel that attraction become vulnerable to deception, deception discovered with the repulsive difference between the face and the "tail," or, in the metaphor, the instability of the "tale" itself. From its initial moments, the *Liber* thus promises both titillation and denial, both identification and destabilization of that identity, all turning on a self-conscious representation of the "tale" and the tale's relationship to its own representations of powerfully attractive monstrous-and-yet-human bodies.

It is no surprise, then, that when the *Liber* promises to begin with the "head of reason" and those marvels "which differ by a rather trifling amount from humankind,"[10] it is drawn immediately to the site of seduction and deception, to the line of demarcation between an attractive and recognizable body, and a body which is not what it seems to be. The narrator claims to have known the first marvel he describes at first hand. This marvel, a "person of both sexes," is "to be trusted" because its description is an eye-witness account. Yet the description of the "person of both sexes," rather than reinforcing the possibility for stable identification of and with the marvel, becomes

[9] "Sirenae sunt marinae puellae, quae nauigantes pulcherrima forma et cantu dulcedinis decipiunt, et a capite usque ad umbilicum sunt corpore uirginali et humano generi simillimae, squamosas tamen piscium caudas habent, quibus semper in gurgite latent," I.6 (*Pride and Prodigies*, pp. 262-63).

[10] "Primoque namque de his ad ortum sermo prorumpit quae leuiore discretu ab humano genere distant...." Prologue (*Pride and Prodigies*, pp. 256-57).

strangely evasive, exactly where it seems to be most emphatically marking out difference:

> Indeed I bear witness at the beginning of the work that I have known a person of both sexes, who although they appeared more masculine than feminine from their face and chest, and were thought male by those who did not know, yet loved feminine occupations and deceived the ignorant amongst men in the manner of a whore; but this is said to have happened often amongst the human race.[11]

To the narrator of the *Liber Monstrorum*, the monstrosity most verifiable by personal experience, more common than even being large, like Higelac, or having dark skin, like the "Ethiopians," is having "both sexes." Furthermore, the presence of "both sexes" is explained not as a mixing or a doubling of genitalia, but as a split between face and chest (here male) and what is below, presumably genitalia through which the "person of both sexes ... deceive[s] the ignorant amongst men."[12] Yet

[11] "Me enim quendam hominem in primordio operis utriusque sexus cognouisse testor, qui tamen ipsa facie plus et pectore uirilis quam muliebris apparuit; et uir a nescentibus putabatur, sed muliebria opera dilexit, et ignaros uirorum more metetricis, decipiebat; sed hoc frequenter apud humanum genus contigisse fertur," I.1 (*Pride and Prodigies*, pp. 258-59).

[12] Lorraine Daston and Katherine Park, in their examination of hermaphroditism in early modern France, suggest that although the contrasting Hippocratic and Aristotelian understandings of hermaphroditism were often interwoven throughout the later Middle Ages, by the sixteenth century, the Hippocratic model of the hermaphrodite as the midpoint in a spectrum of possible sexual formations dominates; "The Hermaphrodite and the Orders of Nature," in *Premodern Sexualities*, ed. Louise Fradenburg and Carla Freccero (New York, 1996), pp. 118-22. Daston and Park argue that "once the hermaphrodite came to be seen primarily as a being of intermediate (rather than doubled) sex, it also became emblematic of all kinds of sexual ambiguity, and associated with all practices that appeared to blur or erase the lines between the sexes" (p. 122). Although discussion of the presentation of the hermaphrodite clearly engages many of the anxieties present in the *Liber's* portrait of the "person of both sexes," and although, as Joan Cadden has demonstrated, Hippocratic material was available, though fragmented, in the early Middle Ages, the *Liber* portrait does not allow its readers even the resolution of identification of the

the precise nature of the deception is occluded: the narrator declines to reveal what, below the face and chest, the "person of both sexes ... deceive[s] the ignorant amongst men in the manner of a whore" *with*. Furthermore, what appears to be a stable point of identification, the "more masculine than feminine" appearance is clearly opposed to another, equally manifest, point of identification: the "person of both sexes ... loved feminine occupations." Performance, on the one hand, seems to indicate femininity. The appearance of the body, on the other, seems to indicate masculinity, but only from the waist up. The lower body, site of the deception "in the manner of a whore," and with it the genitals, sites of sexual, bodily difference, is profoundly absent from the text.

In "Thesis III" of his essay, "Monster Culture (Seven Theses)," Jeffrey Jerome Cohen argues that

> [a] refusal to participate in the classifactory "order of things" is true of monsters generally: they are disturbing hybrids whose externally incoherent bodies resist attempts to include them in any systematic structuration. And so the monster is dangerous, a form suspended between forms that threatens to smash distinctions.[13]

Clearly the *Liber's* opening marvel is presented as a "hybrid," a "person of both sexes." Yet this figure "threatens to smash distinctions" less through the power of its hybridity, and the confusion of interpretive categories that hybridity entails, than by its denial of the possibility for confirmation that its *difference* is actual: the portrait refuses to reveal how the marvel is *not* the same in the lower body as required by *either* his masculine face and chest or his feminine performance.

The split between face and chest and lower body is a familiar one, though in different terms, to readers of monster literature of all kinds. We encounter Centaurs, Satyrs, and

"person" *as* a hermaphrodite; Joan Cadden, *Meanings of Sex Difference in the Middle Ages* (Cambridge, 1993), pp. 13-53.

13 Jeffrey Jerome Cohen, "Monster Culture (Seven Theses)," in *Monster Theory*, ed. Jeffrey Jerome Cohen (Minneapolis, 1996), p. 6.

Cynocephali, for example in a wide range of contexts. These figures which blend human and animal obviously embody questions about interpretive categories. That is, these hybrids demand that the reader ask "What is a man?", "What could it mean if there were such a thing as a man from the waist down, and something else from the waist up?" In the monster catalogs these figures are meticulously detailed, as are the interpretive categories by which we read them. As Bruno Roy argues in his reading of Augustine and Isidore the very effort of listing these monstrosities confirms for both reader and writer exactly those interpretive categories which the monsters seem to call into question: cataloguing what can go wrong, what can fall off or be added on to the human body tells us what has not gone wrong, and thus provides reassurance to both reader and writer that we are not ourselves monsters.[14]

Especially given the narrator's insistence that this is the marvel most common and most verifiable, the occlusion of the site of identifying difference in the *Liber* resonates powerfully, because the very representation of its monstrosity denies to its reader the opportunity to separate himself from the marvel. The description of the "person of both sexes" demands that its reader look at the line of demarcation, the point where he can separate himself from what is not "normal" and then forces the reader at once to imagine the difference and to see that, if difference is imaginary, so too is the "normal," the masculine, the human

Like these episodes from the *Liber Monstorum*, the Old English "Wonders" texts problematize any reading of the monster catalogs as ultimately normalizing. As John Friedman points out, "one of the most important characteristics of the Anglo-Saxon Wonders texts and their illustrations is that the [monstrous] races are seen in some sort of relationship to the

[14] Bruno Roy, "En Marge du Monde Connu: Les Races de Monstres," in *Aspects de la marginalité au Moyen Age*, ed. Guy-H. Allard, et al, (Montreal, 1975), pp. 71-80.

viewer, rather than in the isolation of an empty frame."[15] More clearly, he argues that "the demonic energy that the author of the *Liber* sensed about the monstrous races ... is translated from word to picture in the illustrations for the Anglo-Saxon *Mirabilia* texts." Following Otto Pächt, Friedman notes that "figures, in the developing native English manuscript art, begin to step slightly out of the registers which contain them, as though they 'begin to be ejected from the picture.'"[16]

As Friedman argues, the aggressive interaction of the monstrous figure with the frame is clear in the illustration of the Blemmyae in Cotton Tiberius B. v (figure 19). The "Wonders" text describes these monsters as "men without heads who have their eyes and mouth in their chests. They are eight feet tall and eight feet wide."[17] In the illustration, the monster is not only standing with his cleft feet on the bottom of the frame, but also grasping the frame, both inside and out, as if to indicate that, as a border, the frame is purely cosmetic and easily crossed over.

The Vitellius drawings, in contrast to the Tiberius illustrations, are often described as "perhaps deliberately crude."[18] Kenneth Sisam, for example, remarks that the "bad draughtmanship [of the Vitellius illustrations] gives many of them a ludicrous effect," and that "unless he found them in his original, a scribe so incompetent in drawing would hardly have ventured on illustrations" at all.[19] However "incompetent" the

[15] Friedman, *Monstrous Races*, p. 144.

[16] Friedman, *Monstrous Races*, p. 153. Friedman quotes from Otto Pächt, *The Rise of Pictorial Narrative in Twelfth-Century England* (Oxford, 1962), p. 27.

[17] "Đonne is oðer ealand suð fram Brixonte on þam beoð menn akende butan heafdum, þa habbaþ on heora breostum heora eagan ⁊ muð. Hi syndan eahta fota lange ⁊ eahta fota brade," "The Wonders of the East," section 15 (*Pride and Prodigies*, pp. 192-93). Unless otherwise indicated, citations from the "Wonders" will be from Orchard's edition and translation.

[18] Gibb, "Wonders," p. 5.

[19] Kenneth Sisam, *Studies in the History of Old English Literature* (Oxford, 1953), p. 78.

illustrator may have been, the Vitellius illustrations consistently push at the transgressive relationship between text and image, and between image and viewer which are suggested in the other manuscripts of the "Wonders of the East." I have argued elsewhere that the ant-dog illustration in the Vitellius manuscript (fol. 101r) provides the clearest example of the aggressivity with which the monsters in the images of the Vitellius manuscript crawl through the pages. Whereas the illustrations in the Tiberius version are clearly framed and follow the narrative sequence, in the Vitellius illustration the figures are frameless, and even invading the textual space, so that the body of one ant-dog is literally wrapped around the last word of the text, "fleogan."[20] While the text claims that flight from the monstrous ant-dogs is possible for the man who is sufficiently daring and well informed, the image stops the text with the body of the ant-dog, thus suggesting that the movement is not away from but back into the body of the monster.

Although the illustrations in the Vitellius clearly come from a different exemplar than that of the Tiberius manuscript, still, like most of the illustrations in the Tiberius manuscript, the images in the Vitellius manuscript line up closely with the texts, even images like the ant-dogs which invade the textual space. That is, a text which describes men with no heads and their eyes and their mouths on their chests is paired with an illustration of a man with his mouth and eyes on his chest.[21]

[20] Susan M. Kim, "Man-Eating Monsters and Ants as Big as Dogs: The Alienated Language of Cotton Vitellius A. XV," in *Animals and the Symbolic in Mediaeval Art and Literature*, ed. L.A.J.R. Houwen (Groningen, 1997), pp. 39-51.

[21] Wittkower argues that, unlike the Vitellius A. xv illustrations, the Tiberius B. v illustrations may correspond with a different text than the one they accompany in the manuscript. "The specimen of the race with long ears (fol. 83v, Pl. 43a) has his snakelike ears wound round his arms, but the text says that these people 'have ears like winnowing fans; at night they lie on one and cover themselves with the other.' It is obvious that the picture is derived from a different source from the text. The illustration in the British Museum manuscript Vitellius A XV (fol. 104r, Pl. 43b) shows this man, as one expects to find him, with fan-like ears," "Marvels of the East," p. 173.

The most marked exception to this pattern in the Vitellius manuscript occurs in the illustration for the Donestre episode.

Here is a translation of the Old English text:

> ... there is a race of people called among us "Donestre." They are grown like soothsayers from the head to the navel, and the other part is like a human, and they know all human speech. When they see a man of foreign race, they call him and his kinsmen by the name of familiar men, and with deceitful words they seduce him, and they seize him. And after that they eat him entirely except for his head, and then they sit and weep over that head.[22]

In the Tiberius illustration (figure 17), we can easily follow the narrative in a movement from top to bottom. At the top of the illustration, the Donestre speaks to the foreign man, drawing him to approach; below those figures, in a pose of suggestively sexual as well as literally oral aggression, the Donestre eats the man; and, finally at the bottom of the page, the Donestre weeps over the man's head. Although there is no mention of genitalia in the text, the illustrator has obviously read "mannes lice gelic" as not "like the body of a *human*," but as "like the body of a *man*." The genitals of the Donestre are not merely suggested as are those in the Blemmyae illustration (figure 19), but clearly emphasized. In his description of the illustration, Jeffrey Jerome Cohen argues that the Tiberius Donestre is "at first more virile than bestial.... His hands, calves, and chest bulge with muscles. His genitalia, painted a vibrant red, are prominantly displayed. Compared to this hypermasculine body, the traveler's form is thin, stooped, ill propor-

[22] "Đonne is sum ealand on ðære Readan Sæ, þær is moncynn þæt is mid us Donestre genemned, þa syndon geweaxene swa frihteras fram ðan heafde oð ðone nafelan, ⁊ se oðer dæl byð mannes lice gelic. ⁊ hi cunnon eall mennisc gereord. Þonne hi fremdes kynnes mann geseoð, ðonne næmnað hi hine ⁊ his magas cuðra manna naman, ⁊ mid leaslicum wordum hine beswicað, ⁊ him onfoð, ⁊ þænne æfter þan hi hine fretað ealne butan his heafde ⁊ þonne sittað ⁊ wepað ofer ðam heafde," "Wonders," section 20 (*Pride and Prodigies*, p. 196). Here the translation is my own.

tioned."[23] The second stage of the illustration follows the narration closely. The Donestre devours his victim, literally effacing his victim as he covers the victim's formerly expressive face, and swallows his once gesturing hand. As Cohen suggests, "that this combination of violence, eroticism, and transgression is difficult to contain in the illustration is indicated by the Donestre's very human left foot, which steps out of the picture and into the frame — the only part of the illustration to violate the demarcative power of its border."[24] The final scene of the narrative is represented in the far left corner of the illustration, in which the Donestre, shown here only from the waist up, weeps over the head of his victim. The final expressiveness of the monster is reinforced by an open-handed gesture of grief.[25]

In contrast, the Vitellius illustration (figure 18: Donestre) seems mismatched with the text. It shows the dog-headed monster holding up a dismembered leg, which protrudes from the top of the frame.[26] Beside him a woman, her head projecting from the frame, lifts her skirt around her knees. The emphasis on the male genitalia of the monster, however, links the Vitellius illustration if not immediately to the text, at least to the Tiberius image. This emphasis is perhaps even more

[23] Jeffrey Jerome Cohen, *Of Giants: Sex, Monsters, and the Middle Ages*, Medieval Cultures 17 (Minneapolis, 1999), p. 2.

[24] Cohen, *Of Giants*, p. 2.

[25] C. R. Dodwell has recently examined the gestures of the Roman stage and their resonance in Anglo-Saxon visual art. He notes that Roman actors seem to have favored a gesture of grief in which "the curved or flat hand is laid near or to the side of the cheek," and argues that "it is of some significance, then, to see that it is just this way of expressing grief that is used by Anglo-Saxon artists," *Anglo-Saxon Gestures and the Roman Stage*, Cambridge Studies in Anglo-Saxon England 28 (Cambridge, 2000), p. 111.

[26] The dog- or lion-headedness of the Donestre in both the Tiberius and the Vitellius versions of the illustration does not parallel the text in Old English or Latin (Tiberius Old English: "swa frihteras"; Tiberius Latin: "divine"; Vitellius: "swa frifteras"). Friedman discusses a tradition of "naked wise men," *Monstrous Races*, p. 31. This tradition perhaps may have influenced the representation of the Donestre with exposed genitals, although it does not account for the strange heads on the Donestre.

striking given the fact that the Vitellius illustrator consistently portrays monsters with coverings over genitals which are exposed in the Tiberius manuscript. Where the Tiberius monster is exposed, in the Blemmyae illustration (figure 19), for example, the Vitellius monster wears a triangular covering, which, although it emphasizes his crotch, also conceals his genitals (fol. 102v). In the Donestre episode, in contrast, the Vitellius monster, like that in the Tiberius illustration, has his genitals exposed. The figure looks less naked than he does as if he is wearing a sort of garment which is perversely cut away to reveal his genitals. And if the emphasis on his genitals is not sufficient in isolation, the woman, otherwise fairly inexplicably beside him, with her skirt lifted around her knees, provides graphic contrast: the Donestre is not "like a *human*," but like a *man*, and, furthermore, not like *woman*, but like a *man*, at least from the waist down.

While it is of course entirely possible that the exemplar used by the Vitellius illustrator was simply associated with a different text at this point, pairing this illustration with this text must at least have *made sense* to the illustrator. This pairing might have made sense in part because the emphasis on the monster's human, male genitalia in juxtaposition to the figure of the woman characteristically forces the viewer into a position of recognition of, even identity with, rather than difference from, the monster.

The *Liber Monstrorum* also contains a portrait of the Donestre. This portrait occurs fairly late in the narrative, much closer than the "person of both sexes" to the "scaly tales" of the marvellous.[27] Yet the description of the monsters is minimal: "There is a certain race of mixed nature on an island in the Red Sea, who are said to be able to speak the languages of all nations. In this way they astonish people who come from afar, by naming their acquaintances, in order to deceive them, and

[27] It is number 40 of the 56 portraits in Book One.

eat them raw."[28] Only the anthropophagy at the close of the portrait and the "mixed nature" of these creatures marks them as monsters. The Donestre's "mixed nature" in the *Liber* evokes "category crisis"[29] and at the same time blurs the distinction between the most monstrous and "those things which differ by a rather trifling amount from mankind." Like the "person of both sexes," then, the Donestre becomes both familiar and yet fundamentally disruptive. Eating people may seem to be of a different order than having a "mixed nature." Yet, as Jeffrey Jerome Cohen argues, "the material incorporation of one body into the flesh of another, cannibalism condenses a fear of losing the boundary that circumscribes identity and produces discrete subjects."[30] The Donestre's anthropophagy in the *Liber* thus literalizes for the victims in the episode the loss of identifying difference which the portrait of the "person of both sexes" produces for its reader, and which the introduction of the female figure in the illustration for Vitellius "Wonders" may produce for its viewers.

In the Donestre episode in both the *Liber* and the "Wonders" texts the human victims are vulnerable to the monster's seduction and "deceit" not only as the result of a bodily conflation or confusion, but also because they respond to the names of "familiar kinsmen": they are summoned through language they recognize, even though the names are "familiar" but not their own.[31] In both textual episodes, the victims of deceit are vulnerable to it because they claim identity when difference is manifest. The exposed genitals in the Vitellius Donestre illustration, however, turn the terms of the textual presentation

[28] "Est gens aliqua commixtae naturae in Rubri maris insula quam linguis omnium nationum loqui posse testantur. Et ideo homines de longinquo uenientes, eorum cognitas nominando, adtonitos faciunt, ut decipiant et crudos deuorent," I.40 (*Pride and Prodigies*, pp. 280-81).

[29] Cohen, "Monster Culture," p. 6.

[30] Cohen, *Of Giants*, p. 2.

[31] The sirens in the *Liber*, similarly, "deceive sailors with the outstanding beauty of their appearance ..." ("nauigantes pulcherrima forma et cantu dulcedinis decipiunt"), I. 6 (*Pride and Prodigies*, pp. 262-63).

in the "Wonders," much as does the allusion to the "person of both sexes" in the "mixed nature" of the *Liber* Donestre. If, as the exposed genitals seem to demand, we identify the monster as a *man* from the waist down, we separate out man from monster: we disallow "category crisis": we draw a frame around the monstrous with clear lines of demarcation, "from the head to the navel" and "from the waist down." Geffrey Galt Harpham explains that in the apprehension of the grotesque, readers and viewers fragment the image in order to place it in understandable categories. He suggests that such images

> are grotesque not because they are hideous ... but because, in the midst of an overwhelming impression of monstrousness there is much we can recognize, much corrupted or shuffled familiarity. Knotting the alien whole with more or less familiar parts, these creatures simultaneously invoke and repudiate our conventional, language-based categories. Perceiving them in bits, the mind moves toward a level of detail at which those categories are adequate, at which we can say for certain, "This is an ear," "This is a claw," etc.[32]

Consistently, the "Wonders" illustrations will not allow for the kind of sorting which, by genre, they seem to warrant. Like Harpham's grotesque, as they thus "invoke" and identify differences — differences of gender, of species, of language — they invalidate those distinctions. One way of approaching the Vitellius Donestre illustration without dismissing it as simply misplaced or "incompetent" is to suggest that an illustration that appears to be a gesture providing evidence of additional

[32] Harpham, *On the Grotesque*, p. 5. Campbell argues that the monsters of the "Wonders" cannot be defined as grotesque in Harpham's terms because they are not constructed as art, that is, with the intent of evoking the grotesque: "Harpham tends to avoid the issue of intentionality, positing the grotesque as a type of experience rather than a type of artifact. From this angle, something actual or 'natural' is just as capable as anything else of being grotesque. But that he is somewhat queasy about this position can been seen in the fact that he refers in his study only to works of art, and 'high' art at that," *The Witness and the Other World*, p. 61.

difference — the monster is like a man, not like a woman — ultimately insists on the destabilization of that line of demarcation.

I would like to return one last time to the Tiberius Blemmyae (figure 19) and to note that the very effort of representing the Blemmyae as a man without a head draws the head on the monster, including the chin, the ears, and even the crown of the head. In representing the *absence* of the head, the illustrator has exactly *presented* the head. The representation of the monster's *difference*, in the illustration, outlines its *sameness*, its recognizability, not as a monster, but as a man.

Michael Camille has argued that "during the Middle Ages the edges of the known world were at the same time the limits of representation."[33] What is, in the "Wonders" texts, "the East," and what in the *Liber Monstrorum* is called the "hidden" parts of the world, also marks the limits of representation, and, hence, for their readers, of knowability at all.[34] It is not insignificant that the Donestre are the only monsters in the "Wonders" catalog who "know human speech." These are monsters whose facility with human systems of representation is integral to their

[33] Michael Camille, *Image on the Edge: The Margins of Medieval Art* (Cambridge, 1992), p. 15.

[34] The Prologue to the *Liber* opens, for example, with the following: "You have asked about the secret arrangement [or 'filthiness'] of the lands of the earth, and if as many kinds of monsters are to be credited as are demonstrated *in the hidden parts* [or 'births'] of the world, raised throughout the deserts and the islands of the Ocean and in the recesses of the farthest mountains ..." ("De occulto orbis terrarum situ interrogasti et si tanta monstrorum essent genera credenda quanta in abditis mundi partibus per deserta et Oceani insulas et in ultimorum montium latebris nutrita monstrantur ...", *Pride and Prodigies*, pp. 254-55, my italics). Alexander, in the Old English "Letter of Alexander to Aristotle" which is bound with the "Wonders" in the Vitellius A. xv manuscript, pursues the "hidden" in his travels: "And then I wished to make a trip through the left-hand region of India, in case anything in that land had been hidden or concealed from me" ("On ic þa ða wynstran dælas Indie wolde geondferan þy læs me owiht in þæm londe beholen oððe bedegled wære"), section 26, as edited and translated by Orchard in *Pride and Prodigies*, pp. 242-43.

efficacy against men. Their facility suggests that the linguistic identity claimed by men as *reordberend*, "speechbearers," is never inalienable:[35] on the contrary, it characterizes monsters as well as men. The illustration's juxtaposition of the male monster's genitals with the female figure's gesture of simultaneous concealment and exposure pushes at this suggestion because it poses as the site of identifying difference, the male and female genitals, a difference, following Galenic models, which is not in kind but merely in visibility.

In *Making Sex*, Thomas Laqueur cites Galen: "Turn outward the woman's, turn inward, so to speak, and fold double the man's [genital organs], and you will find the same in both in every respect."[36] Laqueur provides as one explanation for the persistent survival of this model the argument that "in a public world that was overwhelmingly male, the one-sex model displayed what was already massively evident in culture more generally: man is the measure of all things, and *woman does not exist as an ontologically distinct category*."[37] Reading the representation of the Donestre in the Vitellius illustration as that of a *man*, at least from the waist down, establishes the clear difference, the line of demarcation, by the framing of the monstrous as *not a man* from the waist up, and a *man* from the waist down. However, the emphasis on this difference, effected through the juxtaposition with the woman, removes that clear boundary, because the supplemental identifiable point of difference, the difference between man and woman is not a difference in kind, but merely of visibility. Furthermore, if, for the medieval viewer, the woman's genitals are not "other" but inverted and *hidden*

[35] "Reordberend," as it is used in line 3 of "The Dream of the Rood," for example, is clearly a synonym for "man"; "The Dream of the Rood" in *The Vercelli Book*, ed. George Philip Krapp, The Anglo-Saxon Poetic Records 2 (New York, 1932), pp. 61-66.

[36] Thomas Laqueur, *Making Sex: Body and Gender from the Greeks to Freud* (Cambridge, 1990), p. 25.

[37] Laqueur, *Making Sex*, p. 62 (my italics).

versions of the male's, the Vitellius Donestre illustration, like the ant-dog representation, reverses any normalizing trajectory for the monster catalog: if the illustration represents reassuring difference from the monster, at the same time its emphatic representation collapses and conceals that identifying difference.

The dominance of Galenic models of genital identity in philosophical and medical thinking, or in visual art of this period is not by any means indisputable. Joan Cadden has demonstrated, in explicit response to Laqueur, that medieval scholars incorporate a number of often contradictory ancient models, those represented by Hippocrates, Aristotle, and Soranus as well as Galen, even if those models are not always directly accessible to them.[38] Michael Camille has argued, against Laqueur specifically, that by the late medieval period, artists follow a tradition of consistently representing men's and women's bodies, including their genitals, *differently*.[39] Yet the very availability of other philosophical, medical, and artistic models underscores the illustration's emphasis here. Even if we do not pose an explicit Galenic model for the woman's genitalia, the Vitellius illustration, with the woman's contradictory gesture of exposure *and* concealment underscores the emphasis on the "hidden," and thus the illustration's power: with the

[38] "Though there is much evidence in the present study that fits his 'one sex' model, medieval views on the status of the uterus and the opinions of medieval physiognomers about male and female traits suggests evidence of other models not reducible to Laqueur's," *Meanings of Sex Difference*, p. 3. See also pp. 13-53.

[39] "Attempts by modern historians to diminish differences between the medieval conception of male and female bodies is best exemplified by Thomas Laquer who argues that during the Middle Ages a 'one sex model' existed.... But artists clearly distinguished the dangerous female body as different from the more important but also more vulnerable male one, in everything from the scene of the Last Judgement at Bourges, where it is the very voluptuousness of the woman's body that consigns it to the flames, to the horrendous Romanesque luxuria ... whose sexual organs are engorged by the fetishistic phallus of her own desire," Michael Camille, "The Image and the Self: Unwriting Late Medieval Bodies," in *Framing Medieval Bodies*, ed. Sarah Kay and Miri Rubin (Manchester, 1994): pp. 62-99, at 80.

same gesture, the figure of the woman acts as a supplemental point of identifying difference, and insists on the concealing of exactly that point of difference.

The *Liber Monstrorum* promises the reader a journey into the "hidden parts of the world." To send its reader on that journey, from the very beginning, the *Liber Monstrorum* must elide *not* the difference, but the lack thereof, which would render its monsters unrepresentable. Hence it presents the "person of both sexes" as a man from the waist up, but carefully conceals whatever s/he "deceive[s] the ignorant among men" *with*. What the Vitellius Donestre illustration then exposes is that the journey into the hidden world of these monsters folds in on itself: these monsters seduce us and tear us apart not because of their terrifying alterity, but because we recognize them, and in recognizing them we expose their difference as our necessity, because their sameness reveals the limitation of our systems for representation, for interpretation, for coherence, and, hence, we expose the anxiety and desire which compel us to make and to read them, again and again.

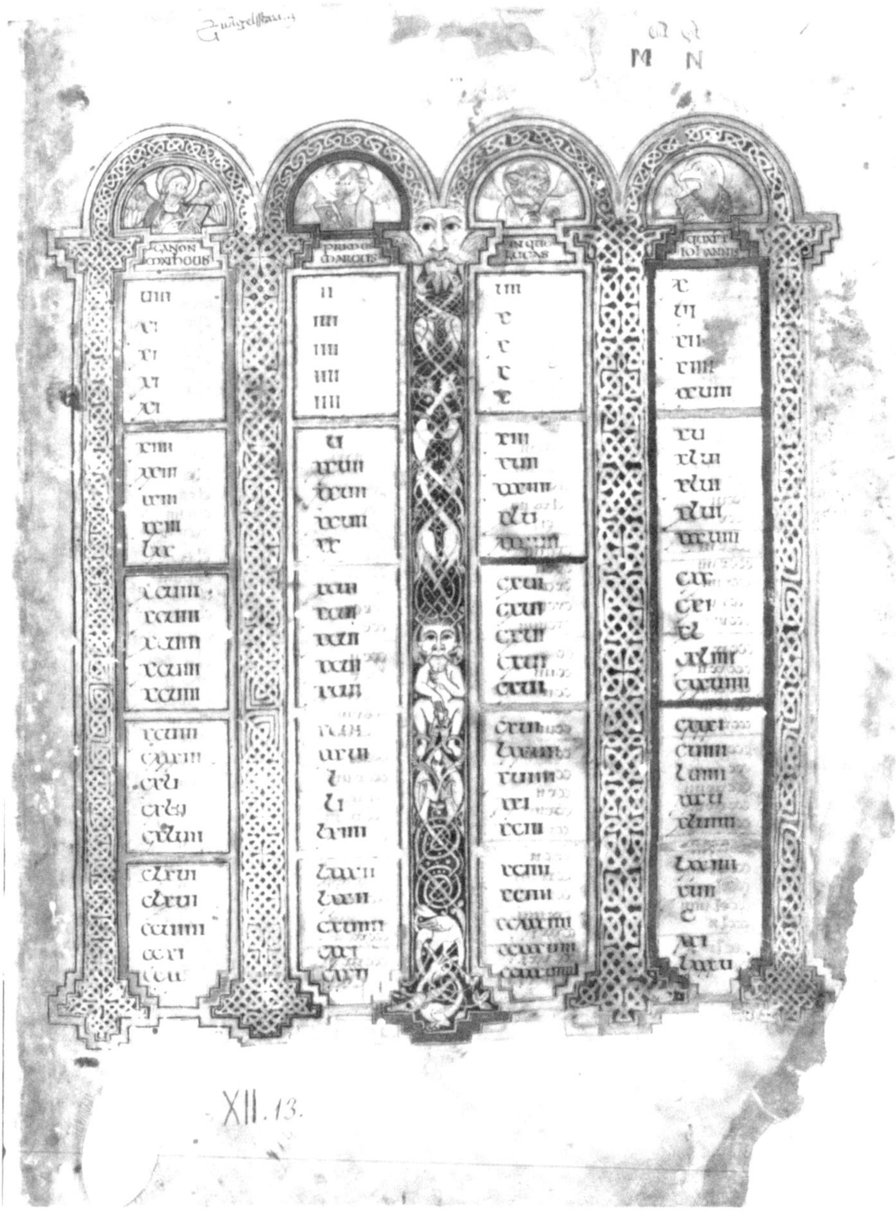

Figure 1. Vatican, Biblioteca Apostolica, Barberini lat. 570, fol. 1 (Barberini Gospels): figure in canon tables. [*Copyright Biblioteca Apostolica Vaticana*]

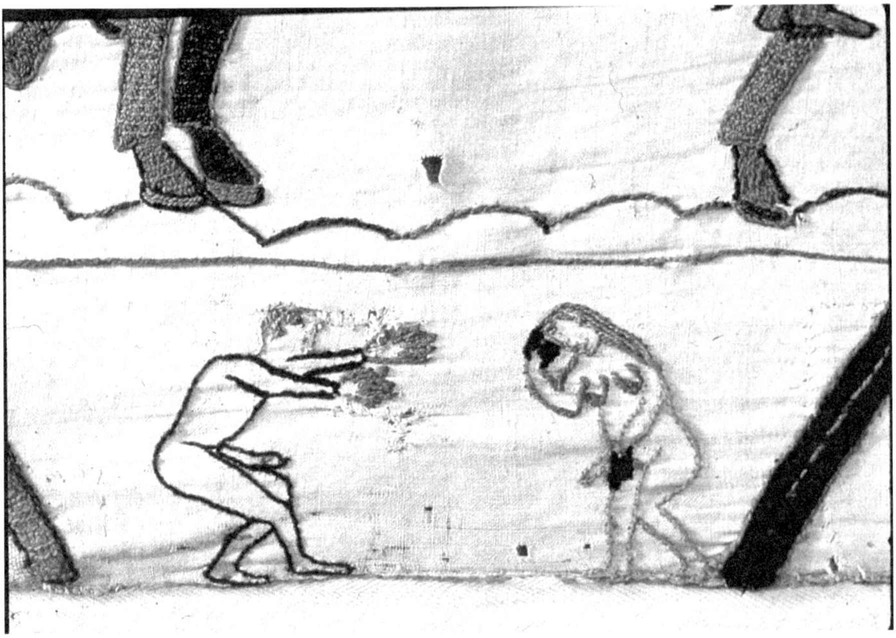

Figure 2. Bayeux Tapestry: nude male and female [*By special permission of the City of Bayeux* ]

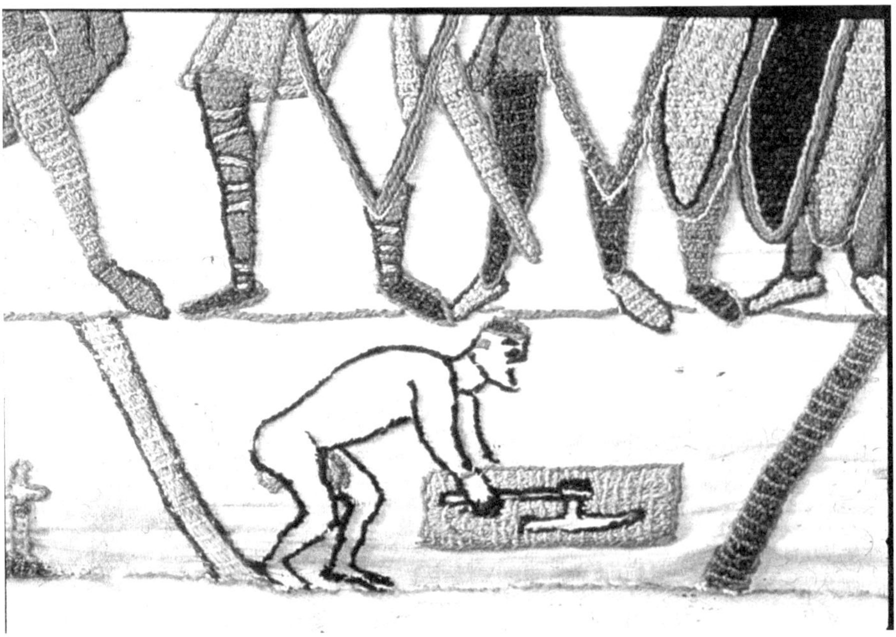

Figure 3. Bayeux Tapestry: nude male with board and axe. Bayeux, Musée de la Tapisserie (photo: Erich Lessing/Art Resource, NY)

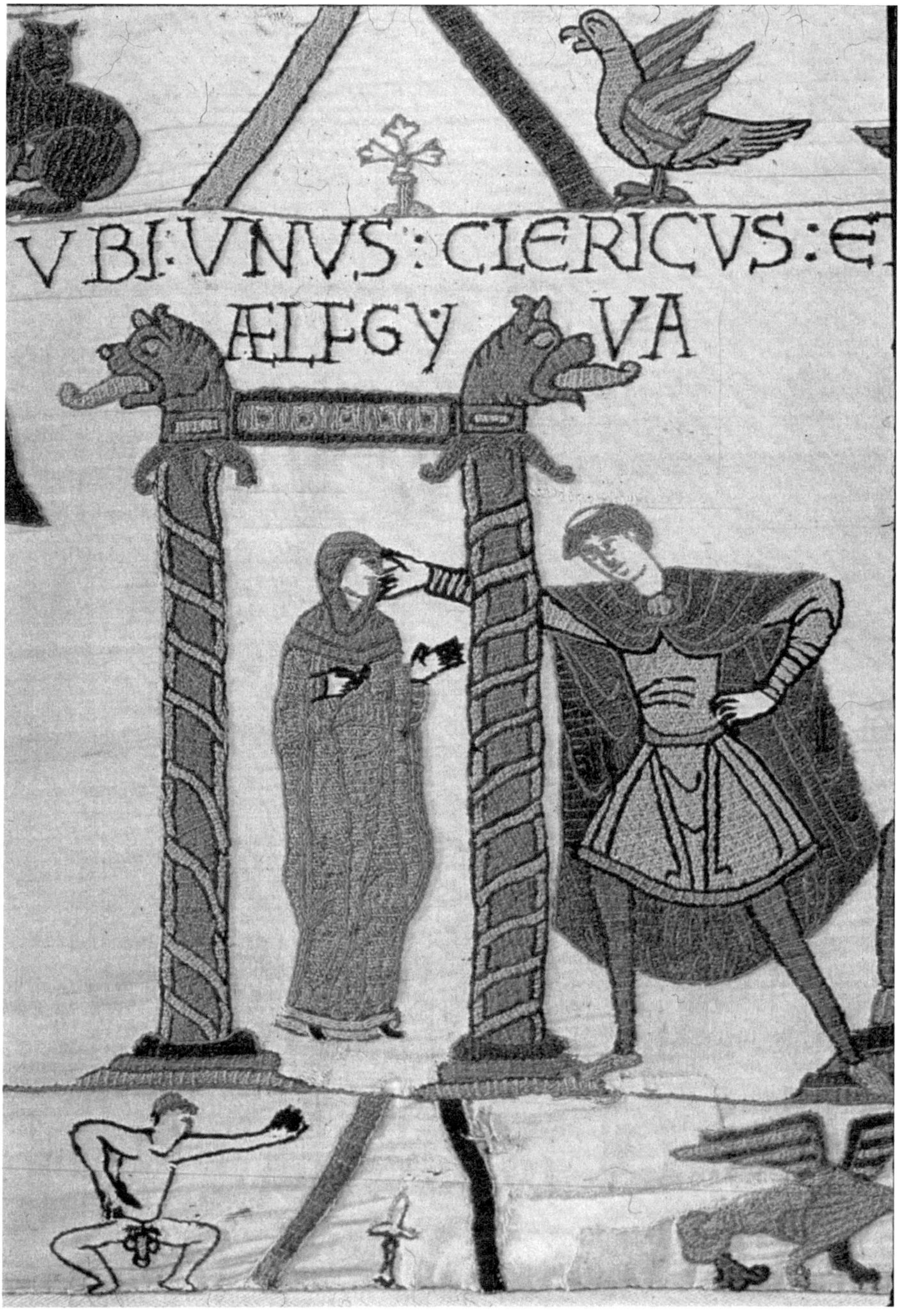


Figure 4. Bayeux Tapestry: nude male. Bayeux, Musée de la Tapisserie (photo: Erich Lessing/Art Resource, NY)

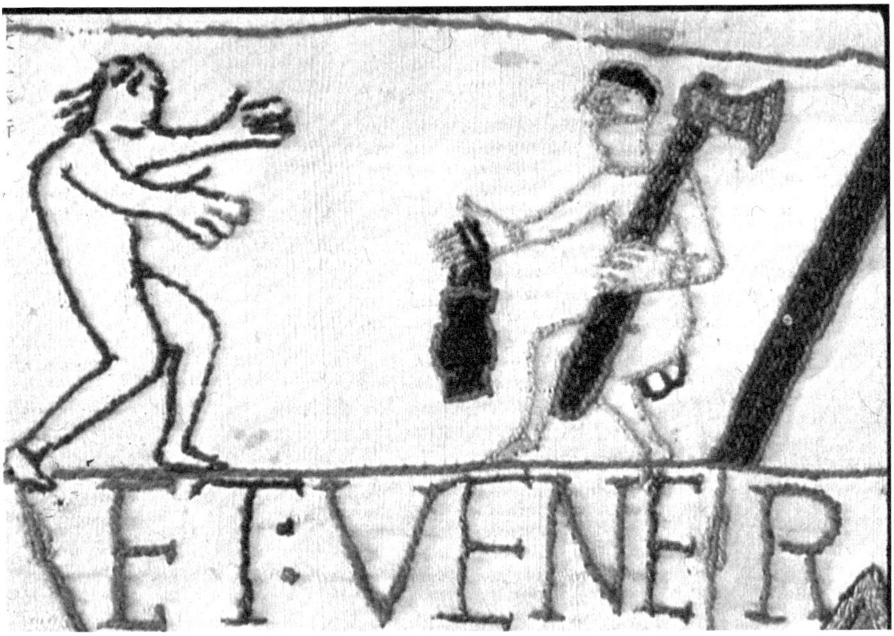


Figure 5. Bayeux Tapestry: nude male and female. Bayeux, Musée de la Tapisserie (photo: Erich Lessing/Art Resource, NY)

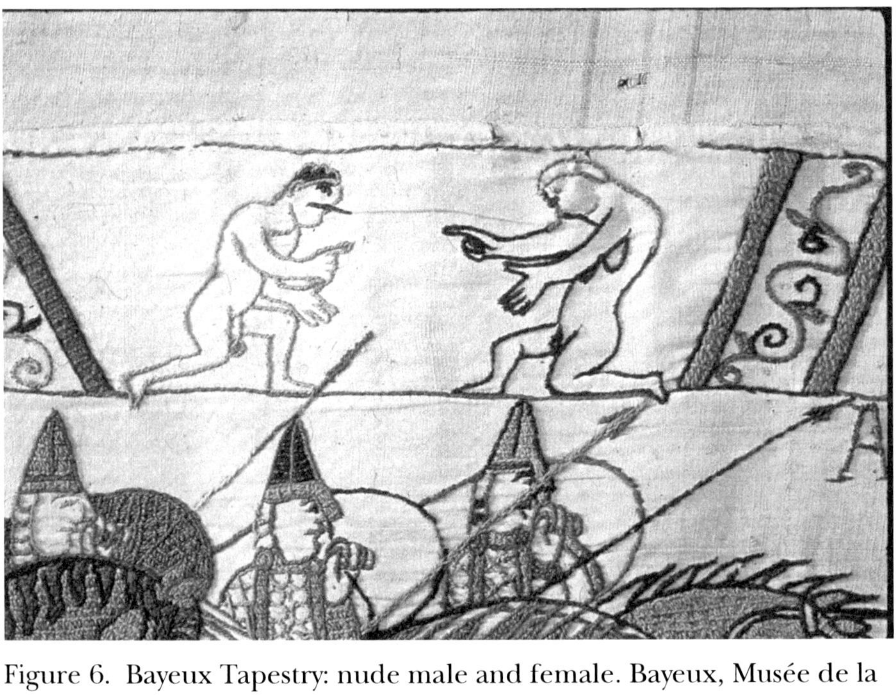

Figure 6. Bayeux Tapestry: nude male and female. Bayeux, Musée de la Tapisserie (photo: Erich Lessing/Art Resource, NY)

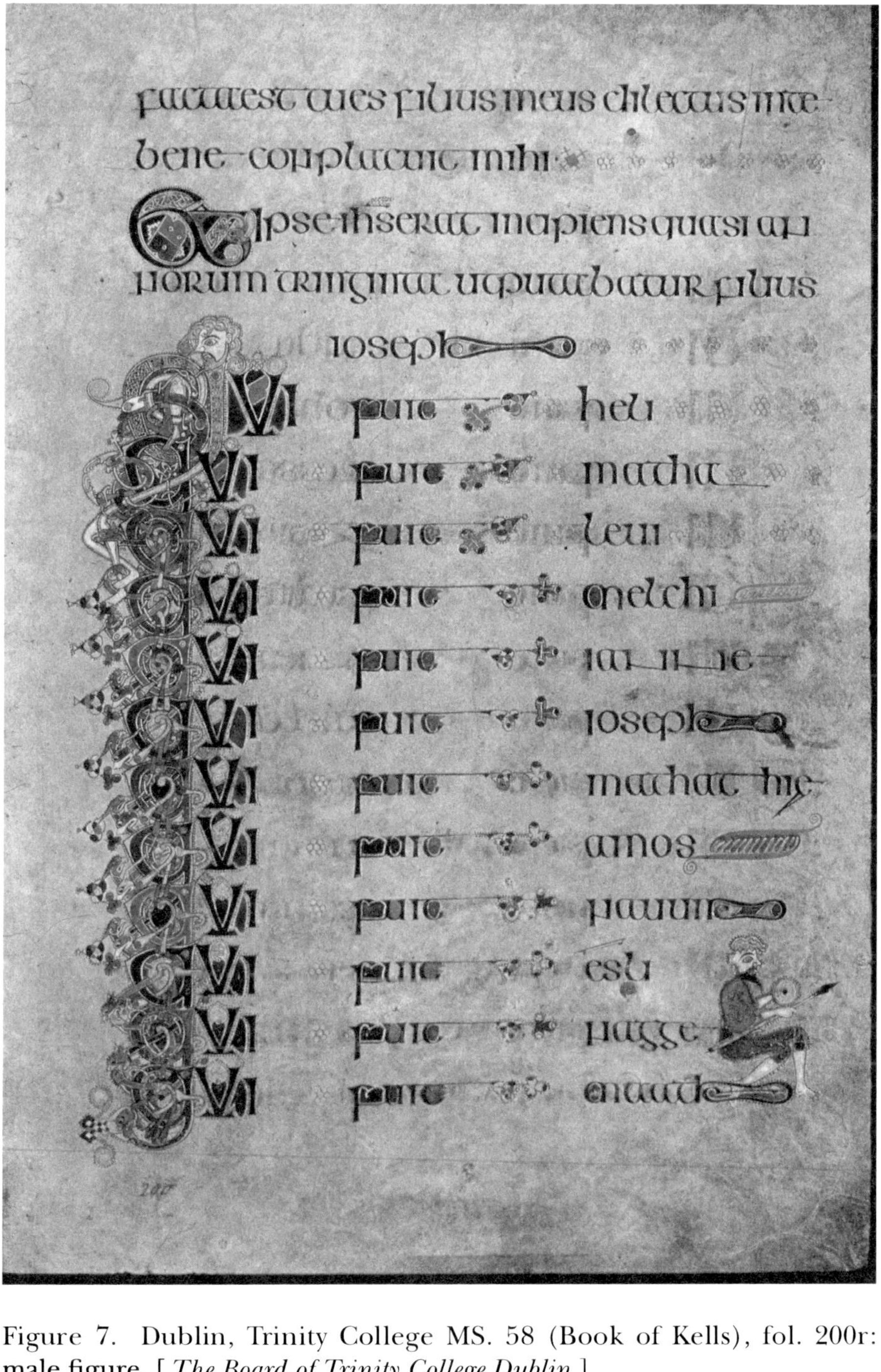

Figure 7. Dublin, Trinity College MS. 58 (Book of Kells), fol. 200r: male figure. [ *The Board of Trinity College Dublin* ]

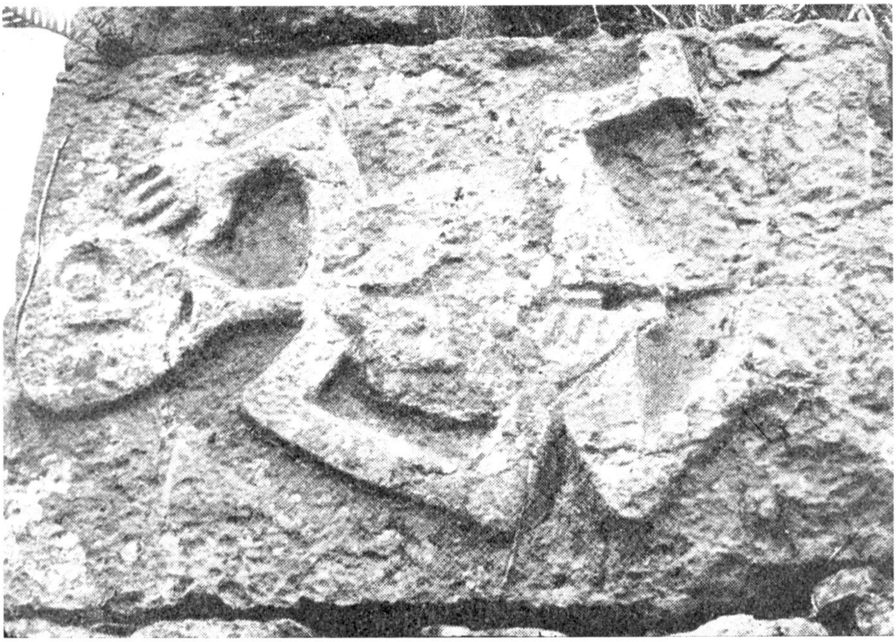

Figure 8. Kiltinane Church: sheela-na-gig relief (photo: Anthony Weir)

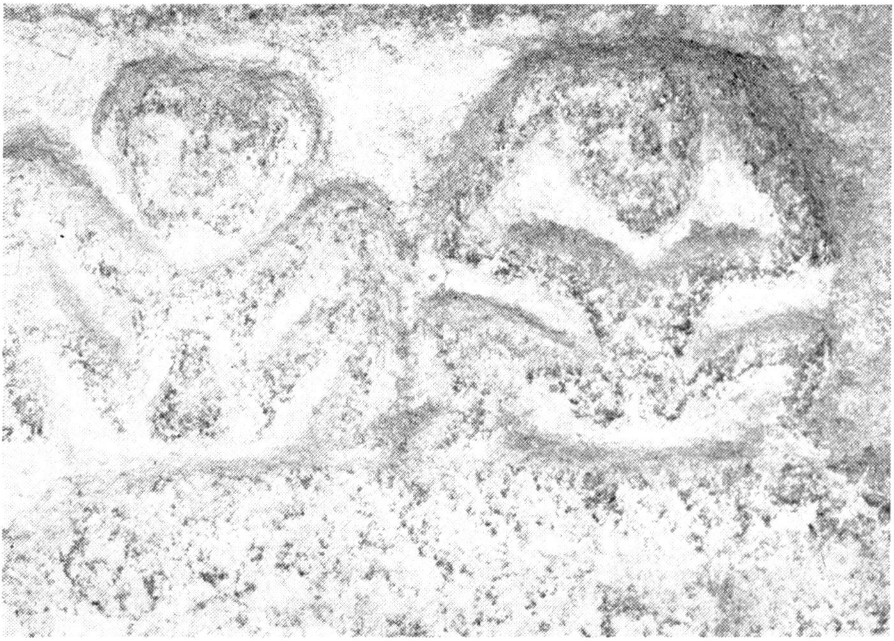

Figure 9. Loctudy, Brittany: exhibiting couple

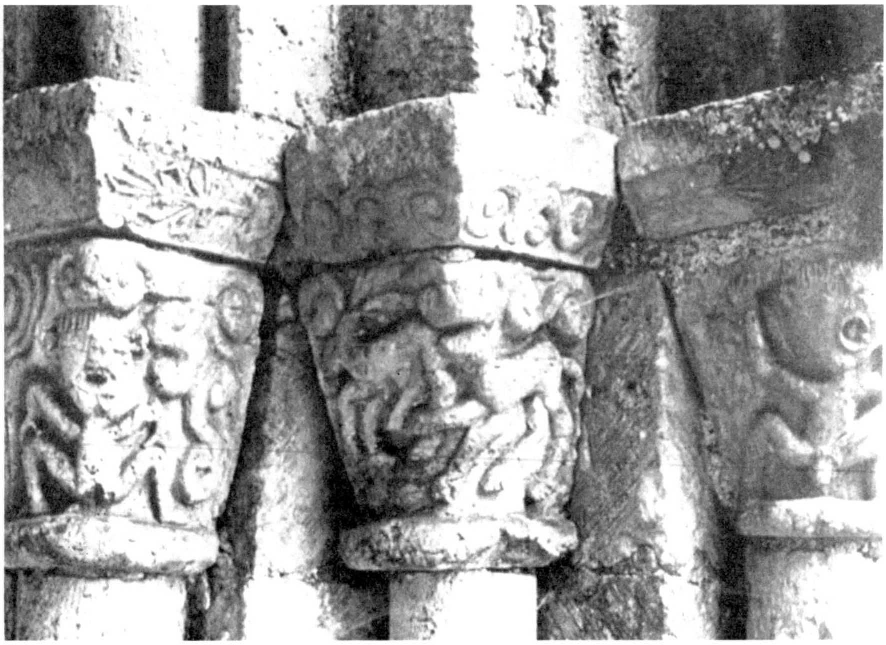

Figure 10. Saint-Front-sur-Nizonne: exhibiting couple (photo: Anthony Weir)

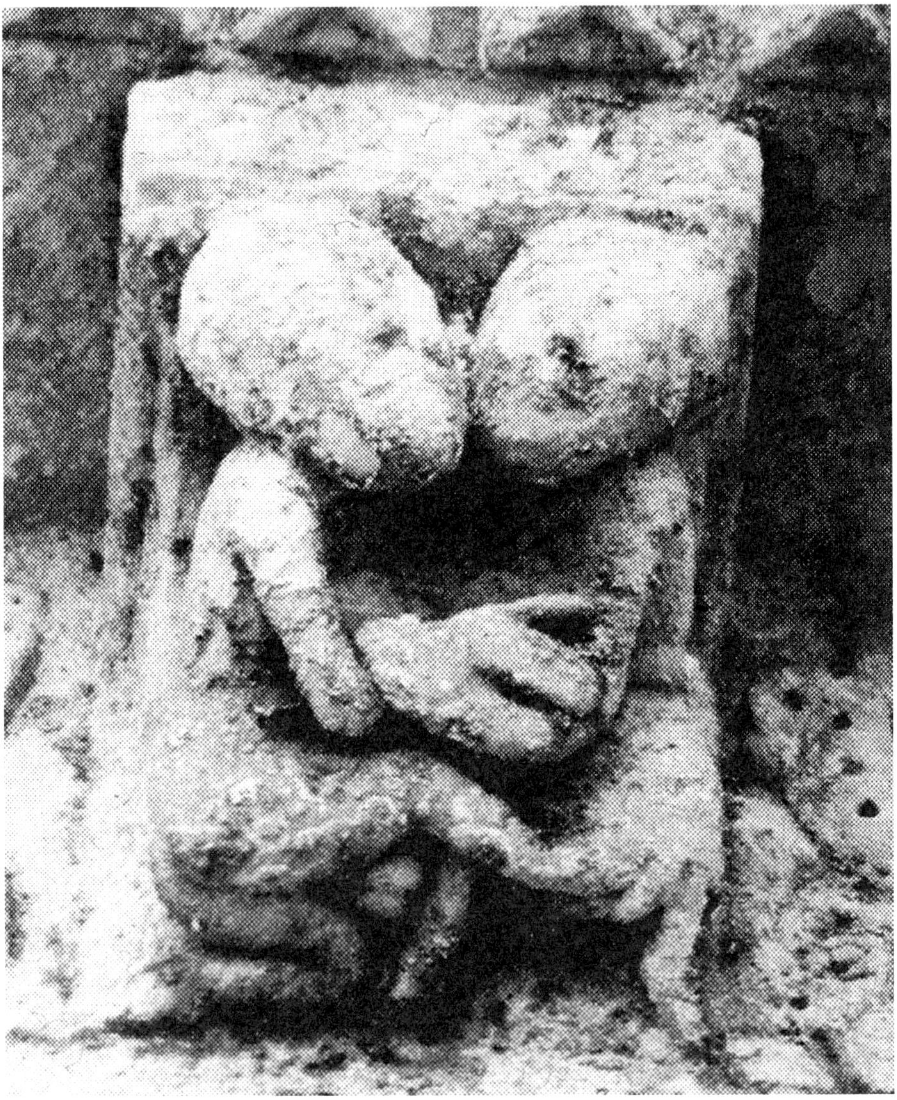

Figure 11. Marignac, St. Supice: embracing couple (photo: Benjamin and Nurith Kedar Archives)

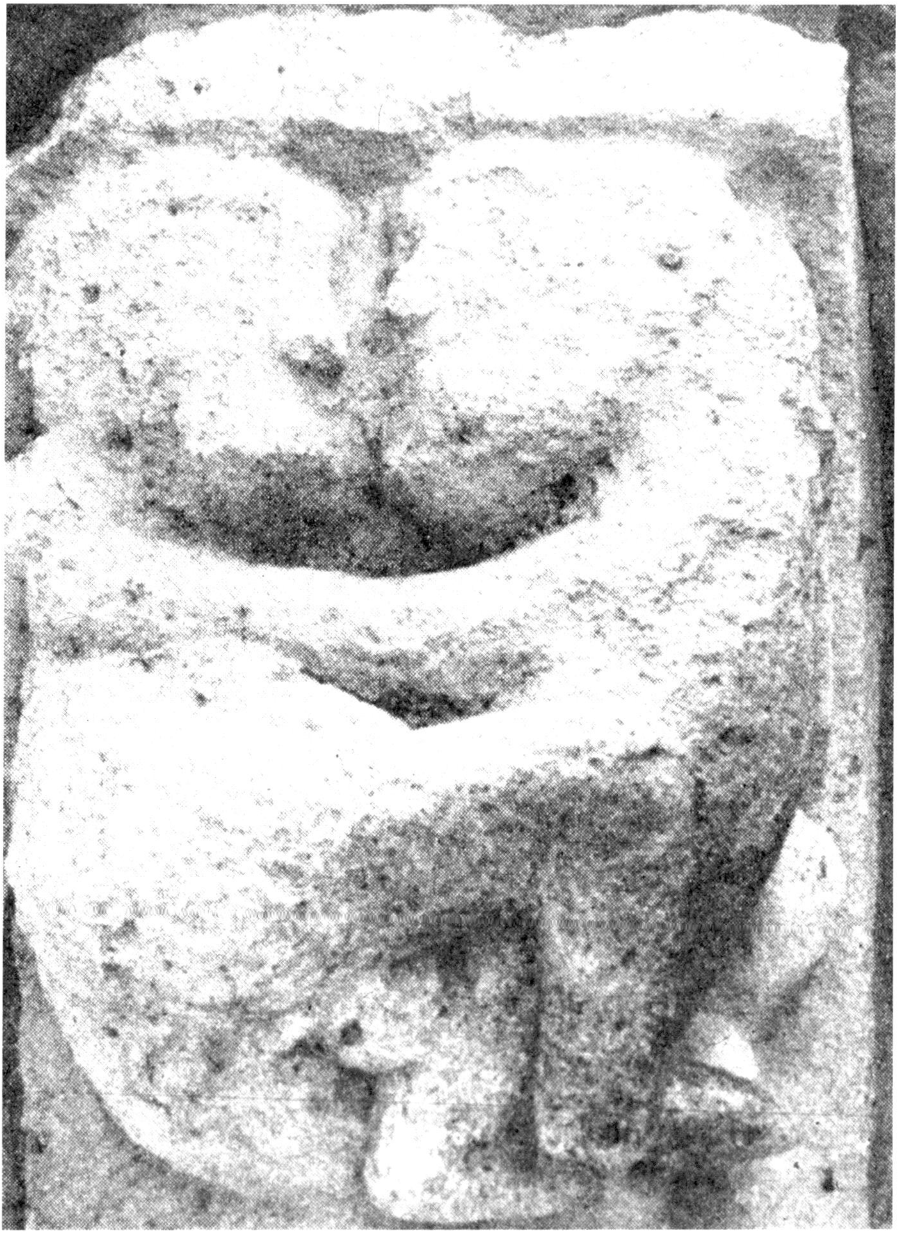

Figure 12. Champagnolles: embracing couple

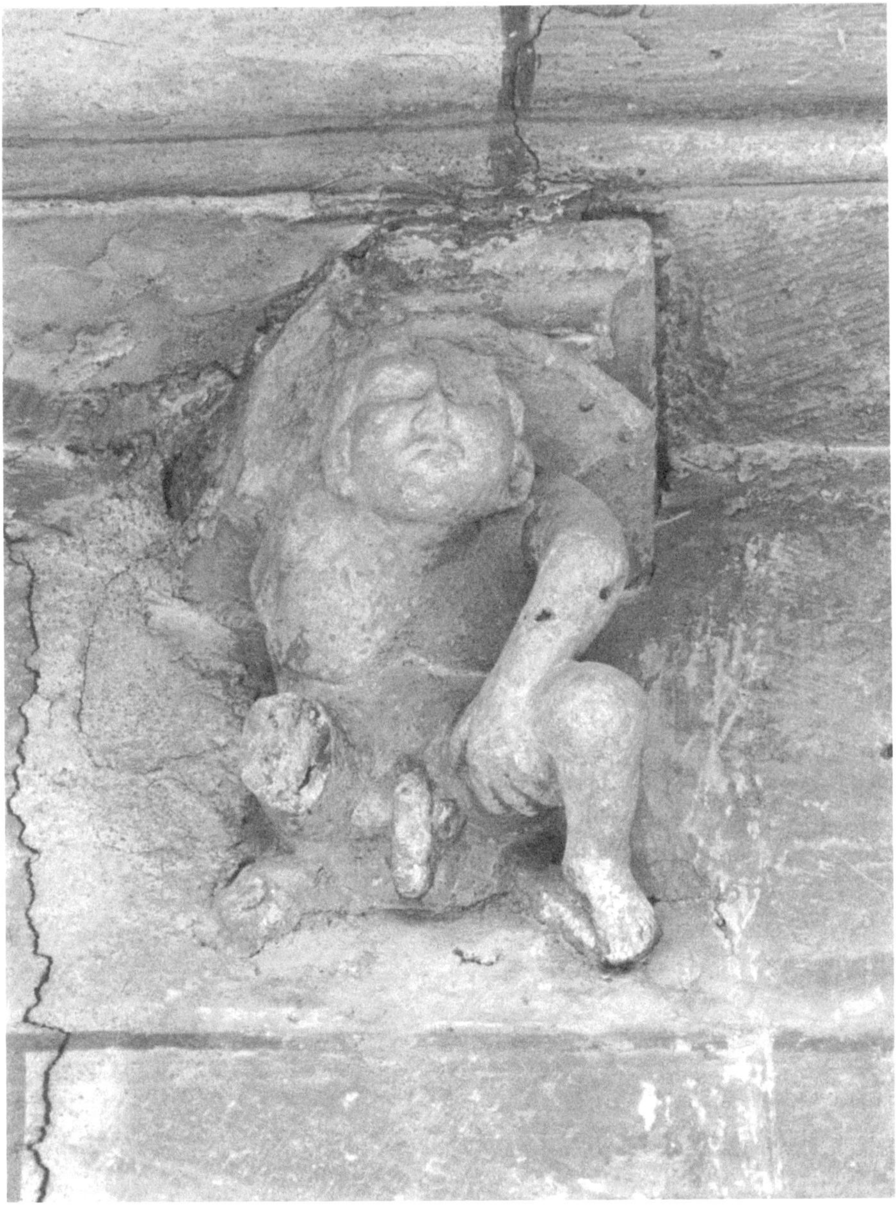

Figure 13. Poitiers, Sainte-Radegonde: male exhibitionist (photo: James Austin)

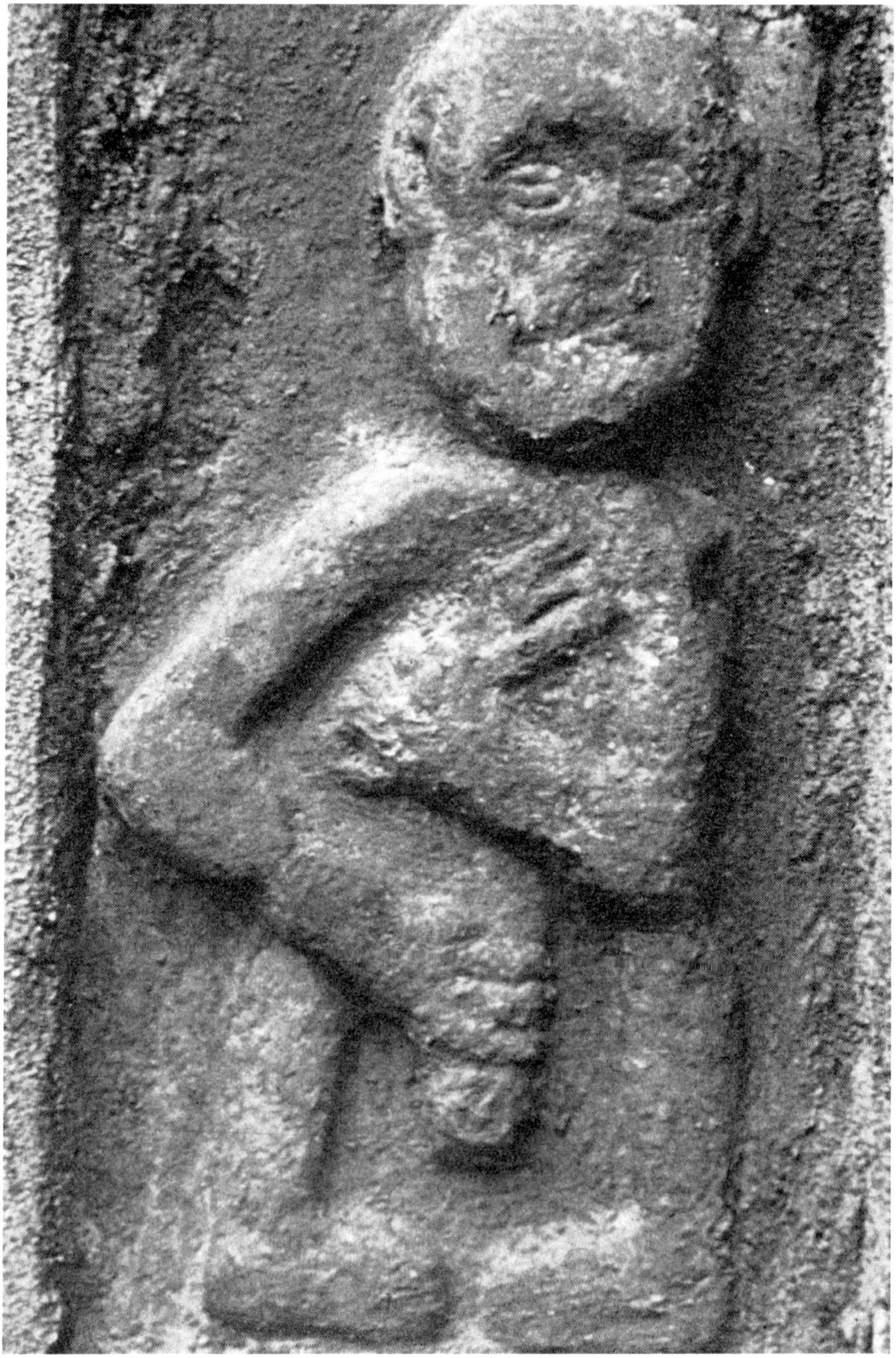

Figure 14. Ballycloghduff: male exhibitionist

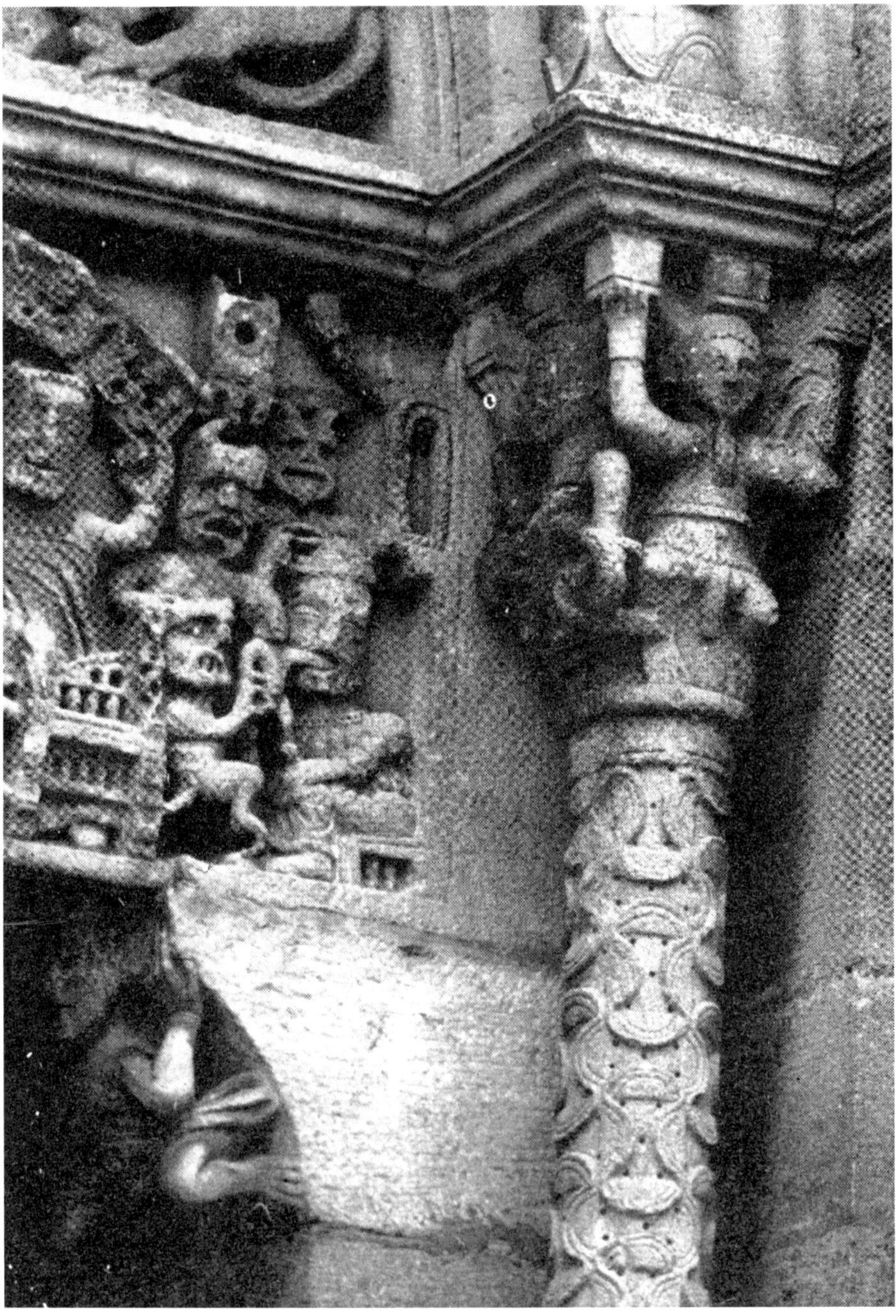

Figure 15. Semur-en-Brionnais: exhibitionist atlas figure (photo: Anthony Weir)

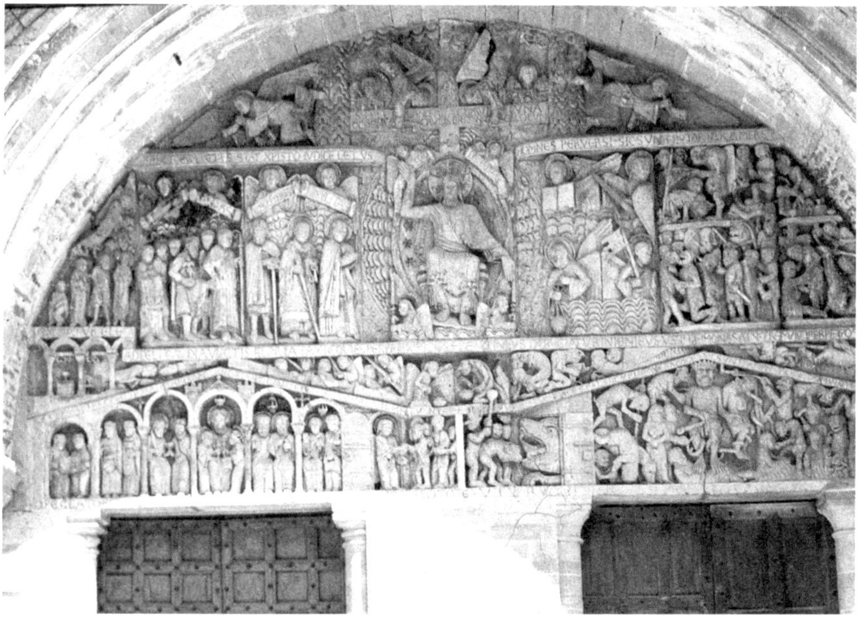

Figure 16. Conques, Sainte-Foi, west portal tympanum: Last Judgment

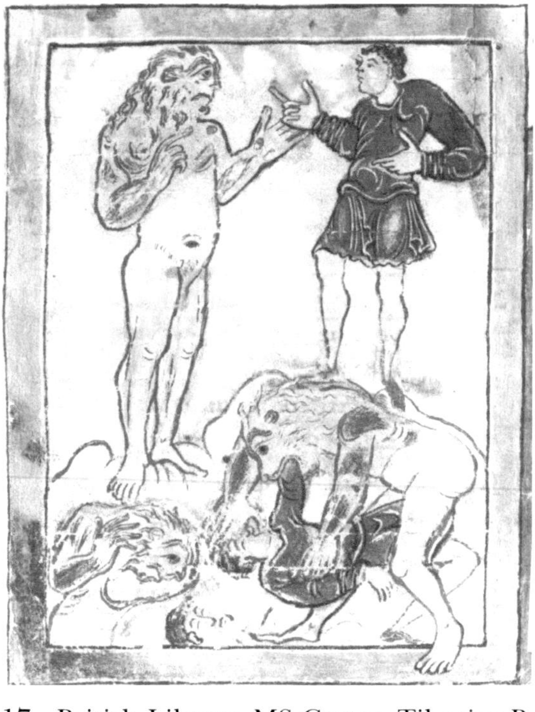

Figure 17. British Library, MS Cotton Tiberius B. v, fol. 83v: Donestre. [*By permission of the British Library*]

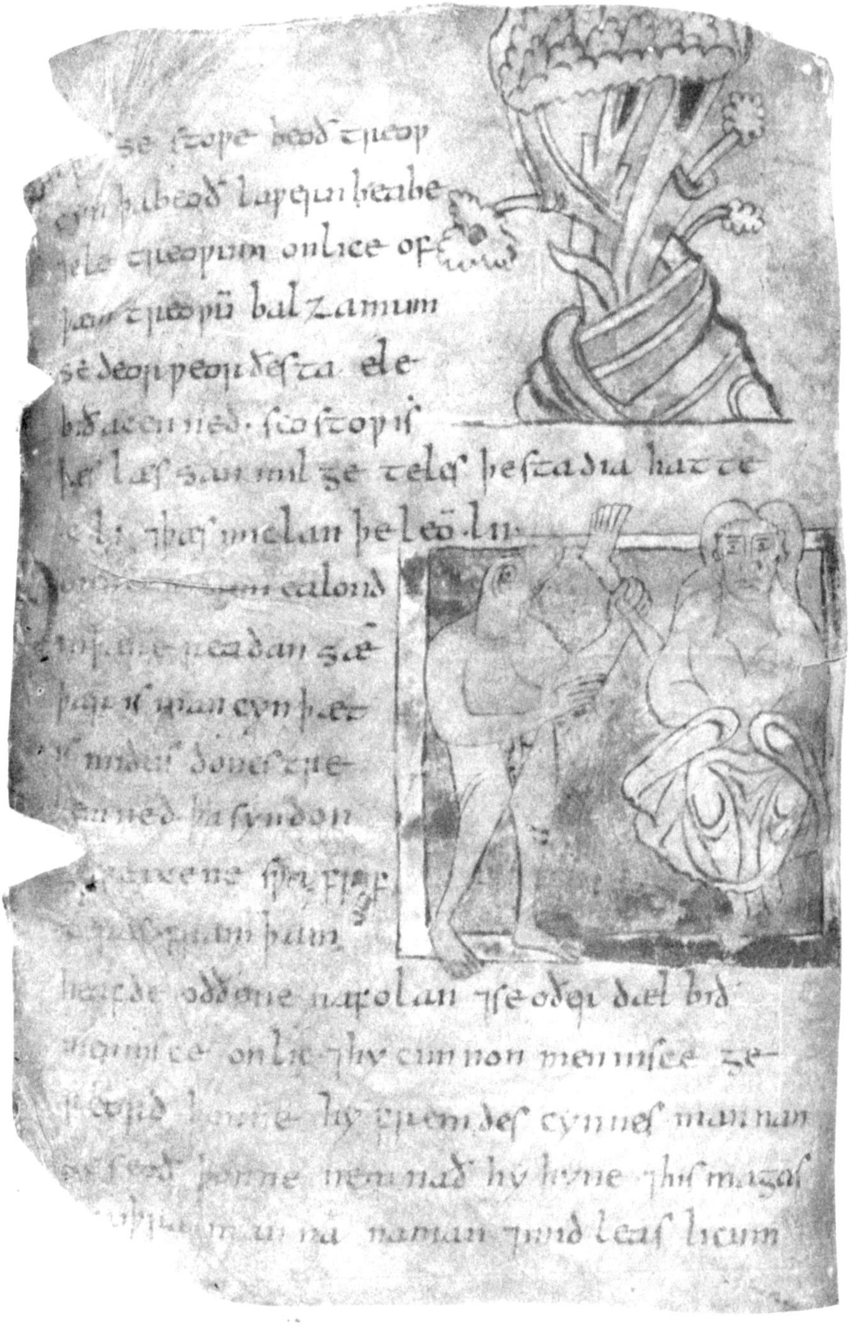

Figure 18. British Library, MS Cotton Vitellius A. xv, fol. 103v: (lower) Donestre. [*By permission of the British Library*]

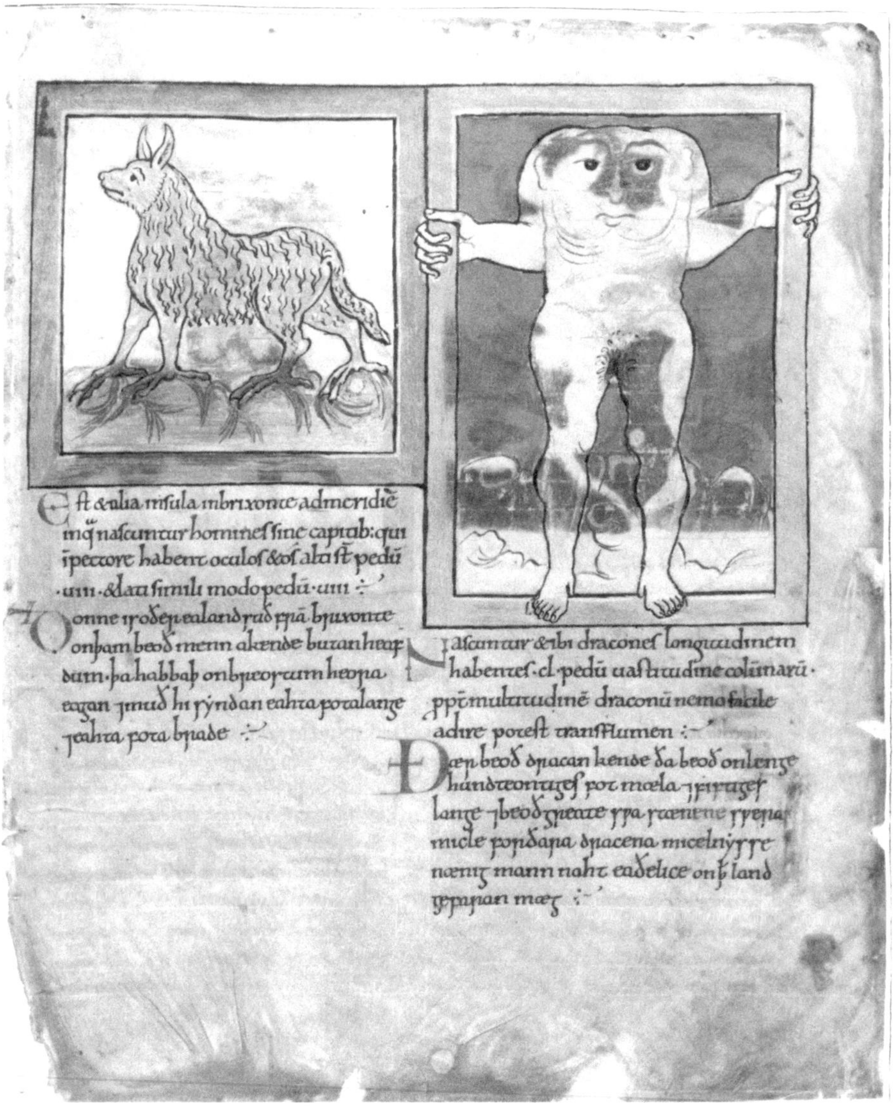

Figure 19. British Library, MS Cotton Tiberius B. v, fol. 82r: Blemmyae. [*By permission of the British Library*]

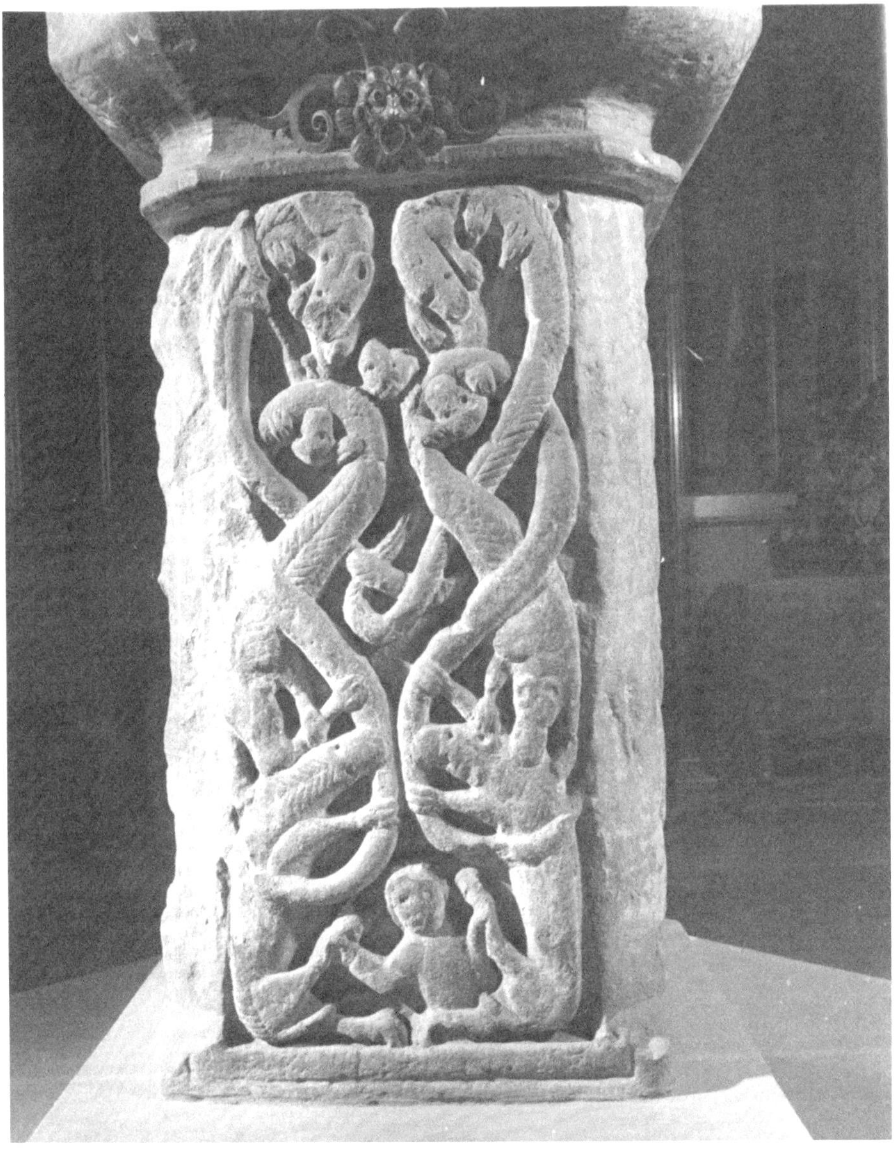

Figure 20. The Rothbury Cross Shaft, base: hell scene. [*Copyright Department of Archaeology, University of Durham. Photographer T. Middlemass*]

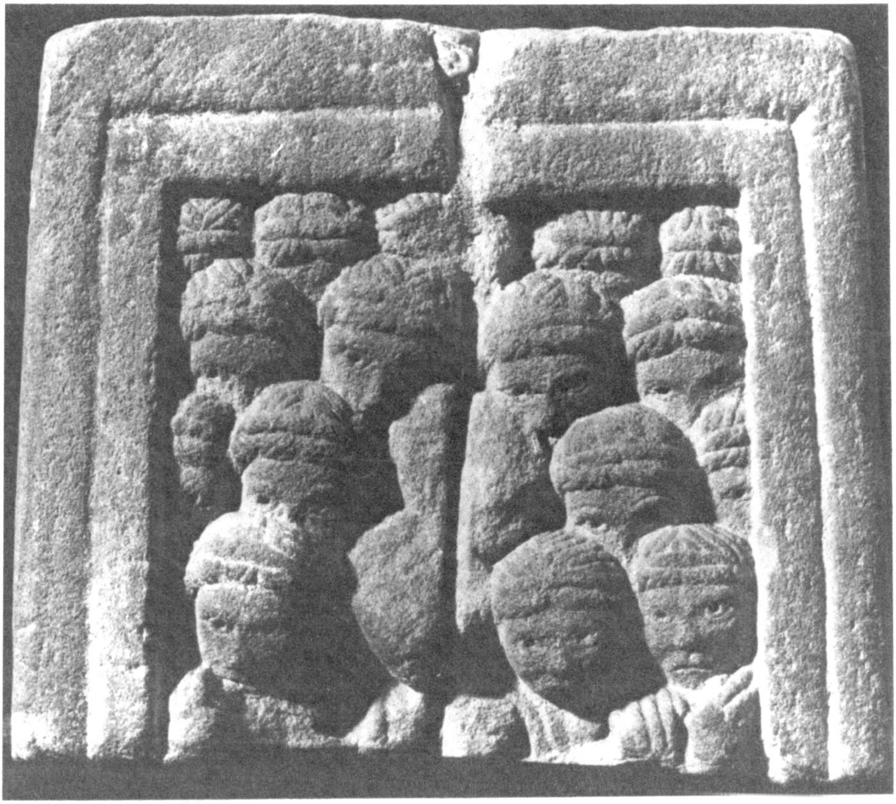

Figure 21. The Rothbury Cross Shaft, top: group of figures [*Copyright Department of Archæology, University of Durham. Photographer T. Middlemass*]

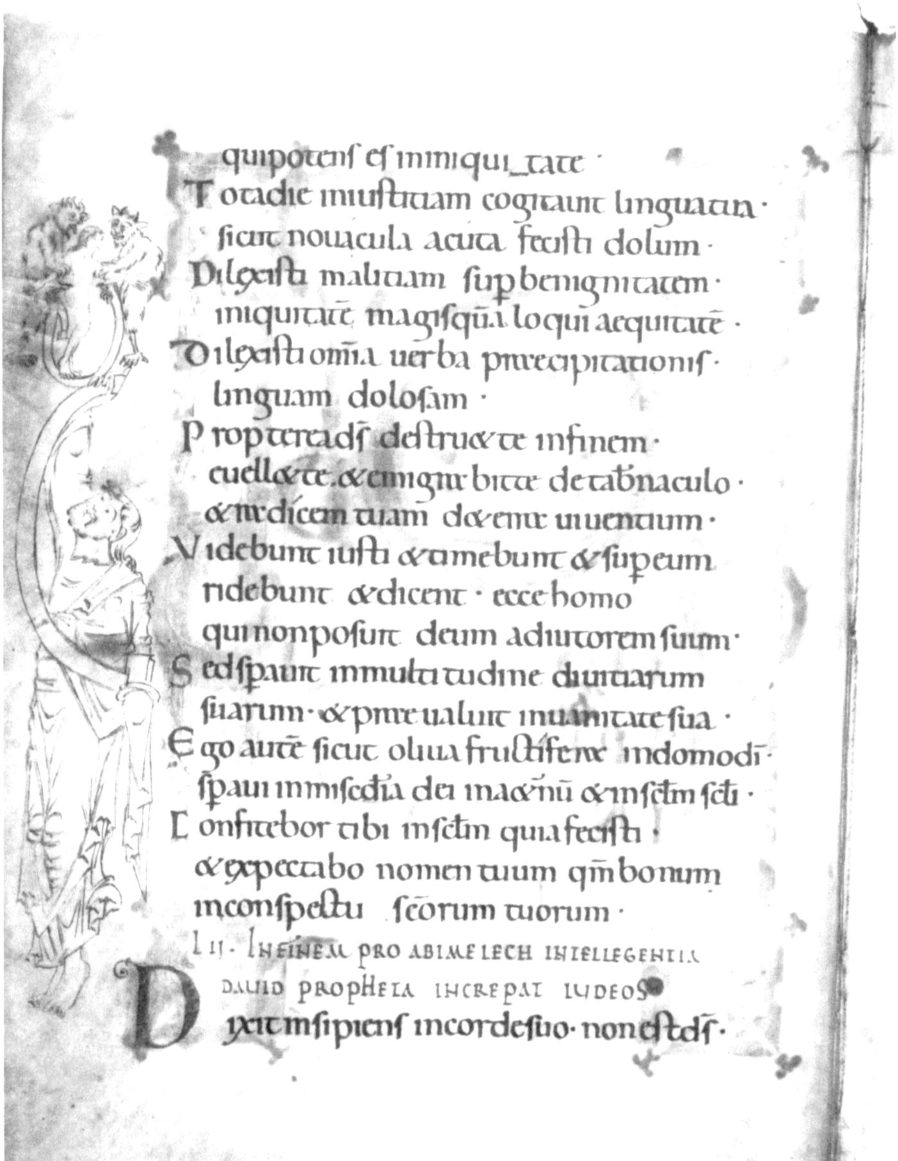

Figure 22. Vatican, Biblioteca Apostolica, Reg. lat. 12 (Bury Psalter), fol. 62v: Psalm 51. [*Copyright Biblioteca Apostolica Vaticana*]

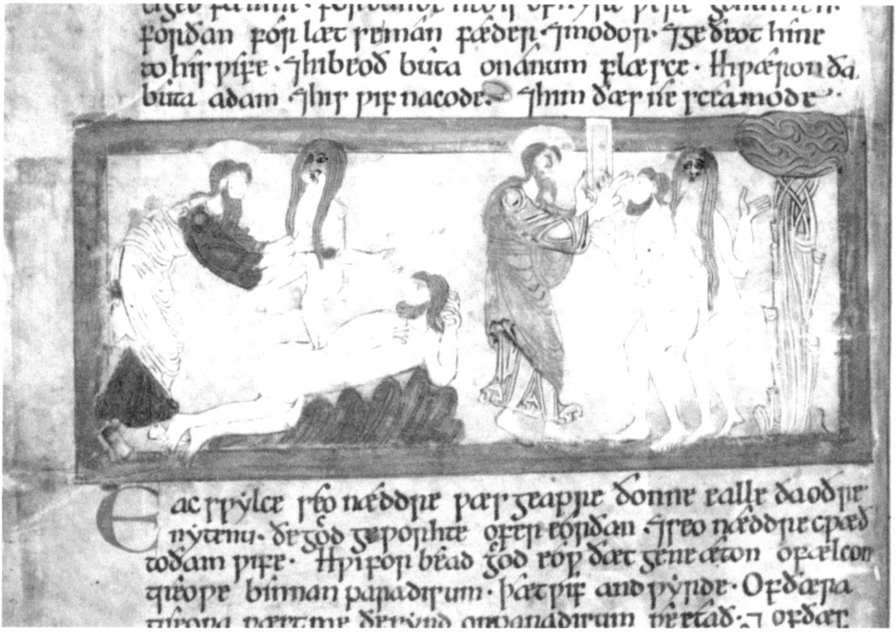

Figure 23. British Library, MS Cotton Claudius B. iv (Illustrated Hexateuch), fol. 6v: Creation of Eve. [*By permission of the British Library.*]

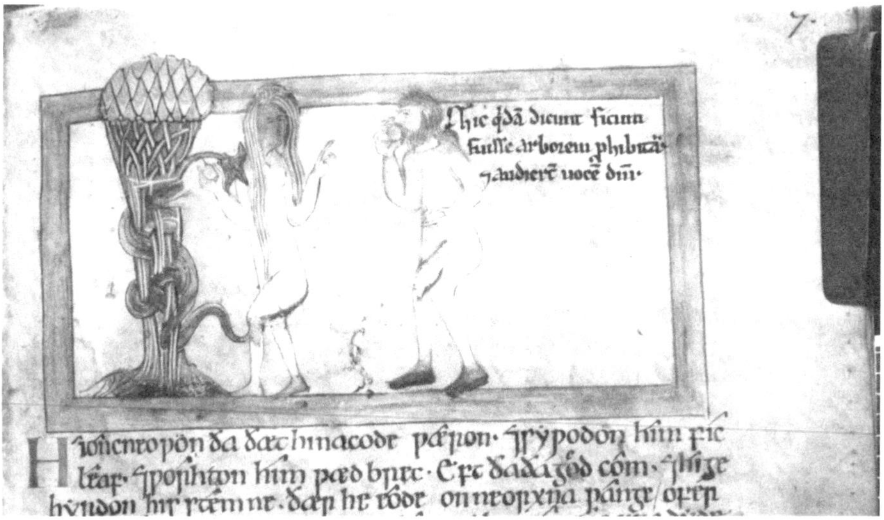

Figure 24. British Library, MS Cotton Claudius B. iv (Illustrated Hexateuch), fol. 7r: Adam and Eve eat fruit. [*By permission of the British Library*]

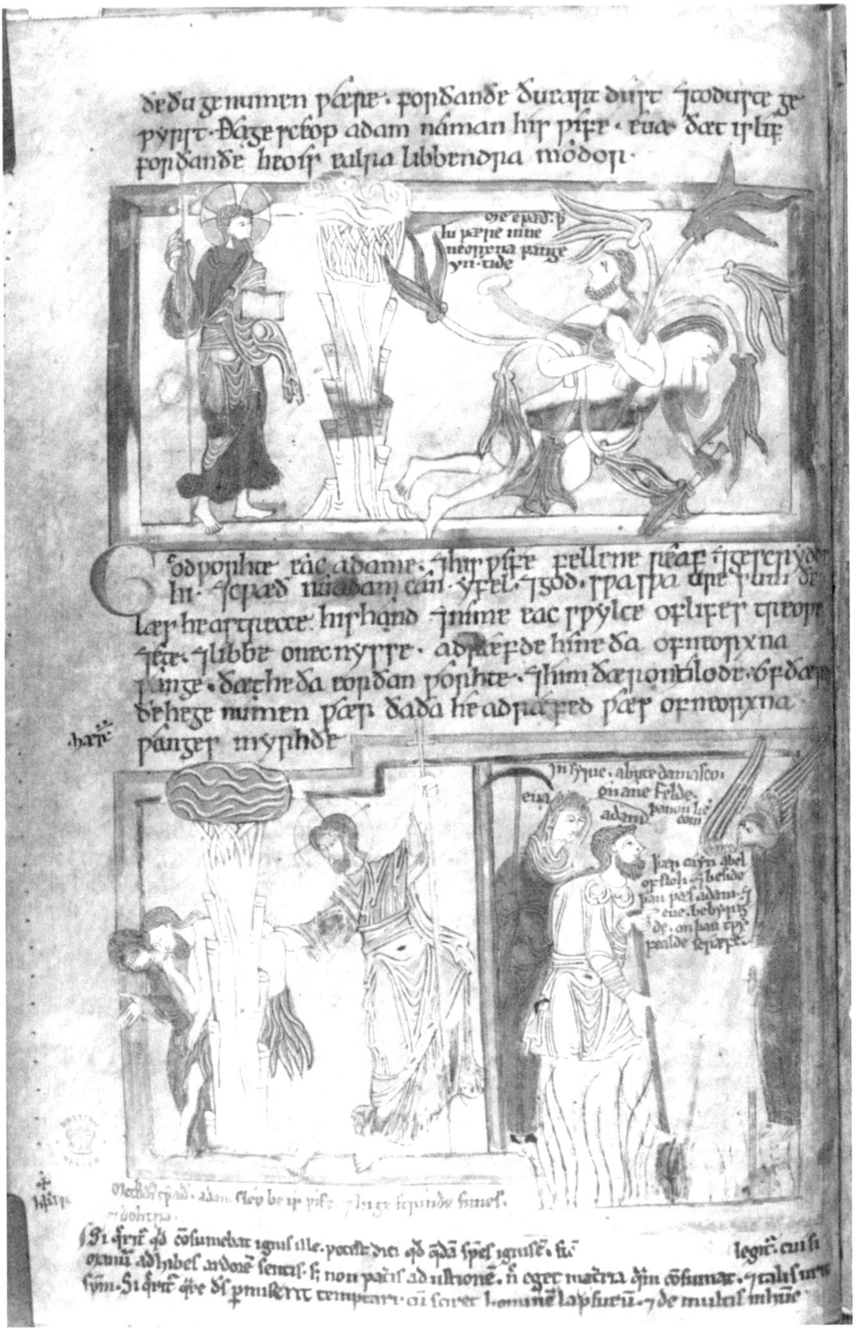

Figure 25. British Library, MS Cotton Claudius B. iv (Illustrated Hexateuch), fol. 7v: (upper) Adam and Eve hide; (lower) Expulsion of Adam and Eve. [*By permission of the British Library*]

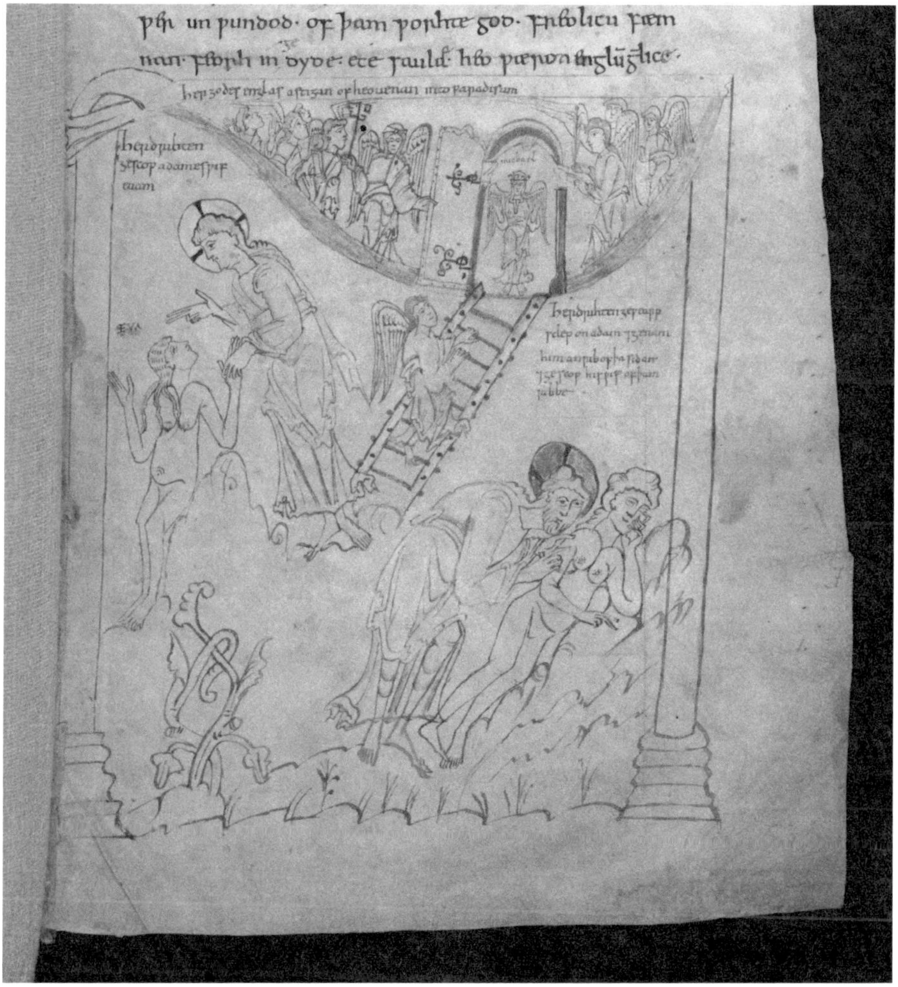

Figure 26. Oxford, Bodleian Library, MS Junius 11, page 9: Creation of Eve. [*B y permission of the Bodleian Library, University of Oxford*]

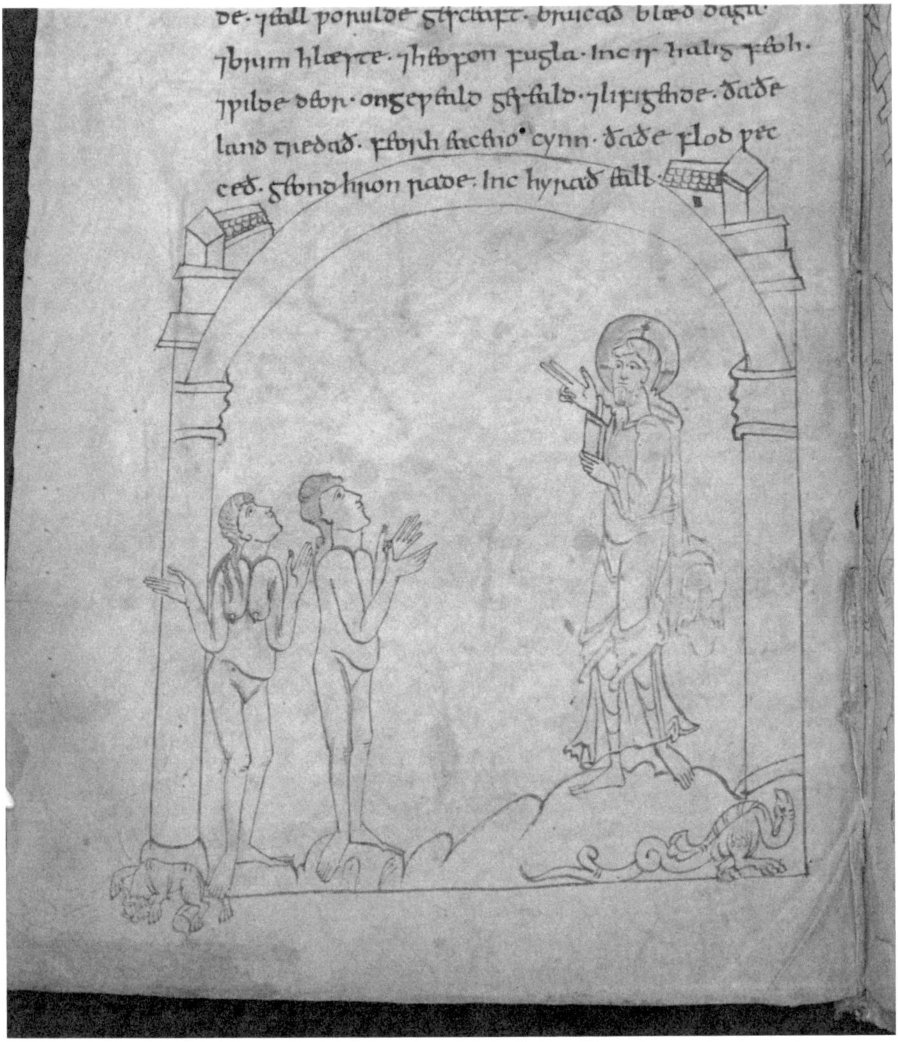

Figure 27. Oxford, Bodleian Library, MS Junius 11, page 10: Adam and Eve. [*By permission of the Bodleian Library, University of Oxford*]

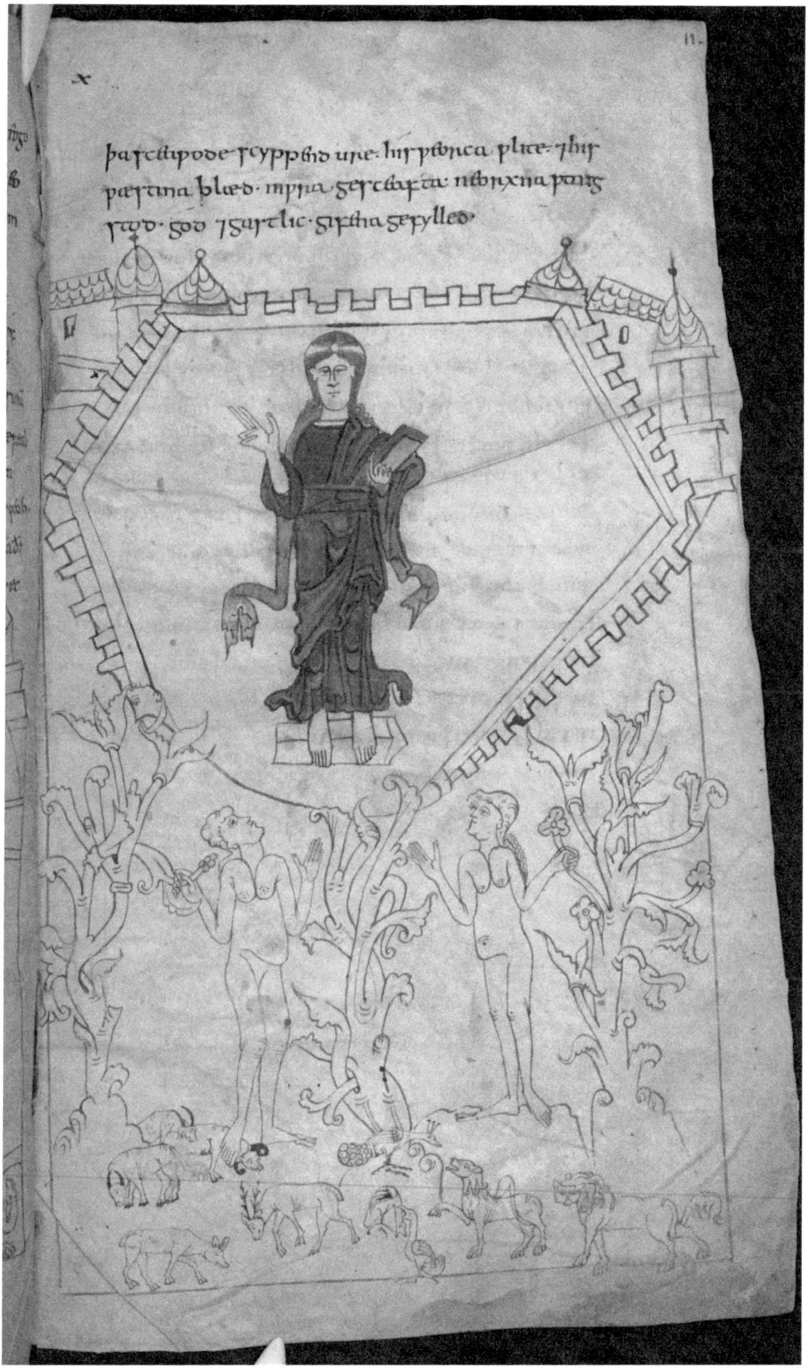

Figure 28. Oxford, Bodleian Library, MS Junius 11, page 11: Creation: God resting. [*By permission of the Bodleian Library, University of Oxford*]

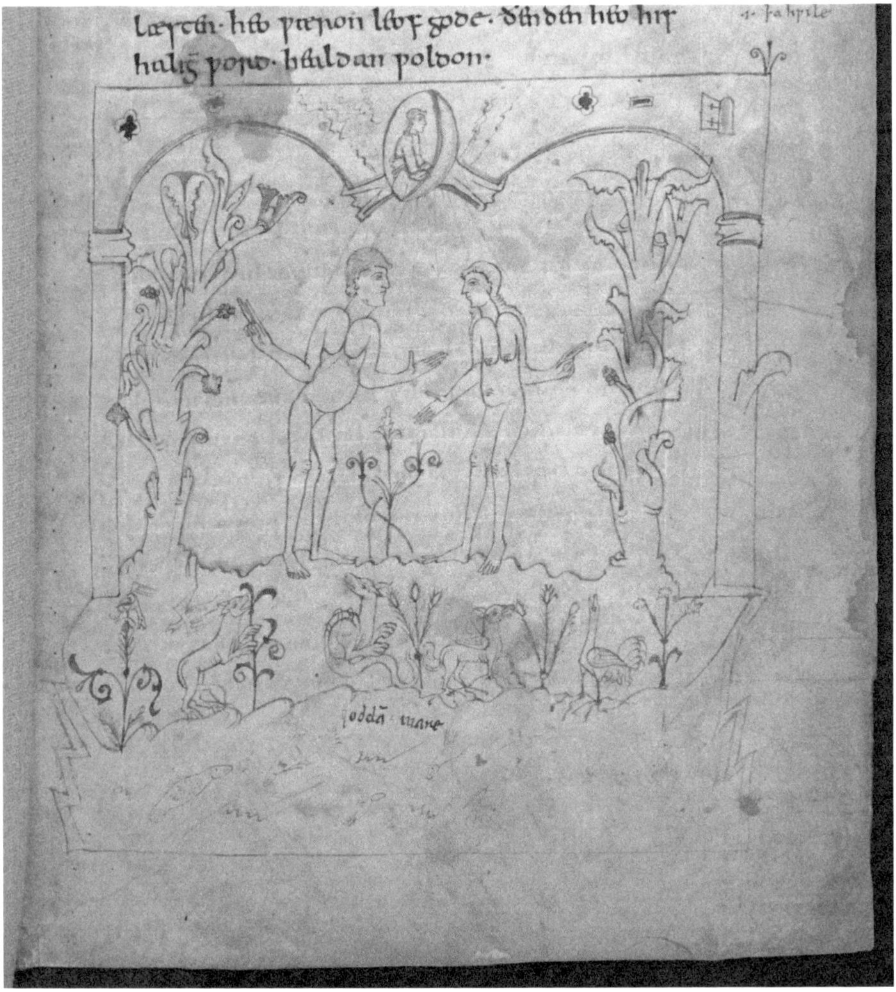

Figure 29. Oxford, Bodleian Library, MS Junius 11, page 13: Adam and Eve. [*By permission of the Bodleian Library, University of Oxford*]

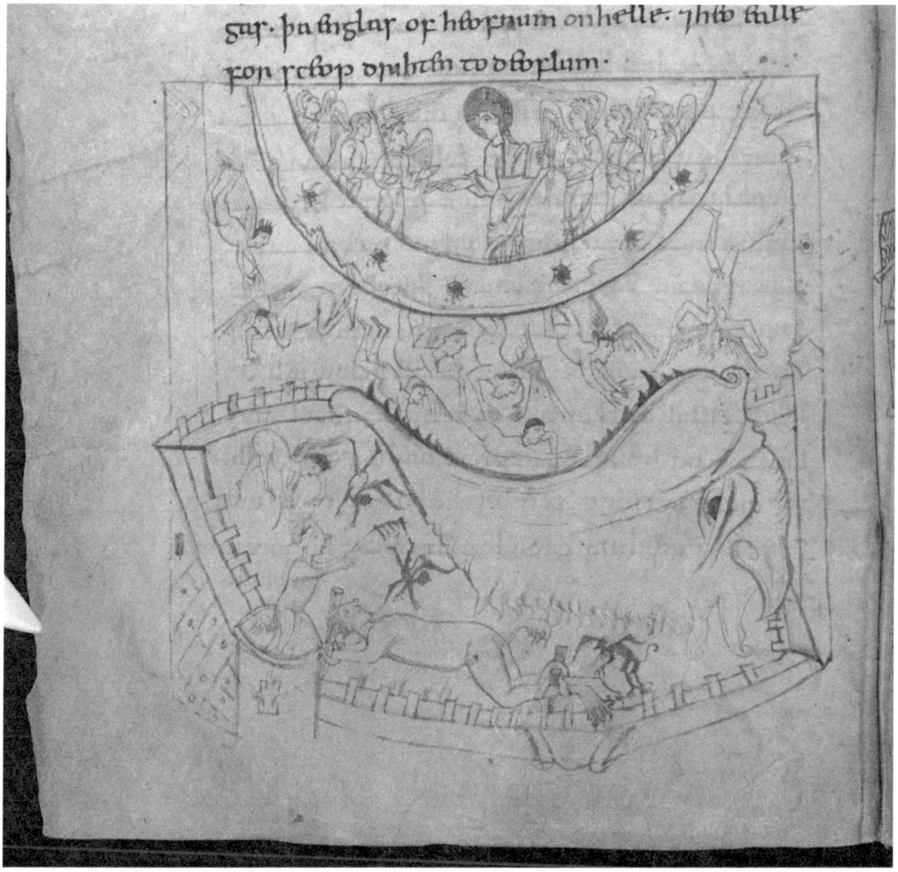

Figure 30. Oxford, Bodleian Library, MS Junius 11, page 16: Fall of the Angels. [*By permission of the Bodleian Library, University of Oxford*]

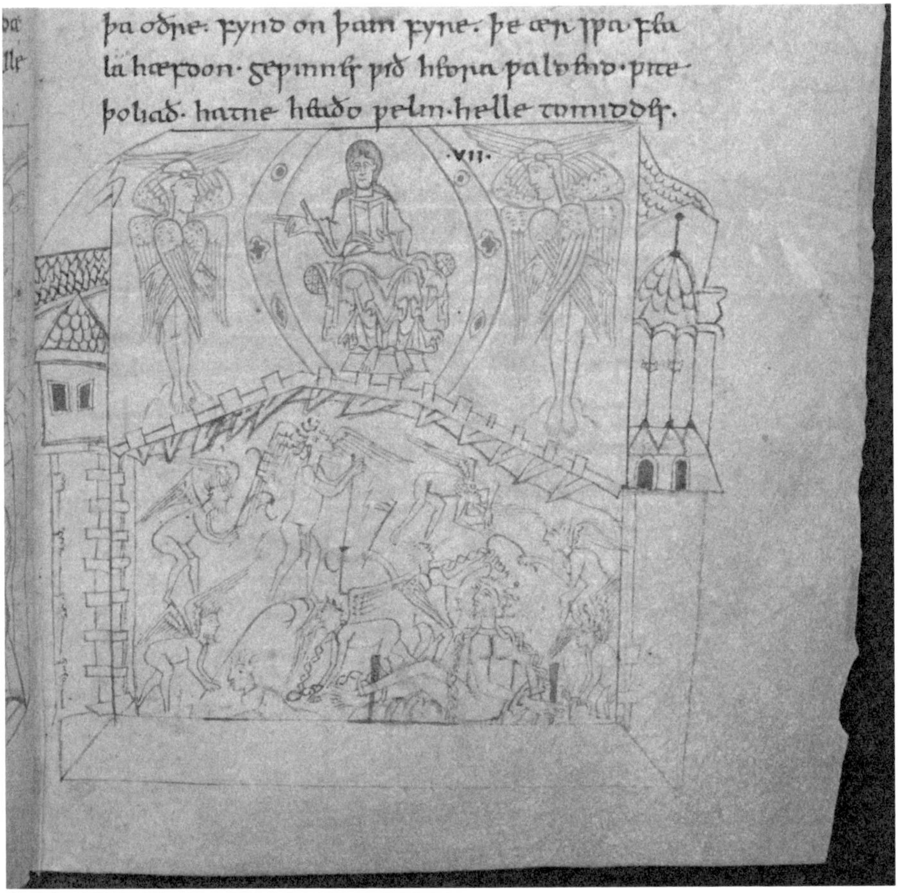

Figure 31. Oxford, Bodleian Library, MS Junius 11, page 17: Fall of the Angels. [*By permission of the Bodleian Library, University of Oxford*]

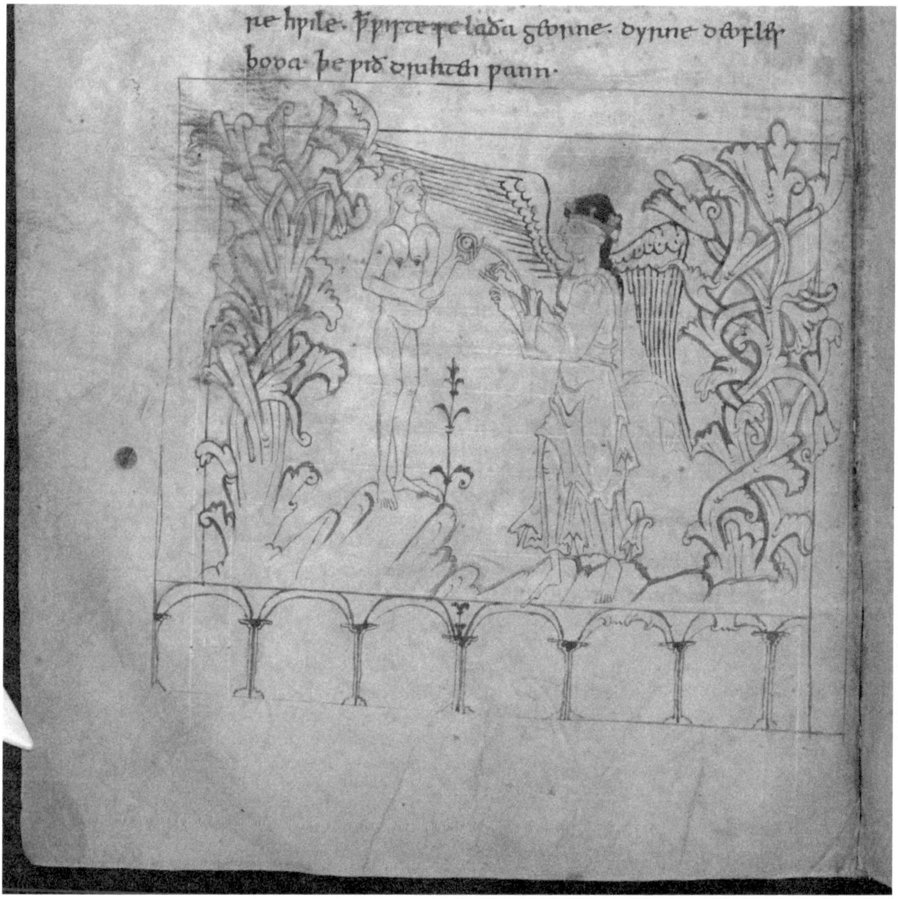

Figure 32. Oxford, Bodleian Library, MS Junius 11, page 24: Eve tempted. [*By permission of the Bodleian Library, University of Oxford*]

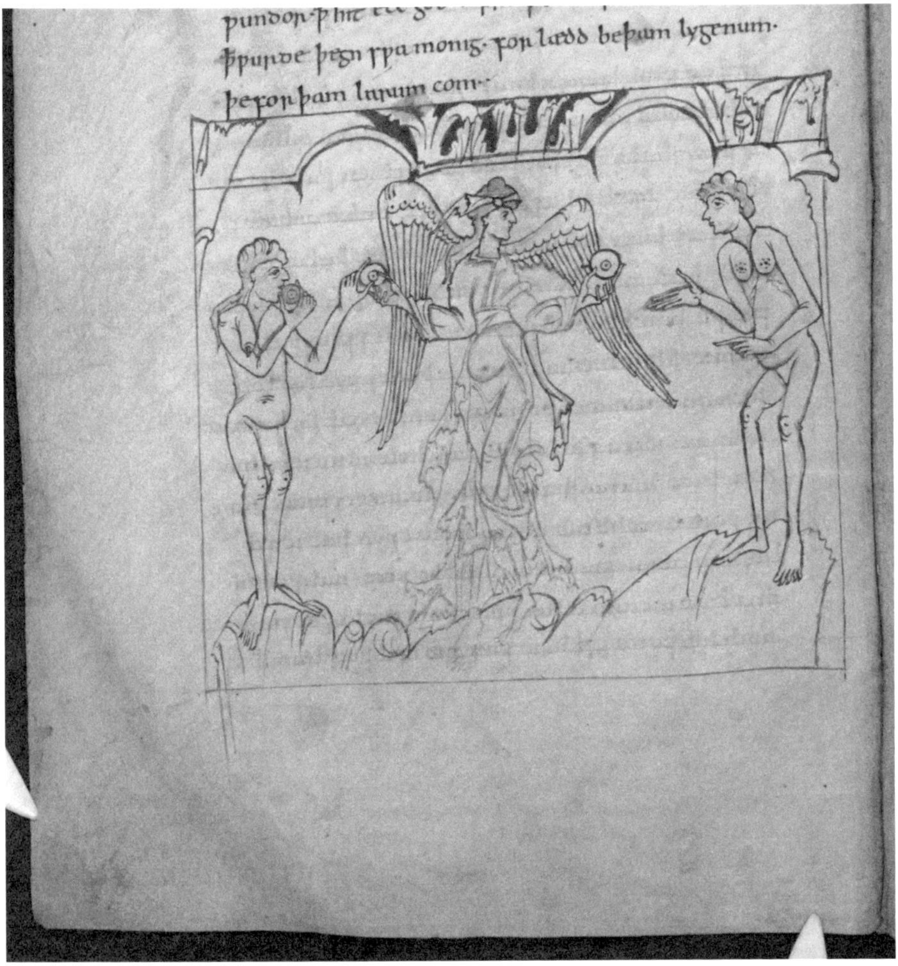

Figure 33. Oxford, Bodleian Library, MS Junius 11, page 28: Adam and Eve tempted. [*By permission of the Bodleian Library, University of Oxford*]

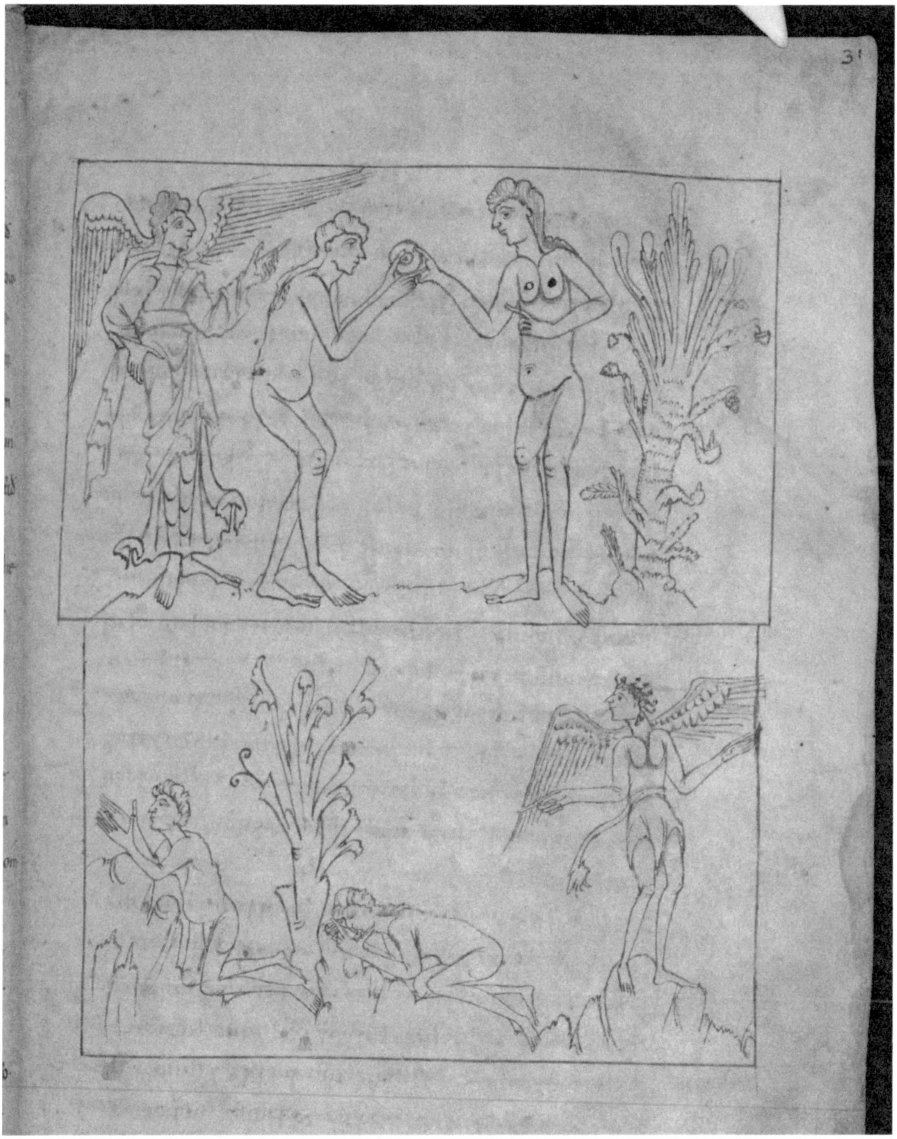

Figure 34. Oxford, Bodleian Library, MS Junius 11, page 31: (upper) Eve tempts Adam; (lower) Adam and Eve's remorse. [*By permission of the Bodleian Library, University of Oxford.*]

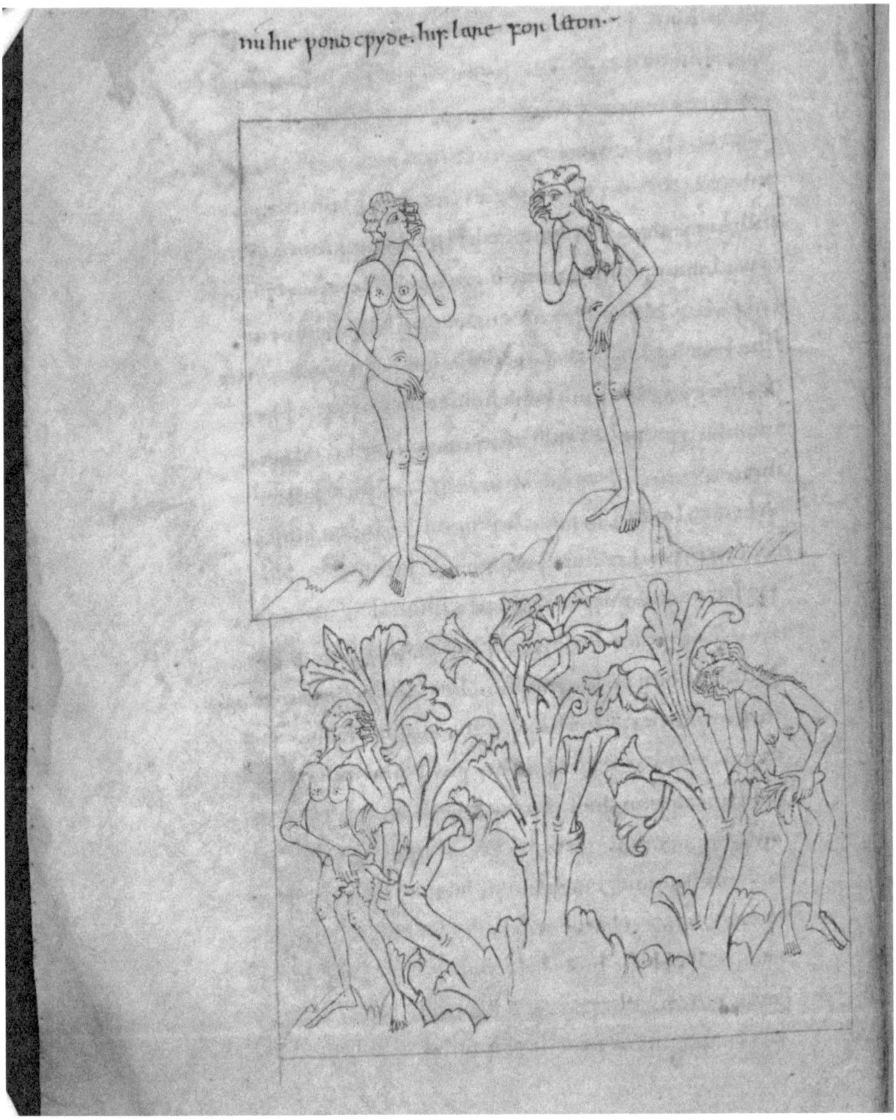

Figure 35. Oxford, Bodleian Library, MS Junius 11, page 34: (upper) Adam and Eve know nakedness; (lower) Adam and Eve hide. [*By permission of the Bodleian Library, University of Oxford*]

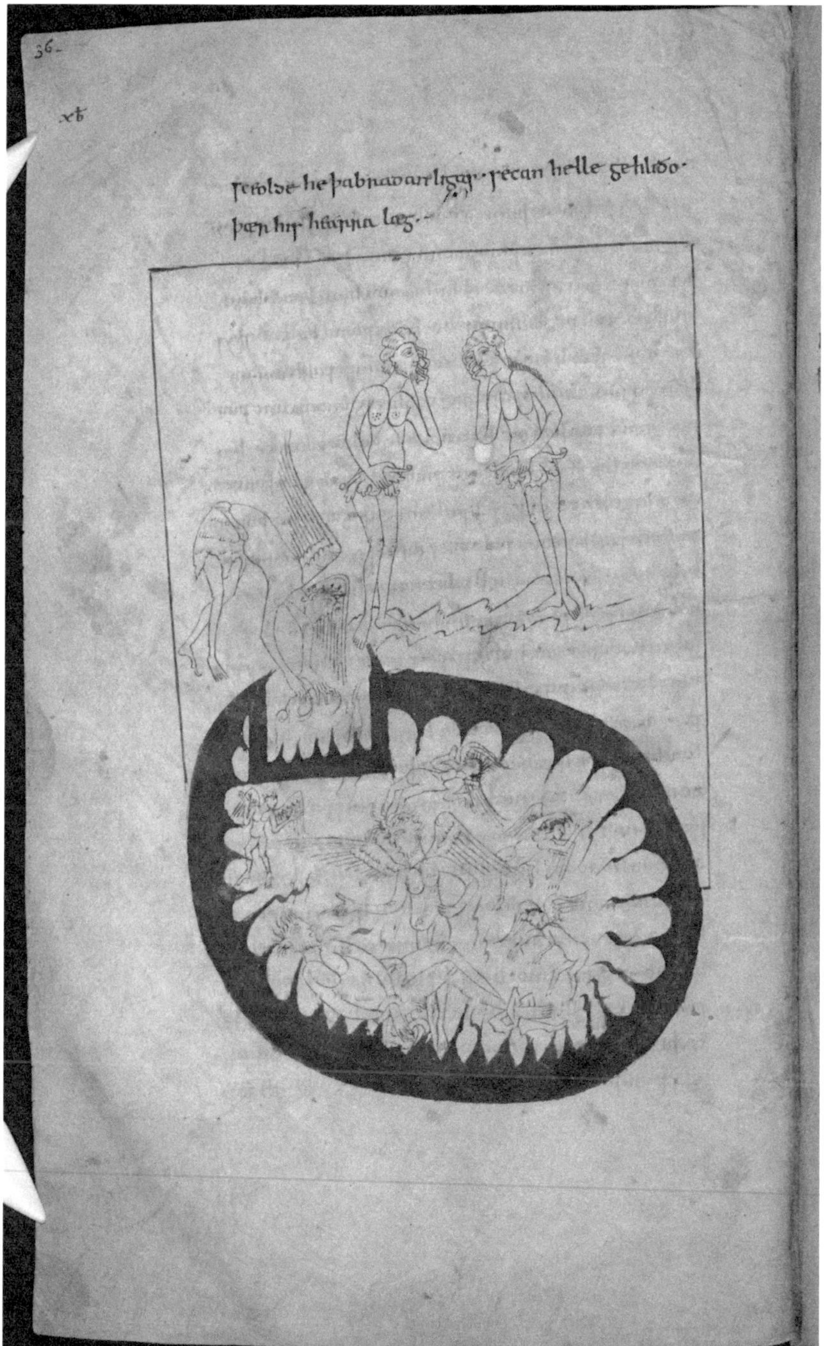

Figure 36. Oxford, Bodleian Library, MS Junius 11, page 36: Tempter returns to Hell. [*By permission of the Bodleian Library, University of Oxford*]

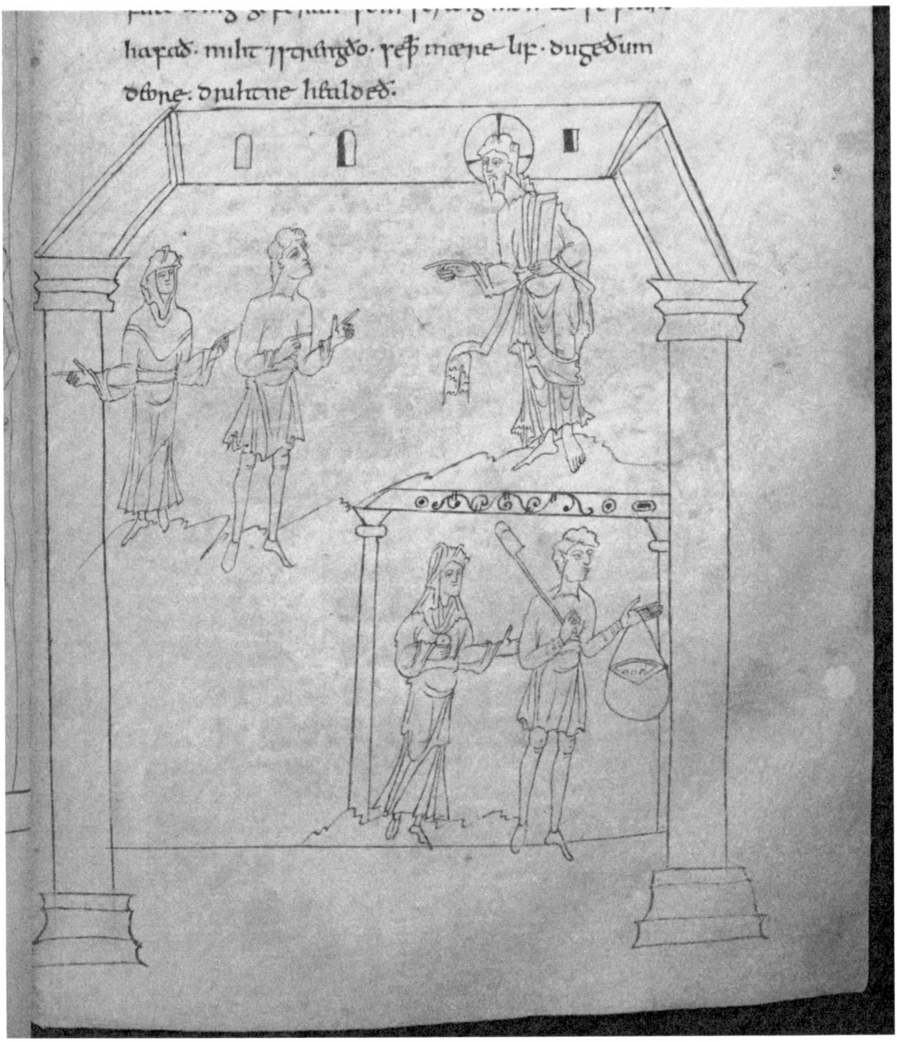

Figure 37. Oxford, Bodleian Library, MS Junius 11, page 45: Expulsion of Adam and Eve. [*By permission of the Bodleian Library, University of Oxford*]

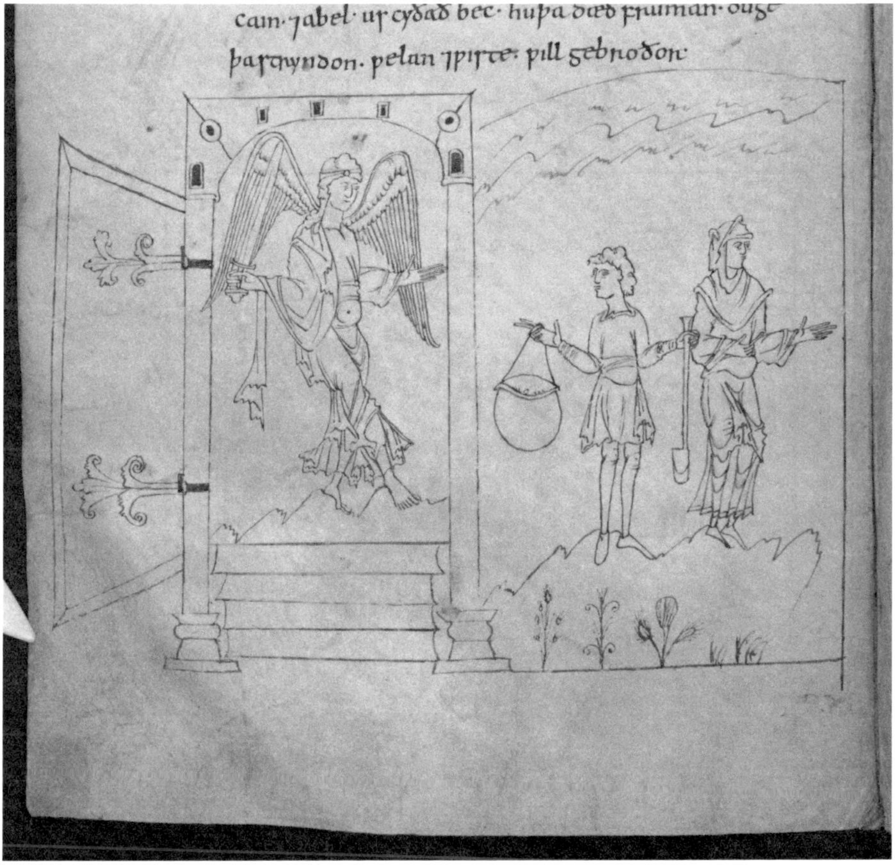

Figure 38. Oxford, Bodleian Library, MS Junius 11, page 46: Expulsion of Adam and Eve. [*By permission of the Bodleian Library, University of Oxford*]

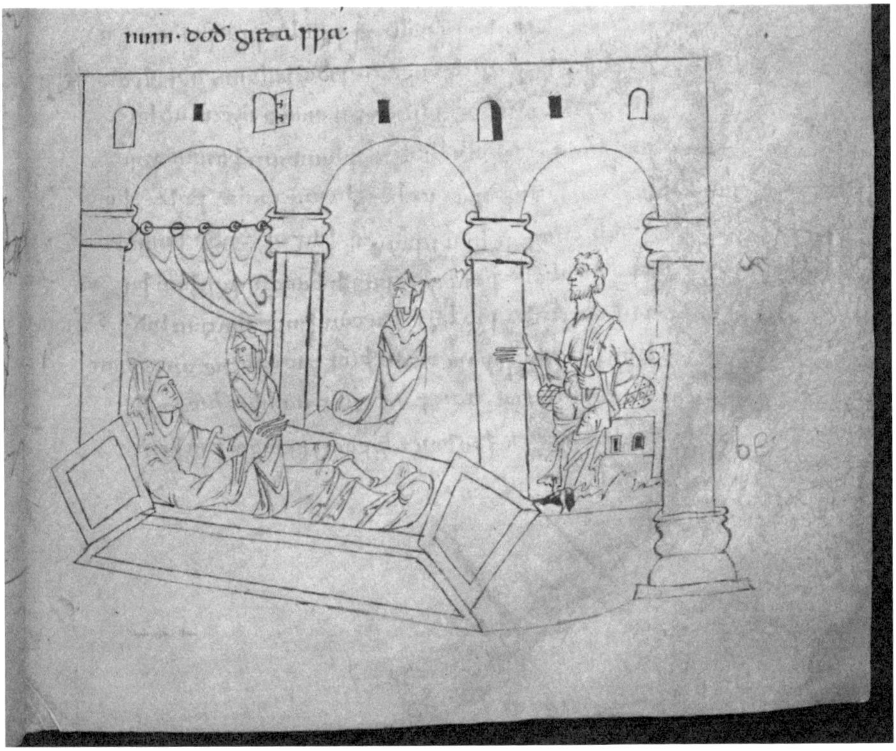

Figure 39. Oxford, Bodleian Library, MS Junius 11, page 47: Eve at childbed. [*By permission of the Bodleian Library, University of Oxford* ]

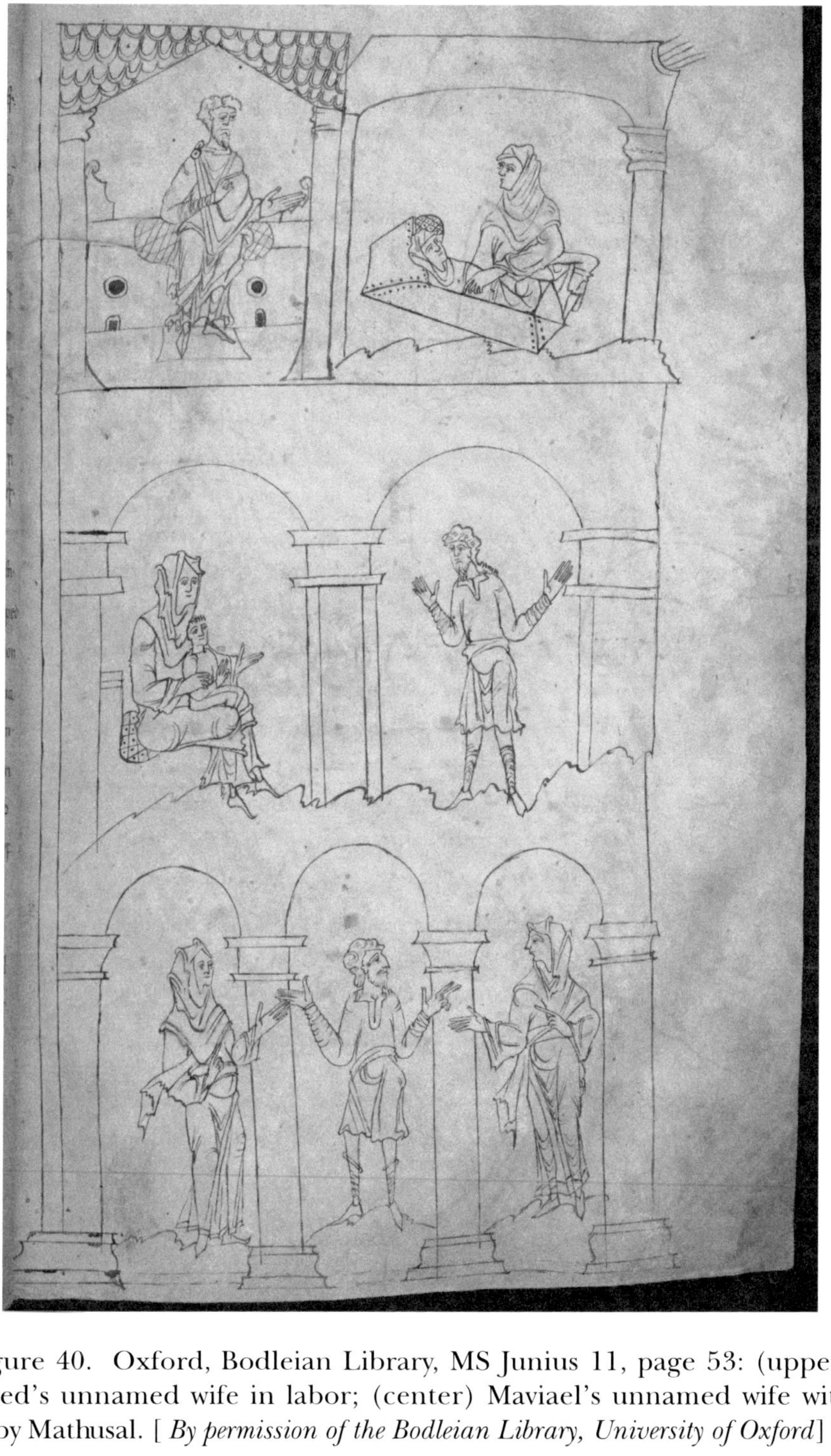

Figure 40. Oxford, Bodleian Library, MS Junius 11, page 53: (upper) Jared's unnamed wife in labor; (center) Maviael's unnamed wife with baby Mathusal. [ *By permission of the Bodleian Library, University of Oxford*]

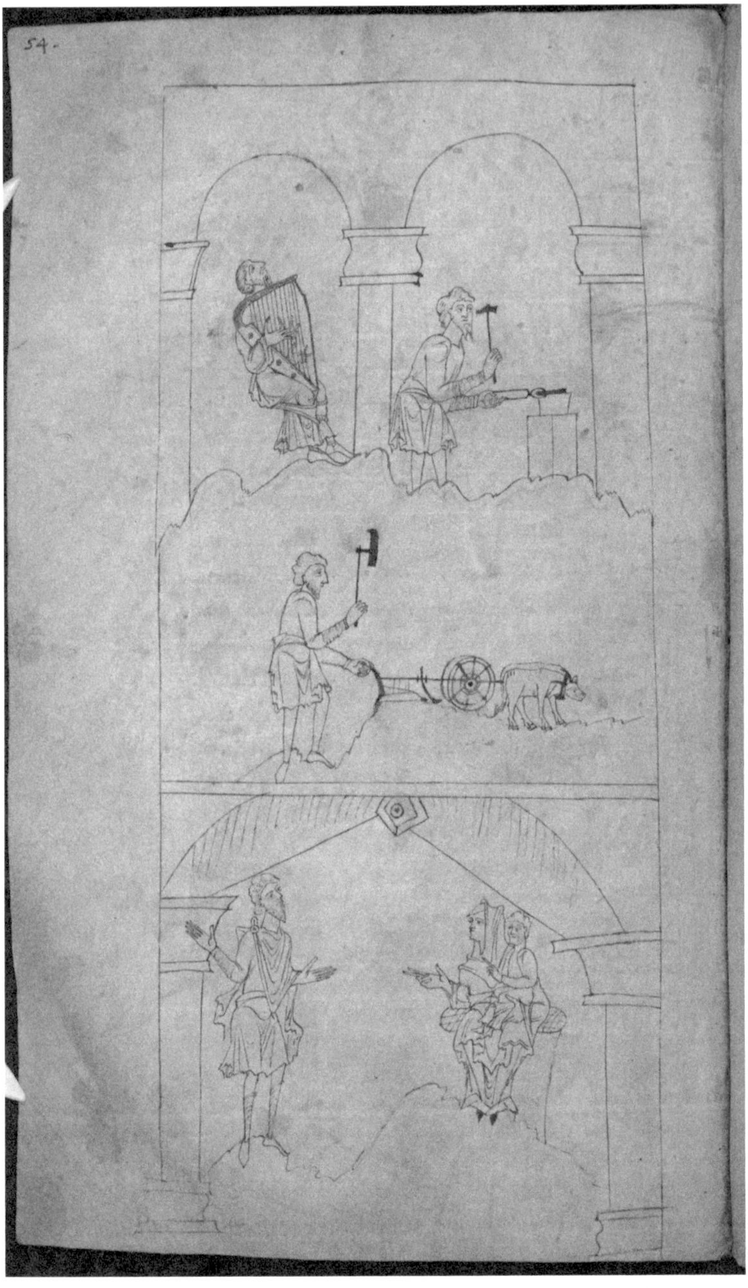

Figure 41. Oxford, Bodleian Library, MS Junius 11, page 54: (lower) Adam and Eve with infant Seth. [*By permission of the Bodleian Library, University of Oxford*]

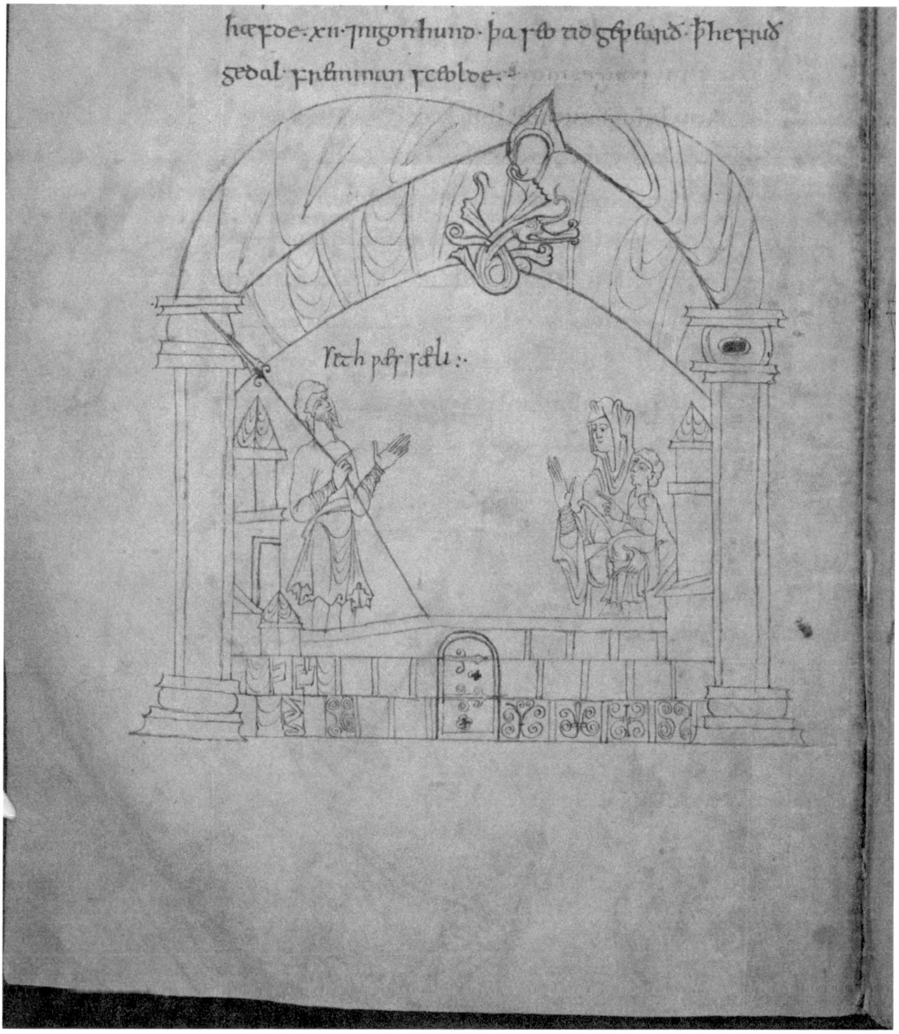

Figure 42. Oxford, Bodleian Library, MS Junius 11, page 56: Seth's unnamed wife with Enos. [*By permission of the Bodleian Library, University of Oxford*]

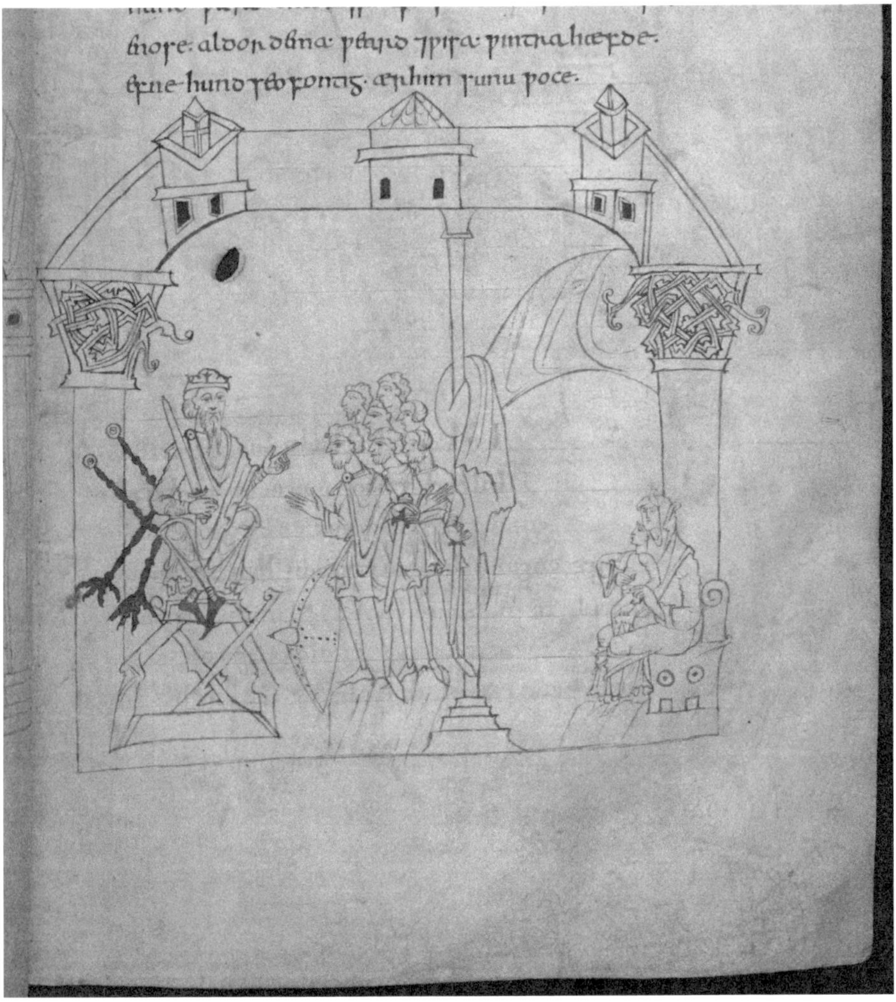

Figure 43. Oxford, Bodleian Library, MS Junius 11, page 57: Cainan's unnamed wife with baby Malalehel. [ *By permission of the Bodleian Library, University of Oxford* ]

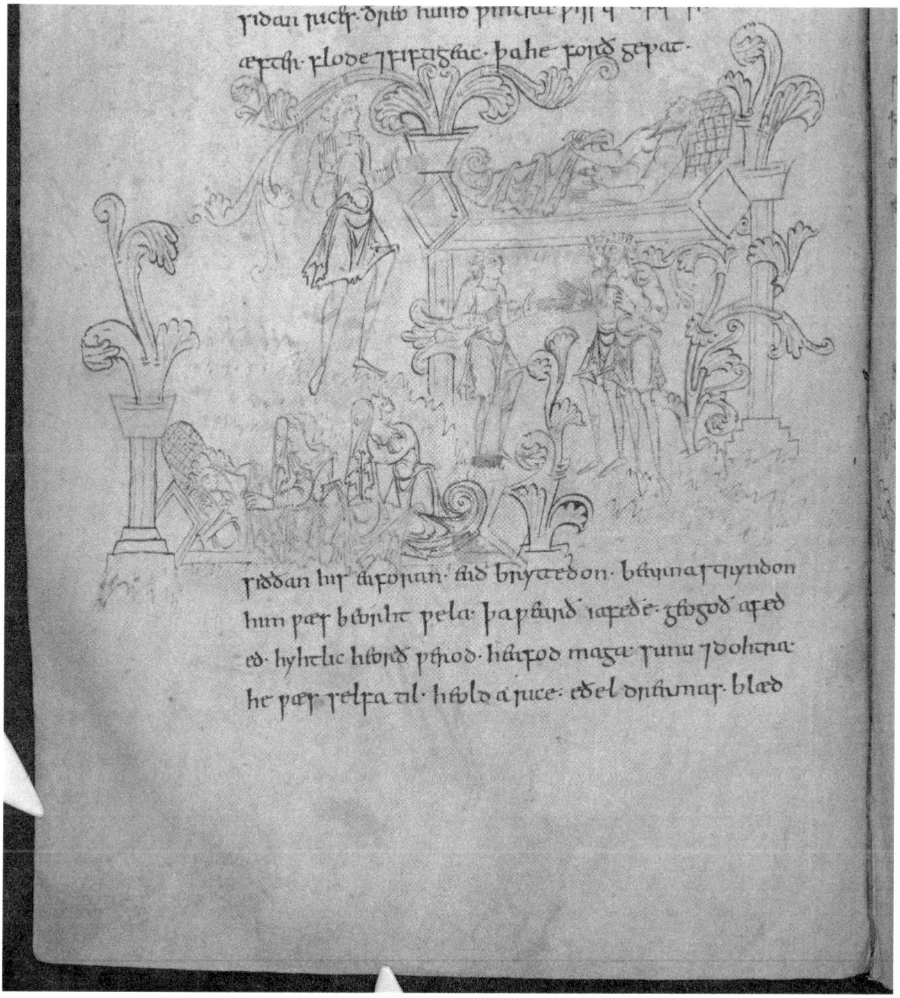

Figure 44. Oxford, Bodleian Library, MS Junius 11, page 78: drunkenness of Noah. [ *By permission of the Bodleian Library, University of Oxford* ]

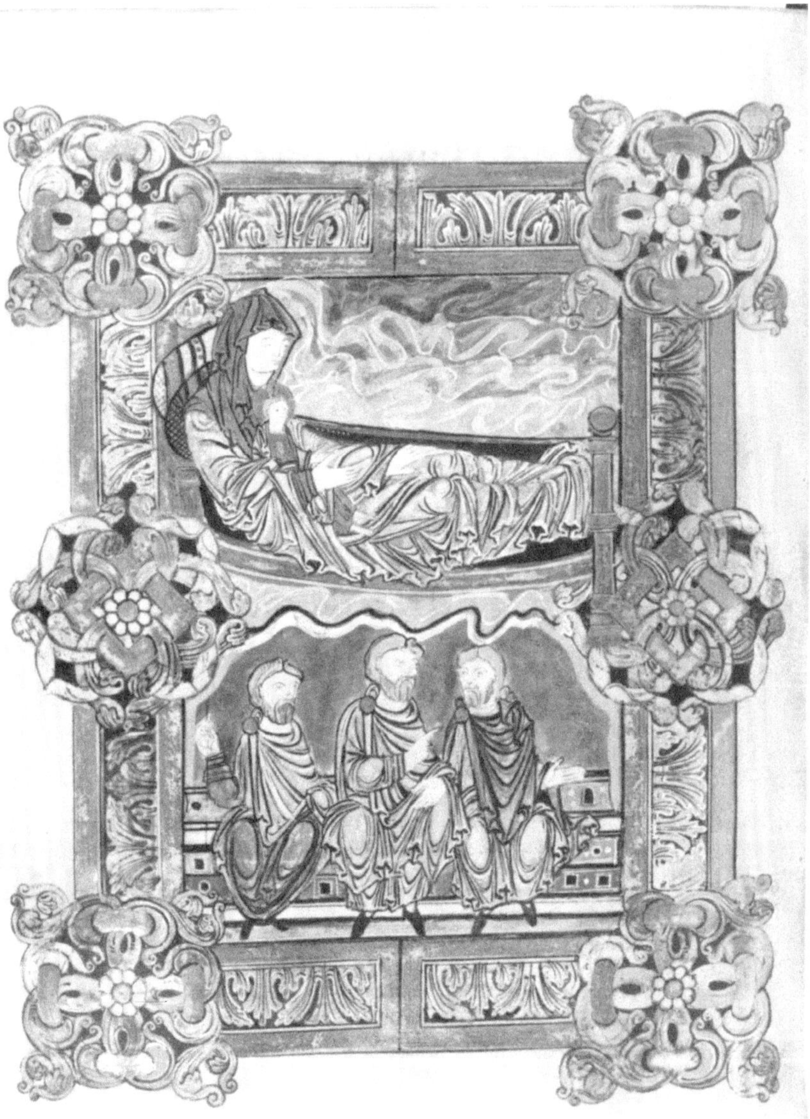

Figure 45. London, British Library, MS Add. 49598 (Benedictional of Æthelwold), fol. 22v: Naming of Christ. [*By permission of the British Library*]

# Exiles from the Kingdom:
# The Naked and the Damned in Anglo-Saxon Art

CATHERINE E. KARKOV

## *Body and Judgment In Anglo-Saxon Art*

The unclothed body is rare in Anglo-Saxon art in any medium, and the naked and sexed body rarer still. Even in the illustration of episodes that we know center on disruptive bodies or sexual encounters — such as the story of Lot and his daughters, or the conception of Ishmael — the body remains clothed. The impropriety of the scene is indicated by the fact that it is depicted at all, and by the way in which depiction positions the viewer as voyeur to an illicit moment. Moreover, art, no doubt because of its physicality, tends to avoid the often violent and eroticized nakedness described in so many saints' lives and other types of texts,[1] although the marginal nudes of the Bayeux Tapestry may well be an exception to this rule.[2] One might also argue that the attention focused on the display of Æthelthryth's virginal, intact, and dead body by both Bede and Æthelwold is erotic, in the case of Æthelwold coming close to

[1] See Clare A. Lees, "Engendering Religious Desire: Sex, Knowledge, and Christian Identity in Anglo-Saxon England," *Journal of Medieval and Early Modern Studies* 27 (1997): 17–45.

[2] The marginal nudes of the Bayeux Tapestry are dealt with elsewhere in this volume. The fact that they occur at key points in the power struggle between Harold and William suggests that they may have been meant as a gendered comment on the battle, with the victors generally associated with the masculine and the losers generally associated with the feminine. See further Catherine E. Karkov, "Gendering the Battle? Male and Female in the Bayeux Tapestry," in *Harold II and the Bayeux Tapestry*, ed. Gale R. Owen-Crocker and David Hill (Woodbridge, forthcoming).

fetishism,[3] but the representation of her body in Æthelwold's Benedictional (London, BL, Add. 49598, fol. 90v) keeps our gaze concentrated on the layers of color and clothing, and the golden letters that separate us from the desired body (the relics) that lie metaphorically beneath.[4] When the naked body does appear in Anglo-Saxon art it is therefore all the more interesting and demands both attention and analysis.

The Anglo-Saxons inherited a tradition in which maleness was connected to salvation and virtue, and femaleness to damnation and sin.[5] Women could achieve salvation by renouncing their female natures and "becoming male." In Anglo-Saxon art this is expressed most notably in the illustrations of the *Psychomachia* of Prudentius, in which the doomed Vices are portrayed as penetrable, feminine and often dismembered bodies, and the victorious Virtues as women become male through their spiritual armor.[6] But the *Psychomachia* was not an

3 Catherine E. Karkov, "The Body of St. Æthelthryth: Death, Desire and Conversion in Anglo-Saxon England," in *The Age of Conversion*, ed. Martin Carver (York, 2003), pp. 397–411.

4 According to Bede, even the sarcophagus for her translation was found miraculously intact. It was "beautifully made of white marble, with a close-fitting lid of the same stone" ("de marmore albo pulcherrime factum, operculo quoque similis lapidis aptissime tectum," Bertram Colgrave and R. A. B. Mynors, *Bede's Ecclesiastical History of the English People* [Oxford, 1969], pp. 394–95). Stone here appears to be a mirror of flesh, with the beautiful, white, unbroken coffin foreshadowing the discovery of the incorrupt body of the saint, miraculously healed of the wound in her neck. All translations from the Ecclesiastical History are taken from Colgrave and Mynors.

5 See, e.g., Margaret R. Miles, *Carnal Knowing: Female Nakedness and Religious Meaning in the Christian West* (New York, 1991); Elizabeth Castelli, "'I Will Make Mary Male': Pieties of the Body and Gender Transformation by Christian Women in Late Antiquity," in *Body Guards: The Cultural Politics of Gender Ambiguity*, ed. Julia Epstein and Kristina Straub (New York, 1991), pp. 29–49. See also Paul E. Szarmach, "St. Euphrosyne: Holy Transvestite," in *Holy Men and Holy Women: Old English Prose Saints' Lives and Their Contexts*, ed. Paul E. Szarmach (Albany, 1996), pp. 353–65.

6 Catherine E. Karkov, "Broken Bodies and Singing Tongues: Gender and Voice in the Cambridge, Corpus Christi College 23 *Psychomachia*," *ASE* 30 (2001): 115-36.

Anglo-Saxon text, and the illustrations, original as they may be in many ways, were built on rules and motifs established in earlier illustrated cycles.

The Anglo-Saxons also inherited the biblical and exegetical tradition that associated women, at least secular women, with Eve, and Eve with the body and sin; although, as we shall see, they transformed this tradition into a positive set of associations. The naked bodies of Eve and Adam are discussed elsewhere in this volume, and I will therefore treat them only in passing.[7] We should note here, however, that Eve's sin in the Junius 11 *Genesis* poem, while it is experienced bodily, is not sexualized as it is in other versions of the Fall.[8] As has been demonstrated many times, she sins out of ignorance and what she believes to be loyalty to Adam.[9] This is an important point,

[7] See the essays by Dockray-Miller, Ericksen, and Wilcox.

[8] See, for example, the depiction of Eve on Bishop Bernward's doors at Hildesheim, where Eve turns to display her body to the audience, and where the apple held next to her breast invites us to equate the two (Adam S. Cohen and Ann Derbes, "Bernward and Eve at Hildesheim," *Gesta* 40.1 [2001], 19–38). See also the Irish *Saltair na Rann*, in which the beautiful Eve is seduced by the voice of the serpent so that she opens the door to Paradise to let him in (David Greene and Fergus Kelly, *The Irish Adam and Eve Story from Saltair na Rann*, 2 vols. [Dublin, 1976], I: 34–43.) In the latter, the "slender hard serpent" ("*ind nathir choel chatot*," line 1206) says to Eve:

> Massa thú ind Eua ro-clos
> co clú fri feba hi Pardos,
> ben Adaim, alainn nad chres,
> furri alim mo lanles. (lines 1189–92)

("If you are the Eve who has been heard of for excellence with fame in Paradise, the wife of Adam, a beauty whose is not miserly, I seek from her my full satisfaction.")

[9] Catherine E. Karkov, *Text and Picture in Anglo-Saxon England: Narrative Strategies in the Junius 11 Manuscript* (Cambridge, 2001); Gillian Overing, "On Reading Eve: *Genesis B* and the Reader's Desire," in *Speaking Two Languages: Traditional Disciplines and Contemporary Theory in Medieval Studies*, ed. Allen J. Frantzen (Albany, 1991), pp. 35–63; Alain Renoir, "Eve's I.Q. Rating: Two Sexist Views of Genesis B," in *New Readings on Women in Old English Literature*, ed. Helen Damico and Alexandra Hennessey Olsen (Bloomington, 1990), pp. 262–72; Kathleen Dubs, "*Genesis B*: A Study in Grace," *American Benedictine Review* 33 (1982): 47–64; Rosemary Woolf, "The

because the Junius 11 manuscript, and especially the work of the first of the two artists who partially illustrated it, places our attention on the naked male body as the primary site of sin and damnation, and locates the sexed male body before that of the female body in the cyclical pattern of falls that help to organize the manuscript. What I intend to do in this essay is to use the Junius 11 manuscript as a point of departure for a consideration of the sexed and gendered body within the larger discourse of crime and punishment in Anglo-Saxon England. As we shall see, it is but one manifestation of the way in which the Anglo-Saxons came to equate demonic actions with human actions, and to unite both in the image of the damned male body.

Creation in the Junius 11 manuscript is interwoven with images of the fall of the rebel angels, in which several of the fallen angels acquire male genitals as part of their fall (figure 30, figure 31, figure 36). These images frame the fall of Adam and Eve, suggesting that male sin and sexuality came into being before female error and the sexed female body. Theologically, and in terms of narrative structure, there is a reason for the primacy of the fall of the angels: it creates the void in heaven that necessitates the creation of Adam and Eve. But there seems no obvious reason for the addition of male genitalia to several of the "angels become demons" in the illustrations on pages 16, 17, and 36, and no surviving model on which the Junius 11 artist might have been basing his work. It seems most likely, therefore, that the images blended the traditional iconography of the fall into hell with a specifically Anglo-Saxon attitude towards the body of the damned.

Male demons have been identified as something of a feature of Anglo-Saxon art. Louis Jordan noted that while Anglo-Saxon artists tended to emphasize "beastly attributes" in their portrayal of demons, they also frequently gave them male

Fall of Man in *Genesis B* and the *Mystère d'Adam*," in *Studies in Old English Literature in Honor of Arthur G. Brodeur* (Eugene, OR, 1963), pp. 187–99.

genitalia.[10] The differing portrayals of the demons in the illustration of Psalm 6 in the Harley Psalter (London, BL, Harley 603, fol. 3v) and its model, the Utrecht Psalter (Utrecht, Bibliotheek der Rijksuniversiteit, 32, fol. 3v), provide one of Jordan's most telling examples. In the Utrecht Psalter (the Carolingian model) the demons are not sexed, while in the Harley Psalter (the Anglo-Saxon copy) they have been given male genitals, along with long talons and grotesque faces.[11] The Junius 11 artist gives us altogether more human devils, drawing our attention to the contrast between their nude, and frequently sexed bodies, and the clothed and genderless bodies of their heavenly counterparts. The *Genesis* poet does not focus on the bodies of the fallen angels so much as on the enormity of their crime and the torments of hell into which they have been exiled; nevertheless, when text and image are read together the naked male body becomes a sign of crime and punishment.[12] In *Christ and Satan*, the final poem in the Junius 11 manuscript, the theme of nakedness reappears with Satan's inclusion of naked men struggling with serpents ("hwilum nacode men winnað ymb wyrmas," lines 134b–35a) in his description of hell. The nakedness of doomed men can thus be equated to the nakedness of the fallen angels, the only other inhabitants of hell that we know of at this point.

The equation between fallen angels and mortal men is made even more specific by the *Genesis* poet's mention of the

[10] Louis Jordan, "Demonic Elements in Anglo-Saxon Iconography," in *Sources of Anglo-Saxon Culture*, ed. Paul E. Szarmach, with Virginia D. Oggins (Kalamazoo, 1986), pp. 282–317, at 295. The possible differences in the gendered portrayal of the demonic and the monstrous in Anglo-Saxon art provide fruitful ground for speculation, although there is not space to examine this issue here. See Susan Kim's essay in this volume and Karkov, "Broken Bodies."

[11] Jordan, "Demonic Elements," p. 295. Jordan's attribution of pendulous breasts to the demons is, however, inaccurate.

[12] See also Dockray-Miller's essay in this volume.

ten orders of angels,[13] a motif also found in the writings of Ælfric[14] and in charters,[15] and one popular in both sermons and apocalyptic literature.[16] Lucifer and his followers constituted the tenth order, an order also connected by Gregory to mankind.[17] While there was much debate over the nature of angels and demons, whether they possessed bodies and, if so, what distinguished the bodies of angels and demons from each other, there was general agreement that a bodily nature of some type could be attributed to demons, though it was not necessarily the same sort of body as that of man.[18] In a much quoted passage from his homily, *Natale Omnium Sanctorum*, Ælfric stated simply that "englas sind gastas buton lichaman."[19]

[13] Hæfde se alwalda engelcynna
þurh handmægen, halig drihten,
tene getrimede þæm he getruwode wel
þæt hie his giongorscipe fyligan wolden

(lines 246–49, "the Ruler of the race of angels, the Holy Lord, had through his mighty hand created ten [orders] in whom he trusted well that they would follow his allegiance"). All citations from the Junius poems of Genesis are taken from A.N. Doane, ed., *Genesis A: A New Edition* (Madison, 1978), and A.N. Doane, ed., *The Saxon Genesis* (Madison, 1991). Translations are my own.

[14] Discussed below; see also "On the Old and New Testament," in *The Old English Version of the Heptateuch*, ed. S. J. Crawford, EETS o.s. 160 (London, 1922), pp. 18–20; Letter to Wulfgeat, in Bruno Assmann, ed., *Angelsächsische Homilien und Heiligenleben*, (Kassel, 1889; repr. with a suppl. intro. by Peter Clemoes, Darmstadt, 1964), pp. 1–12, at 2.

[15] Discussed below; see also, National Library of Wales, Aberystwyth, Peniarth MS 390, edited in C. R. Hart, *The Early Charters of Northern England and the North Midlands* (Leicester, 1975), p. 187.

[16] See Paul Salmon, "Die zehnte Engelchor in deutschen Dichtungen und Predigten des Mittelalters," *Euphorion* 57 (1963): 321–30.

[17] *Homiliae in Evangelia* II.34 (PL 76, 1249).

[18] Dyan Elliott, *Fallen Bodies: Pollution, Sexuality and Demonology in the Middle Ages* (Philadelphia, 1999), chap. 6.

[19] *Catholic Homilies* I.36, lines 16-17; "angels are spirits without bodies," *Ælfric's Catholic Homilies: The First Series*, ed. Peter Clemoes, EETS, s.s. 17 (Oxford, 1997), p. 486. (Hereafter CH I.)

Implicit in his description of the ten orders of angels in his *Sermo de Initio Creaturae*, however, is the idea that it is the body that unites men to the fallen angels:

> He gesceop tyn engla werod; þæt synt englas. ⁊ heahenglas. throni. dominationes. principatus. potestates. uirtutes. cherubim seraphim; her sindon nigan engla werod: hi nabbað nænne lichoman. ac hi sindon ealle gastas swiðe strange. ⁊ mihtige ⁊ wlitige. on micelre fægernysse gesceapene to lofe ⁊ to wyrðmynte heora scyppende; þæt teoðe werod abreað ⁊ awende on yfel.[20]

Here it is the nine orders of faithful angels that have no bodies. The exclusion of the tenth order from the list of angels without bodies implies that it is their lack of *bodilessness* that sets them apart. Their fall into *bodiliness* becomes both a precedent for and a parallel to the fall of Adam and Eve into sinful and sexualized bodies, and their descent into hell, from which they will eventually be rescued by Christ at the Harrowing.

In the lines from *Christ and Satan* quoted above, Satan uses the generic pronoun *men*, a word which can refer to both men and women, but if we turn to the images of human beings condemned to hell in the surviving corpus of Anglo-Saxon art we find that, with the exception of illustrations of the Harrowing, they are almost exclusively male. Even in the famous depiction of the Harrowing of Hell in the Tiberius Psalter (BL, Cotton Tiberius C.vi, fol. 14r), the only naked figures are those of Satan, and short-haired, and thus apparently male, figures. In the equally well-known image of the Last Judgment in the New Minster Liber Vitae (London, BL, Stowe 944, fol. 7) there is only one woman amongst the group being thrust into the hell mouth, and she is clothed.[21] Similarly, on folio 3v of the

[20] CH I.1, lines 22–27; "He created ten hosts of angels, that is angels and archangels, thrones, dominions, principalities, powers, virtues, cherubim, seraphim. Here are nine hosts of angels: they have no body, but they are all spirits, very strong and mighty and beautiful, in great fairness were they shaped, to love and to praise their Creator. That tenth host rebelled and turned to evil."

[21] In fact it is only her long dress that tells us that she is a woman. It is equally important to note here that women are also absent from the kingdom of

Paris Psalter (Paris, BN, lat. 8824), one veiled and presumably female head is included amongst the six heads that stare up from the hell mouth at the bottom of the page.[22] More typical is the male figure surrounded by lacertine animals, his beard and genitals bitten by snakes, who squats in the central column of the canon table on folio 1 of the late-eighth-century Barberini Gospels (Vatican, Biblioteca Apostolica, Barberini lat. 570), possibly a Mercian book (figure 1).[23] Two strands of lacertine sprout from the top of his head suggesting horns, but his appearance is otherwise fully human. If he were intended as a representation of Satan, the serpents looping around his feet would make him the earliest surviving image of the bound Satan in Insular art. The demonic head that fills the top of the column, however, suggests that he is more likely meant to represent one of the human inhabitants of hell, or perhaps one of Satan's followers. He pulls at his beard with one hand, a gesture associated with the sin of anger in Insular art,[24] but the other hand reaches for his genitals, suggesting sin of a more sexual nature. The use of a figure caught up or imprisoned in plant scroll or animal interlace is a common way of representing hell across early medieval Europe.[25] It appears again in Anglo-Saxon art on one side of the shaft of the eighth- or ninth-

heaven at the top of the same page, and from the procession of the saved depicted at the top of fol. 6v, although it is possible to understand the figure of Queen Ælfgyfu/Emma on fol. 6r as forming a part of the procession. See below p. 198.

22 See Thomas Ohlgren, *Anglo-Saxon Textual Illustration* (Kalamazoo, 1992), p. 301.

23 On the provenance of the manuscript see Michelle P. Brown, *The Book of Cerne: Prayer, Patronage and Power in Ninth-Century England* (London, 1996), pp.172, 174, 178.

24 See Helen Roe, *Monasterboice and its Monuments* (Dundalk, 1981), p. 30.

25 See, for example, the carvings on the trumeau now on the inner west wall of the Abbey of Sainte-Marie at Souillac, discussed and illustrated in Michael Camille, "Mouths and Meaning: Towards an Anti-Iconography of Medieval Art," in *Iconography at the Crossroads*, ed. Brendan Cassidy (Princeton, 1993), pp. 43–57.

century Rothbury cross,[26] this time imprisoning a figure who is clearly human rather than demonic (figure 20). The little figure is caught in a mesh of symmetrical writhing and biting animals, which includes a pair of small, partially human, creatures whose underbellies and genitals are being attacked by serpents. (The genitals of the second creature are concealed by the head and paws of the beast that gnaws him, but the two are otherwise identical.) The clearly depicted testicles of the one figure mark them as male. The horror of the scene is magnified by the depth of the carving, but above all by the sensitive rendering of the man's face. The deeply drilled eyes convey absolute terror, while the mouth is open in a silent scream. As Jane Hawkes notes, "viewed in a darkened church, painted and set with paste glass, illuminated by glittering candlelight, and set at eye level at the base of the cross, the deformed figures struggling eternally in the symmetrical coils of the beasts, their genitals threatened by the jaws of the creatures, elicit responses at a very basic level."[27] As reconstructed in the Corpus of Anglo-Saxon Stone Sculpture,[28] the Rothbury cross originally stood just over fifteen feet high, so that its head would have towered above the viewer. At the top of the side of the shaft on which the hell scene is carved, a group of clothed male figures with fillets in their hair looks down at both the viewer and the hell scene below (figure 21). Whether we interpret this group as the saved in heaven or as an earthly audience,[29] there is a strong sense that they look down at us in judgment and as a warning

[26] On the date of the shaft see Rosemary Cramp, *County Durham and Northumberland*, Corpus of Anglo-Saxon Stone Sculpture 1 (Oxford, 1984), pp. 217–21; Jane Hawkes, "The Rothbury Cross: an Iconographic Bricolage," *Gesta* 35.1 (1996): 77–94. See also the Repton Stone on which two men dressed in breeches are being gnawed by a giant serpent (Martin Biddle and Birthe Kjølbye-Biddle, "The Repton Stone," *ASE* 14 [1981]: 233–92).

[27] Jane Hawkes, "Anglo-Saxon Sculpture: Questions of Context," in *Northumbria's Golden Age,* ed. Jane Hawkes and Susan Mills (Stroud, 1999), pp. 204-15, at 214–15.

[28] Cramp, *Corpus* 1, p. 218.

[29] Cramp, *Corpus* 1, p. 220.

that we might suffer the same fate as the little naked man in hell. The sense of downward motion, or fall, on this side of the shaft is subtle, but present nonetheless, connecting our threatened fall with that of the angels. It is balanced by the upward motion of the Ascension of Christ, Raising of Lazarus, and inhabited vinescroll carved on the other three sides of the cross. The iconographic program of the shaft culminates in the image of Christ in Majesty at the top of what was presumably the main face.

A somewhat similar sense of threat, though this time the message is one of ultimate salvation, is depicted in the drawing of the psalmist's soul threatened by demons on folio 62v of the Bury Psalter (Vatican, Biblioteca Apostolica, Reg. lat. 12; figure 22). In this instance the nakedness of the soul may be a sign of its innocence or purity, and the scroll that supports the little figure a sign of the saving words of the psalms — it is balanced by the scroll that curves around the upper part of the clothed and human image of the psalmist below. The demonic creature to the left, with protruding tongue, is an embodiment of the words of the Psalm (51:3–4) written directly adjacent to the image: "Why dost thou glory in malice, thou that art mighty in iniquity? All the day long thy tongue hath devised injustice: as a sharp razor, thou hast wrought deceit." Yet there is also a sexualized threat. The soul's buttocks are turned towards the demon whose phallus, or phallus-like claw, penetrates the outline of the soul's body at the level of his buttocks; below the phallus (or claw), the testicles have been replaced by a leering head. It seems likely that the warning here is specifically against the sin of sodomy. While sodomy was not exclusively a male sin, nor one limited to sexual acts, the naked male figure of the psalmist and the phallic demon allow us to read it as such in this instance.[30]

[30] See Allen J. Frantzen, "Bede and Bawdy Bale: Gregory the Great, Angels and the *Angli*," in *Anglo-Saxonism and the Construction of Social Identity*, ed. Allen J. Frantzen and John D. Niles (Gainesville, FL, 1997), pp. 17–39, at 29: "The term *sodomite* was used to describe those who held unorthodox theological beliefs as well as those who performed sex acts that were considered *contra naturam*, against nature, because they frustrated procreation." For an excellent survey of different approaches to the subject in

The one exception to the general association of the naked male body with damnation, or the threat of it, in Anglo-Saxon art before the Conquest,[31] is the figure of Noah in the drawing of the drunkenness of Noah on page 78 of the Junius 11 manuscript (figure 44). It is possible to explain Noah's nakedness as necessitated by the text, since the forbidden gaze on the genitals of the father is, after all, the subject of the story; yet, despite the text, Noah's genitals are not normally depicted in surviving early medieval versions of the scene, including that in the Old English Hexateuch (London, BL, Cotton Claudius B.iv, fol. 17v). In part, this is a story that incorporates the themes of fertility and rebirth, and Noah's uncovered genitals, combined with the luxurious vegetation that surrounds him, may be read as a sign of both. Noah's genitals and the motion of his two obedient sons as they cover his nakedness at the bottom of the page, point us back to the illustration of Noah ploughing on the previous page, an illustration that is itself a sign of the newly fertile land and human prosperity. The act of reading, on the other hand, directs us forward to the textual account of Noah's sons and their progeny on the facing page. Noah's nakedness thus becomes a sign that his people will be fruitful and multiply, according to God's covenant. Nevertheless, the illustration is also one of shame and condemnation. Noah's drunkenness and Cham's disrespect lead to discord and disharmony, and the eventual breaking up of both understanding and people in the story of Nimrod, Cham's descendant, and the tower of Babel. In this context Noah's nakedness signals his son's punishment, and the fall from grace of one-third of his own line. On waking, Noah curses Cham:

medieval scholarship, see Allen J. Frantzen, "Between the Lines: Queer Theory, the History of Homosexuality, and Anglo-Saxon Penitentials," *Journal of Medieval and Early Modern Studies* 26 (1996): 255–96.

[31] The naked figures in the borders of the Bayeux Tapestry, produced in England immediately after the Conquest, may have nothing to do with damnation *per se*, but as glosses to the figures in the main narrative panel, they are all about the fight for land, power, and the rule of England. See above, note 2.

Þæt þam halgan wæs
sar on mode. ongan þa his selfes bearn
wordum wyrgean, cwæð he wesan sceolde
hean under heofnum hleomaga þeow,
cham on eorþan. him þa cwyde syððan
and his fromcynne frecne scodon.[32]

Noah's condemnation of his son is conveyed visually by the way in which the sleeping Noah's hands and genitals both point directly towards him. Noah's own shame in his son's fall from favor is suggested by the action of his right hand, which appears to be lifting the covers from his body — the activeness of his body indicating that he cannot be considered entirely guilt-free.[33] Neither Noah, nor Cham suffers during his own lifetime, but only through their descendants. Nimrod, like Lucifer, is proud, and his tower is an attempt to reach heaven, as well as a phallic structure.[34] The Junius 11 artist may have been suggesting the direct relationship between the two episodes through his inclusion of a branch of foliate ornament, echoing the foliate ornament under which Noah reclines, in the depiction of the Tower of Babel on page 82. The building of the tower is an act of disobedience "beyond what is fitting for men" (*ofer monna gemet*, line 1677), as Lucifer's attempt to establish his own throne in heaven was an act of pride (*oferhygde*, line 22b) beyond what is fitting for angels. Like Lucifer, Nimrod and his people suffer the loss of their homeland.

In contrast to the male body, there is an ambivalence towards the naked female body, depicted almost exclusively by the body of Eve, in Anglo-Saxon art. In the three representations of Eve that survive in Anglo-Saxon sculpture at Hoddam, Urswick, and Dacre, both Eve and Adam are clothed, and

[32] *Genesis A*, lines 1592b-97; "Because of that the holy one was sad in mind. He began to curse his own son with words, said that he should be miserable under the heavens, the servant to his kinsmen, Cham on earth. Curses then harmed him terribly and his descendants after him."

[33] See Wilcox's discussion of Cham's gesture in this volume, pp. 295-97.

[34] I would like to thank Sarah Larratt Keefer for drawing this to my attention.

therefore will not be considered here.[35] In the illustrations of the Old English Hexateuch, Eve's long wavy hair, sinuous poses, and positioning beneath the figure of Adam in the scene of their shame, point to an awareness of her role as carrier of femininity, the sexed female body, and guilt. Moreover, her coquettish pose in the illustration of the Temptation of Adam (figure 24) implies a sexualized act. This is supported by the text, which reads:

> Ða geseah ðæt wif ðæt ðæt treow wæs god to etenne,
> be ðam ðe hyre ðuhte, ⁊ wlitig on eagum ⁊ lustbære on
> gesyhðe, ⁊ genam ða of ðæs treowes wæstme ⁊ geæt.[36]

While the word *lustbære* does not necessarily carry a sexual meaning, the semantic range of OE *lust* and its compounds does extend to the sensual or sexual,[37] and when read together with the picture we can see the suggestion of such a meaning here.

The illustrations of Eve in the Junius 11 manuscript are more problematic. As argued elsewhere in this volume, her breasts, while they may be signs of the sexed female body, are also signs of the maternal, and maternal care.[38] Read in conjunction with the images of Eve and her female descendants after the Fall, images modeled on contemporary representations of the Nativity and Adoration of the Magi (figure 39,

[35] For Hoddom (late-eighth to early-ninth century), see Richard N. Bailey and Rosemary Cramp, eds. *Cumberland, Westmorland and Lancashire North-of-the-Sands*, Corpus of Anglo-Saxon Stone Sculpture 2 (Oxford, 1988), pp. 91,149, ill. 677; for Urswick (ninth century) see pp. 148–50, ill. 568; for Dacre (tenth to eleventh century) see pp. 91–92, ill. 245.

[36] Genesis 3:6, ed. Crawford, *Old English Heptateuch*, p. 88; "Then the woman saw that that tree was good to eat, because it seemed good to her, and beautiful in her eyes, and desirable in her sight, and then she took the fruit of that tree and ate."

[37] See, for example, "Ælfric's Homily on the Parable of the Vineyard," in *Sweet's Anglo-Saxon Reader*, rev. Dorothy Whitelock (Oxford, 1967), lines 117 and 191, or *Juliana*, line 409.

[38] See Mary Dockray-Miller, "Breasts and Babies: The Maternal Body of Eve in the Junius 11 *Genesis*."

figure 43), they help to moderate our sense of Eve's sin and guilt, and to strengthen her association with the figure of Mary. Moreover, it is through her sexed and gendered body, her role as woman in the act of giving birth, that she achieves her ultimate salvation. Eve explicitly links her own body with that of Mary (her daughter, and Christ's mother) in her appeal to Christ at the Harrowing of Hell in *Christ and Satan*:

> Ræhte þa mid handum   to heofencyninge,
> bæd meotod miltse   þurh Marian had:
> "Hwæt, þu fram minre dohtor,   drihten, onwoce
> in middangeard   mannum to helpe.
> Nu is gesene   þæt ðu eart sylfa god
> and ece ordfruma   ealra gesceafta."[39]

The motif was a relatively popular one in homilies, most notably the Easter homilies in Oxford, Bodleian Library, Junius 121, fols. 14v–154v, and the Blickling Homilies.[40] The interrelationship of the bodies of mothers and Son is emphasized in Junius 121:

> Geara me, min Drihten, for þinre modor lufan of ðære þu wære geadmet þæt ðu menniscne lichaman underfenge. Heo onfeng flæsc of minum flæsce and ban of minum bane.[41]

[39] Lines 435-40, ed. George Philip Krapp, *The Junius Manuscript* (New York, 1931); "Then she reached with her hands to the Heavenly King, asked the Lord's mercy through the person of Mary: 'Lo, from my daughter, Lord, you were born on earth to help men. Now it is seen that you are God Himself, and eternal author of all creation.'"

[40] See Keith Glaeske, "Eve in Anglo-Saxon Retellings of the Harrowing of Hell," *Traditio* 54 (1999): 81–101. Glaeske believes that the entry for the Harrowing of Hell on March 26 in the *Old English Martyrology* is the oldest surviving example of the prose tradition, though he admits that the manuscripts in which Eve's address to Christ is preserved (London, B.L., Cotton Julius A.x and Cambridge, Corpus Christi College, MS 196) are both later than the homiletic tradition (p. 85). See also Günter Kotzor, *Der altenglische Martyrologium.* Abh. Akad. Munich 88, 2 parts (Munich, 1981), II:46–47.

[41] A. M. Luiselli Fadda, "'De descensu Christi ad inferos': una inedita omelia anglosassone," *Studi medievale* 13 (1972): 989–1011, at 1006; "Have pity on me, my Lord, for love of your mother from whom you were humbled so

This same interrelationship of bodies is found in the Blickling homily, but in this case it is the womb of Mary and the maternal body that is stressed:

> Ic þe halsige nu, Drihten, for þinre þeowene, Sancta Marian, þa þu mid heofonlicum wuldre geweorþodest; hire innoþ þu gefyldest nigon monaþ mid ealles middangeardes weorþe; þu wast þæt þu of minre dehter, Driht-en, onwoce; ⁊ þæt hire flæsc is of minum flæsce, ⁊ hire ban of minum banum.[42]

Despite the prominence of the maternal body of flesh and bone in Eve's words, the pictorial tradition centered on the clothed body. It has been suggested that the Harrowing of Hell in *Christ and Satan* may originally have been illustrated.[43] If so, it is likely that Eve would have been shown clothed, as she is in the illustration of the Harrowing in the Tiberius Psalter (London, BL, Cotton Tiberius C.vi, fol. 14), an iconography which might well have been interpreted as continuing her Marian association, but one that can also be understood as representing an ambivalence towards, if not fear of, the exposed female body.[44]

that you received a human body. She received flesh of my flesh and bone of my bone."

[42] Blickling 7, ed. Richard Morris, *The Blickling Homilies of the Tenth Century*, EETS o.s. 58, 63, 73 (London, 1874–80; repr. in one vol. 1967), p. 89; "I entreat you now, Lord, for the soul of your servant St. Mary, whom you have honored with heavenly glory. You filled her womb for nine months with all the earth's prize. You know that you, O Lord, were born from my daughter, and that her flesh is of my flesh and her bone of my bone."

[43] Israel Gollancz, *The Cædmon Manuscript of Anglo-Saxon Biblical Poetry: Juniius XI in the Bodleian Library* (London, 1927), cv; Merrel D. Clubb, *Christ and Satan: An Old English Poem* (New Haven, 1925), ix–x; James R. Hall, "The Old English Book of Salvation History: Three Studies on the Unity of MS Junius 11" (unpub. Ph.D. diss., University of Notre Dame, 1973), pp. 25–43; Barbara C. Raw, "The Construction of Oxford, Bodleian Library, Junius 11," *ASE* 13 (1984): 187–207, at 191 and 203; Karkov, *Text and Picture.*

[44] On the ca. 1050 Bristol Harrowing of Hell relief, a work generally considered Romanesque rather than Anglo-Saxon, she is depicted nude. See George Zarnecki, Janet Holt, and Tristram Holland, eds., *English Romanesque Art 1066–1200* (London, 1984), p. 150.

*The Body in Law and Society*

If the unusual depictions of the fallen angels, the predominance of naked male bodies in hell, and the close relationship between Eve and Mary in Anglo-Saxon art cannot be explained with reference to earlier iconographic models, they might be fruitfully considered as part of a larger Anglo-Saxon cultural tradition. Keith Glaeske notes that while it is likely that a patristic source lies behind Eve's words at the Harrowing, none survives, and it is possible that they may have their origin in Old English literature. It is equally possible that they have their origin in the structure of Anglo-Saxon society, which seems to have aligned Eve, biological "mother of all the living," with Mary, mother of Christ, and spiritual mother of all the living, as well as with Anglo-Saxon queens and abbesses, the mothers of their people and houses respectively. Without doubt Mary served as the model for queens and abbesses, as she did for Eve; and without doubt all of these women functioned as intercessory figures of one kind or another. With the possible exception of the passages from the *Old English Martyrology*, all of the texts of the Harrowing in which Eve takes an active part, pleading with Christ for mercy by means of her maternal relationship with Him and with Mary, date from the tenth or eleventh century. They are thus roughly contemporary with the rise in status of the Anglo-Saxon queen, and the development of an iconography that made the Virgin a "paradigm for the Anglo-Saxon queens as well as for monastic women."[45] Both the iconography of *Maria regina* and the *ordo* that would have been used if Queen Ælfthryth was indeed crowned along with Edgar in 973 include bridal imagery. Byrhtferth's description of the coronation banquet in his *Vita Sancti Oswaldi*, also focuses on the queen's role as bride and producer of royal heirs,[46] a role

[45] Robert Deshman, *Benedictional of Æthelwold* (Princeton, 1995), p. 205.

[46] Deshman, *Benedictional*, p. 205.

that was named, if not highlighted, in the coronation ordo.[47] As both mother, or future mother, of *æthelings*, and protectress of convents, the queen's role and status centered on her fertile and maternal body. Yet, for both earthly queens and *Maria regina*, the maternal body was only a vehicle through which power could be achieved; real power rested in, and was symbolized by the sons (or son) born from that body. A queen was nothing without a son who could rise to and maintain power. Eve's words to Christ at the Harrowing make just this point; she asks for mercy through the children born of her body, rather than through her body itself:[48]

> þu fram minre dohtor, drihten, onwoce (*Christ and Satan*, line 437)
>
> Heo onfeng flæsc of minum flæsce and ban of minum bane (Junius 121 homily)
>
> þu of minre dehter, Drihten, onwoce (Blickling homily 7)

But in *Christ and Satan* Eve also takes on the Marian role of intercessor, pleading to be admitted into heaven with her children ("mid minre mægðe," line 423b). The typological relationship between the two women is conveyed visually in the Junius 11 manuscript by the use of the Nativity as a model for the image of Eve giving birth to Abel in *Genesis* (figure 39). Moreover, Eve is the only one of the inhabitants of hell to speak in this section of the poem, and thus becomes the intercessor on behalf of them all.[49]

Queens too were intercessors, and payments made to queens in wills may be records of this role.[50] Here too, the role of intercessor was couched in Marian terms, and reflected in

47 Deshman, *Benedictional*, p. 205; Janet Nelson, "The Second English *Ordo*," in her *Politics and Ritual in Early Medieval Europe* (London, 1986), pp. 361–74, at 372.

48 A point noted by Glaeske, "Eve," p. 91.

49 Glaeske, "Eve," pp. 94–96; Robert E. Finnegan, *Christ and Satan: A Critical Edition* (Waterloo, 1977), p. 109.

50 Pauline Stafford, *Queen Emma and Queen Edith: Queenship and Women's Power in Eleventh-Century England* (Oxford, 1997), p. 181.

images such as the portrait of Ælfgifu/Emma in the New Minster Liber Vitae, in which Ælfgifu stands beneath Mary on the right side of Christ. The page can be understood as either introducing, or forming part of, the Last Judgment depicted on the following two pages, and Mary's relationship to Christ the Judge paralleled to the queen's relationship to the king as judge and lawgiver. The position of the queen implies that she will eventually be amongst the saved because of her Marian associations. But not all women were types of Mary, and a positivist approach to the representation of women in Anglo-Saxon art, particularly one that limits women to the Marian model, is not enough to explain the lack of women in Anglo-Saxon images of hell, nor the clearly male bodies of the fallen angels and demons that populate it. While such practices may allow for a more sympathetic understanding of Eve in the Junius 11 manuscript, they do not allow generally for a more sympathetic approach to the unclothed female body. The general absence of the naked female body from Anglo-Saxon art is far more likely to be the result of uneasiness towards the female body in general, an uneasiness that is also seen in both the documentary and archaeological records, from which women are almost as absent as they are from art.

The association between men and fallen angels may have had a special relevance for the Anglo-Saxons, and one that originated in part in words attributed to Gregory, whose writings on the ten orders of angels were so influential in early medieval Europe.[51] Both the anonymous author of the Whitby *Life of Gregory* and Bede record the story of Gregory's encounter with Anglo-Saxon boys up for sale in the market in Rome. The author of the *Life of Gregory* tells us that the boys were young, beautiful and/or curly-haired,[52] and on learning that they were

[51] See above, note 17.

[52] "Quos quidam pulchros fuisse pueros dicunt et quidam vero crispos iuvenes et decoros," ed. B. Colgrave, *The Earliest Life of Gregory the Great by an Anonymous Monk of Whitby* (Lawrence, 1968), p. 90. For an exploration of the differences between the Whitby version of the story, Bede's version, and later translations and uses of Bede's version see Frantzen, "Bede and Bawdy Bale."

Angles (*Anguli*), Gregory responded "*Angeli Dei*" ("Angels of God").[53] Bede gives a slightly more elaborate rendition of the encounter:

> Ac uidisse inter alia pueros uenales positos candidi corporis ac uenusti uultus, capillorum quoque forma egregia. Quos cum aspiceret, interrogauit, ut aiunt, de qua regione uel terra essent adlati; dictumque est quia de Brittania insula, cuius incolae talis essent aspectus. Rursus interrogauit utrum idem insulani Christiani, an paganis adhuc erroribus essent inplicati. Dictum est quod essent pagani. At ille, intimo ex corde longa trahens suspiria, "Heu, pro dolor!" inquit "quod tam lucidi uultus homines tenebrarum auctor possidet, tantaque gratia frontispicii mentem ab interna gratia uacuam gestat!" Rursus ergo interrogauit, quod esset uocabulum gentis illius. Responsum est quod Angli uocarentur. At ille: "Bene" inquit; "nam et angelicam habent faciem, et tales angelorum in caelis decet esse coheredes."[54]

In Bede's version of the story, Gregory explicitly links angels and Angles in terms of both bodily appearance and national identity, and laments their fallen (pagan) state and control by "the author of darkness." In other words, they *look* like angels, but they are doomed to dwell amongst demons. This was the version of the story that remained popular in Anglo-Saxon

[53] Colgrave, *Life of Gregory*, pp. 90–91.

[54] Colgrave and Mynors, *Bede's Ecclesiastical History*, pp. 132–35; "As well as other merchandise he saw some boys put up for sale, with fair complexions, handsome faces, and lovely hair. On seeing them he asked, so it is said, from what region or land they had been brought. He was told that they came from the island of Britain, whose inhabitants were like that in appearance. He asked again whether those islanders were Christians or still entangled in the errors of heathenism. He was told that they were heathen. Then with a deep-drawn sigh he said, 'Alas that the author of darkness should have men so bright of face in his grip, and that minds devoid of inward grace should bear so graceful an outward form.' Again he asked for the name of the race. He was told that they were called *Angli*. 'Good,' he said, 'they have the face of angels, and such men should be fellow-heirs of the angels in heaven'."

England, as evidenced by its inclusion in the late-ninth-century Old English translation of Bede's *Ecclesiastical History*,[55] and Ælfric's homily for March 22 on *Sancti Gregorii Pape, Urbis Romane Inclitus*.[56] Ælfric's text follows Bede's closely, the only obvious differences being a slightly greater emphasis on the beauty of the boys and of the English, with the repetition of Gregory's gaze on their attractive bodies, and the identification of the English as being as beautiful (*swa wlitig*) as the boys, rather than just like them in appearance (*talis essent aspectus*):

> þa wæron hwites lichaman. and fægeres andwlitan menn. and æðellice gefexode;
>
> Gregorius ða beheold þæra cnapena wlite. and befrán of hwilcere þeode hí gebrohte wæron; Þa sæde him man þæt hí of engla lande wæron. and þæt ðære ðeode mennisc swa wlitig wære; Eft ða gregorius befrán. hwæðer þæs landes folc cristen wære. ðe hæðen; Him man sæde. þæt hí hæðene wæron; Gregorius ða of innweardre heortan langsume siccetunge teah. and cwæð; Wá la wá. þæt swa fægeres híwes menn. sindon ðam sweartan deofle underðeodde; Eft hé axode hu ðære ðeode nama wære. þe hí of comon; Him wæs geandwyrd. þæt hi angle genemnode wæron; Þa cwæð he. rihtlice hí sind Angle gehátene. for ðan ðe hí engla wlite habbað. and swilcum gedafenað þæt hí on heofonum engla geferan beon.[57]

55 "Eft he frægn, hwæt seo þeod nemned wære, þe heo of cwomon. Ondswarede him mon þæt heo Ongle nemde wæron. Cwæð he: Wel þæt swa mæg: forðon heo ænlice onsyne habbað, ⁊ eac swylce gedafonað, þæt heo engla æfenerfeweardas in heofonum sy" ("Again he asked what the people was called from which they came; they answered that they were called English. He said, 'That may well be; for their look is angelical, and also it is fit that they should be joint-heirs with the angels in heaven'"), ed. and trans. Thomas Miller, *The Old English Version of Bede's Ecclesiastical History of the English People*, EETS o.s. 95, 96, 110, 111 (London, 1890–1898 in 2 vols.), I: 96–97.

56 *Catholic Homilies* II.9, ed. Malcolm Godden, *Ælfric's Catholic Homilies: The Second Series*, EETS s.s. 5 (London, 1979), pp. 72–80. (Hereafter CH II.)

57 CH II.9, lines 57–70; "They were men with white bodes and fair faces and and beautiful hair. Gregory then beheld the beauty of the youths, and

Again, their fairness is fouled through their association with the "dark devil" (*sweartan deofle*).

More importantly, what Bede presented as a story handed down by tradition in words which suggest that he could not guarantee its veracity,[58] Ælfric presents as fact.[59] Ælfric also outlines the story's manuscript tradition; it no longer comes from anonymous forefathers, but from the "Historia Anglorum," and King Alfred's translation of it. What for Bede was a very likely and attractive legend became, for Ælfric, documented history, validated by two of Anglo-Saxon England's most famous authors. Common to all three accounts is Gregory's identification of the Anglo-Saxon boys as the heirs of, or companions to, angels. Rather than simply being created as replacements for the fallen angels, Anglo-Saxon men become the compatriots and mirror images of angels; like the heavenly angels in their beauty, but like the fallen angels in their bodiliness and damned condition. While the words used for the English people in these texts (*incola* and *þeod*) imply both men and women, Anglo-Saxon women are physically absent from both the episode and the equation. They may not be like demons, but neither can they be like angels.

The story of Gregory and the English boys was also part of the history of the conversion of the English and their salvation, albeit a shaky one, from the sin of heathenism, from

asked from which nation they had been brought. Then he was told that they were from England, and that the people of that country were as beautiful. Gregory then asked again whether the people of that land were Christian or heathen. He was told that they were heathen. Gregory then from his inward heart drew a long sigh and said, 'Alas that men of such fair appearance are subject to the dark devil.' Again he asked what the name of that nation was from which they came. He was answered that they were named Angles. Then he said, 'Rightly they are called Angles, because they have the beauty of angels, and thus it is fitting that they be the companions of angels in heaven.'"

58 "Nec silentio praetereunda opinio, quae de beato Gregorio traditione maiorum ad usque perlata est," Colgrave and Mynors, *Bede's Ecclesiastical History*, p. 132. A point also noted by Allen Frantzen, "Bede and Bawdy Bale," p. 19.

59 "Ða gelámp hit…," CH II.9, line 53.

turning away from God and towards Satan. The advent of written law in England was an equally important part of this history, and it too was associated with Gregory and his apostle Augustine. Moreover, we can understand both as concerned primarily with property. To whom do the angelic looking boys ultimately belong: God (and the church), or Satan? And how does one protect what is God's? Æthelberht's law code, the first documented written code of law from Anglo-Saxon England, is introduced by a rubric stating "Ƿis syndon þa domas, þe Æðelbirht cyning asette on Augustinus dæge" ("These are the laws that King Æthelberht established in the time of Augustine").[60] The manuscript in which the laws survive is the much later Rochester *Textus Roffensis,* but Bede also states that it was Æthelberht, the king to whom Augustine was sent by Gregory, who "decreta illi iudiciorum iuxta exempla Romanorum" ("established decrees of judgments for them following the example of the Romans").[61] The code, written in Old English rather than in Latin, opens with a law setting the penalties due for thefts of property from the church, bishop and other clergy.[62] Æthelberht's code emphasized both loyalty and obedience to Lord and lord, with pride of place given to protecting that which belonged to God. The penalty for disobedience or theft from God or His house at this early date was simply monetary compensation, but such thefts were, like rebellion of the angels, acts of disobedience centered on false claims to land, property and power. Like the rebel angels, those guilty of crimes against property led the list of the condemned. The modeling of both the heavenly and hellish courts in the Junius 11 *Genesis* on the relationship between king and retainer, a relationship at the heart of Anglo-Saxon society helps to make this point. The relationship between king and retainer was an

[60] See Mary Richards, "Anglo-Saxonism in the Old English Laws," in *Anglo-Saxonism and the Construction of Social Identity,* ed Frantzen and Niles, pp. 40–59, at 44.

[61] See Patrick Wormald, *The Making of English Law: King Alfred to the Twelfth Century* (Oxford, 1999), pp. 29 and 94; Richards, "Anglo-Saxonism," p. 44; Colgrave and Mynors, *Bede's Ecclesiastical History,* p. 150.

[62] Wormald, *Making of English Law,* pp. 29, 98; Richards, "Anglo-Saxonism," p. 44; Colgrave and Mynors, *Bede's Ecclesiastical History,* p. 150.

aspect of the Anglo-Saxon social order that was exclusively male, and the material and textual records of legal culture in Anglo-Saxon England indicate that the discourse of crime and punishment was also largely a male one. Certainly women were bound by laws, had recourse to the law, committed crimes, and could be punished most severely for them,[63] but laws were made and recorded, and judgments enacted within the predominately male preserves of ecclesiastical and royal council. Allen Frantzen's analysis of the Anglo-Saxon penitentials shows that even the punishment for crimes associated primarily with women, such as adultery, are "not about the act or the person who performs it; rather they are about the husband's status and his vulnerability," and about property.[64] Women owed allegiance to their husbands, as Lucifer had owed allegiance to God, but they were objects rather than subjects when it came to the definition of property. Crimes committed by or against women were thus perceived and judged in relation to their impact on the male body.[65]

[63] See for example, S. Hirst "Death and the Archaeologist," in *In Search of Cult: Archaeological Investigations in Honour of Philip Rahtz*, ed. Martin Carver (Woodbridge, 1993), pp. 41–43. Hirst describes the double burial of two women buried face down in a shallow grave with a heavy rock resting on the spine of the upper burial, a woman possibly buried alive (Sewerby, Yorkshire, Grave 41). The burial has all the hallmarks of an execution burial (see below), though, admittedly, there is controversy over its interpretation. See Andrew John Reynolds, "Anglo-Saxon Law in the Landscape: An Archaeological Study of the Old English Judicial System" (unpub. Ph.D. diss., University College London, 1998), pp. 97–98. I would like to thank both Andrew Reynolds and John Hines for their help in enabling me to read this thesis. See also Wormald, *Making of English Law*, p. 296.

[64] Frantzen, "Between the Lines," p. 272; see also, Vern L. Bullough, "Formulation of Ideals: Christian Theory and Christian Practice," in *Sexual Practices and the Medieval Church*, ed. Vern L. Bullough and James L. Brundage (Buffalo, 1982), pp. 14–21, at 20–21.

[65] Biblical crimes by and against women were also portrayed and judged according to their impact on men. See Mieke Bal, *Murder and Difference: Gender, Genre and Scholarship on Sisera's Death*, trans. Matthew Gumpert (Bloomington, 1988).

This is, of course, even more clearly the case in the secular laws than in the penitentials, and just as the earthly court was a mirror of the heavenly court, so secular law was a reflection of divine law. King Alfred made this abundantly clear in the Mosaic preface to his laws:

> Þis sindan þa domas þe se ælmihtega God self sprecende wæs to Moyse and him bebead to healdanne; and siððan se áncenneda Dryhtnes sunu, ure God, þæt is hælend Crist, on middangeard cwom, he cwæð, ðæt he ne come no ðas bebodu to brecanne ne to forbeodanne, ac mid eallum godum to ecanne; and mildheortnesse and eaðmodnesse he lærde … Ic ða Ælfred cyning þas togædere gegaderode and awritan het, monege þara þe ure foregengan heoldan, ða ðe me licodon ic áwearp mid minra witena geðeahte, and on oðre wisan bebead to healdanne. Forðam ic ne dorste geðristlæcan þara minra awuht fela on gewrit settan, forðam me wæs uncuð, hwæt þæs ðam lician wolde ðe æfter ús wæron. Ac ða ðe ic gemette awðer oððe on Ines dæge, mines mæges, oððe on Offan Mercna cynínges oððe on Æþelbryhtes, þe ærest fulluhte onfeng on Angelcynne, þa ðe me ryhtoste ðuhton, ic þa heron gegaderode, and þa oðre forlét.[66]

[66] F. Liebermann, ed., *Die Gesetze der Angelsachsen*, 3 vols. (Halle 1903–1916, repr. Tübingen, 1960), I, 42–46. "These are the laws that God Almighty spoke himself to Moses, and commanded him to keep; and when the only begotten son of the Lord our God, that is the Saviour Christ, came into the world, he said that he came not to break these commandments nor to countermand them, but to extend them with everything good, and he taught mercy and humility…. Then I, King Alfred, gathered these (*þas*) together and commanded to be written down many of these which our predecessors (*foregengan*) held, those which pleased me; and many of them that did not please me I rejected (*awearp*) with the counsel of my wise men, and ordered that they be observed in other ways. I dared not presume to put in writing at all many of my own, because it was unknown to me which of them would please those that were after us. But those that I found either in the time of Ine my kinsman, or of Offa king of the Mercians, or of Æthelberht, who first among the English received baptism, those that seemed most lawful, I gathered them herein and left out (*forlet*) the others," trans. Wormald, *Making of English Law*, pp. 421–22, 277.

The law for Alfred, like history for Ælfric, had its roots in the Bible but, as with Ælfric's treatment of the story of Gregory and the English boys, it also had a manuscript tradition that could be traced back to Ine, Offa, and Æthelberht, "who first among the English received baptism."

But biblical law was more than just a model for Anglo-Saxon law; it was also a source for legal punishment in the here-and-now. Anglo-Saxon charters, unlike their Continental counterparts, imposed spiritual rather than monetary penalties, and Satan and the fallen angels appeared frequently in sanctions. Criminals thus kept company with fallen angels in diplomatic, just as they did in *Christ and Satan*, and their exclusion from human society in life looked forward to their exclusion from the kingdom of God in death. An 855 grant of privileges to Alhhun, bishop of Worcester, by Burgred, king of Mercia (S. 207) includes the warning:

> Si quis hoc donum cum bona libertate ac voluntate augere voluerit et in omnibus custodire conaverit . sciat se in cælestibus habere consortium cum Deo ⁊ angelis ejus . Et si quis sit qui hoc in pejus mutare voluerit sciat se anathematizatum a consortio omnium sanctorum Dei in celis . et in perpetuum damnatum nisi ante hic Deo et homnibus cum digna satisfactione emendaverit et a malo cesset.[67]

To go against the word of the king, or to interfere with the exchange of property or property rights, thus became equated specifically with Lucifer's betrayal of God, and incurred the same punishment. During the tenth century, apparently as part of the monastic reform, the fall of the angels became a more

[67] "Regesta Regum Anglorum," http://www.anglo-saxons.net. Also accessible via the Anglo-Saxon Charters Website: http://www.trin.cam.ac.uk/chartwww. "And if there be anyone — as indeed we hope there is not — who shall wish to change this and prefer to alter it to evil servitude or constraint, let him know that he will be separated and excommunicated from the fellowship of all the saints of God in heaven, and damned in eternity without end with the devil and his angels, unless previously he shall make amends here with compensation to God and men," trans. Dorothy Whitelock, *English Historical Documents, c. 500–1042* (London, 1955), p. 487.

prominent part of the diplomas in which it was included. It was worked into the creation narratives of several of the expanded religious proems with which charters opened, in which the story served both to set the precedent for and to sanctify Anglo-Saxon social order — as it did in the Junius 11 *Genesis*.[68] One of the most detailed and florid examples of these reform era texts is King Edgar's New Minster Charter (London, BL, Cotton Vespasian A.viii, fols. 2v–33v), produced at Winchester between 966 and 984. The charter opens with the lines:

> ✠EADGAR REX HOC PRIVILEGIUM NOVO EDIDIT MONASTERIO AC OMNIPOTENTI DOMINO EIUS-QUE GENITRICI MARIÆ EIUS LAUDANS MAGNALIA CONCESSIT.
>
> [Chi-Rho (XPI)] Omnipotens totius machinae conditor ineffabili pietate universa mirifice moderatur que condidit.[69]
>
> Qui coaeterno videlicet verbo quaedam ex nichilo edidit . quaedam ex informi subtilis artifex propagavit materia .
>
> Angelica quippe creatura ut informis materia . nullis rebus existentibus divinitus formata . luculento resplenduit vultu .
>
> Male pro dolor libero utens arbitrio . contumaci arrogans fastu . creatori universitatis famulari dedignans . semetipsum creatori equiperans . aeternis baratri incendiis cum suis complicibus demersus iugi merito cruciatur miseria .
>
> Hoc itaque themate totius sceleris peccatum exorsum est . QUARE HOMINEM CONDIDIT ET QUID EI COMMISIT.

[68] See also, David Johnson, "The Fall of Lucifer in *Genesis A* and two Anglo-Latin Royal Charters," *JEGP* 97 (1998): 500–19.

[69] The prominent gold cross and chi-rho that preface the names of Edgar and Christ serve as non-figural signs of their eternal authority. As abstract symbols they stand for "the terrible force or transcendent power that lies behind all subjectivity, power, and law" rather than representing an authority limited to one judge, ruler, or time. See further Costas Douzinas, "Prosopon and Antiprosopon: Prolegomena for a Legal Iconology," in *Law and the Image: The Authority of Art and the Aesthetics of Law*, ed. Costas Douzinas and Lynda Nead (Chicago, 1999), pp. 36–67, at 60.

> I. Evacuata namque polorum sede et eliminata tumidi fastus spurcitia . summus totius bonitatis arbiter lucidas celorum sedes non sine cultore passus torpere . formatis ex informi materia diversarum rerum speciebus . hominem tandem ex limo conditum . vite spiraculo ad sui formavit similitudinem .
>
> Cui universa totius cosmi superficie condita subiciens . seipsum suosque posteros sibi subiecit . quatenus eius exsecutura posteritas angelorum suppleret numerum celorum sedibus superbia turgente detrusum.[70]

In this text the expulsion of the rebel angels is not only part of the Creation story, but part and parcel of the creation of the charter, and of a reformed New Minster. God's cleansing of the

[70] The text is based on Dorothy Whitelock, M. Brett, and C. N. L. Brooke, eds., *Councils and Synods with Other Documents Relating to the English Church*, 2 vols. (Oxford, 1981), I, 121.

KING EDGAR CREATED THIS PRIVILEGE FOR THE NEW MINSTER AND OMNIPOTENT GOD AND HIS MOTHER MARY AND GRANTS IT PRAISING HIS GREAT DEEDS.

The almighty creator of the whole of creation with ineffable piety rules wonderfully all the things that he has created.

He, it is clear, through the coeternal Word, created certain things from nothing; certain things the subtle artificer propagated from formless matter.

Indeed, angelic creation, assuredly, like formless matter, being formed divinely when no things existed, shown forth with brilliant countenance.

Alas, with evil, [Satan] using freewill, proud with contumacious arrogance, refusing to serve the Creator of the universe, making himself equal to the Creator, was plunged with his accomplices into the pit of eternal flames, justly tormented with bonds of misery.

At this occurrence of total crime sin came into being.

WHY HE CREATED MAN AND WHAT HE INTRUSTED TO HIM.

I. When truly, the throne of the heavens having been emptied and the filth of disgusting arrogance eliminated, the supreme judge of all virtue did not allow the gleaming thrones of heaven to be without an occupier, having formed from formless matter the diverse species of things, he at length made man from clay, and formed him in his likeness with the breath of life.

Placing under him all things created on the surface of the whole universe. He subjected man himself and his posterity to Him, so that his posterity, which would follow, would make whole the number of the heavenly angels thrust down from their thrones for their swelling pride.

thrones from the "filth of disgusting arrogance" becomes a model for Æthelwold and Edgar's expulsion of the secular canons from the New Minster, and the creation of man ruled by the Lord, a model for Æthelwold's bringing Benedictine monks loyal to him into the abbey.[71]

The interrelationship of divine and human law and judgment detailed in the text is reinforced in the complex iconography of the frontispiece (fol. 2v), which shows Edgar presenting the charter to Christ. In the portrait Edgar is flanked by the two patron saints of the New Minster, Mary holding a palm-branch and cross, and Peter holding his key. The two saints also intercede for him with Christ, both here in the charter and, by implication, at the Last Judgment. According to Jerome and Augustine, the images of cross and key are united in their ability to open the gates of Paradise.[72] The image of Christ in Majesty above Edgar is a certain reference to the Last Judgment, and the entire composition may have been modeled on images of the Deesis (in which Mary and John the Baptist flank Christ).[73] The charter was written by Bishop Æthelwold of Winchester, the same bishop responsible for establishing the Virgin as the model for the image of the Anglo-Saxon queen, and both the iconography of the frontispiece and the text of the charter establish a typological relationship between Peter, Christ, and Edgar as judges, which parallels the typological relationship between Virgin and queen as intercessors. Robert Deshman has explored this aspect of the page's iconography in some depth,[74] and we need only note here its

[71] Deshman, *Benedictional*, pp. 196, 199–200.

[72] Jerome, *Homilia in Lucam Evangelistam [16, 19–31]*, ed. G. Morin, *Anecdota Maredsolana*, 3.2 (Maredsoli, 1897), p. 385; Augustine *Enarrationes in Psalmos*, ed. E. Dekkers and J. Fraipont, CCSL 38–40, 3 vols. (Turnhout, 1956), p. 518.

[73] Robert Deshman, "Benedictus monarcha et monachus: Early Medieval Ruler Theology and the Anglo-Saxon Reform," *Frühmittelalterliche Studien* 22 (1988): 204–40, at 224; Deshman, *Benedictional*, pp. 200–01.

[74] Deshman, *Benedictional*, pp. 74–76, 197; see also John Higgitt, "The Iconography of St. Peter in Anglo-Saxon England and St. Cuthbert's Coffin," in *St. Cuthbert, His Cult and His Community to AD 1200*, ed. Gerald

applicability to the fall of the angels. Edgar, Christ and Peter were united in their roles as the gate-keepers of their respective kingdoms. Edgar had supported Æthelwold's expulsion of the secular canons from the New Minster, an action which Æthelwold portrayed as parallel to God's expulsion of the rebel angels from heaven, and Edgar was the protector of the church against heresy, as Peter was the protector of the Church against Satan.[75] But in the charter the rebellion and fall of Satan and his angels come first, and thus provide not only a parallel for human crime and sin, but become, as they are in Junius 11, the cause of it. The human criminal again merits the same eternal torment that Satan and his followers received, but the crime itself has become more specific.

There may also have been an historical dimension to Æthelwold's use of the image of Peter as judge, and the typological relationship between the reforming King Edgar and Peter. According to Bede, with whose writings Æthelwold was certainly familiar, Peter had been the authority on which Wilfrid and his Roman party based their arguments at the Synod of Whitby, where the Roman church prevailed over the Irish, and Irish ways were (at least in theory) expelled from the land.[76] It also seems to have been the authority of Peter, and his control over the gates of heaven, that convinced King Oswiu to side with Wilfrid and the Roman church in his final judgment.[77]

Æthelwold had very specific reasons, (his expulsion of the secular canons) for using the fall of the rebel angels as a metaphor for the establishment of just rule and control of a particular piece of land (the New Minster). Nevertheless

Bonner, David Rollason, and Clare Stancliffe (Woodbridge, 1989), pp. 267–85.

[75] Matthew 16:18–19: "Thou art Peter, and upon this rock I will build my church; and the gates of hell shall not prevail against it" (Douay-Rheims translation).

[76] Higgitt, "Iconography of Peter," pp. 273–76.

[77] Colgrave and Mynors, *Bede's Ecclesiastical History*, pp. 306–07; Higgitt, "Iconography of St. Peter," p. 276.

charters were inherently about land and loyalty and, for the most part, the power of the king, and it was Lucifer's betrayal of his Lord, manifested in his attempt to claim land and power in heaven, that brought about his exile and torment. The Junius 11 artist and the *Genesis* poet also emphasized this aspect of the fall of the angels by highlighting Lucifer's claim to a throne and kingdom in heaven. That these were deliberate choices meant to provide a specific reading of the episode is suggested by the fact that neither throne nor land feature in the illustration of the fall of the rebel angels in Claudius B.iv, and the episode is absent from the text of that manuscript.

As already noted in the laws of Æthelberht and the preface to Alfred's laws, betrayal of one's L/lord was the worst of crimes. The parallels between the dispensation of the law in heaven and on earth (particularly when it came to land) that formed the basis for Alfred's law, were addressed explicitly in the opening of Edgar's "*Wihtbordesstan*" Code (IV Edgar) of 962–963.

> ✠ Her is geswutelod on þisum gewrite, hu Eadgar cyningc wæs smeagende, hwæt to bote mihte æt ðæm færcwealme, ðe his leodscipe swyðe drehte and wanode wide gynd his anweald.
>
> I. Đæt is þone ærest, þæt him þuhte and his witum, þæt þus gerad ungelimp mid synnum and mid oferhyrnysse Godes beboda geearnod wære, and swyþost mid þam oftige þæs neadgafoles, þe Cristene men Gode gelæstan scoldon on heora teoðingcsceattum.
>
> I.a. He beþohte and asmeade þæt godcunde be woruldgewunan:
>
> I.1. Gif geneatmanna hwylc forgymeleasað his hlafordes gafol and hit him to ðæm rihtandagan ne gelæst, wen is, gif se hlaford mildheort bið, þæt he þa gymeleaste to forgyfnysse læte and to his gafole buton witnunge fó;
>
> I.2. gif he þonne gelomlice þurh his bydelas his gafoles myngað, and he þonne aheardað and hit þencð to ætstrengenne, wen is, þæt þæs hlafordes grama to ðan swiðe weaxe, þæt he him ne unne naðer ne æhta ne lifes:

I.3. Swa is wén, þæt ure Drihten dó þurh þa gedyrstignysse, þe folces men wiðhæfton þære gelomlican myngunge, þe ure láreowas dydon ymbe þæt neadgafol ures Drihtnes: þæt syn ure teoþunga and cyricsceattas.

I.4. Ðonne beode ic and se ærcebisceop, þæt ge God ne grymman, ne naþer ne geearnian ne þone færlican deað þises andweardan lifes, ne huru þone toweardan écere helle mid ænegum oftige Godes gerihta; ac ægðer ge earm ge eadig, þe ænige tylunge hæbbe, gelæste Gode his teoðunga mid ealre blisse and mid eallum unnan, swa seo gerædnys tæce, þe mine witan æt Andeferan geræddon and nu eft æt Wihtbordesstane mid wedde gefæstnodon.[78]

[78] Liebermann, *Gesetze der Angelsachsen,* I, 206–08; trans. Whitelock, *English Historical Documents,* p. 398.

Here it is made known in this document how King Edgar inquired what could be a remedy in the sudden pestilence which greatly oppressed and reduced his people far and wide throughout his dominion.

I. First, namely, that it seemed to him and his councillors that a calamity of this kind was merited by sins and by contempt of God's commands, and especially by the withholding of the tribute which Christian men ought to render to God in their tithes.

I.a. He has pondered and considered the ways of God by comparison with worldly usage:

I.1. If any tenant disregards the rent to his lord, and does not pay it to him at the appointed day, it is to be expected, if the lord is merciful, that he may forgive the neglect and take his rent without exacting a penalty.

I.2. If, however, he frequently through his bailiffs demands his rent, and the other then proves obstinate and intends to withhold it with defiance, it is to be expected that the lord's anger will so increase that he may grant him neither possessions nor life.

I.3. It is to be expected that our Lord will act in like manner on account of the audacity with which the laymen have resisted the frequent admonitions which our teachers have given about our Lord's tribute, namely our tithes and church-scot.

I.4. Therefore I and the archbishop command that you do not anger God, nor merit either sudden death in this present life or indeed the future death in everlasting hell by any withholding of God's dues; but both poor man and rich, who has any produce, is to render his tithes to God with all gladness and with all willingness, as the ordinance directs which my coun-

As Patrick Wormald points out, in this text God "can be expected to act much like any other landlord confronted with tenants withholding their rent."[79] The code has also become explicitly homiletic in tone, a tone that was to become even more pronounced under the influence of Archbishop Wulfstan during the reigns of Æthelred II and Cnut.[80]

*The Body Punished*

The increasingly homiletic nature of the law in the late-tenth and eleventh centuries is demonstrated not only in abstract rhetorical tone, but also in the very real spiritual and physical punishments imposed. Beginning with the reign of Æthelstan, a king "set on capital punishment for theft," execution became a codified part of the language of charters as well as law codes.[81] Excommunication, which had always been a part of ecclesiastical law, also seems to have been both codified and more systematically enforced in the late-tenth and early-eleventh century.[82] Whereas excommunication, the most severe of punishments, had been prescribed for a host of sins from the sexual to the economic, it was now "employed for sins that infringe upon ordained societal relationships, especially those involving members of the religious orders."[83] For the unrepentant, excommunication meant public exile from the Christian community in both life and death, and eternal damnation in hell. Its enactment paralleled the fall of the rebel angels. The excommunicate was expelled publicly from the church and congregation, a distancing that was reflected in the physical fall of the angels from heaven into hell, and one that certainly had

cillors decreed at Andover, and have now again confirmed with pledging at *Wihtbordesstan*.

[79] Wormald, *Making of English Law*, p. 318.

[80] Wormald, *Making of English Law*, pp. 339–41, 352–55.

[81] Wormald, *Making of English Law*, 306–7.

[82] E. M. Treharne, "A Unique Old English Formula for Excommunication from Cambridge, Corpus Christi College 303," *ASE* 24 (1995): 185–211, at 199, and Wormald as in n. 80.

[83] Treharne, "Excommunication," p. 199.

the potential for imposing a profound psychological awareness of the magnitude of both the crime and the punishment in the psyches of both outlaw and the community from which he was outlawed.[84] Excommunication was also a punishment enacted on the body. The texts of many of the formulae that survive provide an index of body parts that were systematically cursed as part of the public ritual. In the Old English text preserved in the twelfth-century manuscript Cambridge, Corpus Christi College 303, for example, we read:

> Awergoden beon heora hæfdon ⁊ on heora recgan; awergoden beon heora eagan ⁊ heora earan; awergode beon heora tungan ⁊ lippan; awergode beon heora teð ⁊ heora þrotbollan; awergoden beon heora sculdran ⁊ heora breost; awergoden beon heora fet ⁊ scancan; awergode beon heora þeoh ⁊ ealle heora in[n]eweard.[85]

[84] For space as punishment see Valerie I. J. Flint, "Space and Discipline in Early Medieval Europe," in *Medieval Practices of Space*, ed. Barbara A. Hanawalt and Michael Kobialka (Minneapolis, 2000), pp. 149–66. Excommunication was also a punishment enacted on the body — at least symbolically.

[85] Treharne, "Excommunication," p. 211. "Let their heads be cursed, and their necks; let their eyes be cursed and their ears; let their tongues and lips be cursed; let their teeth and their throats be cursed; let their shoulders and breasts be cursed; let their feet and their shins be cursed; let their thighs and all their insides be cursed." The Old English is a translation of the Latin: "Maledicti sint oculi eorum ⁊ colla; maledictæ guttura eorum & lingua; maledictæ sint manus eorum ⁊ brachia; maledictæ sint scapule eorum & dorsa; maledicti sint uentres eorum ⁊ umbilici; maledicti sint coxe eorum & genua; maledicti sint tibie eorum ⁊ pedes, omniaque interiora eorum nisi resipiscant ⁊ ad emendationem ueniant," ed. Terharne, "Excommunication," p. 210. See also Liebermann, *Gesetze der Angelsachsen*, I, 432–41. The formula should be compared with the prayer *Obsecro Te* in which the supplicant implores the cross of Christ to protect his head, eyes, mouth, hands, arms, legs, bowels, feet, and *omnia membra mea ab insidiis diaboli* ("all my parts against the snares of demons"). See Beate Günzel, ed., *Ælfwine's Prayerbook (London, British Library, Cotton Titus D xxvi + xxvii)*, Henry Bradshaw Society 108 (London, 1992), pp. 127–8; Catherine E. Karkov, "Abbot Ælfwine and the Sign of the Cross," in *The Sign of the Cross in*

The formula verbally fragments the body, simultaneously calling attention to the excommunicate as an embodied subject, and symbolically dismembering the body in what might best be seen as a verbal parallel to the sword of the executioner — and perhaps also a foreshadowing of the threat of eternal fragmentation before God.[86] Katherine O'Brien O'Keeffe has noted similar processes at work in secular law codes and descriptions of "schemes of inquiry and punishment" in the period 970–1035, the period framed by the Benedictine reform and the death of Cnut.[87] Excommunicates were also denied burial in consecrated ground, and their bodies may well have been abused in death.[88] It is interesting to note that in contrast to the physically interconnected bodies of Mary, Eve, queens and abbesses portrayed in the homiletic texts and in the art of the reform, there is also a development of the theme of the interconnected bodies of devil and sinner. In Vercelli 22 (line 110) the devil is said to inhabit the heart of the sinner, while in Vercelli 10 (line 88) the sinner is described as longing to reside in the devil's heart (*hardcofan*).[89] There is nothing in the language or grammar of either text to limit this relationship to men, though once again the gendered nature of the discourse of crime and punishment suggests that this is how it may have been received. The bodies of the devil and his servants, be they fallen men or fallen angels, are united not only by their actions,

*Anglo-Saxon England: Papers in Honor of George Hardin Brown*, ed. Karen Jolly, Catherine E. Karkov, and Sarah Larratt Keefer (forthcoming).

86 See Caroline Walker Bynum, *The Resurrection of the Body in Western Christianity, 200–1336* (New York, 1995).

87 Katherine O'Brien O'Keeffe, "Body and Law in Late Anglo-Saxon England," *ASE* 27 (1998): 209–32, at 209.

88 An addition to Vercelli 9, preserved in Oxford, Bodl. Lib., Hatton 115, fols. 140–7, records that amongst the penalties for a priest having sex with a nun, or a secular man either taking a concubine or committing incest are excommunication and burial in a dunghill (?) without a coffin (*ac drage butan cyste butan hi geswicon*), quoted in Treharne, "Excommunication," pp. 197–98, and note 55.

89 Peter J. Dendle, "The Role of the Devil in Old English Narrative Literature," (unpub. Ph.D. diss., University of Toronto, 1998), p. 104.

but through their bodies, which Anglo-Saxon artists showed to be male.

The physical evidence of archaeology demonstrates that the image reflected in and constructed by the documentary and art historical records was a social and cultural, not just a textual reality. Though there are very few textual records telling us who was actually excommunicated or executed for exactly which type of crime (as opposed to which crimes called for excommunication or execution), we might logically expect that both groups included both men and women. The material evidence, however, demonstrates that far more men than women were condemned as criminals. Analysis of the bodies excavated from late Anglo-Saxon execution cemeteries reveals that the execution and/or burial of women at these sites was very rare indeed. Fifty-five female burials out of a total of over 700 from twelve out of a total of around twenty cemeteries are known, and thirty-six of these are from a single cemetery (South Acre, Norfolk).[90] As regards the mode of execution, IV Æthelstan (the Thunderfield Code) directs drowning as a punishment for freewomen, and burning as punishment for female slaves, while male slaves were to be stoned.[91] A charter of 963–75 (S 1377) recording the acquisition by bishop Æthelwold of Winchester and Wulfstan Uccea of an estate forfeit by a woman and her son found guilty of practicing witchcraft records the woman's execution by drowning.

> Her sutelað on þyssum gewrite þet Aþelwold bisceop ⁊ Wulstan uccea hwyrfdon landa on Eadgares cyninge's' ⁊ on his witena gewytnesse. Se bisceop sealde Wulstane þet land æt Hwessingatune . ⁊ Wulstan sealde him þet land æt Jaceslea ⁊ æt Ægeleswurðe . þa sealde Se bisceop þet land æt Jaceslea into Þornige ⁊ þet æt Ægeleswyrðe into Buruh . ⁊ þæt land æt Ægeleswyrðe headde an wyduwe ⁊ hire sune ær forwyrt forþanþe hi drifon serne stacan on Ælsie Wulfstanes feder ⁊ þæt werð æreafe ⁊ man teh þæt morð forð of hire inclifan . þa nam man þæt wif ⁊ adrencte hi æt Lundene brigce ⁊ hire sune ætberst ⁊ werð utlah.[92]

[90] Reynolds, "Law in the Landscape," pp. 165–66, tables 85–104.

[91] Reynolds, "Law in the Landscape," p. 166.

[92] "Regesta Regum Anglorum," as in note 67. Trans. Whitelock, *English Historical Documents*, I, 519. "Here it is made known in this document that

The burial of a female surrounded by stakes on the shore of the Thames at Bull Wharf may represent another execution by drowning.[93] Of the female bodies excavated from execution cemeteries, seven had been decapitated, and a further four showed signs of mutilation, with three of the four showing mutilation of the upper arms.[94] The number of female execution burials known to date is too small for any definitive conclusions to be drawn, but it may well be, as Reynolds has speculated, that the different methods of execution prescribed for women in post-medieval England, "including burning of the corpse instead of disemboweling," have their roots in Anglo-Saxon practices.[95] It may also be that these roots involve an uneasiness about the display of the naked and tortured female body. Burning and drowning are processes that mask the body and its destruction from view as much, if not more, than they reveal it. They are also processes that at least in some cases destroy the body all but completely. The deviant female body thus remains all but absent from the material record of crime and punishment, not because it was not there, but because it was desired not to be seen as being there. Art of course helped to guarantee the veracity of this picture.[96]

Bishop Æthelwold and Wulfstan Uccea exchanged lands in the witness of King Edgar and his councillors. The bishop gave Wulfstan the land at Washington and Wulfstan gave to him the land at Yaxley and at Ailsworth. Then the bishop gave the land at Yaxley to Thorney and that at Ailsworth to Peterborough. And a widow and her son had previously forfeited the land at Ailsworth because they drove iron [?] pins into Wulfstan's father, Ælfsige. And it was detected and the murderous instrument dragged from her chamber; and the woman was seized, and drowned at London Bridge, and her son escaped and became an outlaw."

93 Reynolds, "Law in the Landscape," p. 166.

94 Reynolds, "Law in the Landscape," p. 165.

95 Reynolds, "Law in the Landscape," p. 166; V. A. C. Gatrell, *The Hanging Tree: Execution and the English People 1770–1868* (Oxford, 1994), p. 264.

96 One might also speculate here on the applicability of Freud's theories of the female body and the *unheimlich* to the Anglo-Saxons' apparent ambivalence towards the display and mutilation of the female body. Sigmund Freud, "The Uncanny," in the *Standard Edition of the Complete Psychological Works of Sigmund Freud*, ed. James Strachey, vol. 17, *An Infantile Neurosis and Other Works* (London, 1955), pp. 219–52.

Finally, the cemeteries, about twenty in all, formed an "organized system of execution sites located on the boundaries between individual hundreds," a location which mirrored the exile status of the criminal in both life and death.[97] Execution cemeteries also frequently made use of prehistoric barrows or earthworks, suggesting that they might be seen as located on the boundaries of past and present, Christian and pagan, life on earth and what lies beneath. There was generally little care given to either the body or the grave, and there is frequent evidence for violent decapitation and the display of severed heads.[98] Some graves housed the decapitated bodies of both men and animals, suggesting the sin of bestiality, a sin linked specifically to the devil's power over the bodies of men,[99] and one reflected in the iconography of hell in which men struggled eternally with beasts.[100] Some bodies were buried face down, and Andrew Reynolds postulates a superstitious motive for these types of burial as they are often amongst the deepest graves at a given site.[101] One might also note that bodies in the prone position are literally facing towards hell and away from man and God. The location of the cemeteries and the rituals

[97] Andrew Reynolds, *Later Anglo-Saxon England Life and Landscape* (Stroud, 1999), pp. 105–10. See also Sam Lucy, *The Anglo-Saxon Way of Death* (Stroud, 2000), p. 152.

[98] Reynolds, *Later Anglo-Saxon England*, p. 105.

[99] Mary Clayton and Hugh Magennis, *The Old English Lives of St. Margaret*, CSASE 9 (Cambridge, 1994), pp. 24–25.

[100] In many versions of the fall (Bishop Bernward's doors at the church of St. Michael, Hildesheim, or the illustration of the episode in Claudius B.iv) the serpent winds between or around Eve's legs, suggesting a sexualized fall and punishment; and the woman bitten by a snake (or snakes) was to become a traditional symbol of lust. This motif does not seem to have occurred in Anglo-Saxon England outside of Claudius B.iv. While this fact can be taken as symptomatic of the Anglo-Saxon stress on male punishment, it cannot be taken as supporting a female audience for the Junius 11 manuscript (see Karkov, *Text and Picture*). A relief carving of a woman with a snake coiled around her legs appear on the twelfth-century façade of Modena Cathedral, a church built under the patronage of Matilda of Tuscany, one of the most powerful women of her day.

[101] Reynolds, *Later Anglo-Saxon England*, p. 105.

associated with them, have much in common with the language and image of expulsion and condemnation in Anglo-Saxon England. The executed were banished to the borders of administrative/judicial territories, and their hanging bodies or severed heads were, as Reynolds points out, displayed "hanging effectively between heaven and earth."[102] The reuse of prehistoric features as part of such sites might also reflect the iconography of hell itself through the association of the barrow or earthwork with dragons and demons, and thus the suggestion that here the dead were actually undergoing eternal torment from serpents and other forms of monsters — the torments depicted in the Barberini Gospels canon table, or on the Rothbury cross.[103]

What we see in the fall of the rebel angels, and what we are told of hell by Satan in the Junius 11 manuscript, was then part and parcel of the culture of crime and punishment in Anglo-Saxon England right down to the absence of the female body. The naked and the damned were largely male, or at least were shown publicly to be so. They were banished from heaven and earth, and the location of the majority of their graves may indeed have brought to life the vision of the naked corpse gnawed by serpents. The literal and public mutilation of the body, and the display of hanging, decomposing corpses and severed heads, no doubt also brought to mind the eternal dismemberment and reassembly (the body that is forever in the act of being consumed) suggested by the images surveyed here.[104] Mutilation and burial practice also encourages specula-

[102] Reynolds, *Later Anglo-Saxon England*, p. 109.

[103] Reynolds, *Later Anglo-Saxon England*, pp. 109–10.

[104] Cf. Ælfric, *On Auguries* (LS 7), ed. Walter W. Skeat, *Ælfric's Lives of the Saints*, EETS o.s. 76, 82, 94, 114 (London, 1881-1900; repr. as two vols., 1966), I, 366: "ac gif he ðurh-wunað on yfelnysse . and forsihð his scyppendes beboda . and deofla gecwemð . þonne sceal he unðances on ecnysse ðrowian . on ðam unadwæscend-licum fyre . betwux ðam wyrrestan wurm-cynne . þe næfre ne byð adyd . ac ceowað symle . þæra arleasra lichama . on þam hellican lige" ("but if he continues in evilness and forsakes his Creator's commands and pleases devils, then shall he unwillingly suffer in eternity, in the unquenchable fire, between the worst of serpent-kind,

tion on the complex interrelationship between the bodies and images of men, angels, and fallen angels. If demons and men were separated from the angels and united with each other through their bodiliness, might the prone position and very deep graves of some offenders have been related to the fear of embodied demons? Certainly the depth of the burial, the position of the body, and the frequent mutilation of the corpse suggest an attempt to ensure that the dead stayed dead and buried; but it is quite likely that they also reflect a fear that demons could take bodily form, could even borrow bodies, in order to threaten the living. In his homily on Saul and the Witch of Endor (Pope 29), Ælfric wrote that witches visited the graves of criminals and heathens in order to call upon the devil, and that the devil took on the form of the person buried at the site:

> Gyt farað wiccan to wega gelæton, and to hæþenum byrgelsum mid heora gedwimore, and clipiað to ðam deofle, and he cymð hym tó on þæs mannes gelicnysse þe þær lið bebyrged, swylce he of deaðe aríse þurh hyre drycræft.[105]

In the Junius 11 *Genesis* the Tempter, sent by the devil, reassumes his original form as a beautiful angel in order to bring about Eve's fall. The male genitals and human bodies of the demons in the drawings of the fall of the angels from the same manuscript, might then be understood not only as a reflection of the largely male discourse of crime and punishment in Anglo-Saxon England, but perhaps also as a manifestation of the threat posed by the criminal dead buried outside of consecrated ground. In the Anglo-Saxon landscape, as in hell,

which will never be destroyed, but will chew forever the bodies of the wicked in the fire of hell").

[105] *Homilies of Ælfric: A Supplementary Collection*, ed. John C. Pope, EETS o.s. 259-60 (London, 1967–68), II, 796; "Yet witches travel to crossroads, and to heathen burials with their phantoms, and call to the devil, and he comes to them in the likeness of the person who is buried there, as if he had risen from the dead through their sorcery."

"hwilum nacode men winnað ymb wyrmes," and art may have been a way of making visible not only theological ideas, topographical and social realities, but also, perhaps, invisible cultural anxieties. The fallen angels of the Junius 11 manuscript lived in darkness, just like the heathen English nation which Gregory felt called upon to convert, and were, in appearance, like men, just as the English boys in Rome were in appearance, "non Angli, sed angeli."

# Breasts and Babies:
# The Maternal Body of Eve in the Junius 11 *Genesis*

MARY DOCKRAY-MILLER

IT IS HARD TO ESCAPE the body in the *Genesis* poem of Oxford, Bodleian Library, MS Junius 11.[1] Line drawings of Adam and Eve illustrate many of the first 54 pages of the manuscript, and they are "naked before God" in many of them. Close examination of the interactions between what I will call the "poetic text" and the "illustrated text" reveals the manuscript's uneasy presentation of the biblical narrative of masculine dominance — the story of the Fall, after all, is our primary codification of traditional, oppositional gender roles. The Junius 11 *Genesis* reveals an unresolved tension between its poem and its illustrations: while the poetic text continually reinforces an opposition of masculine Subject/feminine Other, the illustrations present a number of conflicting gender performances of dominant feminine, acquiescent masculine, and even active maternal.

Initial differentiation between the figures of Adam and Eve in the drawings is done most easily by reference to their breasts, specifically their nipples, rather than to the more standard gender markers of hair, dress, or naked genitalia. In the Junius 11 illustrations, Adam can be quickly identified

[1] For detailed descriptions and discussions of the manuscript, see Elzbieta Temple, *Anglo-Saxon Manuscripts 900-1066* (London, 1976); N.R. Ker, *Catalogue of Manuscripts Containing Anglo-Saxon* (Oxford, 1957); Thomas Ohlgren, *Anglo-Saxon Textual Illustration* (Kalamazoo, MI, 1992).

I would like to thank both Benjamin Withers and Jonathan Wilcox for their enormously helpful comments and suggestions as I prepared this essay. I would also like to thank Allen Frantzen, for long term direction and mentoring; Daniel Donoghue, who invited me to give a version of the essay as a talk for the Harvard Medieval Doctoral Conference; and Nina Rulon-Miller, for e-mail encouragement, thoughtful reading, and good wine at Kalamazoo. Any fault that remains is, of course, my own.

through the lack of nipples on his naked breasts. In contrast, Eve's distended and elongated nipples in the illustrations make her easily identifiable while they also mark her as feminine and possibly as maternal, reminding the viewer of the ultimately basic physiological function of female breasts — to feed an infant.

In addition, Eve's body, especially in the illustrations, frustrates the poetic text's attempts to efface biological maternity and maternal performance. The phrase "maternal performance" is indebted, of course, to Judith Butler, who described her theory of gender performance in *Gender Trouble* and elaborated on it in *Bodies that Matter.*[2] Analysis of the place, agency, and action of such maternal performance has begun to appear in Anglo-Saxon studies. Most recently, Clare A. Lees and Gillian R. Overing have discussed a "patristic maternity" that uses the language and concepts of maternity and reproduction in the service of the Anglo-Saxon church.[3] Rather than patristic, Eve's maternity in the Junius 11 *Genesis* is both biological (she is the biological mother of Cain, Abel, and Seth) and performative: she protects and nurtures her babies. This maternal performance is occluded in the poetic text that defines reproduction as a male process and performance,[4] but the illustrations late in the cycle confirm the necessity of her body to the lives of her children. The resulting dissonance colors the seeming finality of the traditional gender roles inscribed in the text of one of western culture's oldest narratives. In addition, this reading of bodies, of breasts and babies, leads to insights about the use of manuscripts in scholarly practice and to speculation about the identity of the artist of

[2] Judith Butler, *Gender Trouble: Feminism and the Subversion of Identity* (New York, 1990) and *Bodies that Matter: On the Discursive Limits of "Sex"* (New York, 1993).

[3] Clare A. Lees and Gillian R. Overing, *Double Agents: Women and Clerical Culture in Anglo-Saxon England* (Philadelphia, 2001).

[4] I borrow the term "occlusion of maternity" from Allyson Newton's essay, "The Occlusion of Maternity in Chaucer's *Clerk's Tale*," in *Medieval Mothering*, ed. John Carmi Parsons and Bonnie Wheeler (New York, 1996), pp. 63-75.

this section of Junius 11, who was certainly and unusually familiar with the way babies look when they rest upon their mothers' bodies.

My argument here attempts to address the drawings (the "illustrated text") and the poem (the "poetic text") as one coherent text — what I term the "full text"; the two are presented together and inform one another. Indeed, the illustrations and the poetry sometimes contradict each other, problematizing the reader's experience of that full text. The maternity illustrations, as I will argue later, are an example of such a contradiction. In her study of the manuscript, Catherine Karkov refers to the illustrations as "active translations" of the written text, highlighting the interaction between the two sorts of media.[5] While some art historians object to the use of the word "text" to discuss visual images, I will follow the example of Mieke Bal, who advocates the use of narrative theory and terms to investigate both literary and visual texts. Bal uses what she terms a "visual narratology" to replace the subjugation of image to text that she perceives to be operating in traditional scholarly practice; she wants to resist the usual assumptions that tend to "subordinat[e] visual to literary narrative."[6] In my discussion of the Junius 11 drawings and poem, I will try not to subordinate one to the other, focusing instead on how the two sorts of texts, the two narrative strategies, both inform and contradict one another. As Thomas Ohlgren says, "to ignore these illustrations is to ignore the manuscript as it was intended to be read."[7]

[5] Catherine E. Karkov, *Text and Picture in Anglo-Saxon England: Narrative Strategies in the Junius 11 Manuscript* (Cambridge, 2001), p. 36. Professor Karkov generously shared her study with with me prior to its publication.

[6] Mieke Bal, *Narratology: Introduction to the Theory of Narrative*, 2nd ed. (Toronto, 1997), pp. 161-70, at 161.

[7] Thomas Ohlgren, "The Illustrations of the Cædmonian Genesis: Literary Criticism Through Art," *Mediaevalia et Humanistica* n.s. 3 (1972): 199-212, at 199.

## *The manuscript and its criticial history*

The Old English poetic version of the Adam and Eve narrative, the first part of the poem *Genesis* contained in Junius 11, offers some striking narratival and visual differences from the biblical story. Most notable among these is that Adam is tempted first by the devil (whom he resists). In addition, both the illustrations and the text show that the devil disguises himself as an angel before appearing to Eve. Most important to an examination of Eve's subjectivity in the poem, another difference from the Vulgate source is the poem's praise of Eve for her loyalty to Adam and for her beauty even as she commits the original sin.

The poem I refer to as *Genesis* comprises 2936 lines and is usually divided into two poems, *Genesis A* and *Genesis B*. *Genesis B*, i.e. lines 235-851, is an Old English translation of an Old Saxon *Genesis* poem, a fragment of which was discovered in the Vatican in 1894.[8] Critics and scholars have tended to treat *Genesis B* separately from the rest of the *Genesis* text since that time, for reasons both aesthetic and critical: *Genesis B* is usually taken to be much better poetry than *Genesis A*,[9] and its 616 lines

[8] Eduard Sievers had hypothesized in 1875 that these lines were a translation from Old Saxon, and the 1894 discovery confirmed that hypothesis as "outstanding among the triumphs of Old English scholarship," according to Israel Gollancz in his facsimile edition, *The Cædmon Manuscript of Anglo-Saxon Biblical Poetry* (Oxford, 1927), p. liii.

[9] Speaking of pre-Sievers readers, Gollancz says, "This passage, telling of the fall of the angels and the temptation of Adam and Eve by Satan's emissary, must have struck many previous readers as being altogether grander in poetic style than any other portion of the volume" (*Cædmon Manuscript,* p. liii). Charles W. Kennedy, in *The Caedmon Poems Translated into English Prose* (London, 1916), states that the account of the angelic rebellion in *Genesis B* "is marked by fullest poetic power" and discusses its possible relationship with Milton's *Paradise Lost* (p. xxxiii). Ann Klinck, in "Female Characterization in Old English Poetry and the Growth of Psychological Realism: *Genesis B and Christ I,*" *Neophilologus* 63 (1979): 597-610, says that "*Genesis B* is distinguished from *Genesis A* by much greater vividness and dramatic intensity in the presentation of its characters" (p. 598), while J.R. Hall calls the *Genesis B* poet "a master of overall dramatic conception" in "*Geongordom* and *Hyldo* in *Genesis B*: Serving the Lord for the Lord's Favor," *Papers on Language and Literature* 11 (1975): 302-07, at 302.

are much more critically manageable than the vast, multi-subject *Genesis A*.[10]

While acknowledging that *Genesis B* has a source separate from that of the rest of the poem, I wish to use one part of the poem, lines 169-1127, as a single unit for an examination of Eve's maternal performance in the poem. Her visual and textual relationships with Adam and with her children are determined in these lines that describe Eve's creation, fall, and life after Eden. While an examination of this section of text may seem odd to readers accustomed to the traditional division between *Genesis A* and *Genesis B*, there is ample justification for examining these lines as a cohesive unit within a single poem called the Old English *Genesis*. Careful examination and analysis of the Junius 11 manuscript shows that these lines can and should be considered a single textual section, even though that section has two distinct sources.

The manuscript does not present what is termed *Genesis B* as a separate poem; there is no break, no notation to indicate that lines 235-851 should be considered different from the rest of the poetry, although twentieth-century scholarship has consistently done so.[11] This argument, (*continued page 227*)

[10] A 616-line poem lends itself to inclusion in anthologies, to individual editions, and to ongoing critical debate about its cruces and interpretations. The critical preference for the separate and shorter poem is evident in its treatment in surveys of the field (like *The Cambridge Companion to Old English Literature*, ed. Malcolm Godden and Michael Lapidge [Cambridge, 1991]) and in the number of critical articles published on *Genesis B* as opposed to *Genesis A*. Michael D. Cherniss even argues that *Genesis B* is not a translation of part of a much longer Old Saxon *Genesis*, but a translation of a nearly complete poem by itself in "Heroic Ideals and the Moral Climate of *Genesis B*," *Modern Language Quarterly* 30 (1969): 479-97.

[11] These lines are on pp. 13-40 of the manuscript (Junius paginated the folios sometime before 1655, so critical references to the manuscript refer to pages rather than to the more usual recto and verso folios). They show no visual differences from the rest of the poem; the system of punctuation is the same for the sections called A and B. *Genesis B* does begin at the top of a page, but the leaves that came before it, which would show the exact place where the Old Saxon translation began, are missing. *Genesis B* ends on line 8 of page 40 and is not visually evident as a separate text on the page. Within *Genesis*, the consistent system of capitals, the continuous (if

irregular) fitt numbering, and the narrative illustrations, all indicate one long *Genesis* poem, not a short separate one clumsily inserted into the middle of a different, longer one. "The large capitals are used at the beginnings of poems or sections of poems, and nowhere else in the manuscript," says George Philip Krapp, ed., *The Junius Manuscript*, ASPR 1 (New York, 1931), p. xx. Large capitals two pages before and two pages after l. 851 indicate the beginning of Eve's renewed temptation of Adam (*Þa spræc Eue eft*, l. 821, p. 38) and the beginning of God's interrogation of Adam (*Him ða ædre god andswarede*, l. 872, p. 42) but no capital indicates an ending to a *Genesis B* section at l. 851. Krapp divides *Genesis* into 41 fitts, though they are not marked consistently throughout the manuscript (see pages xxxix-xl). The first marked fitt is vii at line 325, almost 100 lines into *Genesis B*; the next is xvi at l. 918, 67 lines after *Genesis B* ends. Krapp's suggested divisions into fitts that are not marked does not indicate l. 851 as the end of a fitt, though fitt xiv ends soon after at l. 871. Furthermore, in "Some New Light on the Old English *Caedmonian Genesis*," *Studies in Iconography* 1 (1975): 38-73, Thomas Ohlgren argues that an illustrated Old Saxon *Genesis* served as the source for the drawings of both *Genesis A* and *Genesis B*. This idea was also put forward by Barbara Raw, who noted that the drawings for the A sections conform to the details of the B section in "The Probable Derivation of Most of the Illustrations in Junius 11 from an Illustrated Old Saxon *Genesis*," *Anglo-Saxon England* 5 (1976): 133-148. While much critical debate has centered on the amount of cooperation between the scribe and illustrator, the manuscript was illustrated as a single unit with drawings taken from a single exemplar whether or not the scribe and illustrator worked closely together.

Peter J. Lucas has argued for a thematically-motivated integration of the Old Saxon translation into the Old English *A* section; he details how the interlocking themes of loyalty and obedience connect the two poems at a level deeper than has been previously supposed ("Loyalty and Obedience in the Old English *Genesis* and the Interpolation of *Genesis B* into *Genesis A*," *Neophilologus* 76 (1992): 121-35). In addition, both Barbara Raw and A.N. Doane have analyzed the manuscript construction to conclude that the "two" Genesis poems may have been presented as a single work in other manuscripts, now lost, besides Junius 11. Raw's reconstruction of the damaged and incomplete second gathering of the manuscript shows that "the fragmentary state of gathering 2 ... cannot be used as evidence that *Genesis B* was first combined with *Genesis A* in Junius 11" in "The Construction of Oxford, Bodleian Library, Junius 11," *Anglo-Saxon England* 13 (1984): 187-207, at 195. Doane reaches the same conclusion by analyzing the section, or fitt, numbering. Since the actual marks for fitt division are sporadic, the consistency of the numbering even after some have been missed implies that the scribe was using the numbering from the exemplar; see A. N. Doane, ed., *The Saxon Genesis* (Madison, 1991), p. 34.

detailed more thoroughly in the notes, shows that the "two" poems were considered one poem by the manuscript's compilers in that they were combined more than once and then copied as one work more than once. The Anglo-Saxon scribe, and the community that scribe worked for and in, viewed the poem as one complete entity that was transmitted from manuscript to manuscript as a single unit, generically defined as Old Testament poetry.

Such an examination of the manuscript allows a consideration of Eve as a poetic and illustrated character in one cohesive textual unit. Lines 169-1127 encompass her creation and her disappearance from the text (we hear of Adam's death, but not hers, at l. 1127). These lines were all written by one scribe; their accompanying illustrations were all drawn by one artist.[12] Eve's gender performance encompasses femininity in relation to male figures (God, the devil, Adam) and also maternity after the exile from the garden. Critics have long argued whether to celebrate or excoriate her, but none has examined her *as mother* and questioned whether she actively reared her children.

Criticism of *Genesis,* like that of much Old English poetry, has been heavily source-based. Scholars have delved into the written text and into the illustrations in hopes of determining the sources of the poetry and the art.[13] Most of these source

[12] One scribe wrote pp. 1-212; three others worked on pp 213-29. One artist illustrated pp. 1-68, another pp. 73-84, and pp. 87-88, and a third p. 96. See A. N. Doane, *Genesis A: A New Edition* (Madison, 1978), pp. 3-4 and 16-17.

[13] For discussions of textual sources of the poem, see most recently Paul G. Remley, *Old English Biblical Verse: Studies in* Genesis, Exodus, *and* Daniel (Cambridge, 1996), pp. 94-167, and also J.M. Evans, "*Genesis B* and its Background," *Review of English Studies* 14 (1963): 1-16, 113-123; Brian Murdoch, "The Fall of Man: A Middle High German Analogue of *Genesis B*," *Review of English Studies* 19 (1968): 288-89; and Rosemary Woolf, "The Fall of Man in *Genesis B* and the *Mystère d'Adam*," in Stanley Greenfield, ed., *Studies in Old English Literature in Honor of Arthur G. Brodeur* (New York, 1963), pp. 187-99; see as well Doane's introductions to *Genesis A* and *The Saxon Genesis.* For discussions of a lost Old Saxon *Genesis,* Carolingian Bibles, Apocalypse commentaries, the *Physiologus* and Mediterranean

studies separate the "contents" — i.e., the written text — from the illustrations (and their sources) of the manuscript, a separation that has been constructed by a privileging of poetry over drawing. Doane and other source critics tend to focus on the drawings as indicators of information about dating and sources of the poetry. In her discussion of Junius 11's critical history, Catherine Karkov notes that "Source study . . . continues to fragment this manuscript by failing to consider the poems and drawings as part of a coherent whole" while she argues that reading both the poetry and illustrations provides a necessary perspective on the "manuscript's larger narrative structure."[14] In a similar vein, René Derolez includes the drawings with the poetry, noting that "no interpretation of *Genesis B* (nor of *Genesis A*, for that matter, for it too is illustrated down to p. 96) can afford to ignore the pictorial element."[15]

Although Eve's characterization is thus indicated most completely by the full text, most critical articles about the poem do not mention the illustrations at all, privileging poem over illustration and ignoring the dissonance of the illustrations. In her survey of critical scholarship on Eve in *Genesis B*, Gillian Overing sorts the poem's readers, "loosely grouping them under the more Christian aegis of Rosemary Woolf or under the more Germanic aegis of J.M. Evans."[16] I see the same scholarship (there is very little on *Genesis A*, none focusing on Eve after the Fall) as more definitively, rather than loosely, divided between exegetical[17] and Germanic.[18] The desires of

exemplars as sources for the Junius 11 drawings, see Ohlgren, "New Light"; Raw, "The Probable Derivation"; and Temple, *Anglo-Saxon Manuscripts.*

14 Karkov, *Text and Picture*, p. 6. Later in the same book, Karkov states similarly that "the illustrations were meant to be an integral part of the narrative and an aid in establishing the overall unity of the manuscript" (p. 16).

15 R. Derolez, "*Genesis*: Old Saxon *and* Old English," *English Studies* 76 (1995): 409-23, at 413.

16 Gillian Overing, "On Reading Eve: *Genesis B* and the Reader's Desire," in *Speaking Two Languages*, Allen J. Frantzen (Albany, 1991), pp. 35-63, at 41.

17 The most doctrinally strict exegetical reading of the entire poem is Bernard F. Huppé's in *Doctrine and Poetry* (New York, 1959). Rosemary Woolf argues

the critics who have examined Eve seem to have less to do with blaming or exonerating her and more to do with classifying *Genesis* as an example of a particular genre, with particular sources, be they religious or heroic. My own desires are to examine Eve's feminine and maternal performances rather than to classify the poem as a member of a specific genre; either as a heroic epic (with Eve as tragic lead) or as didactic lyric (with Eve as immoral transgressor), the poem has been read to present its two main figures within the terms of traditional masculine/feminine opposition that subsumes and occludes the maternal as merely a subset of the feminine.

that the poet's "apologetic comments" do not absolve Eve but "reveal his sympathy, not her innocence" in "The Fall of Man," p. 196; most exegetical critics judge Eve for her actions alone: she disobeyed the command of God, and thus is morally wrong. Most recently, Janet Schrunk Ericksen has read *Genesis B* against Augustine in "Lands of Unlikeness in *Genesis B,*" *Studies in Philology* 93 (1996): 1-20. Additional exegetical and theological arguments include Karen Cherewatuk, "Standing, Turning, Twisting, Falling: Posture and Moral Stance in Genesis B," *Neuphilologische Mitteilungen* 87 (1986): 537-44; Margaret J. Erhart, "The Tempter as Teacher: Some Observations on the Vocabulary of the Old English *Genesis B,*" *Neophilologus* 59 (1975): 435-46; Robert Emmett Finnegan, "Eve and 'Vincible Ignorance' in *Genesis B,*" *Texas Studies in Literature and Language* 18 (1976): 329-39 and "God's Handmægen versus the Devil's Cræft in *Genesis B,*" *English Studies in Canada* 7 (1981): 1-14; Constance Hieatt, "Divisions: Theme and Structure of *Genesis A,*" *Neuphilologische Mitteilungen* 81 (1980): 243-51; Thomas Hill, "The Fall of Angels and Man in the Old English *Genesis B,*" in *Anglo-Saxon Poetry: Essays in Appreciation*, ed. Lewis E. Nicholson and Dolores Warwick Frese (Notre Dame, 1975), pp. 279-90; and John F. Vickrey, "The Vision of Eve in *Genesis B,*" *Speculum* 44 (1969): 86-102.

[18] Evans, "*Genesis B* and its Background," pp. 119-20, as well as Cherniss, "Heroic Ideals"; Hall, "Serving the Lord"; Alain Renoir, "The Self-Deception of Temptation: Boethian Psychology in *Genesis B,*" in *Old English Poetry: Fifteen Essays*, ed. Robert Creed (Providence, 1967), pp. 47-67; Thomas Ohlgren, *Anglo-Saxon Art: Texts and Contexts*, Old English Newsletter Subsidia 17 (Binghamton, 1991). More recently, Larry N. McKill has argued for the poem's use of "heroic and exile imagery" in his "Patterns of the Fall: Adam and Eve in the Old English *Genesis A,*" *Florilegium* 14 (1995-96): 25-41.

## *Masculine/feminine opposition*

Most readings of Eve and *Genesis*, whether source-based, exegetical, Germanic, and/or feminist,[19] reinforce traditional notions of gender roles. These readings see masculine and feminine, Adam and Eve, lord and peaceweaver, as opposite and separate, yet dependent on one another for definition. Such opposition is termed by Susannah Mintz the "intensely hierarchized binaries" at work in the poem (she focuses on only *Genesis B*); her examples include "symbolic/semiotic, reason/sense, language/body, [and] self/other."[20] The biblical story of the Fall, after all, is usually interpreted to codify woman's socially constructed inferiority to man; its proponents invoke the story, in stunning circular logic, to show that that inferiority is natural. The Old English version of the narrative follows its source and can be seen as doing much the same thing, even as the narratival differences from the biblical version set it apart. Such a reading reinscribes a construction of gender performance that privileges the masculine side of an opposition (leader/follower) while assuming the naturalization of that opposition as well.[21]

The poetic text of *Genesis* itself overtly reinscribes this opposition. Throughout lines 169-1127, the reader is continually

[19] For feminist readings of Eve that precede Overing's, see Klinck, "Female Characterization"; Pat Belanoff, "The Fall(?) of the Old English Female Poetic Image," *PMLA* 104 (1989): 822-31; and Alain Renoir, "Eve's I.Q. Rating: Two Sexist Views of Genesis B," in *New Readings on Women in Old English Literature*, ed. Helen Damico and Alexandra Hennessey Olsen (Bloomington, 1990), pp. 262-72.

[20] Susannah B. Mintz, "Words Devilish and Divine: Eve as Speaker in *Genesis B*," *Neophilologus* 81 (1997): 609-23, at 611. Mintz's provocative and compelling argument does not address the manuscript illustrations.

[21] Critics who explicitly use this binary opposition in their analyses include Vickrey, "The Vision of Eve," and Hill, "Fall of Angels and Man," who read Adam and Eve as allegory for reason and sense; J.R. Hall, who blames Adam for his failure to lead Eve as he should have in "Duality and the Dual Pronoun in *Genesis B*," *Papers on Language and Literature* 17 (1981): 139-145; and Woolf, whose analysis in "The Fall of Man" assumes that women should not have power over men.

reminded that Eve exists for Adam, not in her own right. God creates her specifically as a support for Adam:

Forþon him heahcyning,
frea ælmihtig fultum tiode;
wif aweahte and þa wraðe sealde,
lifes leohtfruma, leofum rince. (ll.172b-75) [22]

God's initial motivation for creating Eve was simply that Adam not be alone in paradise (ll.170-71a). In the initial temptation scene of Adam, Adam refers to Eve in the same terms, as a woman who exists only in relation to himself: "me þas bryd forgeaf, / wlitesciene wif" (ll.526b-27a, "he gave me this bride, the beauty-shining woman"). Even as he castigates her after the Fall, Adam defines her only in relation to him:

Nu me mæg hreowan þæt ic bæd heofnes god,
waldend þone godan, þæt he þe her worhte to me
of liðum minum, nu þu me forlæred hæfst
on mines herran hete. (ll.816-19a)[23]

Adam's masculine performance in these lines — the performance of speech in narrative — defines the feminine only in relation to his own subjectivity. For him, Eve does not exist outside of her relation to him. The possessive forms in the notations to the illustration of Eve's creation bear out such an existence: Eve is called *his wif* and *Adames wife* in the inscriptions on page nine (figure 26: Creation of Eve); these notations were part of the manuscript's original program—Krapp even suggests that "the intention probably was to provide inscriptions for all of (the illustrations)."[24] Whether *wif* is translated "wife" or "woman," she is most definitively Adam's.

[22]"Therefore for him the high king, the lord almighty, created help; he animated a woman and the light-author of life gave this helpmate to the beloved man" Text throughout from Krapp, *Junius Manuscript*. Translations are my own and are literal rather than poetic. Further line citations appear in my text.

[23]"Now I for myself can regret that I prayed to heaven's God, the good ruler, that here he make you for me from my limbs, now [that] you have deceived me into the hate of my lord."

[24] Krapp, *Junius Manuscript*, p. xvi.

Even as she tempts him to sin, Eve is invoked as a loyal wife to Adam, who follows the tempter's advice to get Adam out of trouble with God. The poet refers to her as *þam þegne* at line 705, underscoring the hierarchy within the pair and her loyalty to Adam. Directly after that reference, the poet explains:

> Heo dyde hit þeah þurh holdne hyge, nyste þæt þær hearma swa fela,
> fyrenearfeða, fylgean sceolde
> monna cynne, þæs heo on mod genam
> þæt heo þæs laðan bodan larum hyrde,
> ac wende þæt heo hyldo heofoncyninges
> worhte mid þam wordum þe heo þam were swelce
> tacen oðiewde and treowe gehet,
> oðþæt Adame innan breostum
> his hyge hwyrfde and his heorte ongann
> wendan to hire willan. (ll.708-17a)[25]

According to the poet, Eve acts in what she feels are her lord's best interests; his needs form the basis of her actions.

The most obvious reinscription of the gender hierarchy comes in the separate curses of God on Adam and Eve (and thus on all men and all women), and it is here that maternity begins to play a part in Eve's gender performance. God tells Adam that he must suffer the curse of mortality: "þe is gedal witod / lices and sawle" (ll. 930b-31a, "for you is the separation of body and soul appointed"). This part of the curse applies to women as well as men, however, as men and women both experience death after the fall. Adam is also cursed to work for his food: "þu winnan scealt / and on eorðan þe þine andlifne / selfa geræcan" (ll. 932b-34a, "you must struggle and you must obtain on earth for yourself your food"). While this curse could be interpreted to apply more specifically to men than did the

[25] "She did it nevertheless through gracious spirit, she did not know there so many of harms, of sinful woes, that must result for the race of men, from what she took in her mind so that she heard the counsel of that hateful messenger, but believed that she, in the grace of the heaven-king, with the words, made that which she showed to the man as such teaching and promised as truth, until his spirit changed for Adam within his breast and his heart began to move to her will."

curse of mortality, working on the earth [in a field] for food is work that can be (and was) performed by male or female bodies. The components of the curse on Adam are simply not as gender-specific as is the curse on Eve.

God's curse to Eve is one that applies only to women, unlike Adam's more neutral punishment. It reinscribes both the inferiority of women to men and the occlusion of maternity within traditional femininity. To Eve he decrees that:

> Þu scealt wæpnedmen
> wesan on gewealde, mid weres egsan
> hearde genearwad, hean þrowian
> þinra dæda gedwild, deaðes bidan,
> and þurh wop and heaf on woruld cennan
> þurh sar micel sunu and dohtor (ll. 919b-24)[26]

In the curse, Eve is ordered into the inferior position in this gender hierarchy, but such a construction is actually nothing new within the gender terms of this poem; she has been oppositionally defined and inferior throughout the written text, as I have shown.

Eve's future motherhood, then, is a curse for her disruption of the gender hierarchy of the text, not a chance for subjectivity and agency. In these terms, motherhood is a punishment, not a joy; it brings sorrow, not power. Motherhood reinscribes the subjected and dominated nature of the feminine. It becomes only a part of that inferior femininity to reinforce the power and dominance of men over women.

Actual maternity is an uneasy affair in this poem. God tells both Adam and Eve to "be fruitful and multiply" in the beginning of the poem:

> Temað nu and wexað, tudre fyllað
> eorðan ælgrene, incre cynne,
> sunum and dohtrum. (ll. 196-98a)[27]

[26] "You must be in male power, constrained firmly with reverence of men, miserable to suffer the error of your deeds, to wait for death, and through weeping and lamentation to bring into the world through great sorrow son[s] and daughter[s]."

These lines and those directly following use the dual second person pronouns, sharing the responsibility for procreating with both the man and the woman. Similarly, when Adam and Eve begin having children, the verbs are initially in the plural: "ongunnon hie þa be godes hæse / bearn astrienan" (ll. 965-66a, "they began then to beget children by God's command").

Later in the poetic text, however, generation seems to be a mostly male affair, as the female contributions to childbearing are neutralized through the grammar of the poem (as, indeed, they are in the Vulgate text as well). Seth is born only to Adam: "þa wearð Adame on Abeles gyld / eafora..." (ll. 1104-05a, "then came to Adam as Abel's replacement a son..."). Children are repeatedly born to fathers, or defined as their fathers': "þanon his eaforan ærest wocan" (l. 1061, "from him [Cain] his sons first were born") is a typical construction in the post-Eden part of the text. Mothers are placed in prepositional phrases — Seth is born *be bryde* (l. 1119), by the bride or woman — like a tool with which a man achieves his goal of having a son who can inherit the family property.

Eve's physical body thus serves Adam's masculine status by producing children that are very specifically defined as his. Two Old English words for birthing or begetting — *cennan* and *(a)strienan* — provide lexical evidence for the subsuming of feminine, maternal work into masculine terminology.

The poet's specific, grammatical changes from the Vulgate source here are dramatic and important. In the Vulgate, Genesis 4:1 separates the work of conceiving and bearing children with third person, singular verbs that refer only to Adam or only to Eve: "Adam vero cognovit uxorem suam Hevam : quae concepit et peperit Cain ... Rursumque peperit fratrem eius Abel" ("In truth Adam knew his wife Eve, who conceived and bore Cain ... and again [conceived] and bore his brother Abel"). The singular, active verbs give Eve the responsibility and the credit for bearing the children. In the

[27] "Teem now and increase, fill with offspring the earth all-green, with both your kin, sons and daughters."

Old English poem, in contrast, the past participle of *cennan* is used to describe the births of Cain and Abel: "Adames and Euan aforan wæron / freolicu twa frumbearn cenned / Cain and Abel" (ll.967-69a, "At first Adam and Eve's two fair first-borns were birthed, Cain and Abel"). The grammatical change from the Vulgate source allows the use of the past participle — *cenned* — to elide the need for an active (maternal) subject to bear the children. The grammar of the sentence then equates Adam's and Eve's roles in their births; just as in the lines before (quoted above), Adam and Eve seem to have equal status as parents.

The other possible meaning of *cennan*, however, tends to impart a "masculine" connotation to the word, despite the specifically maternal associations of giving birth. *Cennan* primarily means "to beget" or "to bear" (the *Dictionary of Old English*'s "A" definition), but it can also mean to declare or to bring forth evidence in court (the "B" definition, with the legal context listed as meaning "B.2.c").[28] The *Dictionary* provides ten examples, clustered in the law codes, for this legalistic use of *cennan*. Through this legal connotation, it can thus be read to impart some of its legal authority when used to describe the birthing process. As such, *cennan* can imply the jural act of producing an heir, not the physical, maternal act of labor and delivery of a newborn infant—the act specifically described in the Vulgate source.

Similarly, *(a)strienan* has economic connotations that color its translation of "beget" or "produce." *Astrienan* is used at line 966 at the beginning of the genealogy of Adam (quoted above), where the unusual plural verb, *ongunnon ... astrienan,* shares the parenting responsibility between Adam and Eve. Another form, *strienan,* is used to mark Seth's birth in Adam's 130th year:

> Adam hæfde, þa he eft ongan
> him to eðelstæfe oðres strienan

[28] *Dictionary of Old English*, ed. Angus Cameron, Ashley Crandell Amos, Antonette diPaolo Healey, et al. (Toronto, 1986–). See similar sets of definitions for *cennan* in Joseph Bosworth and T. Northcote Toller, *An Anglo-Saxon Dictionary* (Oxford, 1898), p. 150; and J.R. Clark Hall, *A Concise Anglo-Saxon Dictionary*, 4th ed. (Toronto, 1960), pp. 66-67.

bearnes be bryde, beorn ellenrof,
XXX and C þisses lifes,
wintra on worulde. (1117-21a)[29]

*Strienan* replaces the Vulgate text's third person singular *genuit* (with Adam as its subject), the usual biblical term for begetting (most often of a son by a man—see Genesis 4:18-24). The Old English poem deviates from the Vulgate to define Seth specifically and unusually as an heir (*eðelstæfe*). The Old English poet's use of the word *strienan* further indicates the economic necessity of Seth's existence. *Strienan* can mean to acquire or amass property as well as to beget children;[30] with Abel dead and Cain in exile, Adam needs an heir to whom he can leave his material wealth.

The associations of these two words for birthing indicate the masculine, public interest in children's relations to legal and property rights of their parents. Eve's maternal body, sidelined in the prepositional phrase *be bryde*, does not figure here. Eve cannot mother these children who are born in past participles so the mother need not be an active subject, either in the grammar of the sentence or, it would seem, in the children's lives.

Children are referred to specifically as Eve's only once in the written text of the poem, when the poet tells us about *hire eaforan*, "her descendents" (l. 623) and these lines indicate her lack of power in matters regarding her children. Right before she takes the apple to Adam, the poet remarks:

[29]"When he again began for himself as a home-staff [heir] to acquire another son by the bride, Adam, the warrior courageous, had 130 winters of this life in the world."

[30] BT, p. 928; Clark Hall, *Concise Anglo-Saxon Dictionary*, p. 324. The *Dictionary of Old English* has not progressed to the letter S; its brief reference to *astrynan* in fascicle A provides only the definition "to beget" but does reference its future work with *strynan/strienan*.

Swa hire eaforan sculon æfter lybban:
þonne hie lað gedoð, hie sculon lufe wyrcean,
betan heora hearran hearmcwyde and habban his
hyldo forð. (ll. 623-25)[31]

In the poem, Eve's actions will necessitate penance (emphasized in the penitential implications of *betan*, l. 624a) for her descendants. But her concerns in her speeches are herself and her husband. She does not comment on those sons and daughters she must bring forth, the pain with which they will arrive, or the death that her action has ordained for them.

These traditional notions of masculinity, femininity, and maternity described and assumed in the Old English narrative and vocabulary are at work in some of the Junius 11 illustrations as well. As a whole, the illustrations are a combination of what are usually termed the Winchester and Utrecht (or Rheims) styles; the Junius 11 drawings take advantage of the narrative possibilities of these styles to illustrate the codification of gender roles demonstrated in the Fall and loss of Eden. The most striking of the many possible examples of the overt gender roles are the illustrations in the two registers on page 45, both of which show the masculine as the leader of the feminine (figure 37: Expulsion of Adam and Eve). At the top of page 45, Adam is foregrounded and in three quarter profile; Eve's body is frontal (and clothed, since they are being expelled from the garden). Her gaze is obscure; it could be directed toward either Adam or God. The illustration literalizes the medieval convention that the man must act as mediator between the woman and God.

In the lower portion of page 45, Adam continues in his traditional masculine role and leads his wife, who takes his arm as they leave the garden. Gollancz notes that Adam carries a spade and bag to conform to his new role of worker; he and

[31] "Thus her descendants must afterwards live: when they do evil, they must work for [divine] love, must atone to their lord for harmful speech and have his grace forthwith."

Ohlgren also contend that Eve is carrying a spindle-whorl.[32] While medieval tradition holds that Eve was a weaver and Adam a gardener, the "spindle-whorl" looks like the apple of the earlier drawings in the manuscript, on pages 24, 28, and 31 (figures 32, 33, 34). The illustrator gave Eve's traditional iconographic symbol the look of the symbol of her weakness. Karkov has noted the typological association of Eve with Mary through the spindle; she acknowledges the spindle's similarity to the apple but focuses on its textile associations as a female-identified object rather than on its visual connection to the apple.[33] In this illustration Adam and Eve leave the Garden with symbols of their gender, but Eve's symbol plays upon another motif in the drawings; the spindle/apple defines the woman as the tempted one who must be led.[34]

## *Breasts as markers*

This opposition so neatly set up in the written text and some of the illustrated text is challenged by the gender roles and subjectivities depicted in other parts of the illustration sequence. This challenge indicates an uneasiness, in the full text, with the reinscribed inferiority of Eve in a binary hierarchy. These drawings lay the groundwork as well for analysis of Eve as maternal subject and agent after the exile from the garden.

In many of these prelapsarian drawings, Eve is the signifying woman who controls representation, upsetting the text's binary construction of masculine Subject and feminine Other. It is Eve, not Adam, who becomes the reference point for

[32] Gollancz, *The Cædmon Manuscript*, p. xliii. Thomas Ohlgren also says this object is a spindle in his electronic *Corpus of Insular and Anglo-Saxon Illuminated Manuscripts* (Provo, Utah, 1991).

[33] Karkov, *Text and Picture*, p. 77. Karkov as well uses the image of the spindle to connect Eve, Sara, and the Virgin Mary as a "matriarchal trinity" in this section of her book.

[34] Illustrations that lend themselves to similar readings of an oppositional, gendered hierarchy include pages 10 (figure 27), 20, 24 (figure 32), and 31 (figure 34).

identification of the nude figures, which have basically no genitalia. Although they are shown together, naked and unashamed in seven illustrations, Adam and Eve look pretty much the same from the waist down. They both have the "spindly legs" that characterize the Utrecht style, abdominal flaps that hang down into the genital area, and blank crotches rather like those of modern Barbie dolls (the illustrations on pages 10, 11, and 13, figures 27, 28, and 29, are good examples). In these illustrations of our primary gender story, Adam has no sign of masculinity; he is not marked as a "have" to oppose Eve as a "have-not."

How, then, to tell the difference between Adam and Eve in the drawings? The viewer must rely on Eve for identification not only of herself but of Adam as well. The Junius 11 artist does not consistently rely on the medieval convention of depicting Adam on the viewer's left-hand side of the image (so that he would be on the right hand of God); while Adam is on the left on pages 11, 13, 34, 36, 39, 41, and 46, he is on the right on pages 9, 10, 20, 28, 31, 44, and 45. Eve's breasts, not Adam's positioning or his (missing) penis, differentiate her from him. In all of the illustrations that show Eve naked, all but two depict her with distended, elongated, and obvious nipples.[35] In these illustrations, the female breast rather than the male penis is the gender marker, the determining factor. Instead of a definition that privileges the masculine, in these illustrations the masculine is defined by lack: Adam does not-have breasts, and that is his defining characteristic. For example, in the illustration of the creation of man and woman (page 9, figure 26), God bends over a figure in the lower right corner of the picture. If the viewer does not see the brief line indicat-

[35] The first of the two illustrations that do not show Eve's breasts is on page 31 (figure 34), where her arms obscure her breasts; in this illustration she offers the apple to Adam, however, so the depiction of the narrative enables us to identify the relatively sexless figures. The second is on page 36 (figure 36); the bodies are covered with leaves and Adam has a beard to differentiate them. While Karkov argues that the "artist is by no means consistent in his use of this detail" (*Text and Picture*, p. 13), this specific analysis of only the prelapsarian drawings shows that this set of illustrations actually is consistent in its use of the nipple as marker.

ing Adam's rib in God's hand, this figure could easily be taken for Eve. The hair is long (Adam's hair changes lengths throughout the cycle) and Adam's breasts look distinctly feminine, round and defined. It is only in a comparison with the figure at the left, which is marked "Eva" and displays obvious female nipples that the viewer can make the sure identification of the righthand figure as Adam, the masculine. Eve's breasts serve as similar signifiers on pages 11, 13, and in both illustrations on 34 (figures 28, 29, and 35): they enable the reader to tell at a glance what is feminine and what is masculine.

Eve's distended nipples imply more than simply easy identification of the nude figures. They also portend some of Eve's sexual and maternal disruption to the narrative, in both the written and illustrated texts. Eve's nipples could be interpreted as a sign of sexual arousal, a reference to her ultimately dangerous sexuality. Viewers could as well read her nipples as a foreshadowing of her postlapsarian maternity and breastfeeding. The sexual and maternal functions of Eve's marked breasts inform readings of Eve as "mother of all the living" as well as a potentially subversive maternal performer in the illustrated text. Eric Jager discusses the function of the word *breost* in the poem, connecting *breost* (which he translates as the more-neutral "chest") with powers of speech and thought; he discusses the *breost* as "the bodily and spiritual center of the Fall."[36] Jager's insightful analysis mentions Eve's powers of "persuasion in its sexual or seductive aspect," but despite an oblique reference to a possible "mammary" function of the *breost*, he focuses on the "chest" as origin of speech as he analyzes the way that "*Genesis B* turns the Fall into a tragedy of oral tradition."[37]

An appropriate contrast to Eve's breasts in the Junius 11 drawings is with the nudes of Cotton Claudius B. iv, an Anglo-Saxon manuscript roughly contemporary with Junius 11. In each of its four illustrations of the creation and Fall, Adam has

[36] Eric Jager, *The Tempter's Voice: Language and the Fall in Medieval Literature* (Ithaca, 1993), p. 176.

[37] Jager, *The Tempter's Voice*; quotations in this sentence from pp. 179 and 188.

a beard and short hair and Eve has long hair (see figures 23, 24, 25).[38] The signs of gender in Cotton Claudius B. iv are apparent from the beginning, even though the artist uses Eve's long hair and carefully placed legs and trees to eliminate the need for portraying breasts or genitals.

Just as Eve's marked nipples upset the hierarchy of masculine and feminine constructed by the poetic text, so do other aspects of the illustrations. The final illustration in the Eden sequence is on page 46 of the manuscript and is the reader's last glimpse of Adam and Eve before they begin their lives defined by God's curse (figure 38). Like the illustrations in which Eve is the signifier of gender, this drawing upsets the gender hierarchy so carefully constructed by the narrative and vocabulary of the poem and reconstructed by the poem's readers and critics.

The page 46 illustration shows Eve as a feminine subject in a part of the tale where the narrative and the critics read only a masculine subject. On the left, the angel closes the door to paradise, which opens almost outside the frame of the picture. Adam and Eve walk away from the door. Adam carries his shovel and his bag, as he does in the similar drawing on page 45 (discussed above).

It is the differences from the drawing on page 45 that are important, however. Eve is not carrying her mark of gender, the feminine spindle/apple. In fact, she is not carrying anything at all and both her arms make evident the motion of her body away from the Garden of Eden and out of the picture into a different life. In a standard iconographical convention, Eve leads Adam from the garden (because she is considered the greater sinner).[39] She is in front, leading Adam, and he manages to hold her arm even though he is also holding his shovel. Their stance is the opposite of the iconographically unusual composition on page 45, where he leads her. He looks back

[38] C.R. Dodwell, and Peter Clemoes, eds., *The Old English Illustrated Hexateuch British Museum Cotton Claudius B. iv*, EEMF 18 (Copenhagen, 1974), fols. 6r, 6v, 7r, 7v.

[39] Hans Martin von Erffa, *Ikonologie der Genesis*, 2 vols. (Berlin, 1989–), I, 239-48.

toward the door and the angel, while she looks toward their destination. Eve is slightly larger than Adam as well. Even if the iconography is conventional, the details of this illustration (Adam's size and gaze, for instance), show Eve as leader, as controller of the action, while the accompanying narrative clearly states she is to spend the rest of her life in male power, as object rather than subject.

## *Maternal subjectivity and illustration*

The feminine subjectivity represented in the illustration of the exile from the garden expands to include a subjectivity of the maternal in the postlapsarian illustrations. The written text extends its presentation of the inferior feminine to an occlusion of the maternal, as the poem attempts to subsume the genealogy and reproduction of the fifth chapter of Genesis into masculine subjectivity (as indeed, does the Old Testament). The Old English text cannot be "blamed" for occluding the maternal, since it follows its source narrative, but that occlusion needs to be remarked upon rather than assumed and dismissed as the production of the source text. Both the Old Testament text and the Old English poem provide a litany of the names of fathers and sons.[40] Lines 1128-1252 comprise a genealogy that lists only masculine names and lengths of lives. A typical segment reads: "He wæs leof gode and lifde her / wintra hundnigontig ær he be wife her / þurh gebedscipe bearn astrynde" (ll. 1146-48, "he was beloved of God and lived here ninety winters before he by a woman here through intercourse begat a child"). This example uses the jural verb *astrienan*, places the woman in a prepositional phrase, and gives the man

[40] Interestingly enough, one Old English text does clarify the Old Testament's occlusion of the maternal; the prose *Genesis* of Cambridge, University Library MS I.i.33 states that: "Adam soðlice æfter þisum breac his wiues, ond heo eacnode" ("Adam truly after this enjoyed his wife, and she gave birth [literally: increased]"). The female pronoun before the verb *eacnian* makes clear that the woman does the labor in this genealogy. For full discussion and edition of this manuscript, see S.J. Crawford, ed., *The Old English Version of the Heptateuch, Ælfric's Treatise on the New Testament and his Preface to Genesis*, EETS o.s. 160 (London, 1922; repr. Milwood, NY, 1990).

sole credit for the production of the child through the singular verb. The rest of the language in this part of the text similarly celebrates patrilineage, but the drawings — and one lone vocabulary word — present active, maternal subjectivity that conflicts with the masculine and patriarchal focus of the poem.

Only one of the three words that describes the births of Eve's children indicates Eve acting as maternal subject. I have already discussed *cennan* and *(a)strienan* and their possible jural and economic connotations above. *Fedan* is the third verb in the poem that is translated "to beget," used to describe the birth of Seth, and it too occurs in the past participle (like *cennan* and *(a)strienan*) to obfuscate the physical maternal body that produces the child:

> þa wearð Adame on Abeles gyld
> eafora on eðle oþer feded,
> soðfæst sunu, þam wæs Seth noma. (ll. 1104-06)[41]

Adam is defined as the parent here, as I pointed out above, but the verb literally means "feed" and other translations include "nourish" or "sustain."[42] The connotations of this verb, unlike *cennan* or *(a)strienan*, point to the maternal body and the physical needs of the infant. Although the verb is a past participle, it reflects the Vulgate text in that it acknowledges the integral female contribution to childbearing (Genesis 4:25 echoes the phrasing and vocabulary of 4:1: "Cognovit ... Adam uxorem suam: et peperit filium"). The Old English poet's unusual choice of *fedan* (why not repeat *cennan* or *strienan*, as the Vulgate repeats *peperit*?) forces the reader to acknowledge the physicality of children and their mothers. Until the production of baby formula and sterilized bottles, only a lactating female body could feed a newborn. *Fedan* equates nourishing with birthing, or with begetting, and although Eve is not mentioned in this sentence, the verb used subtly reminds the text's reader that the mother's body was an absolutely necessary part of birthing and feeding the child.

[41] "Then came to Adam as Abel's replacement a son in the home, another begotten, a truth-fast son, whose name was Seth."

[42] BT, p. 273; Clark Hall, *Concise Anglo-Saxon Dictionary*, p. 113.

We have no visual or textual evidence (of which I am aware) that provides any information about breastfeeding practices in Anglo-Saxon England. Even religious iconography is missing: the common later medieval image of *Maria Lactans* has no counterpart in Anglo-Saxon England.[43] The one literary allusion to Christ nursing at Mary's breast occurs in *Christ I* (sometimes called the *Advent Lyrics*).[44] While some aristocratic women may have used wet nurses (as was common throughout Europe in the High Middle Ages[45]), the majority of Anglo-Saxon women must have fed their own children.[46] For a reader of the Junius 11 *Genesis* who is also a viewer, the word *fedan* may thus resonate with the previous illustrations of the naked Eve, whose elongated nipples marked the gender assignment in the early parts of the visual text. The figure of the prelapsarian, nude Eve certainly reminds viewers of the basic physiology of lactation and feeding.

The two illustrations of Eve as mother bear out such an acknowledgement of the mother's body. Indeed, in the drawings the infants Cain, Abel, and Seth are noticeably separated from their father, as if the illustrator (and the illustrators of the manuscript's exemplars) could not conceive of drawing an infant close to his father and far from his mother. Iconographically, of course, the image of Virgin and Child was much more readily drawn upon than any scene of father and infant.[47] It

[43] See Mary Clayton, *The Cult of the Virgin Mary in Anglo-Saxon England* (Cambridge, 1990), for a discussion.

[44] See Mary Dockray-Miller, "The Maternal Performance of the Virgin Mary in the Old English *Advent*," *NWSA Journal* 14.2 (2002): 38-55.

[45] See Clarissa W. Atkinson, *The Oldest Vocation: Christian Motherhood in the Middle Ages* (Ithaca, 1991), pp. 57-61 and 157-58.

[46] See Sally Crawford, *Childhood in Anglo-Saxon England* (Stroud, Gloucs., 2000), for a discussion of a clay artifact that may be an early medieval attempt at a baby bottle. The artifact was found in a child's grave, however, indicating the failure of the bottle experiment (if Crawford's identification is correct).

[47] Much of the Mother and Child iconography used by the Junius 11 artist is also evident in the *Benedictional of Æthelwold*, produced at Winchester, probably in the 970s. The *Benedictional*, London, BL, MS Add. 49598, includes a Nativity (fol. 15v), a Naming of Christ (fol. 22v), and an Adora-

may be dependence on such iconography (which gives precedence to the Virgin over Joseph) that places Eve on the left (presumably on God's right hand) and Adam on the right. In addition, these depictions of infants specifically with their mother rather than with their father indicate a culture wherein a father holding a baby might have been unusual, an image not readily available in the artist's store of usable compositions. Despite the poem's lexical insistence that these are Adam's children, in the drawings they are very much Eve's, and we get a glimpse of her performing maternal work that does not appear in the poem. But the poem and the drawings were meant to be experienced as one text, and the two drawings of Eve as mother are examples of the conflict, or dialogue, between the poem and the illustrations.

The first faces the page 46 drawing; when the illustrations are viewed as a dual set, Eve seems to lead Adam from the garden (p. 46, figure 38) to her childbed (p. 47, figure 39) where she delivers Abel. She is unattended (who could be her midwife?). Adam sits off to the right, separated from the other figures by columns. Cain is also separated, an infant hanging/standing in space between two columns, his future exile already ordained by the composition of the drawing. Eve's bed is foregrounded and fills most of the left part of the drawing; she looks intently at Abel, whom she holds up in his swaddling clothes so she and Adam can see him better. In her discussion of this illustration, Karkov focuses on iconographic connections of Eve with Mary (and of Abel with Christ); she points out that in this illustration "Eve's labour takes precedence over Adam's."[48]

Eve demonstrates maternal agency in two ways in this scene. First, she fills the space and commands the drawing. The placement of the bed and the detailed curtain above it draw the viewer's eye to Eve; it is hard *not* to look at her as she rests,

tion of the Magi (fol. 24v), all three of which bear striking iconographic resemblance to the Junius motherhood illustrations. For thorough discussion and reproduction of the *Benedictional*, see Robert Deshman, *The Benedictional of Æthelwold* (Princeton, 1995).

[48] Karkov, *Text and Picture*, p. 79.

postpartum — although the vocabulary of the poem resists acknowledging that postpartum body at all. Karkov notes that the composition of the illustration is "suggesting woman's dominant role in the process of procreation."[49] Second, she nurtures her child. She holds him, swaddled, keeping him warm and happy. Her other child, Cain, is close by and swaddled as well. While Cain is the older, they are both *frumbearn* (l. 968, "first-born"), and Eve seems quite calm, her children placid during this postpartum moment with twins, a situation that many parents and non-parents alike would find distinctly unnerving. Adam seems happy as well as he gestures toward the baby in his mother's arms.

The second illustration of Eve as mother emphasizes some of these differences from the text even more strongly. On page 54 (figure 41), Eve holds Seth on her lap on the lower right, gesturing to Adam, who stands in the lower left. While the written text defines Seth as Adam's son, in this drawing Seth is Eve's baby, and his little feet dangle from her legs as he perches on her knee. We see her hand grasping his side, supporting and securing him. This scene, like the other mother and child scenes in the manuscript, calls upon conventional iconography of the Virgin and Child even as it emphasizes a facet of the genealogy — the necessity of the mother's body — elided in the poetic text. (A similar illustration of Maviael's unnamed wife with baby Mathusal in the middle of the previous page [p. 53, figure 40] uses the same gestures, the same compositional separation of the father, the same definite association of the infant son with the mother rather than the father.) In these drawings, Eve demonstrates subjectivity and agency both before and after the Fall, especially in the scenes with her children. Hers is a feminine and maternal subjectivity that refuses to acquiesce to acting as Other to a privileged masculine — a subjectivity revealed only in the drawings.

Investigating Eve as mother leaves more questions asked than answered: what was her reaction to Cain's murder of Abel? At Cain's exile, we are told that he must "hweorfan / meder

[49] Karkov, *Text and Picture*, p. 79.

and magum" (ll.1047b-48a, "go from his mother and kin"). Aside from its convenience as a poetic formula, does the specific mention of Eve as *meder* here mean that the Anglo-Saxon poet thought that Cain had an especially close relationship with her? The poetic text even blames Eve, indirectly, for Cain's sin; while murder does lead to more murder (the poet uses the image of twigs stemming on a tree), "us hearde sceod / freolecu fæmne þurh forman gylt" (ll. 997b-98, "the beautiful woman more sorely harmed us through first guilt"). Her sin was worse than her son's, and without hers, his would not have been committed. Did Eve similarly blame herself for Abel's death? Furthermore, the poet twice calls Seth Abel's replacement (ll. 1104 and 1109); did Eve think of Seth that way? why does she not give thanks to the Lord, as Adam does, for Seth (ll. 1111b-16)? Is it because women are traditionally silenced or because she didn't think that one child could simply replace another?

Speculation like this, of course, draws us away from the text, from the silenced and occluded mother to a questioning of the mother's place in biblical narrative in general, in this specific poetic and illustrated text, and in Anglo-Saxon England. Eve's maternal performance leaves us with these speculative, unanswerable questions, observing the uneasy dialogue between the text and the drawings, watching Eve mother in the illustrations as the poem faithfully follows its sources to perform grammatical sleight of hand and make her disappear.

The obvious maternal focus of these illustrations plays out through the genealogical illustrations in the manuscript. Catherine Karkov has remarked on the unusual number of mothers depicted in Junius 11, connecting their postpartum images to Marian iconography of the Nativity and a celebration of late Anglo-Saxon dynastic mothers who "attained and manipulated power, shaping their own histories through their bodies and their sons."[50] Prominently depicted in the manuscript are not just Eve but Enoch's unnamed wife with baby Jared (p. 51), Jared's unnamed wife in labor (p. 53 top, figure

[50] Karkov, *Text and Picture*, p. 86.

40), Maviael's unnamed wife with baby Mathusal (p. 53 middle, figure 40), Seth's unnamed wife with Enos (p. 56, figure 42), Cainan's unnamed wife with baby Malalehel (p. 57, figure 43), Mathusal's unnamed wife postpartum as a midwife holds her baby (p. 62), and Noah's unnamed mother postpartum (p. 63). In one of the primary contradictions within the full text, all the mothers are not named in the written text but are important parts of the illustrative composition. All but one (Maviael's wife on page 57) of the mothers and motherhood scenes are comparable (if not precisely equal) in size to other figures and narrative illustrations on their pages. Karkov notes that the illustration cycle "keeps the viewer's eyes firmly on the procreative body";[51] motherhood is an integral part of the narrative, in these illustrations, even as it is ignored in the written text.

This prominence leads to speculation about the identity of the illustrator of the manuscript or its illustrative exemplar. Whoever made these drawings was familiar with the ways that babies rest upon their mothers' bodies. While conventional, all of the drawings show the mothers' arms believably positioned to support the babies and toddlers. Historical accuracy or believability is not a phrase usually associated with Anglo-Saxon manuscript illustration. Martin Carver has discussed the inclusion of realistically depicted contemporary artifacts in manuscript illustration, focusing on Anglo-Saxon swords, shields, and other objects that have made their way into illustrations adapted from earlier exemplars (Carver uses BL, MS Harley 603, a copy of the Utrecht Psalter, as his primary example).[52] Babies' positions in adult laps are not as readily identifiable — or period-specific — as sword pommels, but any adult who has held a baby, in any time period, knows that the sorts of positions and supports depicted in the Junius 11 maternity illustrations are accurate and usual. The artist who made these illustrations had carefully observed postures that were then rendered in a readily identifiable manner. Stylized iconography

[51] Karkov, *Text and Picture*, p. 143.

[52] M.O.H. Carver, "Contemporary Artifacts Illustrated in Late Saxon Manuscripts," *Archaeologia* 108 (1986): 117-45.

blends with physical reality when mothers hold babies to support their necks, balance their weight against the mothers' bodies, and provide the security of bodily contact. For example, on page 57 (figure 43), Cainan's wife grasps the forward-facing Malalehel around the belly, while on page 56 (figure 42) Seth's wife holds the sideways Enos by his calf, his thighs and buttocks firmly supported by her forearm.

These details of positioning in these illustrations contrast with less physically believable but more usual Marian conventions, like those exemplified in the *Benedictional of Æthelwold*. In the two nativities in the *Benedictional*, those of Christ and John the Baptist, the babies are separate, swaddled in cribs rather than in their mothers' laps (fols. 15v and 92v).[53] In the Adoration of the Magi (fol. 24v), Christ sits on his mother's lap, but this miniature is supremely conventional rather than physically accurate like the images of Junius 11. Christ's arms and legs are proportionately the length of an adult's rather than an infant's; his feet dangle in the middle of his mother's calves (contrast with Seth's more accurately-lengthed legs in Junius p. 54, figure 41, which reach only to his mother's bent knees, or the other babies whose feet are covered by swaddling and look to be more accurately proportioned). Mary's left hand is enlarged to fit around both Christ's arm and his upper thigh. Besides the unlikelihood of a parent holding both arm and leg, any parent knows that holding a baby's arm to stabilize it is a useless endeavour. Babies must be held at the center of gravity — which is not the forearm.

The only recognizably familiar depiction of the infant Christ in the *Benedictional* is the one Deshman deems "remarkably precocious and original" — Christ in Mary's lap in her bed on folio 22v, depicting the Naming of Christ (figure 45).[54] A somewhat accurately-proportioned Christ child (he does not look simply like a miniature adult), much smaller than his mother, uses her chest as a backrest as they both touch an

[53] Deshman, *Benedictional*, plates 12 and 30. Karkov discusses the ways in which the Marian imagery of the *Benedictional* was associated with Anglo-Saxon queens in *Text and Picture*, pp. 149-50.

[54] Deshman, *Benedictional*, p. 31.

object (Deshman calls it a "gold book") balanced in her lap. Christ's feet stick out daintily from under her right arm in this miniature that Deshman calls an "unusually intimate group of mother and child."[55] It is significant to my argument about physical accuracy that the most unconventional and intimate mother and child depiction in the *Benedictional* is also the most believable. Like the Junius 11 maternity illustrations, the *Benedictional*'s "Naming of Christ" is an illustration that a parent in any time period can view and identify with — this is an accurate and usual position for mothers (or fathers!) and babies.

This sort of accurate depiction of babies and mothers in the Junius 11 maternity illustrations implies an illustrator intimately familiar with babies and their needs. I would not propose that the artist must have been a woman, for to assert that only women can draw women with babies is to indulge in essentialist sexism just as surely as to assert that only men would have been permitted to work on such an obviously important manuscript. Karkov has recently argued that "There is no . . . reason to assume that Junius 11 could not have been produced for a woman, or at least with an audience that included aristocratic women";[56] I would like to suggest in addition that the manuscript may have been been produced by as well as for women. While our modern concept of "nuns" does not include women who have had babies, a significant number of the individual Anglo-Saxon nuns about whom we have information — usually aristocratic abbesses — were widowed mothers.[57] It is reasonable to assume that a similar number of the nuns who were not abbesses were widows as well. Anglo-Saxon religious houses for women, then, housed a number of nuns who would

[55] This quotation and that in the previous sentence from Deshman, *Benedictional*, p. 32.

[56] Karkov, *Text and Picture*, p. 151.

[57] For a discussion of widowed mothers as abbesses in seventh- and eighth-century Anglo-Saxon England, see Mary Dockray-Miller, *Motherhood and Mothering in Anglo-Saxon England* (New York, 2000), pp. 9-41. Men as well may have had extensive secular contact with small children before and during their monastic lives, of course.

have had intimate contact with babies and toddlers before their retirements and who could have used or shared that experience in the scriptoria in which manuscripts were made. The drawings of mothers and babies do not show that the illustrator of Junius 11 was a woman; they do force us to question the scholarly community's unthinking assumption of the maleness of the creators of manuscripts.[58]

Scholarly discussion about the dating and provenance of the manuscript and the poem places composition of *Genesis* all over Anglo-Saxon England at any point between 680 and 1000 A.D.[59] Doane suggests that the poem was originally composed sometime late in the seventh century, substantially modified with the inclusion of the Old Saxon translation at about 900, and changed again, less substantially, by the time of the creation of Junius 11 in c. 1000. He equivocally notes that "there are no reasons against the old assignment of the poem to Bede's Northumbria, though a Mercian or south-western home is also possible."[60] In contrast, Derolez follows Schwab's argument to suggest that the translation from Old Saxon be dated to Alfred's time, almost 100 years after Doane's dating.[61]

[58] For example, Doane states that the plain capitals were "presumably drawn by the scribe *him*self" (*Genesis A*, p. 12) while the zoomorphic capitals were likely careful copies of "capitals *he* found already in *his* exemplar" (*Genesis A*, p. 18, emphases added). Most egregious is Richard Gameson's discussion of manuscript inscriptions, legends, and tituli, wherein he both assumes and naturalizes the male scribe: "Naturally, this information could only have been appreciated fully by a literate man, or with the help of a literate man" (*The Role of Art in the Late Anglo-Saxon Church* [Oxford, 1995], p. 74). Gameson here does not even acknowledge the possibility of the existence of a literate woman. I must acknowledge that later in this book, Gameson does include the female: "Another point of obvious relevance is that the individual artist himself (or herself) might work in a number of different fields" (p. 123). Even Karkov, who argues for a female reception of Junius 11, refers to the artist as "he" (for example, see *Text and Picture*, p. 33).

[59] Doane, *Genesis A*, pp. 5-37.

[60] Doane, *Genesis A*, p. 37.

[61] Derolez, "*Genesis*: Old Saxon *and* Old English," p. 416.

While scholars consistently date the manuscript (as opposed to the composition of the poem) to c.1000 AD, there is much less agreement about where the manuscript was created. Gollancz suggests Winchester's New Minster as the manuscript's provenance and its abbot Ælfwine as its artist (because of the medallion portrait marked "Ælfwine" on p. 2).[62] David Johnson suggests a Winchester connection as well because of the poem's analogic connection with the description of the fall of the rebel angels contained in the charter known as "King Edgar's Privilege to New Minster," a known Winchester document.[63] Temple argues for Canterbury,[64] while Richard Gameson calls Canterbury "unlikely."[65] Peter J. Lucas argues that the manuscript originated at Malmesbury and identifies the Ælfwine of the medallion portrait as the abbot of Malmesbury from c.1043-1045.[66] Mildred Budny agrees with Gameson that the manuscript was not made at Canterbury but notes that it was "made somewhere in Southern England in the late tenth or early eleventh century" in her discussion of Junius 11's second artist's illustration of a Prudentius manuscript that is now Cambridge, Corpus Christi College MS 23.[67]

This range of suggested dates and geography indicates that many scriptoria in Anglo-Saxon England could have produced Junius 11 c. 1000; the possibilities include not just New Minster (a house for monks) but its sister house Nunnaminster (a convent founded by Alfred's wife Ealhswith), not just the all-male Malmesbury in Wiltshire but the all-female Shaftesbury in Dorset (probably founded for or by Alfred's daughter Æthelgifu).

62 Gollancz, *The Cædmon Manuscript*, p. xviii.

63 David Johnson, "The Fall of Lucifer in *Genesis A* and Two Anglo-Latin Royal Charters," *Journal of English and Germanic Philology* 97 (1998): 500-21.

64 Temple, *Anglo-Saxon Manuscripts*, p. 77.

65 Gameson, *Role of Art*, p. 37.

66 Peter J. Lucas, "MS Junius 11 and Malmesbury," *Scriptorium* 34 (1980): 197-220, at 219.

67 Mildred Budny, *Insular, Anglo-Saxon, and Early Anglo-Norman Manuscript Art at Corpus Christi College, Cambridge: An Illustrated Catalogue*, 2 vols. (Kalamazoo, MI, 1997), I, 283.

While the idea of female artists and scribes may seem novel, there is ample evidence to suggest that women made art throughout the Anglo-Saxon period. Most of this evidence comes from the early part of the period, from the seventh and eighth centuries. This early evidence ranges from the Boniface correspondence, in which Boniface asks Abbess Eadburh of a double monastery (possibly Thanet) for elaborately illuminated books,[68] to Rosamond McKitterick's paleographical analyses of the activity in nun's scriptoria in eighth-century England and Francia.[69] Of eighth-century religious houses, Bernhard Bischoff writes, "Even the inmates of English nunneries were versed in writing and were active too as scribes."[70] This early activity by women in the process of literary and artistic production, while not directly applicable to Junius 11, establishes substantial cultural precedent for female involvement in manuscript creation.

That precedent continued to be set throughout the ninth and tenth centuries despite the devastation of the Viking invasions of the ninth century. There was a definite decline in the learning and status at women's monastic houses from the eighth to the tenth centuries (as, indeed, there was in the men's houses); Patricia Coulstock states that "there was a deterioration in the state of English monasticism after 980" even as she notes that "the survival of Anglo-Saxon nunneries has not been adequately investigated."[71] Despite the Vikings, the eighth-century tradition and precedent of women making manuscripts survived in some form into the Benedictine Reform that produced the Junius manuscript. Stephanie Hollis

[68] See Ephraim Emerton, ed. and trans., *The Letters of St. Boniface* (New York, 1973); the letter from Boniface to Eadburh is letter 26, on pp. 64-65.

[69] Rosamond McKitterick, "Nuns' Scriptoria in England and Francia in the Eighth Century," *Francia* 19.1 (1992): 1-35; reprinted with the same pagination as Essay VII in *Books, Scribes and Learning in the Frankish Kingdoms, 6th-9th Centuries* (Aldershot, Hamps., 1994).

[70] Bernhard Bischoff, *Latin Palaeography: Antiquity and the Middle Ages*, trans. Dáibhí Ó Cróinín and David Ganz (Cambridge, 1990), p. 199.

[71] Patricia Coulstock, *The Collegiate Church of Wimborne Minster* (Woodbridge, 1993), p. 97.

has discussed female saints' lives composed and transmitted through the female monastic tradition from seventh- and eighth-century composition to tenth- and eleventh-century manuscript preservation.[72] Michelle Brown discusses just such a survival in her work on female ownership of prayerbooks from ninth-century Mercia (one of which may have been produced at Nunnaminster).[73]

Early eleventh-century evidence for women's involvement in artistic production brings the sketchy trail of female-produced manuscripts to the period that produced Junius 11. In her edition of the Vercelli Book manuscript facsimile, Celia Sisam includes an intriguing footnote suggesting a female house such as Barking Abbey as a possible provenance for the Vercelli Book (also c. 1000).[74] More substantial is C.R. Dodwell's discussion of the artistic ability of Wilton's St. Edith (961?-984), daughter of King Edgar; Goscelin's *Life of Edith* celebrates her skills in embroidery, music, calligraphy, and painting. Dodwell suggests that only her sanctity led to the preservation of descriptions of Edith as an artist.[75] All of this seemingly disparate scholarly work focused on a variety of texts and time periods shows that women were involved in manuscript production throughout the Anglo-Saxon period, up to and including the early eleventh century.

[72] For a specific discussion of a Life of St. Mildrith, see Stephanie Hollis, "The Old English 'Ritual of Admission of Mildrith' (London, Lambeth Palace 427, fol. 210)," *Journal of English and Germanic Philology* 97 (1998): 311-21; for a more general analysis of the body of texts known as the "Mildrith Legend," see Hollis "The Minster-in-Thanet Foundation Story," *Anglo-Saxon England* 27 (1998): 41-64; see also her book-length analysis, *Anglo-Saxon Women and the Church: Sharing a Common Fate* (Woodbridge, 1992).

[73] Michelle P. Brown, "Female Book-Ownership and Production in Anglo-Saxon England: the Evidence of the Ninth-Century Prayerbooks," in *Lexis and Texts in Early English: Studies Presented to Jane Roberts*, ed. Christian J. Kay and Louise M. Sylvester (Amsterdam, 2001), pp. 45-67. Dr. Brown has been most generous in her sharing of this work with me prior to publication.

[74] Celia Sisam, ed., *The Vercelli Book*, EEMF 19 (Copenhagen, 1976), p. 44, n. 2.

[75] C.R. Dodwell, *Anglo-Saxon Art: A New Perspective* (Ithaca, NY, 1982), pp. 48, 53-55.

We have very few clues to point to the identity of the scribes or artists of Junius 11. While Junius 11's second artist (not the artist of the maternity illustrations) was also the artist of the Corpus Christi *Prudentius* (see n. 61), this connection is not evidence that rules out a female idenity of the first artist. Budny states that CCCC 23 was "[a]pparently not made in the same center as the Junius Manuscript." The first artist of Junius 11 — the one working at an "apparently provincial" scriptorium, the one who was not "the better artist,"[76] — was the artist who departed from conventional Marian iconography just enough to indicate a working familiarity with the bodily interactions of mothers with babies and toddlers. The illustrations of the babies in Junius 11 demand the inclusion of women in the list of possible illustrators of the manuscript; scholars need to use the cumbersome but accurate "he or she" when discussing the manuscript's creators.

In the full text of the Junius 11 *Genesis*, feminine and maternal subjectivity are actually represented, and represented accurately with unusual frequency. Because of the poem's publication history, however, very few readers have the opportunity to view the drawings and the text simultaneously. There were only 250 copies of the Junius 11 manuscript facsimile made in 1927 and this is the only hard copy publication that reproduces the text and illustrations together — reproducing them in black and white, which does not give any sense of the delicately colored inks of some of the drawings.[77] To read just the poem or see just the illustrations gives the reader/viewer a circumscribed view of the poem or the drawings. Only the full text — the version intended by the scribe and artist and by their exemplar — allows the reader/viewer of *Genesis* to see Eve as maternal performer disrupting the poem's careful construction of masculine domination and exploitation of the maternal and the feminine for masculine ends. Although Eve is a mother — of Cain, of Abel, of Seth, and (according to some creation-

[76] Quotations in this and the previous sentence from Budny, *Manuscript Art*, p. 283.

[77] Gollancz, *The Cædmon Manuscript*, endleaf; Ohlgren, *Textual Illustrations*.

ists) of all humanity — she is not maternal, except in the two pictures of her in the postlapsarian genealogy, a genealogy devoted to the celebration of patrimony passed from fathers to sons through occluded maternal bodies. The full text is crucial to this understanding of the ultimate ineffectuality of an attempt to occlude maternity from genealogy and reproduction.

The editorial practices of separation — institutionalized in separate editions of *Genesis A* and *Genesis B* and in reproduction of the drawings without the text — has led to a reception of *Genesis* fragmented by modern publication practices. A reading of *Genesis,* rather than of *Genesis A* or *Genesis B,* entails the use of Krapp's 1931 edition, *The Junius Manuscript*; a reading that can refer to drawings while reading the poetry presented next to those drawings entails using the manuscript facsimile (hard copy or electronic) as a core text, not an option even for most scholars, certainly not for more casual students. The Bodleian Library's digitally reproduced facsimile (available on the world wide web at http://image.ox.ac.uk/pages/bodleian/MSJUNI~1 /Main.htm) is perhaps the best solution to the fragmentation of reception wrought by nineteenth- and twentieth-century scholarship.[78] This accessible edition of the full text finally makes generally available the subversive dissonances of the maternity illustrations; it reveals the breasts and babies of Junius 11. Furthermore, an accessible electronic facsimile can reveal other, as yet unremarked, dissonances within the text whose most famous characters begin "naked before God."

[78] See Karkov, *Text and Picture*, pp. 182 and 202, for reservations about the electronic facsimile project.

# Penitential Nakedness and the Junius 11 *Genesis*

Janet S. Ericksen

An injunction in an Old English guide for assigning penances, the "Scrift boc" usually tagged as of "Pseudo-Egbert," asserts that "Ceorle ne gedafenað þæt he his wif æfre nacode geseo" ("it is not right for a man that he ever see his wife naked").[1] Despite its potential impracticality and peripheral-seeming status in a list of more dramatic moral transgressions, the restriction is not alone among Anglo-Saxon texts in identifying nakedness as both the focal sign of sin and part of an encouragement to confess and receive penance. The illustrated Old English *Genesis* narrative in Oxford, Bodleian Library Manuscript Junius 11, usually known by the conventional titles of its two parts, *Genesis A* and *Genesis B,* as well as at least two Old English anonymous homilies corroborate the penitential. In early Anglo-Saxon law, as Mary Richard's essay indicates, "the unclothed, wounded body . . . conveyed the evidence of a crime and the means to determine restitution."[2] In a vernacular poetic narrative, a homily, and a penitential handbook, nakedness itself, rather than the marks upon the naked body, is a sign of sin and a demonstration of the clothing that confession and

[1] Robert Spindler, ed., *Das altenglische Bussbuch (sog. Confessionale pseudo-Egberti)* (Leipzig, 1934) XIV.17.a, p. 182. The OE survives in three manuscripts, CCCC 190, Oxford, Bodleian Library, Junius 121 and Laud Misc. 482; for discussion of the attribution, name, and date of the contents, see Allen J. Frantzen, *The Literature of Penance in Anglo-Saxon England* (New Brunswick, NJ, 1983), pp. 133-36. The same injunction appears in the twelfth section, "Of Matters Relating to Marriage," in the Penitential of Theodore, for which see John T. McNeill and Helena M. Gamer, *Medieval Handbooks of Penance* (New York, 1938, 1990), p. 211, #31, as well as pp. 243-48 on the Pseudo-Egbert penitential.

[2] See Mary P. Richards, "The Body as Text in Early Anglo-Saxon Law," in this collection.

penance might provide. The language of the penitential restriction expressly recalls Adam's recognition of Eve's nakedness, and though the homilies do not directly evoke the Fall, the persuasive power of nakedness in the homilies and the penitential remains inextricably tied to the Genesis narrative, to the ramifications of that first recognition of nakedness. Indeed, the most developed evidence for a perception in Old English of nakedness as a penitential motif occurs in *Genesis A* and *B*, where a remarkably vivid verbal and visual emphasis on nakedness accompanies the inclusion of Adam and Eve's repentance. The Fall story, particularly as it appears in these two Old English poems, offers a quite precise originary narrative moment for an explicitly penitential view of nakedness in Anglo-Saxon England, one that allows the good Christian little room for bare bodies and unconfessed sin.

The Junius 11 *Genesis* narrative, like the homilies, uses literal nakedness to emphasize the need for figurative clothing and defines part of that clothing as confession and penance.[3] The dramatic presentation of penance in the poem and the more directly dogmatic connection of nakedness to penance in the penitential and the homilies imply the potential usefulness of multiple approaches to the same topics in conveying church

[3] The majority of the surviving Old English references to nakedness stem from the New Testament vision of Judgment Day offered at the end of the parable of the talents in Matthew 25:31-46. Of these, most focus on the duty of each person to clothe the poor; this is one means of working towards salvation on Judgment Day. The connection between nakedness on Judgment Day and clothing the soul by such actions as giving garments to the poor is a related trope in Old English religious literature. One of the best articulations of this is in the first Dialogue of Gregory, in the story of Boniface: "While he was still at home with his mother, he would sometimes leave the house and later return without his coat or even without his shirt, for, as soon as he saw anyone in need of clothes, he would give up his own. By divesting his body in this way, he wished to clothe his soul in the sight of God with merits for heaven." Gregory I, *Dialogues*, trans. Odo John Zimmerman, Fathers of the Church 39 (New York, 1959), p. 40. Wærferth's translation of the Dialogues includes the story, describing as "nacodne" those that Zimmerman translates "in need of clothes," *Bischofs Wærferth von Worcester Übersetzung der Dialoge Gregors des Grossen*, ed. Hans Hecht (Leipzig, 1900) I, 68.

teachings.[4] The practice of confession was encouraged in the early medieval church primarily by a proliferation of penitential handbooks, written by and for the clergy. The handbooks offered lists of sins and accompanying penances, although as Allen Frantzen points out, "[n]o single list of sins and no one set of instructions for the confessor prevailed" and the "texts were frequently altered by interpolation or excerpted with a notable lack of system."[5] The lack of uniformity suggests the developmental aspect of the practice of confession, while the simple existence of the handbooks also indicates that confession was clearly an ongoing concern of the church. Frantzen argues that a unity of purpose guided religious, literate Anglo-Saxons in the creation of penitential literature, whether prose or poetry:

> The acts and ideas substantiated by the [penitential] handbooks, homilies, and instructional passages are mirrored in the [penitential] poems. . . . In an important way the poems are one with the prose: they never invoke confession and penance without exhorting their audience to practice them. In this respect, the poems are more than reflections of the Anglo-Saxon penitential tradition; they are part of the reformers' spiritual and social design.[6]

While *Genesis A* and *B* do not explicitly invoke the system of confession and penance — and Adam confesses directly to God, of course, rather than privately to a confessor — the text does present and, by way of that presentation, encourage acts of repentance, confession, and penance. The narrative offers an account not just of original sin, but of the original need to confess and repent. The penitential reinforcement in the

[4] Not until the *Decretum* of Gratian appeared in the twelfth century did canon law begin to be formulated in a more widely agreed upon way. See James A. Brundage, *Medieval Canon Law* (New York, 1995), for an overview of the development of medieval canon law.

[5] Frantzen, *The Literature of Penance*, p. 17.

[6] Frantzen, *The Literature of Penance*, p. 174. Frantzen reviews other critics' use of the term "penitential poetry" and focuses his own discussion on *Christ III*, *Judgment Day II*, "Soul and Body," *Elene*, and *Juliana*.

sustained, dramatic narrative of the Junius 11 *Genesis* and in its accompanying body-focused illustrations might, moreover, have made it an especially effective vernacular conveyor of the penitential message, particularly in conjunction with homiletic exhortations.[7]

Despite its continuous presentation, the Junius *Genesis* consists of two distinct poems, *Genesis A* and *Genesis B*. The repeated attention to Adam and Eve's physical condition — a condition that so clearly conveys their spiritual vulnerability as well — is primarily a feature of the end of the 616 line *Genesis B*, but is also the result of the interpolation of *Genesis B* into the longer *Genesis A*, a closer biblical paraphrase than *Genesis B*. When and why the two poems were brought together is not known; a late ninth or early tenth century date has been suggested, and it is generally agreed that they were already integrated in the exemplar for the manuscript in which they survive.[8] Whatever the reason for the interpolation, the poems

[7] The potential ongoing usefulness of the poems might suggest why *Genesis A* and *Genesis B* continued to be copied — both are given earlier composition dates than the copying of Junius 11 in c.1000; see A.N. Doane, ed., *Genesis A: A New Edition* (Madison, 1978), pp. 36-37.

[8] The two poems, *Genesis A* and *Genesis B*, are generally treated separately. *Genesis A* is often considered the older of the two, but no precise evidence for dating has been found; Doane only goes so far as to say that it "differs from the poems known to be late" and "[a]ny date in the eighth century seems reasonable" (*Genesis A*, pp. 36-37). The most plausible arguments so far for the date of *Genesis B* put the original Saxon composition in the mid-ninth century and the Old English version slightly later, around the beginning of the tenth century. See B. J. Timmer, ed., *The Later Genesis* (Oxford, 1948), pp. 19-42, and A. N. Doane, ed., *The Saxon Genesis* (Madison, 1991), pp. 43-54, but see also Ashley Crandell Amos's work on dating, particularly his response to one of Timmer's arguments, *Linguistic Means of Determining the Dates of Old English Literary Texts* (Cambridge, MA, 1980), p. 101. The manuscript, Oxford, Bodleian Library, MS Junius 11, is usually dated to the first half of the eleventh century; no visual or clear textual marker separates the two *Genesis* poems. On the idea that the poems were integrated in the Junius exemplar, see Doane, *Genesis A*, p. 11. The date of their interpolation is not agreed upon; Doane and Timmer suggest the late ninth or early tenth century. A facsimile of the manuscript can be found in Israel K. Gollancz, ed., *The Cædmon Manuscript of Anglo-Saxon Biblical Poetry* (Oxford,

are presented in the manuscript as a single account of Genesis material, with no formal markers distinguishing between them and with a continuous cycle of illustrations.[9] Across the end of *Genesis B* and the resumption of *Genesis A*, moreover, is a coherent and well-developed example of nakedness emphasizing not just the exposure of bodies but of language. Nakedness here functions both literally and metaphorically to dramatize the result of sin and the need for confession and penance, amplifying and specifying an aspect of the briefer biblical counterpart. While a priest might encourage sinners directly to confess, Adam's lament and the narrator's commentary on his condition might have made the results of not repenting more emotionally charged and more threatening — a point that the abundant illustrations in MS Junius 11 offer as well. Not only does the poetic text make strikingly clear that the Fall is the moment when nakedness is transformed and clothing becomes necessary for the first time, but also that the figurative clothing

1927), or the full manuscript can be viewed in color, page by page, online at the Bodleian Library's website, http://image.ox.ac.uk/.

9 On the issue of where *Genesis B* begins and ends, see, most recently, Paul G. Remley, *Old English Biblical Verse* (Cambridge, 1996), pp. 154-57 and pp. 159-60. Remley asserts that "The currently accepted 'end' of *Genesis B* at line 851 finds no codicological or palaeographical support whatsoever," and the "internal evidence of the verse itself, mostly of a linguistic or metrical nature" must be the basis for distinguishing between the two poems. While I do not want to suggest that the references to nakedness indicate a different end line for *Genesis B*, they do suggest that the interpolator might have revised *Genesis A* in particular as he worked in order to improve the meshing (see Remley, p. 157 n. 138). Peter J. Lucas, "Loyalty and Obedience in the Old English *Genesis* and the Interpolation of *Genesis B* into *Genesis A*" *Neophilologus* 76 (1992): 121-35, argues that an Anglo-Saxon audience would probably not have been substantially bothered by the stylistic differences between the two poems, and that more may be gained from reading the two poems together: "Whatever the motivation for the interpolation [of *B* into *A*] it certainly had the effect of widening the scope of the thematic content of *Genesis A*. It is plausible to suggest that the effect reveals something of the purpose" (123). For an argument that all the poems in the manuscript are thematically unified, see J. R. Hall, "The Old English Epic of Redemption: The Theological Unity of MS. Junius 11," *Traditio* 32 (1976): 185-208.

God delivered — including penance — is an ongoing postlapsarian necessity, an idea reiterated in the anonymous homilies.

The biblical account of Adam and Eve's actions immediately after eating the forbidden fruit asserts, in Genesis 3:7, that they became aware of their nakedness and devised fig-leaf coverings for it. When God appears in Paradise that afternoon, Adam and Eve hide themselves until Adam is forced to admit, with shame, his nakedness (Genesis 3:8-10). The Old English fused *Genesis* poems multiply these two references to seven in the same narrative space, that is from the recognition to the admission of nakedness, before God questions the source of Adam's knowledge and shame (Genesis 3:11). Emphasizing the corporeal condition of Adam and Eve dramatizes their plight in terms directly accessible to a postlapsarian audience; if the fall from purity to sin cannot be fully imagined in a postlapsarian world, the shift from clothing to unprotected nakedness can (perhaps particularly in a British climate). That shift acts as a crucial piece of explanation for why inhabitants of the fallen world need clothing in the form of God's guidance, and connecting the multiple references to nakedness to images of confession and penance yields the didactic message. The Old English narrative emphasizes, more clearly than a more literal translation of biblical text does, that the Fall is not just an end to Edenic existence, but the beginning of the teacher/Church-student/sinner relationship promoted in religious texts such as the homilies and penitential handbooks.[10] In Junius 11, the language of confession and penance surrounds the revelation of and repeated references to Adam's and Eve's nakedness,

[10] While the Junius *Genesis* poem does not elaborate on the actual penance undertaken by Adam and Eve after confession, reading their initial postlapsarian actions as explicitly penitential suggests an affinity with the tradition of continental Adam books such as the *Vita Adae et Evae*, in which an explicit and developed account of Adam and Eve's penance does appear. See the edition and translation by R.H. Charles in *The Apocrypha and Pseudepigrapha of the Old Testament in English*, Vol.II: Pseudepigrapha (Oxford, 1977) pp. 134-54, as well as Gary A. Anderson, "The Penitence Narrative in the *Life of Adam and Eve*," *Hebrew Union College Annual* 63 (1992): 1-38, and Michael E. Stone, "The Fall of Satan and Adam's Penance: Three Notes on *The Books of Adam and Eve*," *Journal of Theological Studies* 44 (1993): 142-56.

whereas in the biblical Genesis, Adam and Eve's first postlapsarian action is to cover themselves, then to attempt to hide from God. One example of the confessional interests of the Old English text comes at the moment of the devil's triumph, when the narrator announces the tempter's departure (the tempter is, in *Genesis B*, not Satan himself but one of his minions), and the first information provided about Adam's and Eve's fallen condition reveals their immediate inclination toward confession despite their fears of punishment:

> Sorgedon ba twa,
> Adam and Eue, and him oft betuh
> gnornword gengdon; godes him ondredon,
> heora herran hete, heofoncyninges nið
> swiðe onsæton; selfe forstodon
> his word onwended. ...
> Hwilum to gebede feollon
> sinhiwan somed, and sigedrihten
> godne gretton and god nemdon,
> heofones waldend, and hine bædon
> þæt hie his hearmsceare habban mosten,
> georne fulgangan, þa hie godes hæfdon
> bodscipe abrocen. Bare hie gesawon
> heora lichaman. (765b-84a) [11]

The praying that Adam and Eve undertake is not confession itself, although their penitential attitude is certainly a step towards it, one that the illustrations of the poem underscore.

Six pages before the narrative account of Adam and Eve's recognition of what they have done comes the first illustration

[11] "Both of them sorrowed, Adam and Eve, and often passed sad words between them; they dreaded, intensely feared, their lord God's punishment, the heaven-king's enmity; they realized that his word had been transgressed.... At times the wedded pair fell to prayer together and spoke to the good Lord of victories and called on God, heaven's ruler, and begged him that they might receive his punishment, willingly undergo it, since they had broken God's command. They saw their bodies were naked." This and all quotations from *Genesis A* and *Genesis B* are from George Philip Krapp, ed., *The Junius Manuscript*, The Anglo-Saxon Poetic Records 1 (New York, 1931). The translations of the *Genesis* poems and other Old English works are, unless otherwise noted, my own.

of it, in the lower register on page 31. George Henderson describes the apparent disjunction: "Before we have read that Adam yields to temptation or that Eve's euphoria has passed, they are shown suffering the bitterness of their sin, cast down in anguish on the ground while the undisguised tempter, a naked devil with a tail and serpent hair, spits at them" (figure 34).[12] Each of the next seven images of Adam and Eve after this shows them covering their nakedness, and three of these appear before the narrative itself addresses their recognition of their sin (as on page 34, see figure 35).[13] Before confession occurs, the narrator and the illustrations together thus make vividly clear the need and the desire for God's guidance that Adam and Eve now desperately have.[14] The initial narrative assertion of their shameful nakedness, summing up their new, exposed condition, prefaces the enumeration of Adam's and Eve's repentant actions, but punishment and guidance do not come until Adam and Eve sink still lower into despair, with Adam blaming Eve and Eve sorrowing deeply.

Adam fearfully details their new physical vulnerability as they await God's appearance in the Garden, a condition stressed by the starkness of the upper register in the illustration

[12] George Henderson, "The Programme of Illustrations in Bodleian MS Junius 11," *Studies in Memory of David Talbot Rice*, ed. Giles Robertson and George Henderson (Edinburgh, 1975), p. 125.

[13] The upper register illustration on page 34 shows Adam and Eve covering their genitalia with one hand; the lower register shows them covering themselves with leaves, as does the illustration on page thirty-six. The illustrations are reproduced in Thomas H. Ohlgren's *Anglo-Saxon Textual Illustration* (Kalamazoo, 1992), pp. 541-46, and at the Bodleian Library's website (see note 8).

[14] The emphasizing role of illustration is evident, too, in the expressions of sorrow. The five narrative descriptions of Adam and Eve's grief or sorrow are, notes C.R. Dodwell, "emphatically taken up by the illustrator, who signifies it no less than eight times in the brief space of six pages," *Anglo-Saxon Gestures and the Roman Stage* (Cambridge, 2000), p. 116. Catherine E. Karkov's study, *Text and Picture in Anglo-Saxon England: Narrative Strategies in the Junius 11 Manuscript* (Cambridge, 2001), is particularly relevant here, but came out too late to be used in the present essay.

on page 34 (figure 35).[15] Their Fall has brought them into a world in which not only perception but also environment has changed — no trees, no aspects of the Garden, appear in the upper illustrations of Eve and Adam on pages 34 and 36; the lower register on page 34 shows the Garden, but only as a place where Adam and Eve seek to hide their nakedness. Distance from God is described, visually and verbally, in ways that intensify the need for clothing. The initial response to this shift is blame and fear. Adam accuses Eve of bringing hell into their vision: "Hwæt, þu Eue, hæfst yfele gemearcod/ uncer sylfra sið. Gesyhst þu nu þa sweartan helle/ grædige and gifre" (791-93a, "Listen, Eve, you have marked our fortune with evil. Do you now see that dark hell, greedy and voracious?"). The sight of hell alone does not push Adam to focus on his spiritual condition. It is, instead, the first in a series of ominous observations. Adam and Eve now perceive threats both in and to their own bodies, and Adam focuses on the anticipated bodily discomforts that accompany nakedness:

> Hu sculon wit nu libban  oððe on þys lande wesan,
> gif her wind cymð  westan oððe eastan,
> suðan oððe norðan?  Gesweorc up færeð,
> cymeð hægles scur  hefone getenge,
> færeð forst on gemang,  se byð fyrnum ceald.
> Hwilum of heofnum  hate scineð,

[15] The physical aspects of the Fall are heightened by the manuscript's repeated and unusually plentiful illustrations of Adam's and Eve's nakedness. Illustrated accounts of the Fall often conflate the temptation and fall of Adam, as in the Carolingian Bibles that Barbara Raw links to the sequence of Adam and Eve illustrations in Junius 11; see Barbara Raw, "The Probable Derivation of Most of the Illustrations in Junius 11 from an Illustrated Old Saxon *Genesis*," *Anglo-Saxon England* 5 (1976): 133-48. Later examples, too, such as the Ripon Bible, show Adam and Eve already covering their nakedness at the same time as they consume the forbidden fruit; see Wilhelm Neuss, *Die katalanische Bibelillustration um die Wende des ersten Jahrtausends und die altspanische Buchmalerei* (Bonn, 1922), taf. 2, 3. For discussion of the distinctness of the Fall illustrations in Junius 11, see Janet Schrunk Ericksen, "Offering the Forbidden Fruit in MS. Junius 11," *Gesture in Medieval Drama and Art*, ed. Clifford Davidson, Early Drama, Art, and Music Monograph Series 28 (Kalamazoo, 2001), pp. 48-65.

blicð þeos beorhte sunne, and wit her baru standað,
unwered wædo. (805-12a)[16]

Adam and Eve have fallen into a realm of heightened physical awareness, one in which the body is no longer subject wholly to the mind, but is instead a locus of pain and shame. Although the bodies, for the moment, remain in Paradise, the comforts of the Garden are gone, replaced in the Old English text by menacing physical sensations, by the vision of dark hell, and by the new, shameful perception of nakedness, which the illustrations particularize in the covering of genitalia and which Adam refers to before he and Eve separately go into the woods: "Ac wit þus baru ne magon bu tu ætsomne/ wesan to wuhte" (838-39a, "But we two, thus naked, cannot be together at all").

Both Adam and Eve are stripped of material and spiritual comforts, and their position and comments dramatize the despair of the unconfessed soul awaiting judgment. They cannot cover themselves adequately either physically or figuratively, for they perceive their spiritual shame as keenly as Adam dreads the feel of hail on his bare skin. The protection that they attempt to fashion for themselves is described in such a way as to demonstrate the inadequacy of individual initiative without God's guidance. Adam recognizes that "þus baru" it is impossible for him to remain with Eve and he first suggests the loose cover of the forest, "Uton gan on þysne weald innan,/ on þisses holtes hleo" (839b-40a, "Let us go into this wood, into this forest's covering"). Once in that shelter, Adam and Eve devise what the narrator immediately defines as temporary, not permanent, clothing: "Þa hie heora lichoman leafum beþeahton,/ weredon mid ðy wealde, wæda ne hæfdon" (845-46, "Then they covered their bodies with leaves, clothed themselves with foliage; they had no garments"). Their nakedness is only superficially covered until God provides true

[16] "How will we now live or exist in this land, if wind comes here, from west or east, south or north? A dark cloud will appear, a hailstorm will come pelting from the sky, frost will come in the midst of it, which will be wickedly cold. At times the bright sun will glare, gleam down hotly from the heavens, and we stand here naked, unprotected by clothing."

garments (which occurs in Genesis 3:21 and in *Genesis A*, lines 941-43). Adam and Eve's own ability to conceal or clothe shame is inadequate, just as any subsequent individual's isolated efforts to do the same are inadequate; only with confession do real clothes or comfort appear.

As if anticipating the possibility that his audience might miss this point, the narrator pairs the comment on Adam and Eve's leafy attire with a reiteration of their repentant actions as they await the moment of confession. Once screened by foliage,

> wæda ne hæfdon;
> ac hie on gebed feollon   bu tu ætsomne
> morgena gehwilce,   bædon mihtigne
> þæt hie ne forgeate   god ælmihtig,
> and him gewisade   waldend se goda,
> hu hie on þam leohte forð   libban sceolden. (846b-51)[17]

Both the biblical account and *Genesis A* indicate that God appears in the afternoon of the same day as Adam and Eve eat the forbidden fruit, despite the reference here, at the end of *Genesis B*, to "morgena gehwilce." If the function of the passage is to stress the penitential attitude, then A. N. Doane's reading, in his edition of the poem, sounds especially plausible: "This formulaic phrase, suggesting that Adam and Eve spent several days repenting before they were judged, is probably used loosely to indicate the fervor of their penitence rather than the passage of time."[18] But Doane's reading can be taken one step further. The penitential formula offers an exemplary model, while at the same time, the emphasis on Adam and Eve's nakedness suggests the results of incomplete penance. Though they pray diligently and fittingly, Adam and Eve focus on the unfamiliar insecurity of their condition until God lays out their penance and, by so doing, shows them "how they should live in that light henceforth."

[17] "they had no garments, but they fell in prayer, both, the two of them together each morning, prayed the mighty one that he, God almighty, not forget them, and that the good Ruler would show them how they should live in that light henceforth."

[18] Doane, *Saxon Genesis*, p. 302, note to l. 848a.

The metaphor of the naked body as the revealed condition of the unconfessed soul culminates in despair. Although Adam and Eve have veiled their nakedness with leaves, they are still "blæde bereafod" (859b, "bereft of dignity" or "blessedness"), and the narrator describes Adam facing God as "hean ... hrægles þearfa" (866, "the wretched one ... destitute of clothing"). Twice in his speech of confession, Adam bemoans his nakedness. The translation from Genesis 3:10 of his admission of nakedness — "Ic wreo me her wæda leasne, / liffrea min, leafum þecce" (867-68, "I am hiding myself here lacking in clothes, my Lord of life, I cover myself with leaves") — becomes in the Junius 11 *Genesis* a repetition of the narrator's own earlier distinction between covering and clothing. To this is added the climax of the penitential scene, Adam's anguished admission to God, "ic eom eall eall nacod" (871b, "I am all, *all*, naked!").[19] In response, God confirms Adam's bared condition as he casts him out of Paradise: "Þu scealt oðerne eðel secean,/ wynleasran wic, and on wræc hweorfan/ nacod niedwædla, neorxnawanges/ dugeðum bedæled" (927-30a, "You must seek another homeland, a more joyless place, and turn, a naked poor wretch, into exile, deprived of the benefits of paradise"). In so stressing the bleakness of exposure, the poetic narrative follows patristic commentary. Ambrose, in *De Paradiso*, makes the metaphor more direct than does the poet of the Old English text: "ergo posteaquam spoliatos se illa sinceritate et simplicitate uiderunt integrae incorruptaeque naturae, quaerere mundana et manu facta coeperunt, quibus nuda suae mentis operirent" ("When, therefore, they saw that they had been despoiled of the purity and simplicity of their untainted nature, they began to look for objects made by the hand of man wherewith to cover the nakedness of their minds").[20]

[19] I follow Krapp and Doane in leaving the manuscript reading of the double "eall" unemended. Both editors suggest the repetition may have been for rhetorical stress rather than an accident. See Doane, *Genesis A*, p. 241.

[20] *Sancti Ambrosii Opera*, pars I, ed. Carolus Schenkl, Corpus Scriptorum Ecclesiastorum Latinorum 32 (Vienna, 1897) 13.63. Trans. John J. Savage, *Saint Ambrose: Hexameron, Paradise, and Cain and Abel*, Fathers of the Church 42 (New York, 1961), p. 343. Eric Jager, *The Tempter's Voice: Language and the*

Ambrose's formulation of nakedness, like the homilies and the penitential, also pushes its application from the original sin to all sinners: "quicumque praeuaricatur mandatum dei spoliatur atque nudatur et fit ipse sibi turpis" ("Whoever . . . violates the command of God has become naked and despoiled, a reproach to himself)."[21] The concern with corporeal exposure in the Old English *Genesis* poem aligns it with such commentary, but the poet has translated the image into more than vernacular language and dramatic circumstance. Adam's despair at his exposed body remains a warning, but the references to nakedness are paired with an implied exhortation to confession and the example of the necessity and usefulness of God's guidance.[22] The nakedness reveals the sin, the sinners then begin to repent and seek guidance ("on gebed feollon," 847a), and then God begins to show the path to clothing the nakedness. The narrative dramatization of penitential need and behavior thus indicates a way out of despair even though it so stresses the sorrow of nakedness. This use of the image of nakedness is crystallized in abbreviated form in homiletic literature.

According to two anonymous Old English homilies, unconfessed, unrepentant sinners will be stripped naked before all creation on Judgment Day; they will return, in other words, to the desperate condition of the unclothed Adam. In both homilies, however, the image of the naked sinner is explicitly coupled with an exhortation to confess. Both penitential passages may, in fact, be the work of the same anonymous

*Fall in Medieval Literature* (Ithaca, NY, 1993), discusses the trope of clothing in Ambrose's works as well as in other patristic commentary.

21 *De Paradiso* 13.65; Savage, *Saint Augustine*, p. 344. Augustine, too, employs the metaphor, though he reverses its emphasis, describing the pre-lapsarian Adam as "naked of dissimulation" and "clothed with the divine light." The quotation is pointed out by Jager in his discussion of the clothing that Adam and Eve fabricate (*The Tempter's Voice*, p. 128); Augustine, *De Genesi contra manichaeos* 2.16.24, *PL* 34: 173-220.

22 The words are further reinforced, too, by the abundant illustrations of Adam and Eve sorrowing and/or attempting to cover their nakedness: page thirty-one, page thirty-four, page thirty-six, page thirty-nine, page forty-one, and page forty-four.

author interpolated into different works, but they suggest that at least twice the image was found appropriate to the encouragement of confession.[23] In both instances, the image of the naked sinner follows the articulation of a penitential motif identified by M. R. Godden, a motif that, as Jonathan Wilcox points out, "occurs in some fifteen Old English works, primarily homilies or works of advice for a confessor," although only twice does nakedness figure into it.[24] The motif is a contrast between shame now and shame on Judgment Day. Godden sums it up this way: "it is better to be shamed for one's sins before one man (the confessor) in this life than to be shamed before God and before all angels and before all men and before all devils at the Last Judgement."[25] While Godden's concern is the contrast itself and Wilcox's is the embarrassing spectacle that nakedness becomes in this context, the homiletic contrast in potential shame is made both more threatening by recollection of that first exposure in the Garden and more hopeful by encouragement to confess and receive penance. A non-Ælfrician addition to Ælfric's homily for the sixteenth

[23] Implied rather than explicit connections between nakedness and the need for penance appear in other Old English homilies. In the anonymous homily Vercelli 22, for instance, confession is not directly urged, but sinners — those who gather wealth, in particular — are reminded that they will be naked on Judgment Day:

> He goldhord samnað, ac he ne wat hwam he hit samnað. For ðam þe we ealle nacode ⁊ forlætene arisað swa swa we geborene wæron, ⁊ to þam andrysenlican [dome] we ferað nacode ⁊ earme ⁊ unrote ⁊ gesworcene mid ege ⁊ mid fyhrðu. Beforan heahsetle þæs ecan deman we beoð alædde. (179-84)

"He collects a treasure of gold, but he does not know for whom he gathers it. Therefore we all will arise as naked and lost as we were born, and we will go naked and destitute and sad and troubled with fear and with dread to that dreadful judgement. Before the highseat of that eternal judge we will be led." See D. G. Scragg, ed., *The Vercelli Homilies and Related Texts,* EETS o.s. 300 (Oxford, 1992), pp. 366-80.

[24] Jonathan Wilcox, "Naked in Old English: the Embarrassed and the Shamed," in the present collection.

[25] Malcolm Godden, "An Old English Penitential Motif," *Anglo-Saxon England* 2 (1973): 222.

Sunday after Pentecost (*Catholic Homilies* II. 36) not only employs the Fall-resonant image of the exposed body, but lays out explicit directions for clothing it:

> Hit his eall soð þæt we gyt secgan wyllað: Ðam þe nele her nu his synna andettan his scrifte, ⁊ betan swa he him tæcð, him sceal on Domes-dæg sceamian beforan Gode sylfum, ⁊ eallum his halgum ⁊ eallum deoflum, swa þam menn dyde þe wurde færinga nacod beforan eallum folce, ⁊ nyste þonne mid hwam he his sceamigendlican bewruge: swa him byð on Domesdæge buton he his synna ær bewreo mid andetnesse, ⁊ mid dædbote, ⁊ mid ælmyssum. (114-21) [26]

John Pope, in his edition of the homily, suggests no source for the image of the naked man, but it does appear in almost identical wording in an anonymous homily printed by Napier as homily 46:[27]

> we eow sæcgað to soðan, þæt, se þe nele her his synna nu andettan his scrifte and betan, swa he him tæcð, hine sceal on domes dæg gesceamjan beforan gode and eallum his halgum and eac eallum deoflum, swa þam men dyde, þe wurde færinga nacod beforan eallon

[26] "It is all true what we yet will say: that who will not here now his sins confess to his confessor, and atone as he instructs him, he shall be shamed on Judgment Day before God himself, and all his angels and all devils, as that man did who was suddenly naked before all people, and knew not then with what he might cover his shaming body: just so is he on Doomsday unless he before clothes his sins with confession, and with penitence, and with almsgiving," John C. Pope ed., *Homilies of Ælfric: A Supplementary Collection,* EETS o.s. 259-60 (London, 1967), homily 27 (II, 770-81). Godden, in "An Old English Penitential Motif," uses "deoflum" as the end point for the motif he identifies. The reference to almsgiving touches on an extension of the metaphor of nakedness; by giving alms, one literally clothed the naked as well as figuratively clothed the giver's own naked soul. The Fall story articulates only the starting point for the need to clothe nakedness, and both the Bible and commentary extend the metaphor substantially, primarily in the direction of almsgiving.

[27] The homily is not by Wulfstan; see Dorothy Bethurum, *The Homilies of Wulfstan* (London, 1957), p. 43.

folce, and he nyste þonne, mid hwam he þone sceamjendan lichaman bewruge. (238, 10-16) [28]

Both homilies use nakedness to stress an idea more often found in soul and body literature: that on Judgment Day, punishment or reward for the life of the body is rendered, and death alone does not sever the connection to the body. But the image of exposed nakedness, rather than simply the abstraction of exposed sin, invokes the threat of shame in terms vividly understandable to a person still able to repent. In the homilies, as in the Old English poems, nakedness functions as a focal, graphic encourager of confession and penance. The exposed body itself becomes the sign of sin yet makes clear at the same time the need for the clothing that might come with confession and penance. The context of Judgment Day stresses that the sinner anticipate, and seek to avoid, eternal nakedness. But like Adam, the exposed *mann* cannot hide nakedness once it is revealed except by turning to God. Like Adam and Eve, the sinner must seek penance, and through confession can be clothed. Though Adam, by his originary circumstance, must confess directly to God, the rules for postlapsarian existence — part of what *Genesis B* refers to as God showing Adam and Eve "how they in that light henceforth should live" — allow his descendants to confess to God's representative rather than being stripped before all creation.

Only the homilies directly name as a remedy for nakedness the confession of sins and the undertaking of penance and atonement. The *Genesis* poem itself does not, and cannot in the

[28] "We say to you in truth, that, he who will not here (in this world) confess his sins now to his confessor and atone, as he directs him, shall on domsday be ashamed before God and all his saints and also all devils, as the man did, who was suddenly naked before all people, and he knew not then with what he might cover that shamed body," Arthur Napier, ed., *Wulfstan: Sammlung der ihm zugeschriebenen Homilien* (Berlin, 1883), pp. 232-42. Pope, and Godden point out overlaps between this homily and the *Visio Pauli* and Vercelli Homily 8. See also Antonette DiPaolo Healey, *The Old English Vision of St. Paul*, Speculum Anniversary Monographs 2 (Cambridge, MA, 1978), pp. 43, 51, 54. The material that precedes it, translated from the *Vitae Patrum*, may have been derived originally from one of Ælfric's homilies. See the notes in Pope's edition of the homily.

confines of its historical narrative, outline a postlapsarian system of confession and penance in detail. As Frantzen points out, "[p]enitential literature has to date been vaguely defined chiefly because penance has not been distinguished from repentance. This is a crucial distinction. Repentance, a state of mind in which one experiences and then expresses sorrow for sin, is an attitude endemic to the Christian consciousness.... Penance, on the other hand, is an idea embodied in an act and has, as an ecclesiastical tradition, a high degree of specificity."[29] Yet the repeated use of nakedness as a metaphor for the state of the soul before confession allows the *Genesis* poem to anticipate and reinforce, if not directly name, the more explicit dictates of the confession ritual. The penitential direction of the Fall images of nakedness is made concrete by the "Scrift boc" dictate that "Ceorle ne gedafenað þæt he his wif æfre nacode geseo" ("it is not right for a man that he ever see his wife naked").[30] The prohibition calcifies the nakedness metaphor, generalizing it even further than does the threat of the exposed sinner, and making physical nakedness itself a sin in a confessor's guide for administering penance. While it rejects the explanations of Eve's act offered in *Genesis B* and resists any narrative complications, the injunction's language and force derive from the immediacy of the Fall narrative and perhaps specifically from the kind of salient depictions of nakedness tied to penance that *Genesis A* and *B* and their illustrations offer. The penitential constructs a physical sin through that sin's metaphorical relation to the spiritual state defined by Adam's perception of nakedness. The body is being constrained on the basis of its symbolic relationship to a spiritual condition.[31] The image of Adam and Eve's post-lapsarian

[29] Frantzen, *The Literature of Penance*, p. 12.

[30] See n. 1 above.

[31] The Junius *Genesis* poem, moreover, also underscores the general need for religious law. When Adam asks, "Hu sculon wit nu libban oþþe on þys lande wesan" (805, "How will we now live or exist in this land?"), the answer presents itself to the audience: by reading — or listening to — formulations of God's guidance, the very act in which they are currently engaged as the poem's audience.

nakedness resonates beneath the metaphor even as it shifts from a threat to encourage penance to the penitential prohibition; the church dictates rely on the Genesis narrative and the attendant belief that the first man should not have seen that his wife was naked.

# Naked in Old English: The Embarrassed and the Shamed

JONATHAN WILCOX

IN THE FAMOUS legend, Lady Godiva agrees to ride naked through the marketplace of Coventry — an *impossibilia* posed by her husband — in order to free the citizens of Coventry from oppressive taxation. This she does,

> nuda equum ascendens, crines capitis et tricas dissolvens, corpus suum totum præter crura candidissima inde velavit, et itinere completo, a nemine visa, ad virum gaudens, hoc pro miraculo habentem, reversa est.[1]

Thus the most famous naked Anglo-Saxon that never was plays with the taboo of public exposure in a vision of nudity that fired the imagination of subsequent eras. Although the story is not Anglo-Saxon — it was first recorded by thirteenth-century chroniclers and is dependent upon a sense of property rights in marriage and even of a marketplace in Coventry that are more probable in the Anglo-Norman than the Anglo-Saxon period[2] — it encapsulates a paradoxical sense of exposure and con-

[1] Matthew Paris, *Chronica maiora*, ed. Henry Richards Luard, Rolls Series 57.1 (London, 1872), s.a. 1057 (pp. 526-57): "mounting her horse naked and loosening the hair and tresses of her head, [which] covered her whole body except her beautiful legs; and when she had finished her journey, not seen by anyone, she returned with joy to her husband, who took this as a miracle," trans. Donoghue, as next note, p. 198. I wish to thank Stacy Klein and Ben Withers for helpful critiques of earlier versions of this essay.

[2] See, most recently, Daniel Donoghue, "Lady Godiva," in *Literary Appropriations of the Anglo-Saxons from the Thirteenth to the Twentieth Century*, ed. Donald Scragg and Carole Weinberg, CSASE 29 (Cambridge, 2000), pp. 194-214. See also Katherine L. French, "The Legend of Lady Godiva and the Image of the Female Body," *Journal of Medieval History* 18 (1992): 3-19 and H. R. Ellis Davidson, "The Legend of Lady Godiva," *Folklore* 80 (1969): 107-21.

cealment of the naked body, of shame and of defiance, that proves emblematic for an investigation of the spectacle of nudity in Anglo-Saxon England.

Nudity and sexuality seem not to be much of an issue in a literary and artistic corpus as decorous as that of Anglo-Saxon England. The literature of the period centers on lords a-fighting or monks a-praying and so the surviving works give little attention to the naked body: in *Beowulf* the only *nacod* things are two swords and a dragon and Ælfric is more concerned with the naked narrative of uninterpreted text than with actual hot and sweaty bodies.[3] Such decorousness is unsurprising in a manuscript tradition that survived only by means of a monastic culture.[4] With the famous exception of a handful of riddles, the naked or sexualized body is not an obvious part of the surviving Anglo-Saxon record.[5] But that is no good reason for not asking questions about the naked body. Anglo-Saxon culture is also reticent about portraying women or discussing gender for many of the same reasons, yet questions about the role of women and the nature of gender have been particularly fruitful sites of enquiry for recent work.[6] In this essay I will

[3] See *Beowulf: An Edition*, ed. Bruce Mitchell and Fred C. Robinson (Oxford, 1998), lines 539a, 2585a (naked swords) and line 2273a ("nacod niðdraca," glossed by Mitchell and Robinson as "bare or smooth hostile dragon") and *Ælfric's Prefaces*, ed. Jonathan Wilcox (Durham, 1994), preface 4, lines 42-43. For more on *Beowulf*, see the essay by Hill in this volume.

[4] See further my "Transmission of Literature and Learning: Anglo-Saxon Scribal Culture," in *A Companion to Anglo-Saxon Literature*, ed. Phillip Pulsiano and Elaine Treharne (Oxford, 2001), pp. 50-70.

[5] For a survey of the literature, see the aptly-titled essay by Hugh Magennis, "'No Sex Please, We're Anglo-Saxons'? Attitudes to Sexuality in Old English Prose and Poetry," *Leeds Studies in English* n.s. 26 (1995): 1-27. On the sexual riddles, see further the essays of Higley and Salvador in this volume.

[6] A first wave of such work was evident in the new and reprinted essays of *New Readings on Women in Old English Literature*, ed. Helen Damico and Alexandra Hennessey Olsen (Bloomington, 1990) and in the historical study by Christine Fell with Cecily Clark and Elizabeth Williams, *Women in Anglo-Saxon England* (Oxford, 1984). For recent studies of interest, see Clare A. Lees and Gillian Overing, "Birthing Bishops and Fathering Poets: Bede Hild and the Relations of Cultural Production," *Exemplaria* 6 (1994): 35-65; Allen J. Frantzen, *Before the Closet: Same-Sex Love from "Beowulf" to "Angels in*

investigate Anglo-Saxon nudity by considering the presentation of the naked body in a broad range of surviving Anglo-Saxon literature and its manuscript illustrations. Although generally unremarked, I will uncover a surprisingly rich crop of naked bodies lurking in Old English biblical literature, in visions of judgment, and in the hagiographical corpus, as well as in the riddles.

If the human body has changed scarcely at all over the last thousand years, the cultural significance ascribed to that body and to its uncovering is far more rooted in a particular habitation and is likely to have changed significantly through a millennium. The very reticence of representation suggests one difference between Anglo-Saxon England and today. Much good recent work has advanced understanding the cultural significance of the body in Anglo-Saxon England.[7] Nudity has received less attention, although other essays in this volume, particularly those of Ericksen and Salvador, advance such investigations by considering the symbolic significance of the naked body in Anglo-Saxon Christian thought. I propose to explore the meaning of the naked body at a level that is more skin-deep. In particular, I will focus on an issue that has so far eluded scholarly attention, namely, the intersection of nudity and embarrassment in Anglo-Saxon England. I will approach representations of the naked form in relation to the ideas of shame and embarrassment and thereby refine an Anglo-Saxon

*America*" (Chicago, 1998); Jane Tibbetts Schulenburg, *Forgetful of Their Sex: Female Sanctity and Society, ca. 500-1100* (Chicago, 1998); Pauline Stafford, "Queens, Nunneries and Reforming Churchmen: Gender, Religious Status and Reform in Tenth- and Eleventh-Century England," *Past and Present* 163 (1999): 3-35; Catherine Cubitt, "Virginity and Misogyny in Tenth- and Eleventh-Century England," *Gender & History* 12 (2000): 1-32.

[7] Katherine O'Brien O'Keeffe, "Body and Law in Late Anglo-Saxon England," *Anglo-Saxon England* 27 (1998): 209-32; Clare A. Lees, "Engendering Religious Desire: Sex, Knowledge, and Christian Identity in Anglo-Saxon England," *Journal of Medieval and Early Modern Studies* 27 (1997): 17-45; Clare A. Lees and Gillian R. Overing, "Before History, Before Difference: Bodies, Metaphor, and the Church in Anglo-Saxon England," *Yale Journal of Criticism* 11 (1998): 315-34.

sense of these emotions at the same time as uncovering Anglo-Saxon attitudes to the uncovered body.

Lady Godiva's ride has all the ingredients for a story of embarrassment — the body exposed, to be gazed upon by the public at large — and fear of such embarrassment clearly underlies the nature of the challenge. Yet it fails to deliver the expected — Lady Godiva returns with joy unseen by anyone. In its exceptional nature, the episode is seen to constitute a miracle, giving it something of the status of a saint's life, where, as will be seen, the regular rules of embarrassment do not apply. Yet the story carefully presents the exposed body to be viewed by the mind's eye of the audience, as later retellers well knew. Later versions of the story make explicit the role of the viewer/voyeur in the character of the eponymous Peeping Tom, who embodies a transgressive and gendered gaze, and who is duly punished for his (scapegoat) transgression by being struck blind or, in some versions, struck dead. The legend dramatizes a need to take embarrassment and nudity seriously.

Embarrassment as a concept needs defining. Contemporary psychological literature provides experimental and theoretical insight into the state. An embarrassed subject feels "conspicuous, foolish, awkward and uncomfortable, mortified and chagrined, all at once."[8] Modern psychologists distinguish embarrassment from the related idea of shame: shame is a more serious, more internalized breach of a moral code, whereas embarrassment is more situational, more spontaneous, and more dependent upon an observer. While the two are clearly interlinked, they differ in both duration and seriousness. Embarrassed people feel temporarily awkward but are often subsequently able to laugh at their predicament; people who are shamed feel immoral and view themselves as bad when reflecting back on the situation. A consciousness of shame may be triggered by embarrassment, but embarrassment itself is also triggered by less fundamental transgressions. Embarrassment

[8] Rowland S. Miller, *Embarrassment: Poise and Peril in Everyday Life* (New York, 1996), p. 6; cf. Robert J. Edelmann, *The Psychology of Embarrassment* (Chichester, 1987).

depends above all upon a public self-consciousness — "the ability to think about and be concerned with what other people are thinking about us"[9] — and to this extent may be one of the defining characteristics of humanity; the experimental evidence suggests that embarrassibility is a predictable stage in child development, that it is universal to all peoples but not present in other creatures. As Mark Twain put it: "Man is the Only Animal that Blushes. Or needs to." Thus, despite Ricks's implicit argument in *Keats and Embarrassment* that the emotion was invented by the English in the eighteenth century with the development of the novel, and reached exquisite heights in romantic poetry, embarrassment can reasonably be expected in ancient and medieval cultures as well as modern.[10] Such embarrassment can have many causes, but I will confine the discussion in this essay to embarrassment triggered by nudity and exposure.[11]

Literary studies of embarrassment, like all studies of emotion in cultures past, need to balance constructionist and essentialist assumptions about human development. While Ricks implies a developmental view, William Ian Miller is far more careful to maintain a balance.[12] In a stimulating study, he examines embarrassment in action within the social economy of the Norse sagas, showing how shame is ever-present as the flip side of honor, while humiliation and embarrassment are related to shame as emotions of self-attention and self-consciousness but can be differentiated from it through careful attention. While Miller goes furthest in examining embarrassment in a culture close to Anglo-Saxon England, Gail Kern Paster makes the link between embarrassment and the expo-

[9] Miller, *Embarrassment*, p. 1.

[10] Christopher Ricks, *Keats and Embarrassment* (Oxford, 1974).

[11] I will therefore not discuss the full range of Anglo-Saxon embarrassment, omitting such examples as Apollonius's blushes or Cædmon's discomfited departure when faced with a harp.

[12] William Ian Miller, *Humiliation* (Ithaca, 1993).

sure of the body in her important study of Elizabethan drama.[13] But nobody has yet given much attention to embarrassment in Old English.

The vocabulary of Old English discourages such study since it includes many potentially relevant terms but without the same distinctions as Modern English feeling terms have. The term *embarrassment* itself is first recorded in English in the seventeenth century, somewhat preceded within that century by another nominal form, *embarrass*, but developing its contemporary sense in the eighteenth century.[14] Even without this particular word, the idea is available in Old English through a rich vocabulary, albeit with fuzzy boundaries that are necessarily simplified in translation. The obvious Old English term is *sceamu*, a feminine noun cognate with Modern English "shame" (defined by BT as "the emotion caused by consciousness of unworthiness or of disgrace" as well as "what causes a feeling of shame" but at times occupying the realm of embarrassed exposure) and its related derivatives, such as the adjective *sceamlic*, the adverb *sceamlice*, and verb *sceamian*. Another common series clusters around *sceand*, a feminine noun meaning "shame, disgrace, infamy" (according to BT), and its derivatives *sceandful*, *sceandlic*, and so on. A more common form in Old English is the term *bysmor*, a masculine or neuter noun defined by DOE as "shame, disgrace, humiliation" (*inter alia*), and its cluster of related terms such as the adjective *bysmorful* and the verb *(ge)bysmorian*, primarily meaning "to mock." This cluster survives through Middle English but dies out in Modern English apart from some Scottish dialect uses. Rarer forms in Old English include *æwisce* (DOE "disgrace, foulness") and its

13 Gail Kern Paster, *The Body Embarrassed: Drama and the Disciplines of Shame in Early Modern England* (Ithaca, 1993).

14 See *The Oxford English Dictionary*, 2nd edn. (Oxford, 1981), s.v. embarrassment and embarrass. Old English dictionaries and their abbreviations are as follows: Joseph Bosworth and T. Northcote Toller, *An Anglo-Saxon Dictionary* (Oxford, 1898) and *Supplement* (Oxford, 1921) = BT(S); *Dictionary of Old English*, ed. Angus Cameron, Ashley Crandell Amos, Antonette diPaolo Healey, et al. (Toronto, 1986 - ) = DOE.

derivatives, while other terms shade off more into humiliation and disgrace than into embarrassment.[15] These word-clusters provide a rich range of opportunities for expressing ideas of both shame and embarrassment but, as always when dealing with nuances of meaning, it will be necessary to consider a particular scene and its context in detail to pinpoint the precise overtones of any of these words and the feelings that are conveyed by them.

The interconnection of embarrassment and the body becomes apparent in considering the Old English word-hoard for the sexual anatomy. A common term for genitalia is *ge-cyndlimu,* literally "generative limbs," a term applied to both male and female sexual organs. Unease with the sexual body is suggested by an alternative formation building on part of this term, *sceamlim,* literally "shame-limb, embarrassment-limb," which occurs uniquely as a gloss beside *gecyndlim* (for *dedecus* and *turpitudinem* [shame, unsightliness]).[16] The noun *sceamu* itself sometimes serves to describe the sexual member, as will be seen in the analysis below, presumably on the model of Latin *pudenda.*[17] The term *sceamigendlic* is a substantive use of the adjectival form derived from the present participle of the verb for giving off shame or embarrassment. The term, which occurs only in a single passage that will be considered in a moment, is particularly revealing of an attitude of unease towards the sexual body.

15 Jane Roberts and Christian Kay with Lynne Grundy, *A Thesaurus of Old English,* 2 vols. (King's College London, 1995) sort these words under the classification "07.09 Shame, disgrace" classed under 07 Opinion rather than 08 Emotion; they do not have a classification for embarrassment as such.

16 The terms occur in glosses to Prudentius's *Psychomachia* in MS Boulogne-sur-Mer, Bibliothèque Municipale, 1890, ed. H. D. Meritt, *The Old English Prudentius Glosses at Boulogne-sur-Mer* (Stanford, 1959). BT define *sceamlim* as "the private member"; on the euphemistic treatment of Old English sexual vocabulary in the dictionaries, see Julie Coleman, "Old English Sexual Euphemism," *Neuphilologische Mitteilungen* 93 (1992): 93-98.

17 See further J. N. Adams, *The Latin Sexual Vocabulary* (Oxford, 1982).

The overlap evident in the relevant Old English vocabulary between *embarrassment* and *shame* might lead to the assumption that Old English does not differentiate the observed moment of squirming from the inner self's breaking of a serious moral code. While the two ideas are clearly related, a passage about Judgment Day in two different homilies demonstrates that some Old English writers did choose to make the distinction. In one example, Pope 27, an anonymous homilist warns that it is better to confess and be ashamed of one's sins before one man here in the world than to be shamed at Judgment Day before God, the angels, the citizens of earth, and the devils:

> (Đam) þe nele her nu his synna andettan his scrifte, ⁊ betan swa he him tæcð, him sceal on Domes-dæg sceamian beforan Gode sylfum, ⁊ eallum his halgum ⁊ eallum deoflum, *swa þam menn dyde þe wurde færinga nacod beforan eallum folce,* ⁊ *nyste þonne mid hwam he his sceamigendlican bewruge*: swa him byð on Domes-dæge buton he his synna ær bewreo mid andetnesse, ⁊ mid dædbote, ⁊ mid ælmyssum. (Pope 27, lines 114-21)[18]

The context here is the homilist's concern with a fundamental Christian idea of shame: the sinner will feel shame — an individual and internalized reflection of breaking the code — because he has unconfessed sins on his conscience at the Day of Judgment. The preacher's message is important and so he makes it pellucid: you had better confess to your confessor and atone in this life in order to avoid being fundamentally shamed after death with the consequence of eternal damnation. The

[18] "That one who will not here now confess his sins to his confessor, and atone as he teaches him, must be ashamed on Judgment Day before God himself, and all his saints and all the devils, *just like it occurred to that man who was suddenly naked before all the people, and did not know then with what he might cover his private parts*: so will it be for him on Judgment Day unless he cover his sins beforehand with confession, and with repentance, and with alms." John C. Pope, *Homilies of Ælfric: A Supplementary Collection*, EETS o.s. 259-60 (London, 1967-68), II, 770-81; emphases mine. All translations from Old English are my own.

preacher is so concerned that his message should be unmissable that he illustrates it with an example, an extended simile of sorts, starting with *swa*. That example appeals directly to something different from the fundamental lack of inner worth that comes from sins unshriven. In a rhetorical turn not essential to the context of the passage, the homilist appeals to something more sensational, more attention grabbing, but less fundamentally important, than the shame of unshriven sins. Specifically he appeals to a squirming sense of situational inappropriateness that comes from finding oneself, like Lady Godiva, naked in front of a crowd — in other words, to embarrassment. In this context, the *sceamigendlican* that need covering up might be translated, in the English vernacular, as "his naughty bits," i.e. a part of the body whose public exposure will cause non-lasting but acute social discomfiture. Contemplating those naughty bits provides a good entry point to an Anglo-Saxon sense of embarrassment.

The biblical source for the homilist's idea does not make this specific appeal to embarrassment and lacks the relevant simile. The underlying thought is expressed by Paul in his second epistle to the Corinthians, alluding to Matthew 25:31-32:

> For we must all be manifested before the judgment seat of Christ, that every one may receive the proper things of the body, according as he hath done, whether it be good or evil.... (II Corinthians 5:10)[19]

The idea expressed by the homilist makes up part of a common stock of penitential motifs. Malcolm Godden, who has studied this motif, formulates it as follows: "it is better to be shamed for one's sins before one man (the confessor) in this life than to be shamed before God and before all angels and before all men and before all devils at the Last Judgement."[20] Such a motif occurs in some fifteen Old English works, mostly homilies or

[19] All translations of the Bible are from the Douay-Rheims version.

[20] M. R. Godden, "An Old English Penitential Motif," *Anglo-Saxon England* 2 (1973): 221-39, at 222.

works of advice for a confessor. It ultimately derives from a letter by Alcuin or a homily attributed to Boniface, but many of the Old English writers probably drew it from the vernacular stock of penitential commonplaces rather than from the Latin source.[21] The recurring motif makes heavy use of the idea of shame conceived as a realization of a lack of moral worth, but only in two versions does a conjuring of the sinner's exposed vital parts add a specific appeal to embarrassment.

One of these two is the formulation in Pope 27 cited above, which occurs in the context of a homily by Ælfric, although this part is not by him. Pope 27 is an insertion into Ælfric's *Catholic Homilies* II.36, a homily for the Sixteenth Sunday after Pentecost. The augmented homily was added to MS Cotton Vitellius C. v as part of the systematic interpolations made into that manuscript during the first half of the eleventh century.[22] The central part of the addition is a vision of departing souls, drawn from the *Vitae Patrum* and written by Ælfric in his characteristic style. This has been embedded by an anonymous homilist in a generalized introduction and conclusion, including the relevant passage.[23] The context of the motif, then, reinforces the general nature of the homiletic advice, which is good for a general audience on any occasion.

The same motif, including the image of the naked and exposed sinner described here, proved useful enough to be used by another anonymous homilist. The relevant passage occurs almost identically in Napier 46, an anonymous general homily on Judgment Day composed by the first half of the eleventh century.[24] The Napier 46 version has one significant

[21] Sources: PL 100:52 or PL 89:351; see Godden, "Penitential Motif," pp. 235-36.

[22] See Pope, *Homilies*, I, 27-30.

[23] See Pope, *Homilies*, II, 771-74.

[24] *Wulfstan: Sammlung der ihm zugeschriebenen Homilien nebst Untersuchungen über ihre Echtheit*, ed. Arthur Napier (1883; repr. with a bibliog. suppl. by Klaus Ostheeren, Dublin, 1967), pp. 232-42. The homily survives in MSS CCCC 419, of the first half of the eleventh century, and in Oxford, Bodleian Library, Bodley 343, of the second half of the twelfth century.

difference in the relevant simile; here it will go for the one with sins unshriven:

> swa þam men dyde, þe wurde færinga nacod beforan eallon folce, and he nyste þonne, mid hwam he þone sceamiendan lichaman bewruge. (Napier 46, 238/14-16)[25]

The concern of the suddenly naked person is "þone sceamiendan lichaman" ("the embarrassing/shaming body"). This is probably a euphemistic substitute for "his sceamigendlican" ("his private parts"),[26] and results in a warning that sounds more like an allusion to the Emperor's New Clothes than to the story of Priapus in view of the focus on the suddenly perceived nakedness of the whole man rather than a gaze directed specifically to the sexual anatomy.

Two anonymous homilists, then, exploit the startling idea of embarrassment at sudden nakedness to get at the more fundamental but less immediately arresting idea of exposing shame at sins unshriven. Underlying the simile used in both homilies is a sense that it is obvious to the audience that such public exposure is a trigger for embarrassment, an assumption that can be made as readily in Anglo-Saxon England as by Freud in his dream of an analogous scene.[27] This idea is worth stressing since it runs counter to the absence of the self-conscious body in much of the surviving Old English corpus. Heroic literature knows of shame but it is a result of cowardly conduct, as in the ignominious epithet, *scamiende* ("bearing shame," *Beowulf* 2850a), applied to the cowards who abandoned Beowulf in his final fight. While the body is an interesting locus for certain heroic concepts, as Hill shows in his essay in this volume, it is not usually a paradable source of embarrassment

[25] "as it did for that man, who was suddenly naked before all the people, and he did not then know with what he might cover the embarrassing/shaming body."

[26] As Pope suggests, *Homilies*, II, 781.

[27] See Sigmund Freud, *The Interpretation of Dreams*, trans. James Strachey (New York, 1955): pp. 242-48.

in the manner of Lady Godiva's ride. But public exposure of the naked body is seen by two preachers as an idea that will grab their audience's attention: embarrassment at nakedness is already in Anglo-Saxon England a predictable part of the Christian construction of the body.

Anglo-Saxon Christian literature is deeply engaged with bodily shame and, incidentally to this, with the embarrassment of the body. The *locus classicus* for the very idea of nakedness in Christian culture is, of course, an incident in the Garden of Eden where shame enters this world along with all our woe — and shame's entry comes with an associated residue of embarrassment. This incident from Genesis is treated numerous times in Anglo-Saxon art and literature. In view of the foundational nature of the event and the opportunity it presents for discussing both nudity and embarrassment, it will be worth looking with care at the nuances of the various Old English handlings of the Fall from un-self-conscious grace.

As so often in the Old Testament, the original narrative unfolds with a spareness and paucity of editorial direction that makes it difficult to be certain of the tone. This reticence is closely replicated, as so often, in Ælfric's biblical translation. The issues are first raised when the creation of Eve leads the Genesis-narrator, and Ælfric after him, to reflect upon the primal couple's lack of clothes. When God has created Eve from Adam's rib and brought her to Adam, the narrator is explicit about their prelapsarian state:

> 2:25 Hi wæron ðа buta, Adam ⁊ his wif, nacode ⁊ him ðæs ne sceamode. (*OE Heptateuch*, Genesis 2:25)[28]

It is unsurprising that, before the Fall, nakedness "him ... ne sceamode." Indeed, the observation only makes sense from a postlapsarian perspective where the connection of nudity and shame is so automatic that its absence needs remarking upon.

[28] "They then were both naked, Adam and his wife, and it was not shameful/embarrassing to them." *The Old English Version of the Heptateuch*, ed. S. J. Crawford, EETS o.s. 160 (1922; repr. with the text of two additional manuscripts transcribed by N.R. Ker, London, 1969).

Eve and then Adam eat the fruit of the forbidden tree:

> 3:7. ⁊ heora begra eagan wurdon geopenode; hi oncneowon ða ðæt hi nacode wæron, ⁊ sywodon him ficleaf, ⁊ worhton him wædbrec.
>
> 3:8. Eft ða ða God com, ⁊ hi gehyrdon his stemne ðær he eode on neorxnawange ofer midne dæg, ða behydde Adam hine, ⁊ his wif eac swa dyde, fram Godes gesihðe on middan ðam treowe neorxnanwonges.
>
> 3:9. God clypode ða Adam, ⁊ cwæð: Adam, hwær eart ðu?
>
> 3:10. He cwæð: Đine stemne ic gehirde, leof, on neorxnawange, ⁊ ic ondræde me, for ðam ðe ic eom nacod, ⁊ ic behyde me.
>
> 3:11. God cwæð: Hwa sæde ðe ðæt ðu nacod wære, gyf ðu ne æte of ðam treowe ðe ic ðe bebead ðæt ðu ne æte? (*OE Heptateuch*, Genesis 3:7-11)[29]

The couple's concealment, first through the sewing of the figleaf, then through the vain attempt to hide from God among the trees, indicates their embarrassment. While this should result from the shame of their transgression, Adam's response displaces his discomfiture to their clothelessnes (3:10). Rather than being an internalized sense of wrong-doing, i.e. shame,

[29] "3:7. And the eyes of them both were opened: and they perceived then that they were naked, and they sewed figleaves for themselves, and they made for themselves breeches.

3:8. Again when God came, and they heard his voice where he walked in paradise in the middle of the day, then Adam hid himself from the sight of God in among the trees of paradise, and his wife also did so.

3:9. God then called out to Adam, and he said: Adam, where are you?

3:10. He said: I heard your voice, dear one, in paradise, and I was afraid, because I am naked, and I hid myself.

3:11. God said: Who said to you that you were naked, if you did not eat from the tree which I commanded that you might not eat from?"

At 3:10, MS London, BL, Cotton Claudius B. iv has "gehire" in the present tense, which is printed in Crawford's text, while MSS Oxford, Bodleian Library, Laud Misc. 509 and Cambridge, University Library, Ii. 1. 33 have the more probable past, "gehirde/gehyrde."

the couple are made uncomfortable by a viewer, albeit one who is omniscient. The couple, then, are preoccupied with the embarrassment of their nakedness which continues even after their sewing of the breeches. God, on the other hand, does not remark on their nakedness except in order to steer their thoughts back to their more fundamental sin by drawing an inference from Adam's answer (3:11). God subsequently relieves their situational embarrassment by going on to clothe them (Genesis 3:21).

This scene defines the first example of nakedness in the Christian story in the sense of self-consciousness in a naked body which can for the first time be contrasted with a clothed body. Now that they perceive themselves as naked, Adam and Eve evidently feel the embarrassment they were lacking at 2:25. While the Genesis narrator, and Ælfric following in his track, does not explicitly name the feeling here, the couple acts on their discomfiture with all the marks of embarrassment — a temporary and conduct-based reaction to their predicament, requiring the idea of an onlooker — in their adoption of the fig-leaves and in their move behind the trees.

Ælfric's view of this scene becomes apparent elsewhere in his writings. He omits discussion of nudity from his translation of Alcuin's *Interrogationes Sigewulfi in Genesin*, but touches upon the incident in the opening homily of his first series of *Catholic Homilies*, "De Initio Creaturae," where he retells the action in a compressed form:

> Ða wæron hí butu deadlice. ⁊ cuðon ægðer ge gód ge yfel. ⁊ hí wæron ða nacode. ⁊ him ðæs sceamode. (CH I.1, 140-42)[30]

In this shorthand account of the incident, Ælfric makes explicit the connection implied in the biblical narrative. While *þæs* could refer back to the sequence of consequences (mortality,

[30] "Then they were both mortal, and they knew both good and evil, and they were then naked, and they were ashamed/embarrassed about that." CH I is ed. Peter Clemoes, *Ælfric's Catholic Homilies: the First Series*, EETS s.s. 17 (Oxford, 1997). Citation is by homily and line number from this edition.

knowledge of good and evil, and nudity), the echo of Genesis 2:25 makes it clear that the couple *sceamode* on account of being naked.

Ælfric's analysis of the event is altogether briefer and less nuanced than Augustine's. Augustine spends considerable time on the idea in the *City of God*, seeing the embarrassment as a result of the loss of control over sexual desire. Augustine explicitly insists that the bodies of the first couple were fully sexually formed and that they would have gone forth and multiplied through sex driven by desire, but that desire before the Fall would have been in obedience to the will.[31] After the Fall lust rose in disobedience to the will — "there appeared in the movements of their body a certain indecent novelty, which made nakedness shameful. It made them self-conscious and embarrassed."[32] Embarrassment for Augustine, then, follows from the lack of control over the sexual body that comes from nudity after the Fall, which is a bodily mark of the shame of primal disobedience.

Anglo-Saxon understanding of this key scene is further visible in a pictorial presentation. The actions of the first couple are represented — and their feelings embodied — in the illustrations of MS Cotton Claudius B. iv.[33] Nudity is immediately an issue. On fol. 6v (figure 23), Eve is shown being created from Adam's rib and Adam and Eve are shown receiving the command not to eat of the forbidden fruit. Even though the illustration comes on the page immediately beneath

[31] Augustine, *City of God*, Book XIV, chs. 17-24; see also Augustine, *The Literal Meaning of Genesis*, Book 11, ch. 34.

[32] "extitit in motu corporis quaedam inpudens nouitas, unde esset indecens nuditas, et fecit adtentos reddiditque confusos," *De civitate Dei*, CCSL 47-48 (1955), XIV, 17, 18-20; translation from *Concerning the City of God against the Pagans*, trans. Henry Bettenson (Harmondsworth, 1972): p. 578.

[33] Text and illustrations are reproduced in a facsimile edition: *The Old English Illustrated Hexateuch: British Museum Cotton Claudius B. iv*, ed. C.R. Dodwell and Peter Clemoes (Copenhagen, 1974). The manuscript is discussed in *The Old English Hexateuch: Aspects and Approaches*, ed. Rebecca Barnhouse and Benjamin C. Withers (Kalamazoo, Mich., 2000).

the observation of their nakedness from 2:25, "⁊ him ðæs ne sceamode," Eve's sexual parts are covered by the presence of Adam, the fall of her hair, and the turn of her leg, while Adam is pictured lacking his male sexual member. The illustrator has suggested innocent nakedness while strategically draping it from the postlapsarian gaze of the picture's viewer. On fol. 7r (figure 24), the illustrator presents the couple eating of the forbidden fruit. Here one of Eve's breasts is visible, while her hair strategically drapes over the remainder of her body. The line of the hair is taken up by the line of the serpent's tail, which suggestively enters between her legs, perhaps hinting at a visual level at Eve's seduction by the serpent. Adam's *gecyndlim* is concealed by a strategic blemish in the parchment, which surely calls attention to the question of prelapsarian bodily representation even as it obviates the need for the illustrator to decide what to do in that space.

The next illustration (fol. 7v upper, figure 25) is particularly interesting for portraying the key moment of the birth of bodily self-consciousness. It presents Adam and Eve in the moment of their attempted concealment. They present an impossible tangle of limbs, intertwining both each other and the palm frond vegetation. The oddly entwined bodies of the couchant couple might be viewed as suggestive of a sexual act but that the heads are facing in opposite directions. Eve cups her face in one hand while breaking off a frond of vegetation with the other, perhaps intending it for concealment. Adam casts a guilty stare across to God, who returns his gaze, their eyes interlocking across the picture space, suggesting that Adam's embarrassed concern is triggered by the onlooker. Embarrassment and nudity and a hint of sexuality are all present in a drawing that appears to present a literal illustration of the biblical text but in fact shows how fraught nakedness is for the postlapsarian imagination. When, in the next scene (fol. 7v lower left, figure 25), the couple are expelled bodily from paradise — with Adam receiving a physical shove from the touch of the Lord — they are now clothed, while their downturned postures clearly embody their internalization of a sense of shame and of humiliation at their nakedness more enduring and more fundamental than their earlier situational embarrassment.

This same biblical passage was translated another time into Old English in the verse paraphrase known as *Genesis A*, where the rendition is by no means so literal as Ælfric's.[34] Because the anonymous poetic translator does not hesitate to flesh out the spare narrative, his understanding of the incident is much more apparent than Ælfric's. This can be seen in his expanded translation of Genesis 3:8-11:

gewitan him þa gangan   geomermode
under beamsceade,   blæde bereafod.
hyddon hie on heolstre   þa hie halig word
drihtnes gehyrdon   and ondredon him
þa sona ongann   swegles aldor
weard ahsian   woruldgesceafta.
het him recene to   rice þeoden
his sunu gangan.   him þa sylfa oncwæð,
hean hleoðrade   hrægles þearfa:
"Ic wreo me her   wæda leasne,
liffrea min,   leafum þecce.
scyldfull mine,   sceaðen, is me sare
frecne on ferhðe,   ne dear nu forðgan
for ðe andweardne.   ic eom eall eall nacod."

(*Genesis A*, 858-871)[35]

[34] Ed. A. N. Doane, *Genesis A: A New Edition* (Madison, 1978); my translations and interpretation of this poem draw upon Doane's thoughtful commentary and glossary. For a more theologically-centered reading of this incident, see the essay by Ericksen in the present volume.

[35] "They then departed to go, sad in mind, under the shadow of a tree, deprived of blessedness. They hid in the darkness when they heard the holy speech of the Lord and they feared him, when immediately the lord of heaven began to ask for the guardian of worldly-creation. The powerful lord commanded his son quickly to go to him. He himself then answered him, the miserable one spoke, needy of clothing: 'I hide myself here, my Lord of life, lacking clothes, I cover myself with leaves. A guilty, injured conscience is grievously dangerous to me in spirit. I do not dare now to come forth in front of your presence. I am all completely naked.'" Translation of the obscure prepenultimate sentence is drawn from Doane, *Genesis A*, note to lines 869-70a (p. 241).

The poet's amplifications fill in many of the blanks of the original story. His poetic variation immediately pinpoints a specific state of mind for the couple — *geomermode* (858b, "sad in mind"), *blæde bereafod* (859b, "deprived of blessedness"), while Adam is *hean* (866a, "miserable") — with an explicitness about interior states that is alien to Ælfric's closer rendering of the deadpan original. The spelling out of causation continues with the explanatory *ondredon him* (861b, "they feared him"), which is here explained by the narrator rather than coming dramatically from Adam's mouth. Adam's speech of Genesis 3:10 amplifies upon his guilt ("scyldfull mine, sceaðen" 868, "my injurious guilt") and makes the perception of nudity highly climactic with the reiterative "ic eom eall eall nacod" (871b, "I am all completely naked"). The narrator makes clear that this is the immediate cause of Adam's discomfort, since he is miserable *hrægles þearfa* (866b, "needy of clothing").

When God speaks, he provides the most explicit analysis of Adam's state in an explanatory speech inconceivable in the original:

> Him ða ædre god    andswarede:
> "saga me þæt, sunu min,    for hwon secest ðu
> sceade sceomiende?    þu sceonde æt me
> furðum anfenge,    ac gefean eallum
> for hwon wast þu wean    and wrihst sceome,
> gesyhst sorge    and þin sylf þecest,
> hean hygegeomor    þæt þe sie hrægles þearf
> nymþe ðu æppel    ænne byrgde
> of ðam wudubeame    þe ic þe wordum forbead?"
> (*Genesis A*, 872-881)[36]

[36] "God then quickly answered him: 'Tell me, my son, why you seek the shadow, acting in shame? You took shame/embarrassment in my presence immediately, but amidst every joy why do you know sorrow and cover your shameful parts, see sorrow and cover yourself, abject, sad of mind, so that you are in need of clothing, unless you tasted an apple from that tree in the forest which I forbade to you in words?'"

*Sceomiende*, *sceonde*, and *sceome* chime through the poet's amplification of Genesis 3:11, collocating with the oppressive *sceade* and associating with *sorge* for the *sylf*. While God harps rather mercilessly on Adam's requisite sense of shame at the fundamental sin of disobedience, he observes that shame from a conduct-based squirming ("You took *sceonde* in my presence") which he remarked in the naked Adam. Embarrassment is one marker of shame and such embarrassment is triggered by the exposure of bodily nakedness, itself a metaphor for a more metaphysical vulnerability. Adam and Eve give themselves away here because they discover embarrassment at their nakedness. That embarrassment and that nakedness can be seen as metaphors for the more fundamental failing of disobedience (through pride) and the shame that acknowledges that disobedience. Embarrassment and shame enter the world here together. The shame is long-lasting and important and relates to a moral lapse; the embarrassment is temporary and almost comic and relates to a perception of public nakedness.

The *Genesis A* account continues in the traditional way, with Adam trying to pass the blame for eating the fruit to Eve, but this is followed by another amplification which may point to the sexually self-conscious body:

> "nu ic þæs tacen wege,
> sweotol on me selfum." (885b-86a) [37]

Presumably this is the initial signification (*tacen*) of the sexual part as shameful (*sceome*), a marker that continues beyond the temporary nakedness which is alleviated by clothing. If the poet were following Augustine's interpretation of this scene, the *tacen* would be the sexual movement of the body beyond the control of the will — the first unwilled erection.[38]

Just how clearly that token is inscribed upon the self of Adam may be seen in another illustrated cycle. The poetic translation of *Genesis A* and *B* is embodied in a series of draw-

[37] "now I carry the token of it, clear on my self."

[38] See Augustine's discussion cited in note 31 and the suggestion of Doane, *Genesis A*, note to lines 885b-86a (p. 242).

ings in MS Oxford, Bodleian Library, Junius 11, which closely renders the story of the poem.[39] Here the first couple is illustrated in numerous scenes before the Fall, duly un-self-conscious about their lack of clothing. In these scenes Eve's breasts and nipples are prominent, serving to mark sexual difference, while Adam's body lacks the expected sexual marker, even when shown full-frontally (see, for example, the illustrations on pp. 10 and 13, figures 27, 29).[40] While Adam and Eve are portrayed at this stage without bodily self-consciousness, the viewer's postlapsarian sense of bodily embarrassment is anticipated in Adam's anatomical absence. After the Fall, the bodies look the same, but bodily self-consciousness is now present: both Adam and Eve hold a hand, or a hand with an acanthus-shaped fig-leaf, in front of their *sceome* (see the two illustrations on p. 34, figure 35), while, with their spare hand, they produce a gesture of grief.[41] In the terms suggested here, the hand in front of the vitals is a gesture of embarrassment, while the hand in front of the face is a mark of their shame, here indicated by grief. A few frames after the Fall, from page 36 onwards, Adam first begins to sport a beard: apparently, secondary sex characteristics have now come into this world.

The Fall from Paradise, then, provides a crucial originary moment in the Christian construction of the naked body and its association with shame and embarrassment. If Anglo-Saxon

[39] The complete manuscript is reproduced in facsimile in Israel Gollancz, *The Cædmon Manuscript of Anglo-Saxon Biblical Poetry* (Oxford, 1927); the illustrations alone are reproduced in *Anglo-Saxon Textual Illustration*, ed. Thomas H. Ohlgren (Kalamazoo, 1992), pp. 526-76. The complete manuscript is available on the world wide web at http://image.ox.ac.uk/pages/bodleian/MSJUNI~1/Main.htm. It is discussed by Catherine E. Karkov, *Text and Picture in Anglo-Saxon England: Narrative Strategies in the Junius 11 Manuscript* (Cambridge, 2001).

[40] For a fuller reading of Eve's nipples in Junius 11, see the essay by Dockray-Miller in this volume.

[41] See C.R. Dodwell, *Anglo-Saxon Gestures and the Roman Stage* (Cambridge, 2000), pp. 114-17.

commentators were less eager than Augustine to expand and expound upon this scene, nevertheless, they did not avoid depicting it and, in the process, showed the connection between shame and embarrassment and between embarrassment and nakedness. Through repeated presentation in Old English text and image, the Fall from Eden explains the birth of bodily self-consciousness, offering an explanation for the origin of shame and embarrassment. Both feelings are an essential part of the biblically explained postlapsarian world.

The association between nudity, embarrassment, and shame continues elsewhere in Genesis, reinforcing the initial presentation, most notably in the story of Noah, when the patriarch's exposed body is laughed at by his son, Ham. Again, Ælfric gives a deadpan translation close to the style of the original:

> 9:21. ⁊ ða ða he dranc of ðam wine, ða wearð he druncen ⁊ læg on his getelde unbehelod.
>
> 9:22. His sunu ða, Cham, geseah his gesceapu unbeheled, ⁊ cydde hit his twam gebroðrum ut on felda.
>
> 9:23. Hwæt, ða Sem ⁊ Iapheth dydon anne hwitel on heora sculdrum, ⁊ eodon underbæc ⁊ beheledon heora fæderes gecynd, swa ðæt hi ne gesawon his næcednysse.
>
> (Genesis 9:21-23)[42]

In Ælfric's voice, as in the Vulgate, the offense of Ham seems slight and enigmatic in the telling; its severity becomes apparent only through the curse that Noah subsequently visits upon his peeping and prattling son. In this instance, as in the case of Peeping Tom, the taboo of nakedness is reinforced through the

[42] "9:21. And when he drank from that wine, then he became drunk and lay in his tent uncovered.

9:22. His son, Ham, then saw his genitals uncovered, and made it known to his two brothers out in the fields.

9:23. Lo, then Sem and Japheth placed a blanket on their shoulders and went backwards and covered their father's nature, so that they did not see his nakedness."

punishment of the voyeur who gazes without proper acknowledgement of the embarrassment. Like Ælfric, the illustrator in Cotton Claudius B. iv also presents the scene straightforwardly, with Noah's *gesceapu* uncovered, and so available to the viewer, but not emphasized.

Once again, a more illuminating version comes in the poem *Genesis A*, where the extended handling of this scene (lines 1562-88a) makes explicit what is at stake in Ham's gaze. The poet's version is remarkably sensitive to Noah's drunkenness, which is described with sympathy and imagination as the cause of his exposure,

> þa him on hreðre heafodswima
> on þæs halgan hofe heortan clypte
> (lines 1568-69),[43]

with the unique use here of the term *heafodswima*, "head-swimming, dizziness." Ham's disrespect is made explicit through the addition of derisive laughter when he catches sight of his father's nakedness (lines 1579b-84a). But the poet's most revealing addition is to slow the narrative down by equating *sceome*, here a naming of Noah's shameful vital parts, with the *gesceapu*, "genitals," but perhaps also punning on "fate," which is the human lot since the expulsion from Eden:

> ... sceome... swa gesceapu wæron
> werum and wifum siððum wuldres þegn
> ussum fæder and meder fyrene sweorde
> on laste beleac lifes eðel.
> (lines 1573b-76)[44]

[43] "when, in that holy man's home, a dizziness in his breast embraced his heart"

[44] "shameful parts, such were the genitals in men and women since the thane of glory closed the homeland of life for our father and mother with a fiery sword on the track." The punning use of *gesceapu* as genitals is brought out in the analysis by Frantzen, *Before the Closet*, p. 221.

The very term *sceome* is enough to trigger in the poet an awareness of the origin of the shame of human sexuality and the poet stresses the association in order to explain the embarrassment of the naked body.

When this scene is drawn in MS Junius 11, this illustrator, too, feels obliged, unusually, to insert the *gesceapu* (p. 78, figure 44), which are the more prominent for being reflected in (or perhaps parodied by) the gesture of Ham's finger in the central register. By this stage in Christian narrative, bodily embarrassment is firmly established within the fallen world. The story of Noah and Ham shows that disregard of the embarrassment that should surround the naked body redounds to the discredit of the one looking on in the wrong spirit, more than of the one who disregards the taboo by exposing himself. The same pattern will be evident in the lives of many saints, where shame falls to those who look on in the wrong spirit – generally the pagan persecutor.

The firm association between shame and nudity within Anglo-Saxon culture is evident in an intriguing translation error in a different biblical passage. Shame is a recurrent point of appeal for the psalmist, who repeatedly invokes the shame of his enemies, usually with no particular reference to nakedness. In Psalm 108, the psalmist curses his enemies with an elaborate image of shame itself as clothing:

> induantur qui detrahunt mihi pudore; et operiantur sicut deploide confusione sua. (Psalm 108:29)[45]

Within the image, shame is one level of attire while confusion is a redoubling of that attire. This psalm is translated into Old English verse in the Paris Psalter:

> Syn ða butan are  ealle gegyrede
> þe me tælnysse  teonan ætfæstan,
> and him si abrogden  swa of brechrægle
> hiora sylfra sceamu  swyþust ealra.[46]

[45] "Let them that detract me be clothed with shame: and let them be covered with their confusion as with a double cloak."

[46] "May those be clothed completely without honor who inflict on me the reproof of enmity, and may they be uncovered so from their breeches, the

The translator has rendered the image of clothing in shame with a more literal clothing without honor, after which the doubling brings him trouble. The translator assumes that the only way of increasing the force of the image is to imagine removal of the *brechrægle* for an idea of explicit exposure, piling bodily embarrassment on explicit shame. Such exposure is glossed as *sceamu.* For the Old English poet and audience, the removal of clothing signals an extremity of shame through embarrassment more obviously than the psalmist's elaborate image of clothing.

Shame is associated with inappropriate dress elsewhere in the Bible and picked up in its Old English reflexes. In the parable of the wedding feast at Matthew 22:1-14, an inappropriately garbed guest is cast by the kingly host into outer darkness. As Ælfric explains in his homily for the Twenty-First Sunday after Pentecost (CH I.35), the wedding garb stands for the true love of God and of men:

> witodlice ge geseoð þæt gehwam sceamað gif he gelaðod bið to woruldlicum gyftum þæt he waclice gescryd cume to þære scortan blisse; Ac micele mare sceamu bið þam þe mid horium reafe cymð to godes gyftum þæt he for his fulum gyrelan fram þære ecan blisse áscofen beo. into ecum þeostrum. (CH I.35, 152-56)[47]

The fundamental shame is the stained moral state, here imagined as foul clothing ("fulum gyrelan"), that will lead to

greatest of all shame/embarrassment for themselves." Psalm 108:28; ed. George Philip Krapp, *The Paris Psalter and the Meters of Boethius*, ASPR 5 (New York, 1933), p. 94. The translation of *abrogden* draws on the DOE s.v. *abregdan*, definition A.8 "rendering *operire* 'to cover' perhaps as if *aperire*, 'to uncover'."

[47] "Truly you see that everyone is embarrassed/ashamed if he is invited to a worldly feast if he were to come meanly clothed to that brief pleasure. But it will be much more shameful/embarrassing for that one who comes with a dirty garment to God's feast such that he may be shoved from that eternal bliss into eternal darkness on account of his foul outfit."

eternal damnation. In an elaboration that builds upon his source in Gregory, Ælfric contrasts this with the temporary discomfiture — the embarrassment — of sartorial inadequacy ("waclice gescryd") at a merely human gathering.[48] Just as in the anonymous homilist's judgment scene, the pains of eternity are figured by Ælfric in relation to, albeit worse than, the human embarrassment of inappropriate garb. It is characteristic of Ælfric's decorousness that the embarrassment in his version stems from shoddy clothing rather than from downright nakedness.

As Ælfric's analysis suggests, the fear of shame is most forcefully apparent in a Christian context in the moment of judgment. Judgment scenes abound with the portrayal of the naked and exposed body. These scenes help demonstrate the distinction between shame and embarrassment because they focus on fundamental issues of Christian morality. The two homilists already discussed appeal to embarrassment to emphasize the fundamental fear of exposure. Other writers present the naked body in association with shame but no embarrassment. In a judgment scene associated with Wulfstan's *Institutes of Polity*, for example, a homilist displays the sexual body in unembarrassed terms for unambiguous punishment. Those in clerical orders who failed to curb sexual desires stand with their lower bodies immersed in flames, along with the women with whom they fornicated,

> And se deofol hi beswang swyðe gelome on heora gecyndlimum, swa swa seo boc us segð. (section 4)[49]

[48] The source is Gregory's homily 38; see Malcolm Godden, *Ælfric's Catholic Homilies: Introduction, Commentary and Glossary*, EETS s.s. 18 (Oxford, 2000), pp. 289-98.

[49] "And the devil scourged them very often on their genitals, just as the book tells us." Oxford, Bodleian Library, Junius 121, ed. Karl Jost, *Die "Institutes of Polity, Civil and Ecclesiastical"*, Swiss Studies in English 47 (Bern, 1959), p. 217. The book from which this is drawn is identified by Jost as Ayto, *Liber de Visione et Obitu Wetini Monachi* (PL 105, 774): "semper in locis genitalibus virgis caederentur" (Jost, p. 218).

Here the body is tormented with an obvious appropriateness to the sin of lust. The body is an object to be disciplined, and the presentation of that discipline is apparently an edifying sight. Even though the exposed body within the world comes with a residue of potential embarrassment, in eschatological time such embarrassment is irrelevant. This judgment scene makes its moral point through the staightforward presentation of brute force with none of the appeal to social embarrassment of the two anonymous homilists or even of Ælfric.

Other judgment scenes, too, present the exposed body stripped of the social concerns that enable embarrassment. In the poem *Christ and Satan,* Satan describes the fate of cursed mortals in his fevered imaginings of hell even before any doomed souls have had the chance to occupy the place. Among the torments of hell that he envisages, the doomed are explicitly naked in a Bosch-like scene:

hwilum nacode men
winnað ymb wyrmas. (134b-35a)[50]

The nakedness here is part of the general sense of horror. Once again, there is no suggestion that the doomed are embarrassed in their nudity, even if the phallic opponents hint at a sexual overtone to the torments.[51]

The idea of the unembarrassable body at the Last Judgment is seen even more clearly in the poetic account of *Christ III.* The poet describes three torments of sinners at Judgment (1262-1312). The second is that they will be exposed and suffer shame:

þonne is him oþer earfeþu swa some
scyldgum to sconde, þæt hi þær scoma mæste
dreogað fordone. (1272-74a)[52]

[50] "sometimes naked human beings strive against serpents." Ed. George Philip Krapp, *The Junius Manuscript,* ASPR 1 (New York, 1931).

[51] See further Karkov's analysis in this volume, pp. 194-95.

[52] "Then there is likewise a second difficulty for them as a shame to the guilty, that they must suffer there the greatest of shame." Ed. George Philip Krapp and Elliott van Kirk Dobbie, *The Exeter Book,* ASPR 3 (New York, 1936). The poet is not drawing closely from an identified source for this passage; see

The poet is emphatic about the shame to be received (*scyldgum to sconde*, "a shame to the guilty," *scoma mæste*, "the greatest of shame"). The exposure is not that of naked bodily flesh that causes embarrassment, but rather a more fundamental form of shame. The Lord, the angels, the people, and the devils will view a person's every sin:

manwomma gehwone
magun þurh þa lichoman, leahtra firene,
geseon on þam sawlum. Beoð þa syngan flæsc
scandum þurhwaden swa þæt scire glæs,
þæt mon yþæst mæg eall þurhwlitan.
(1279b-83)[53]

The shame here (*scandum*, "shamingly") is at the sins which can be seen *through the body* ("þurh þa lichoman"). The body has transparency. These onlookers see *through* the body as if through clear glass "swa þæt scire glæs" (1282). Such a trope of transparency is the opposite of bodily embarrassment: the body no longer operates in the social world or has any surface significance. Where the body has lost its surface significance, embarrassment is doubly irrelevant, since it is a social phenomenon of this world and the poet is describing an event beyond human society (although the body is still the subject of attentive gazes, consciousness of which are designed to control conduct) and because nakedness is a phenomenon of the surface that requires taking the surface seriously and is punctured by a truly transparent body. The moment of judgment here is analogous to that described by the homilists in Pope 27 and Napier 46, and the poet proceeds to use the same broad motif, but here without any attempt to appeal to embarrassment. Instead the poet observes how much better it would have

Frederick M. Biggs, *The Sources of "Christ III": A Revision of Cook's Notes*, OEN Subsidia 12 (Binghamton, NY, 1986).

[53] "through the body they can see in those souls every guilty stain, transgressions of sins. Those sinful bodies will be shamingly pierced through just like clear glass that one can most easily completely see through."

been for the sinners to have confessed in the world — "ær gescomeden/ fore anum men" (1302b-03a, "to have shamed/ embarrassed themselves before one man") by confessing their sins to the confessor – than to be faced with this shame after death. The poet emphasizes the striking image of the transparent body by reflecting upon its opposite, the opaque body in this world:

> Ne mæg þurh þæt flæsc se scrift
> geseon on þære sawle. (1305b-06a)[54]

The poet is reflecting upon the unfortunate ability of the sinner to thereby conceal sins within the world but the same bodily opacity creates the possibility of embarrassment. At judgment only those fundamental (and internal) sins matter, for which the body will provide no cover.

Such an idea of the transparency of the body at Judgment is also made explicit by the Blickling homilist in a homily centered on the need for repentance in this life in view of the imminence of the end of the world:

> Ne þearf þæs nán man wenan þæt his lichama móte oþþe mæge þa synbyrþenna on eorþscrafe gebetan; ah he þær on moldan gemolsnaþ ⁊ þær wyrde bideþ, hwonne se ælmihtiga God wille þisse worlde ende gewyricean, ⁊ þonne he his byrnsweord getyhþ ⁊ þas world ealle þurhslyhþ, ⁊ þa lichoman þurh sceoteð, ⁊ þysne middangeard tocleofeð, ⁊ þa deadan upastandaþ, biþ þonne se flæschoma ascyred swa glæs, ne mæg ðæs unrihtes beón awiht bedigled. (Blickling 10)[55]

[54] "The confessor cannot see through the flesh into the soul."

[55] "Concerning that no man need think that his body may or can atone those burdens of sin in the grave; but he will moulder there in the earth and will there await the fate, when the almighty God will work the end of this world, and when he will draw his fiery sword and will completely chop through this world, and pierce through those bodies, and cleave asunder this earth, and the dead will rise up — the body then will be made clear like glass, and nothing of sin may be concealed." *The Blickling Homilies*, ed. R. Morris, EETS o.s. 58, 63, 73 (1874-1880; repr. as one vol. London, 1967), pp. 109-11.

The grave is a fine and private place, but none, the homilist warns, do there find grace. When the Final Judgment comes, the individual will not be able to hide the inner self with the outer form. Instead, the body is again made transparent with the same image as in *Christ III*: "biþ þonne se flæschoma ascyred swa glæs" ("the body will then be made clear like glass"). Here any possibility of bodily embarrassment is dismissed with the opacity of the body itself, leaving only the possibility of inner and fundamental shame. This rendering of the scene of judgment makes clear what is so distinctive in the Pope 27/Napier 46 version. There the vehicle to impel the audience to act on their sins was contemplation of the analogy of bodily embarrassment in this world. Here, as in *Christ III*, the homilist poses a competing analogy of a transparent body to emphasize instead the exposure of a transparent inner state. The image of transparency erradicates the body and with it both bodily nakedness and bodily embarrassment.

Inattentiveness to the worldly body is an essential aspect of the Last Judgment with its move beyond human time. It is also a sign of piety within this world in narratives of exemplary Christians. As such, lack of embarrassment at bodily exposure is a familiar trope in saints' lives, where it is particularly triggered by scenes of torture. Ælfric makes the trope explicit in his treatment of the persecution of Hippolitus in his Life of St. Lawrence (CH I.29). Hippolitus is the deputy prefect of Rome and as such ought to be on the side of the persecuting emperor, Decius. After witnessing the martyrdom of Lawrence, however, he buries the martyr's body and converts to Christianity. The emperor has him stripped and tortured and gloats:

> lá hú nære ðu geornful biggenga ura goda. ⁊ nu þu eart swa stunt geworden þæt furþon ðe ne sceamað þinre nacednysse; Ypolitus andwyrde; Ic wæs stunt. ⁊ ic eom nu wis. ⁊ cristen. (CH I.29, lines 236-39)[56]

[56] "'Lo, were you not an eager worshipper of our gods? And now you have become so foolish that you are not even ashamed of/embarrassed by your nakedness.' Hippolitus answered: 'I was foolish and now I am wise — and a Christian'."

The pagan torturer who can see only the literal level expects embarrassment at bodily exposure. The empowered Christian saint can see further: for him the body is as glass and he has the wisdom to ignore such taunting and to formulate a position based upon transcendent values.

Within the economy of saints' lives a saint's divine transcendence of the distractions of this world commonly includes transcendence of bodily embarrassment while the pagan persecutor over-values embarrassment. The paradox is particularly clear when the saint is a woman, which may explain the frequency of the trope in female saints' lives. Other than Ælfric's Hippolitus, the saint whose exposure is designed by the torturer to elicit embarrassment and yet who transcends that expectation is most often a woman, as in the cases of Juliana and Margaret, Agnes and Agatha.[57] This is the aspect of Anglo-Saxon nudity that has probably received most discussion in recent years and so can be dealt with summarily here.[58] The defiant transcendence of the exposure of the body in these scenes is the hagiographical trope deployed by Lady Godiva's ride; indeed, Lady Godiva's miraculous concealment by her hair is anticipated by Agnes.

In some instances, though, a more worldly attitude to the body and its potential for embarrassment creeps into saints' lives, particularly where the saint is not martyred. The issue of bodily embarrassment hovers interestingly around the anony-

[57] Cynewulf, *Juliana*, ed Rosemary Woolf (London, 1955); *The Old English Lives of St Margaret*, ed. Mary Clayton and Hugh Magennis, CSASE 9 (Cambridge, 1994); *Ælfric's Lives of Saints*, ed. Walter W. Skeat, EETS o.s. 76, 82, 94, 114 (London, 1881-1900; repr. as two vols., 1966), lives 7 and 8.

[58] For fuller discussion of torture and exposure in female saints' lives, see Clare Lees, "At the Crossroads: Old English and Feminist Criticism," in *Reading Old English Texts*, ed. Katherine O'Brien O'Keeffe (Cambridge, 1997); Lees, "Engendering Religious Desire"; Leslie A. Donovan, *Women Saints' Lives in Old English Prose* (Cambridge, 1999); Shari Horner, *The Discourse of Enclosure: Representing Women in Old English Literature* (Albany, 2001), chs. 3 and 4.

mous life of Mary of Egypt.[59] This anonymous translation of Paul the Deacon's eighth-century Latin version of a sixth-century Greek original circulated in the context of Ælfric's lives even though it is significantly less guarded than Ælfric in its treatment of sexuality.[60] The desert hermit is approached through Zosimus, who provides the narrative's point of view. He is repeatedly characterized as an old man, while Mary's age is also stressed.[61] Perhaps such maturity is designed to distance them from any potential for sexual desire. Despite that, their first meeting in the desert is fraught with embarrassment over the issue of Mary's nakedness.

Mary's body is introduced as sunburned and exposed, with hair to the neck providing no opportunity for a protecting veil in the manner of Agnes or Godiva (lines 174-77). Zosimus runs after her and she retreats. When he finally catches up enough to have a shouted exchange, he learns why she is running from him:

> ic ne mæg mé þé geswutelian. and ongean-weardes þe gewenden. forþon ic eom wíf-hádes mann. and eall-unga lichamlicum wæfelsum bereafod. swá swá þu sylf

[59] "De Transitu Mariae Aeyptiace," ed. Skeat, *Ælfric's Lives of Saints*, homily 23B, II, 2-52. References are to this edition by line number. For a recent edition, see Hugh Magennis, *The Old English Life of Saint Mary of Egypt* (Exeter, 2002). For the tradition of this saint's life, see *The Legend of Mary of Egypt in Medieval Insular Hagiography*, ed. Erich Poppe and Bianca Ross (Dublin, 1996).

[60] The Latin source is discussed, edited, and translated by Jane Stevenson, "The Holy Sinner: The Life of Mary of Egypt," in *Mary of Egypt*, ed. Poppe and Ross, pp. 19-98. The character of the Old English life and its circulation is discussed by Hugh Magennis, "St Mary of Egypt and Ælfric: Unlikely Bedfellows in Cotton Julius E. vii," in *Mary of Egypt*, ed. Poppe and Ross, pp. 99-112. For a fuller analysis of Mary's body, see Andrew P. Scheil, "Bodies and Boundaries in the Old English Life of St. Mary of Egypt," *Neophilologus* 84 (2000): 137-56, and Lees and Overing, "Before History, Before Difference."

[61] We are told that Zosimus is 53 years old and that Mary has been in the wilderness for 47 years; see lines 244, 47, and 563.

> gesihst. and þa sceame mines lichaman hæbbende ún-oferwrigene. (205-09)[62]

Her answer insists on the visibility of her *sceame*, "swá swá þu sylf gesihst," presenting her naked sexuality with rhetorical forcefulness to the reader as well as to Zosimus. She asks for his cloak so that she might cover "þa wíflican tyddernysse" ("the female frailty"). Zosimus throws her the cloak while turning his back and she secures it with more emphasis on the body:

> And gegyrede hire be þam dæle þe heo mæst mihte. and mæst neod wæs to beheligenne. (219-20)[63]

The very periphrasis of the unnamed part where "mæst neod wæs to beheligenne" along with the awkwardness of Zosimus throwing the cloak and turning his back enacts embarrassment at the *sceome* and at its exposure to this point. Both the nakedness and the embarrassment it creates are emphasized in the telling, which revels in displaying Mary's naked body through the provision of these details.

Mary's naked body is particularly charged in this text because the story she will tell is of exploiting her body in her youth for sexual pleasure and for advantage, "unsceandlice swá swá ic gewuna wæs" (372, "shamelessly, as was my wont"). In her shameless past, she was particularly unembarrassed about offering her naked body for pleasure and for gain: she offers her favors, for example, in exchange for passage to Jerusalem the better to satisfy her desires (356-57, 371). The bodily embarrassment of the present serves as a guarantor of upstandingness in contrast with the lasciviousness of Mary's past in which embarrassment at bodily display was suppressed. Mary's exploitation of her nude body has given way to embarrassment

[62] "I cannot reveal myself to you and turn towards you because I am a person of the female kind and completely lacking in bodily clothes, just as you yourself see, and having the shame of my body uncovered."

[63] "And she covered herself about that part which she was most able to and which there was most need to conceal."

at her naked body and so the story of her life has switched from pornographic display to the comedy of embarrassment.

The way the Life of Mary of Egypt plays with the display of the naked body is like the legend of Lady Godiva and strikingly unlike the lives by Ælfric, who goes out of his way to downplay the emphasis on sex and bodily exposure, even when retelling lives where the exposed body is essential to the story, such as those of Agnes and Agatha. In contrast with Ælfric, the Life of Mary of Egypt suggests a fascination with the taboo of nudity, a fascination which is also symptomatic of the most complicated Old English literary engagement with the embarrassment of the exposed body, the sexual riddles of the Exeter Book.

Some eight riddles offer blatantly sexual clues that can nevertheless also be resolved with innocent solutions, while many other riddles briefly toy with such *double entendre.*[64] Paradigmatic is riddle 44 with its account of a wondrous thing hanging by the thigh of a man under the clothing of that lord, pierced in front, stiff and hard, that often fills a familiar hole of equal size. For a riddle such as this to work as a *double entendre* game requires a joy in the potential sexual answer but also a repressive sense that it is wrong to enjoy the sexualized possibility, which cannot possibly be uttered.[65] Of riddle 44, if you cry out *gecyndlim,* or even *sceamiendlican,* the riddler can reply, no, it is only a key. Providing the obvious anatomical answer would make you like the one "suddenly naked before all the people, [who] did not know then with what he might cover his private parts." The nexus of embarrassment and sexual display explored in this essay provides a necessary context for an under

[64] The best edition of the riddles is Craig Williamson, ed., *The Old English Riddles of the Exeter Book* (Chapel Hill, 1977), while the numbering adopted here is that of Krapp and Dobbie, *The Exeter Book.* On the sexual riddles, see Reinhard Gleissner, *Die "zweideutigen" altenglischen Rätsel des Exeter Book in ihrem zeitgenössischen Kontext* (Frankfurt, 1984). See also the essays by Higley and Salvador in this volume.

[65] This dynamic is most successfully explored in D.K. Smith, "Humor in Hiding: Laughter Between the Sheets in the Exeter Book Riddles," in *Humour in Anglo-Saxon Literature,* ed. Jonathan Wilcox (Cambridge, 2000), pp. 79-98.

standing of these sexual riddles, while the solution of Riddle 44 may, in its turn, provide the key to the homiletic appeal of the exemplar discussed in this essay.

Both embarrassment and shame prove to be crucial concepts for understanding attitudes to the unclothed body in Anglo-Saxon England. In spite of a general reticence around overt depictions of sexuality, this survey has shown that the art and literature of the period contain a startling number of scenes featuring naked individuals who experience embarrassment on account of their bodily exposure. The idea is central to a Christian conception of nakedness. Within a Christian rhetoric, embarrassment as triggered through self-perception of the naked body is a metaphor for the more profound feelings of shame that ought to be experienced on account of the individual's continual and inevitable transgressions against God. Christian writers and illustrators explore this concept in accounts of the Fall from Eden, which motivates and explains the birth of such bodily self-consciousness. Ideas about the body are bracketed at the other end of Christian time by an inevitable moment of exposure that is more than skin-deep: at the Last Judgment bodily nakedness is inevitable but irrelevant as the individual will be judged on an exposed state of inner worth, which makes embarrassment beside the point.

Between these two moments of eschatological time, Christian preachers emphasize that the individual has the opportunity to alleviate his or her inevitably sinful state through confession of shame to a priest. Such confession requires contrition: a state of self-conscious reflection related to both shame and embarrassment which is a prelude to exposure to a confessor. The appropriate state of contrition can be inhibited by too much concern for the embarrassment of this world, as the homilists warn. It is to encourage the right level of self-consciousness that preachers are direct about the shames of the Last Judgment. In the process, two anonymous preachers chose to appropriate the idea of bodily embarrassment as an image to emphasize the importance of the Last Judgment. Their example is valuable to this discussion as they clarify a distinction in Old English between shame and embarrassment.

While shame is clearly the more important and more productive emotion within a Christian rhetoric, potentially leading to the salvation of souls, embarrassment plays an important role, not only in encouraging appropriate social conduct (such as appropriate dress), but also, in the hands of a gifted homilist, allowing an understanding of transcendent values through a comparison with worldly ones.

Bodily embarrassment is far more visible in Christian than in heroic literature. It is a paradoxical issue in the lives of martyrs, who always present a special case. Through their acceptance of bodily martyrdom for a metaphysical good, these Christian heroes transcend bodily embarrassment. Only the benighted pagan persecutor is foolish enough to believe in the power of regular social and physical constraints, including the power of embarrassment, to control such exceptional individuals. More revealing of quotidian bodily embarrassment are the occasional other stories of exposure — such as the drunken Noah or Mary of Egypt or the more complicated case of the riddles. Such scenes suggest how a sense of embarrassment at bodily exposure was powerfully present, if but rarely displayed, in Anglo-Saxon England.

Pursuing such a fleeting feeling as embarrassment in a long-past culture requires a careful attentiveness to nuance in both the literature and the art. Such attentiveness allows us to complicate the picture of Anglo-Saxon England as either flatteningly decorous or unrecognizably alien to modern emotions. The exposed body sporadically shows itself in the surviving works and, in the process, reveals a complex tangle of feelings. Even as temporary and foolish an emotion as embarrassment proves to be a useful key in opening up an understanding of an Anglo-Saxon sense of bodily self.

# Index


Abel, 197, 222, 234-36, 243-47, 255
Adam and Eve, 16, 139, 183-84, 187, 192-93, 221-27, 231-74, 286-94; see also Eve
*Adrian and Ritheus,* 73-74n.
*Adrian and Epictetus,* 87n.
Agatha, St., 23
Agnes, St., 304-05, 307
Alaman law code, see Law Codes, continental
Alcuin, 284; *Interrogationes Sigewulfi in Genesin,* 288
Aldhelm, 36, 94; "Riddle 26," 63n.; "Riddle 76" 94n.; "Riddle 77," 94n.; "Riddle 78," 91-92; "Riddle 70," 82n.; "Riddle 80," 92-93
Alfred, king, 114, 120, 251-52; translation of "Historia Anglorum," 201; preface to law code, 204-05, 210; see also Law Codes, Anglo-Saxon
Alhhun of Worcester, bishop, grant of privileges, 205
Ambrose, St., *De Paradiso,* 268-69
*Andreas,* 133
angels, 145, 184-87, 190, 192, 198-202, 205-07, 210, 212, 214, 218-220, 252
*Anglo-Saxon Chronicle,* 97
Anthony of Egypt, St., 89
Antoninus Liberallis, *Metamorphoses,* 47
Aristotle, 179; *Nicomachean Ethics,* 27
Athelstan, king, 120, 133, 212; see also Law Codes, Anglo-Saxon
Augustine of Canterbury, archbishop, 202
Augustine of Hippo, St., 169; *Enarrationes in Psalmos,* 208; *City of God,* 139n., 289; *De Genesi contra manichaeos,* 269n.
Ælfgifu (Ælfgyva), queen, 143, 152, 158, 198
Ælfric, 30, 93, 186, 205, 276, 286, 307; *Catholic Homilies*: *Sermo de Initio Creaturae* (*CH* I.1), 187, 288-89, 291-92; Life of St. Lawrence (*CH* I.29), 303-05; homily for the Twenty-First Sunday after Pentecost (*CH* I.35), 298-300; *Natale Omnium Sanctorum* (*CH* I.36), 186; *Sancti Gregorii Pape, Urbis Romane Inclitus* (*CH* II.9), 200-01; homily on Mid-Lent Sunday (*CH* II.12), 65, 85n.; homily for the Sixteenth Sunday after Pentecost (*CH* II.36), 270-71, 284; homily on Saul and the Witch of Endor (Pope 29), 219; *Glossary,* 88n.; *Grammar,* 67; *Lives of the Saints*: On Auguries (LS 7), 218n.; Life of St. Oswald (LS 26), 127-28, 135-36; translation of Genesis (OE Heptateuch), 89-90, 286-88, 291-92, 295-96
Ælfthryth, queen, 196
Ælfwine of Malmesbury, abbot, 252
Ælfwine of Winchester, abbot, 252; "Prayerbook": see

Manuscripts, London, BL, Cotton Titus D.xxvi and xxvii
Æthelberht of Kent, king, 204-05; see also Law Codes, Anglo-Saxon
Æthelgifu, daughter of Alfred, 252
Æthelred II, king, 115, 120, 133, 212; see also Law Codes, Anglo-Saxon
Æthelthryth, abbess, 181-82
Æthelwold of Winchester, bishop, 208-09, 215; "Benedictional": see Manuscripts, London, BL, Additional 49598

Bacchus, 91
Bamborough, 127
"Barberini Gospels": see Manuscripts, Vatican, Biblioteca Apostolica, Barberini lat. 570
Barking Abbey, provenance of Vercelli Book, 254
*Battle of Brunanburh,* 120, 129, 132
*Battle of Maldon,* 116, 119-20, 128-29, 132-34
Bavarian law code, see Law Codes, continental
Bayeux Cathedral, 154, 159
Bayeux Tapestry, 140-61, 181
Bede, 251; *In Principium Genesis,* 88-89; *Ecclesiastical History,* 127-28, 136, 181-82, 198-201, 209
Pseudo-Bede, *Flores,* 64n.
Benedictine Reforms, 61-62, 97, 214, 253
*Beowulf,* 114, 116-19, 122-32, 276, 285
Blickling Homilies, see Homilies
*Boethius* (OE prose version), 52, see also *Meters of Boethius*
Boniface, 253, 284; *enigmata,* 89n., 90, 94
"Book of Kells": see Manuscripts, Dublin, Trinity College MS. 58
Burgred of Mercia, king, 205
"Bury Psalter": see Manuscripts, Vatican, Biblioteca Apostolica, Reg. lat. 12
Byrhtferth, *Vita Sancti Oswaldi,* 196-97
Byrhtnoth of Essex, ealdorman, 120, 128-29, 133-37

Cain, 222, 234-36, 244-47, 255
Cainan, 248-49
*Cambridge Songs,* 61, "Lyric 49," 77-78
*Canons of Theodore,* 44
Canterbury, provenance of Junius 11 manuscript, 252
cemeteries and burial practices, 214-19
*cennan,* 233-35, 243
Cham (Ham), 191-92, 295-97
Chaucer, Geoffrey, 29, 46, 50, 53, 55, 69-70n., 86n.
*Christ I* (The Advent Lyrics), 79, 143, 244
*Christ II* (The Ascension), 46-47
*Christ III* (The Judgment), 35, 300-03
*Christ and Satan,* 185, 187, 194-95, 197, 205, 300
Churches: Autun, 157; Ballycloghduff, Ireland, 153; Champagnolles, 152; Conques, Sainte-Foi, 157; Frómista, Spain, 151; Kitinane, Ireland, 148; Loctudy, Brittany, 151; Marignac, St. Supice, 152;

Poitiers, Saint-Hilaire, 151; Poitiers, Sainte-Radegonde, 153; Saint-Front-sur-Nizonne, 151; San Pedro de Tejada, Spain, 151; Semur-en-Auxois, Notre Dame, 153; Semur-en-Brionnais, 153
Clovis, 101
Cnut, king, 115, 212, 214; see also Law Codes, Anglo-Saxon
Cologne, 80
condoms, 47-50
"Corpus of Anglo-Saxon Stone Sculpture," 189, 193n.
Coventry, 275
Cuchulainn, 118
Cynewulf, *Juliana*, 304

Dacre, 192
demons, 184-90, 264
dildoes, 42-48
Donestre, 162-80
Dore, 120
*double entendres*, 30, 41-47, 56-58, 60-61, 66, 82-86, 91-96, 307
*Dream of the Rood*, 178n.

Eadburh, abbess, 253
Ealhswith, wife of Alfred, 252
Eanulf Penearding, reeve, 52
Edgar, king, 196, 206-12, 254; "New Minster Charter": see Manuscripts, London, BL, Cotton Vespasian A.viii; "Wihtbordesstan" law code, see Law Codes, Anglo-Saxon
Edith, St., daughter of Edgar, as artist, 254
Edmund, St., king, 120, 132
Egbert, king, 120
Pseudo-Egbert, "Scrift-boc," 257, 273, see also Manuscripts, Cambridge Corpus Christi College 190, Oxford, Bodl. Lib. Junius 121, and Oxford, Bodl. Lib. Laud Misc. 482
*Egills saga*, 118
*Ely Book*, 134, 136-37
*enigmata*, 60, 63, 91-94
Enoch, 247
Enos, 248-49
Eusebius, 94
Eve, associated with Virgin Mary, 193-98, 244-45
*Exodus*, 67-68

*Flateyjarbók*, 43

Galen, 178-79
*Genesis*, 71n., 129n., 134, 183-86, 192, 197, 202, 205, 210, 219, 221-74, 291-93, 296-97
Godiva, Lady, 275-76, 278, 283, 285-86, 304-305, 307
Goscelin, *Life of Edith*, 254
Gregory the Great, pope, 198-202, 220, 298; *Dialogues*, 258n.; *Homiliae in Evangelia*, 186

"Harley Psalter": see Manuscripts, London, BL, Harley 603
Harold, king, 157
Herod Antipas, 91
Herodias, 91
Hilton, Walter, *The Scale of Perfection*, 30, 34, 57
Hippocrates, 179
"Historia Anglorum," 201
Hlothhere and Eadric, law code, see Law Codes, Anglo-Saxon

Hoddon, 192
Homilies, anonymous in OE: Blickling Hom. 7, 194-95, 197; Blickling Hom. 10, 302-03; Napier 46, 271-72, 284-85, 301, 303; Pope 27, 271, 282, 301, 303; Vercelli Hom. 10, 214; Vercelli Hom. 15, 79-80; Vercelli Hom. 22, 214, 270n.
*Hrolfs saga kraka,* 118

Ine, king, 204-05
injury tariffs, 97-115
Isidore of Seville, 169, *Etymologiae,* 71n., 73n., 88n.

Jared, 247
Jerome, St., *Homilia in Lucam Evangelistam,* 208
Junius 11: see Manuscripts, Oxford, Bodl. Lib., Junius 11
Justin the Martyr, 135

Lady Godiva, see Godiva
Lantfred, *Translatio et miracula S. Swithuni,* 97
Law Codes, Anglo-Saxon: Alfred, 99-100, 108-113, 204-05, 210; Athelstan, 125, 215; Æthelberht, 99-108, 112-13, 202, 210; Æthelred II, 24; Cnut, 121, 125-26; Edgar, "Wihtbordesstan," 210-12; Hlothhere and Eadric, 102
Law Codes, continental: Alaman, 100; Bavarian, 100, *Lex Salica,* 101; Merovingian, 98; Rothari (Lombard), 100n., 103n.
*Leechdoms,* 45
"Letter of Alexander to Aristotle," 177n.
*Lex Salica,* see Law Codes, continental
*Liber Monstrorum,* 163, 165-70, 174-80
Lindisfarne, 127
Lot, 87-91, 95-96, 181

Malalehel, 248-49
Malmesbury, provenance of Junius 11 manuscript, 252
*Mankind,* 74-75n.
Manuscripts:
Boulougne-sur-Mer: Bibliothèque Municipale 1890, 281n.
Cambridge: Corpus Christi College 23, 252, 255; Corpus Christi College 190, 257n.; Corpus Christi College 196, 194n.; Corpus Christi College 303, 213-14; Corpus Christi College 419, 284n.; University Library Ii.1.33, 242n., 287n.; University Library Gg.5.35, 61n.
Dublin: Trinity College MS. 58, 146
London: BL, Additional 49598, 181-82, 244-45n., 249-50; BL, Cotton Claudius B.iv, 191, 193, 210, 217n., 240-41, 287n., 289-91, 296; BL, Cotton Julius A.x, 194n.; BL, Cotton Julius E.vii, 305n.; BL, Cotton Tiberius B.v, 162-64, 170-74, 177; BL, Cotton Tiberius C.vi, 187, 195; BL, Cotton Titus D.xxvi and xxvii, 213n.; BL, Cotton Vespasian A.viii, 206-10, 252; BL, Cotton Vitellius A.xv, 162-64, 170-

80; BL, Cotton Vitellius C.v, 284; BL, Harley 603, 145, 185, 248; BL, Sloane 2839, 143n.; BL, Stowe 944, 80-81n., 187, 198
Oxford: Bodl. Lib. Ashmole 1431, 144n.; Bodl. Lib. Bodley 343, 284n.; Bodl Lib. Hatton 115, 214n.; Bodl. Lib. Junius 11, 16, 144, 183-86, 191-94, 197, 202, 206, 210, 218-74, 294, 297, provenance, 252-55; Bodl. Lib. Junius 121, 194, 197, 257n., 299n.; Bodl. Lib. Laud Misc. 482, 257n.; Bodl. Lib. Laud Misc. 509, 287n.
Paris: Bibliothèque Nationale, lat. 8824, 187-88, 297-98
Utrecht: Bibliotheek der Rijksuniversiteit 32, 185, 248
Vatican: Biblioteca Apostolica, Reg. lat. 12, 190; Biblioteca Apostolica, Barberini lat. 570, 145-46, 188, 218
Mary of Egypt, anonymous Life of, 305-07, 309, see also Manuscripts, London, BL, Cotton Julius E.vii
masturbation, female, 42-47, 50
Mathusal, 246, 248
Matthew, St., Gospel, 85, 91, 283
Matthew Paris, *Chronica Majora*, 275
Maviael, 246, 248
Merovingian law codes, see Law Codes, continental
*Meters of Boethius*, 51-52

"New Minster Liber Vitae": see Manuscripts, London, BL, Stowe 944
Nimrod, 191-92
Noah, 144, 146, 191-92, 248, 295-97, 309
Nunnaminster, provenance of Junius 11 manuscript, 252

Odin, 118, 122
Odo of Bayeux, 159
Offa of Mercia, king, 204-05
Old English Heptateuch, see Ælfric
Old English Hexateuch, see Manuscripts, London, BL, Cotton Claudius B.iv
*Old English Martyrology*, 194n., 196
Oswald, St., king, 127-29, 134-36
Oswiu, king, 127, 136, 209

*Palladium*, 50
*Panther*, 51
"Paris Psalter": see Manuscripts, Paris, Bibliothèque Nationale, lat. 8824
Paul, St., *1 Corinthians*, 84; *2 Corinthians*, 283
Paul the Deacon, 305
Penda of Mercia, king, 127, 135
*Penitential of Bede*, 43-44
Peter, St., 79-81, 208-09
Petrarch, 57
*Phoenix*, 94
Pliny, *Historia Naturalis*, 69n.
Prudentius, 252; *Psychomachia*, 182-83, glosses, 281n.

Rabanus Maurus, *De Universo*, 68-70n.; commentary on Gospel of Matthew, 91
Ramsey *Life of St. Oswald*, 134-36
Repton Stone, 189n.
Riddles (OE, in Exeter Book):
Riddle 12: 29-59, 69; Riddle 20: 60; Riddle 25: 69; Riddle 32:

51; Riddle 37, 83; Riddle 40: 61; Riddle 42: 63-72, 74-76, 95-96; Riddle 43: 63, 72-76, 88, 95-96; Riddle 44: 60, 76-82, 95-96, 307-08; Riddle 45: 40, 82-86, 95-96; Riddle 46: 86-96; Riddle 54: 54; Riddle 61: 45-46, 48-50, 55; Riddle 62: 45; Riddle 63: 42, 46
Rothbury Cross, 147n., 188-90, 218

Satan/Lucifer, 185-92, 201-03, 205, 209, 218-19
*sceamu, sceand,* and derivatives, 280-307
Sedulius Scotus, 84n.
Seth, 222, 234-36, 243-49, 255
Shaftesbury, provenance of Junius 11 manuscript, 252
Shakespeare, William, *Love's Labours Lost,* 42
sheela-na-gig, 147-50, 152
Snorri Sturluson, *Edda,* 118
Song of Songs, 77-78, 96
Soranus, 179
*Soul and Body II,* 73, 85
*Soul's Address to the Body,* 22
*stician,* 32-36, 40-49
*strienan* (and compounds), 234-36, 242-43
"Stuttgart Psalter," 144
*swifan,* 29, 34, 36, 40, 45, as *double entendre,* 50-58
Symphosius, *enigmata,* 94

Tacitus, *Germania,* 119-20
Tatwine, 94
*Textus Roffensis,* 100n., 202
"Tiberius Psalter": see Manuscripts, London, BL, Cotton Tiberius C.vi
Tisbury, 52
Tower of Babel, 191-92
Tyr, Norse god, 118-19, 122, 125, 127, 129, 133, 136-37

Urswick, 192
"Utrecht Psalter": see Manuscripts, Utrecht, Bibliotheek de Rijksuniversiteit, 32
Utrecht (or Rheims) style of illustration, 237, 239

*Vainglory,* 83-84, 90
Vercelli Book, 254
Vercelli Homilies, see Homilies
*Vita Adae et Evae,* 262n.
*Vitae Patrum,* 284

*Waldere,* 129, 132
*wergild,* 100-01, 105, 110
Whitby *Life of Gregory,* 198-99
Whitby, Synod of, 209
*Widsith,* 120
Wilfrid, abbot, 209
William the Conqueror, king, 157
Willibrord, 128
Wilton, 254
Winchester, provenance of Junius 11 manuscript, 252
Winchester style of illustration, 237
*wlonc* (and compounds), 39-41, 84-85, 90-91
"Wonders of the East," 144, 162-65, 169-80; see also Manuscripts, London, BL, Cotton Tiberius B.v, London, BL, Cotton Vitellius A.xv
Wulfstan of York, archbishop, 115, 212; *Institutes of Polity,* 299-300
Wulfstan Uccea, 215